OUT OF THE BOX

Ready to Use Pack

BOXES: READYTO USE PACK

Edited and distributed in Europe and Latin America by:
INDEX BOOK, SL
Consejo de Ciento, 160 local 3
08015 BARCELONA, SPAIN
Tel: +34 93 454 5547
Fax: + 34 93 454 8438
ib@indexbook.com
www.indexbook.com

Cover design: EMEYELE
www.emeyele.com

Published in 2006 by
Page One Publishing Private Limited
enquiries@pageonegroup.com
www.pageonegroup.com
First published 2006 by Liaoning Science and Technology Press
Editor: Zhou Jianzhong

Model making :Li Xiaoyu
Model drawing :Wang Ranran
Editor :Wang Li Xia
Project Manager :Dawn Teo
Cover design :Feng Dexian

ISBN: 84-96309-72-X
ISBN 13: 978-84-96309-72-2

Printed and bound in China

Contents

Packaging is an essential aspect of retailing any manufactured product. On many occasions, it is the packaging, rather than product itself, that catches the consumer's eye – and influences him or her to buy it.

In some instances, products are easily identifiable by characteristic packaging forms; in other cases, manufacturers use unusual, quirky packaging design to make their products stand out from the crowd.

At the same time, structural packaging is extremely functional. It has traditionally served to protect and ship goods securely, yet with maximum economy in terms of costs and space.

Well-designed packaging always strikes a balance between logistics and cost, and **Out of the Box: Ready-to-Use Structural Packaging** is an invaluable sourcebook for anyone who needs practical designs and ideas for the taking. A handy, easy-to-understand reference for anyone seeking to design inexpensive, yet structurally sound packaging, this volume presents each design template on its own spread, along with the finished product.

The design of any package should also involve decisions on the dimensions, material, and the thickness of the material used, and whether these are appropriate for the size, weight and nature of the product. Other techniques such as scoring or creasing will further increase the strength of the packaging, and these should be taken into consideration to ensure the success of any structural packaging design.

About the CD-ROM

The template for each design can be found on the accompanying CD-ROM. They can easily be scaled and adapted according to the specific requirements of any product. While the designs can be used to develop new packaging solutions, the images themselves cannot be used for any type of commercial application without prior permission from the publishers. While every effort has been made to ensure that the CD can be used on most operating systems, the publishers do not accept any responsibility should it not be compatible with any platform.

Introduction

International Standards

A . L = Length of Box

B . W = Width of Box

C . D = Depth of Box

Terms

R.T.E.	Reverse Tuck End
S.T.E.	Straight Tuck End (For window box)
French R.T.E.	French Reverse Tuck End (For cosmetics)
Auto Bottom	Auto Assemble
123 Bottom	Snap Lock Bottom (For cosmetics, wine and food)
Six/Four-points-glued Box	Beer Tray

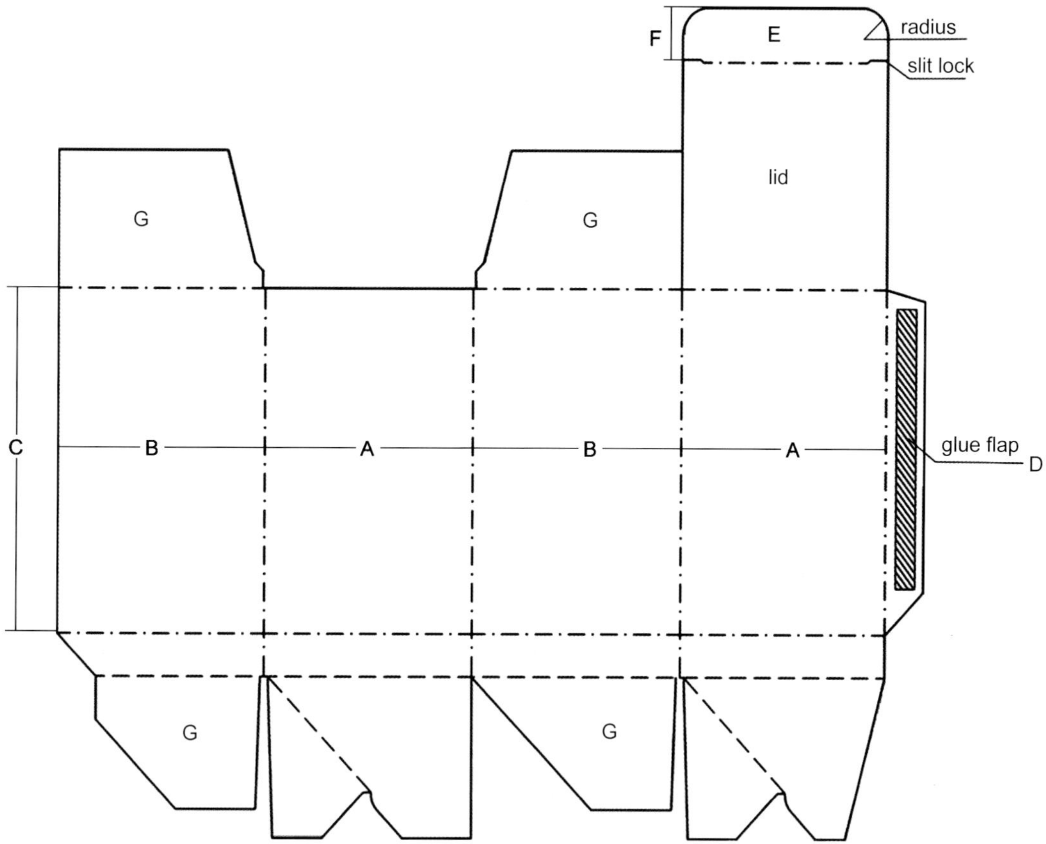

A. L=Length
B. W=Width
C. D=Depth
D. Glue flap
E. Tuck
F. Shoulder
G. Dust flap

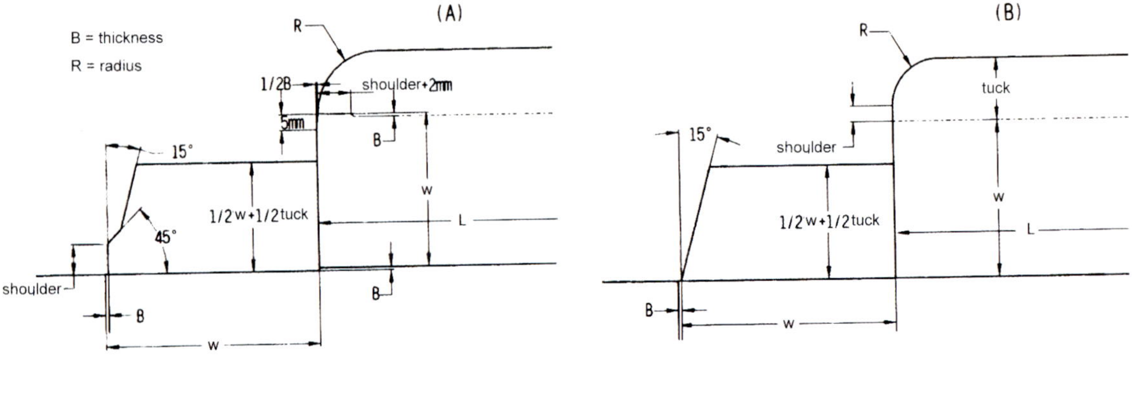
B = thickness
R = radius
(A)
R
1/2B
shoulder+2mm
5mm
15°
B
45°
1/2 w+1/2 tuck
w
L
shoulder
B
B
w
(B)
R
tuck
15°
shoulder
1/2 w+1/2 tuck
w
L
B
w

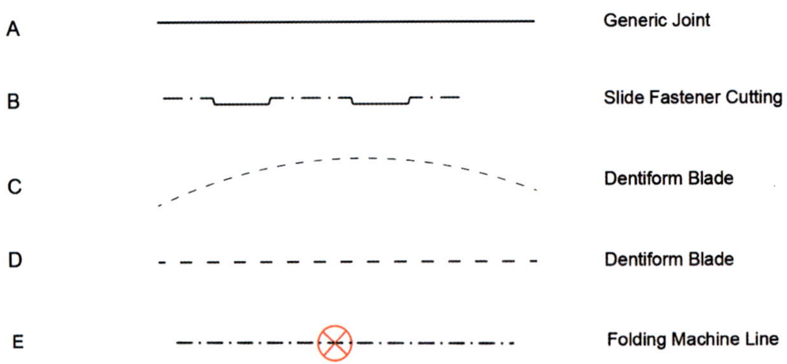
A
Generic Joint
B
Slide Fastener Cutting
C
Dentiform Blade
D
Dentiform Blade
E
Folding Machine Line

Locking Methods

1 . Auto Locks

2 . Top Panel Locks

3 . Side and End Panel Locks

4 . Click Locks

5 . Foot Locks

6 . Double Locks

7 . Gusseted Dust Locks

8 . Dust Flap Locks

9 . Butterfly Locks

10. Floral Locks

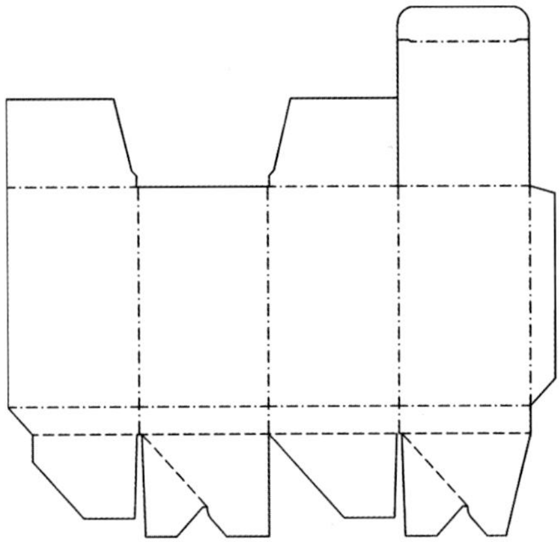

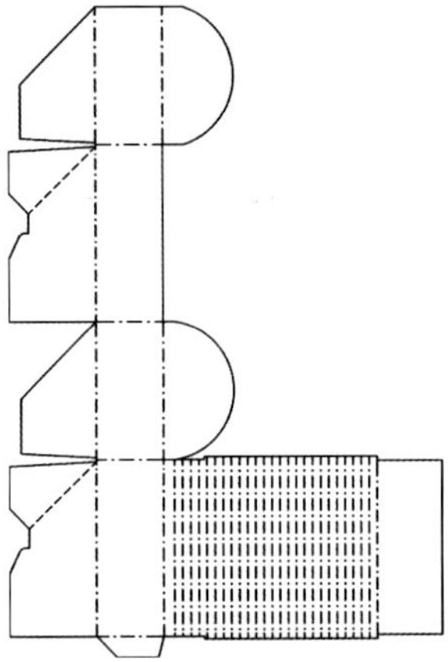

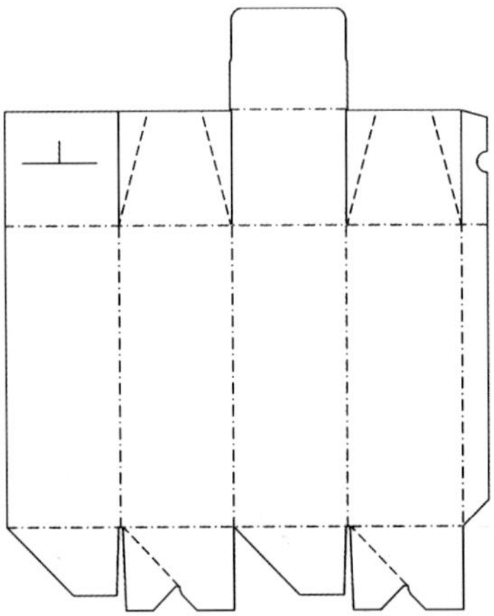

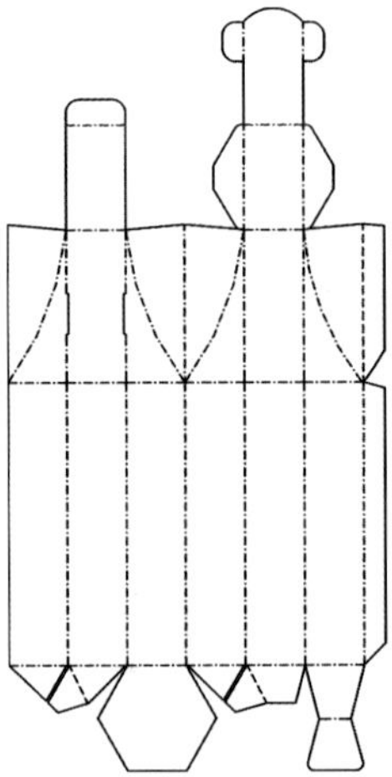

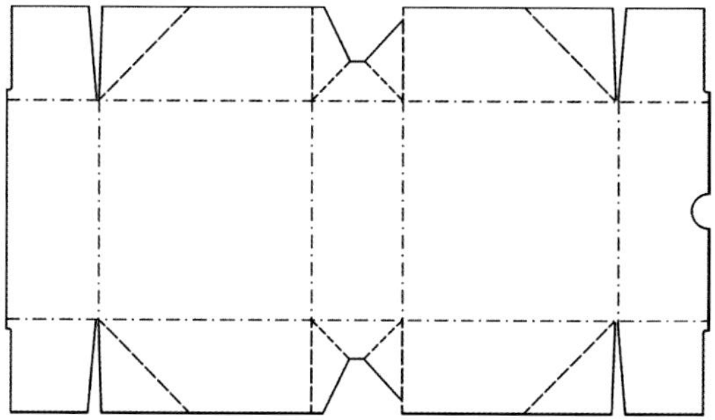

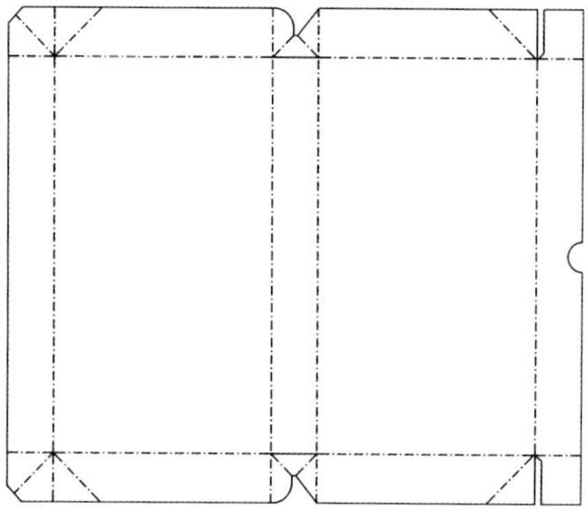

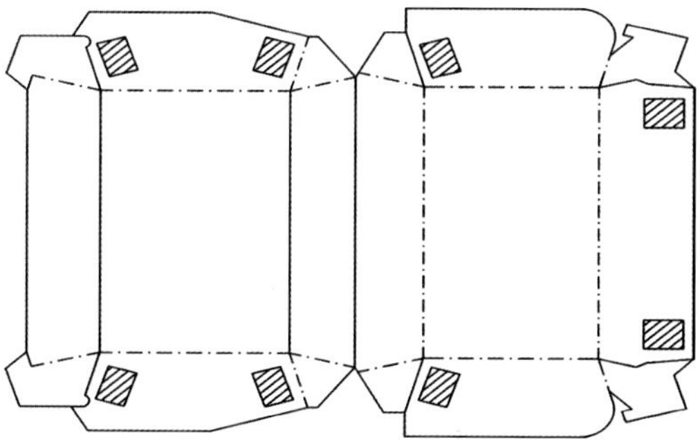

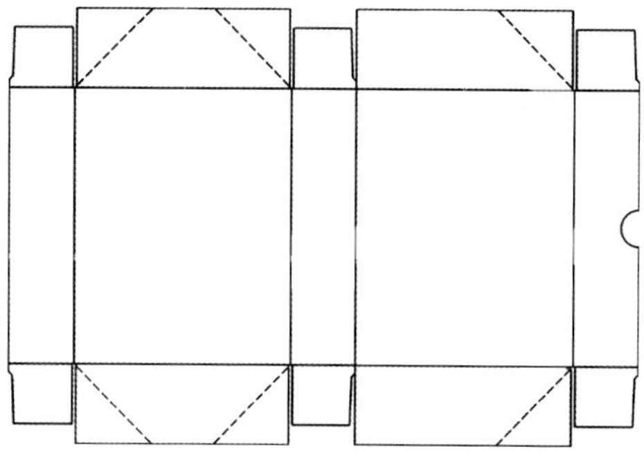

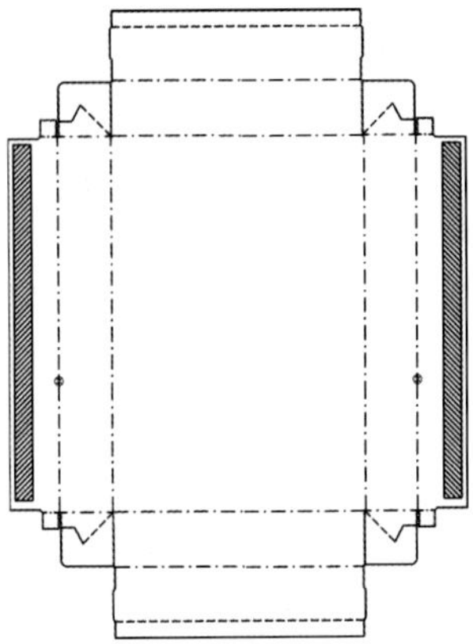

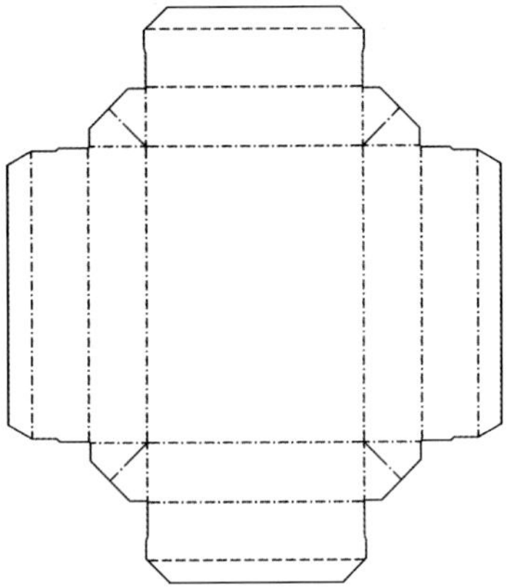

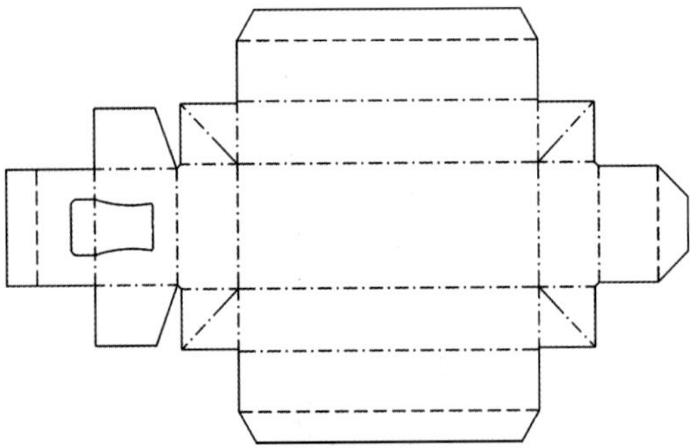

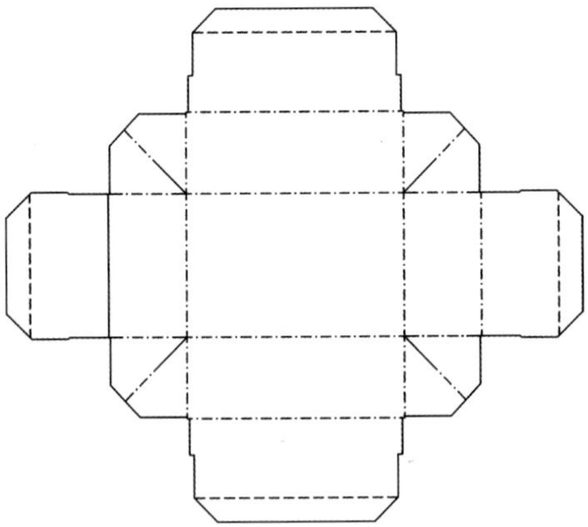

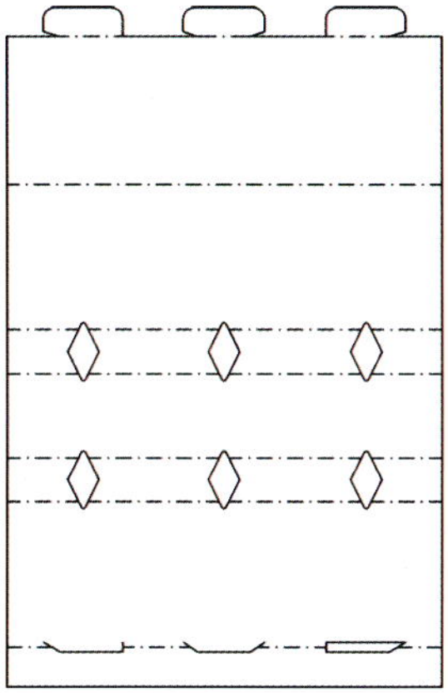

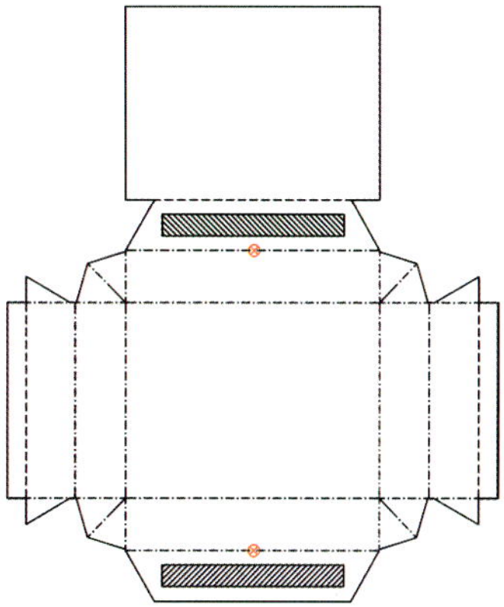

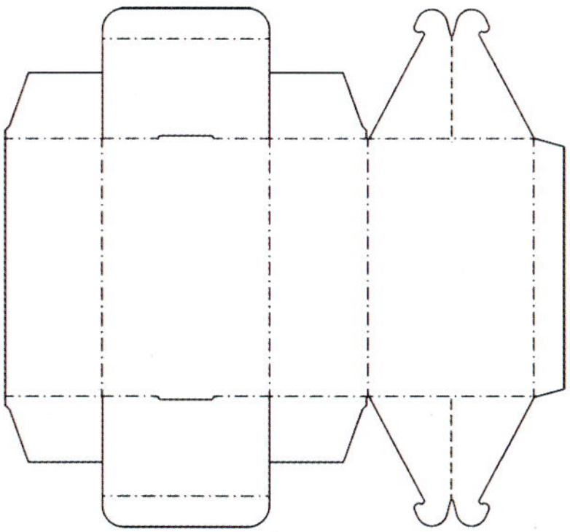

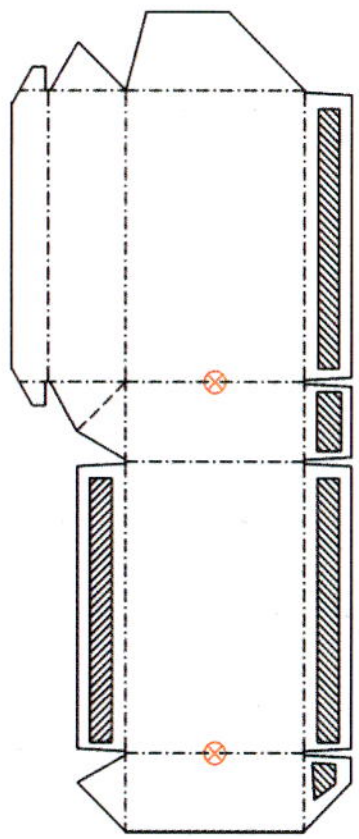

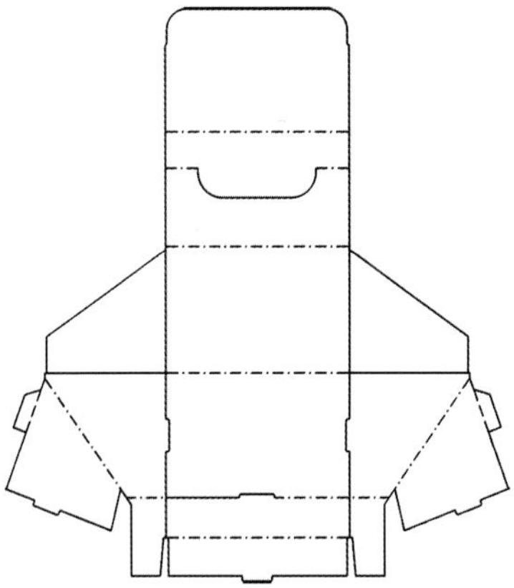

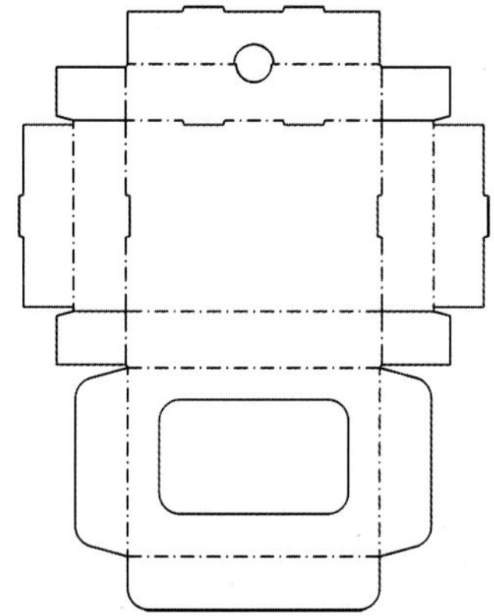

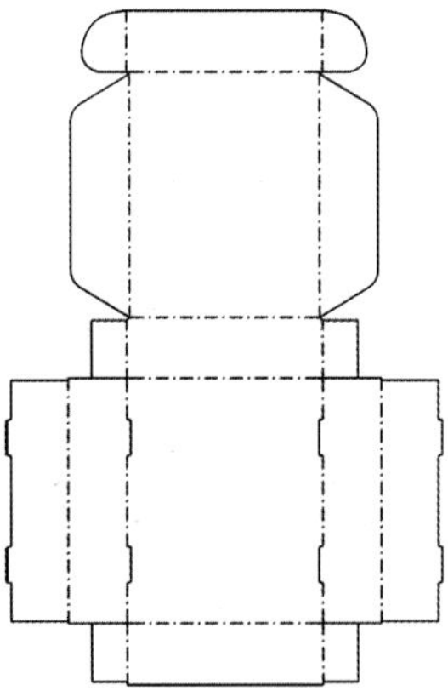

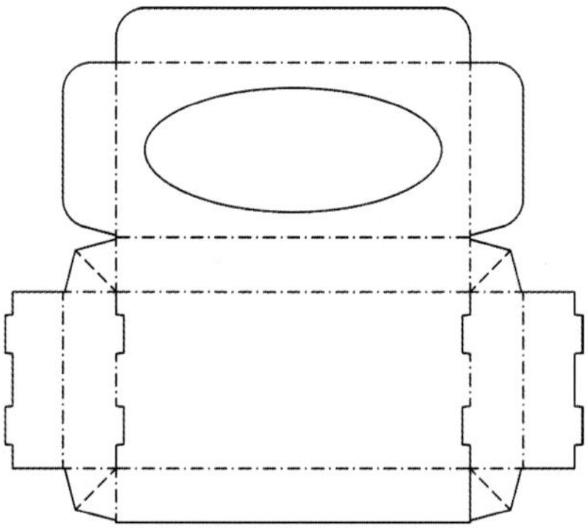

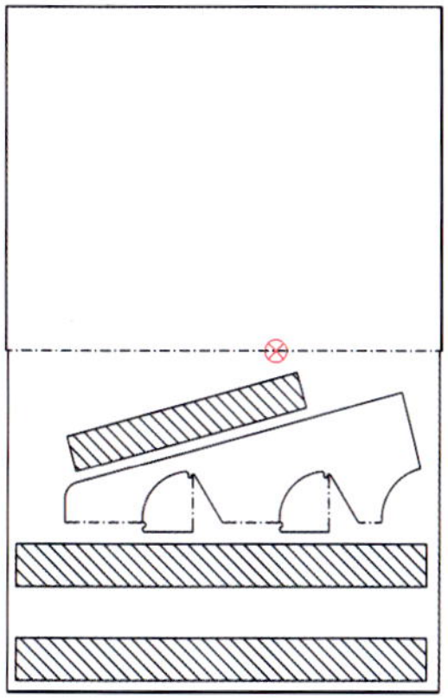

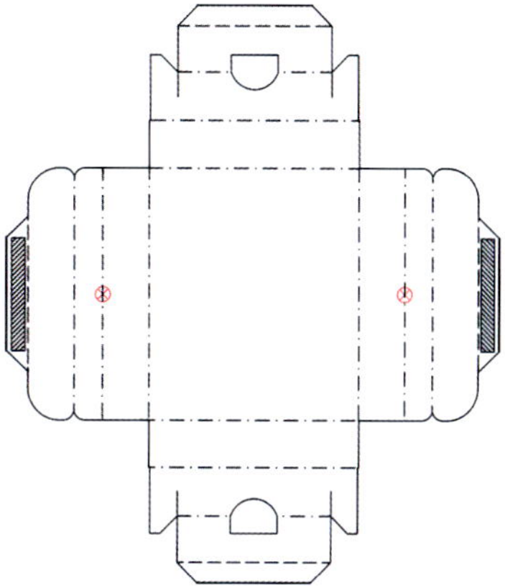

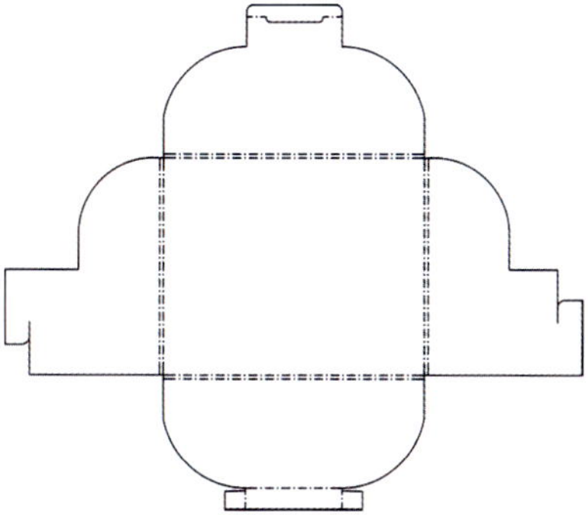

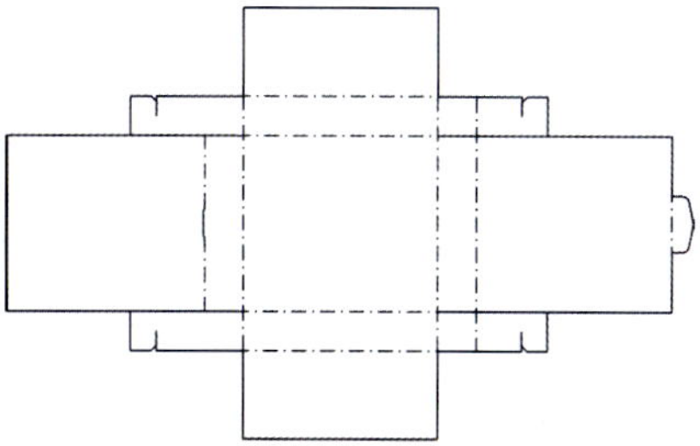

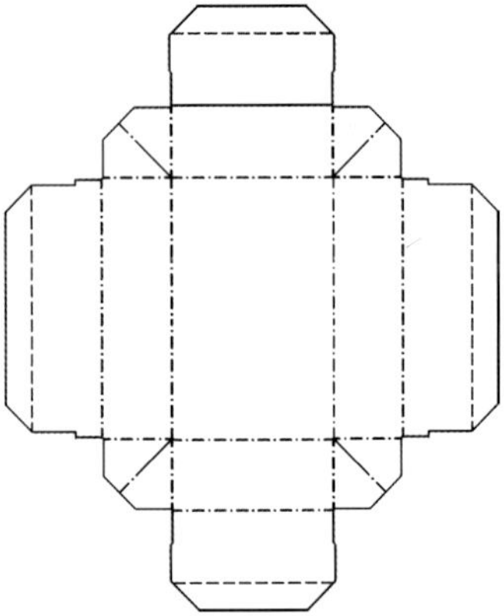

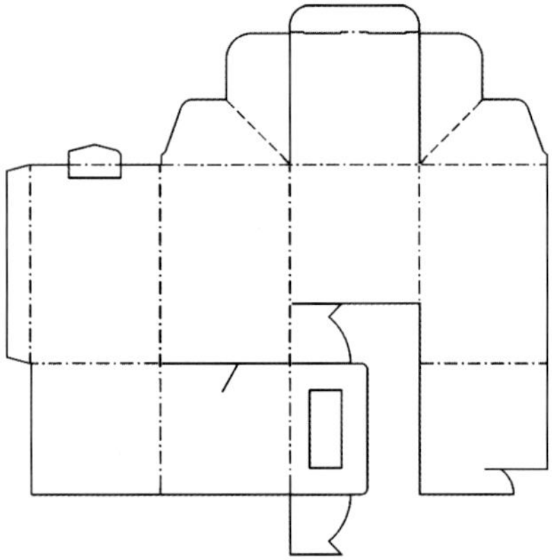

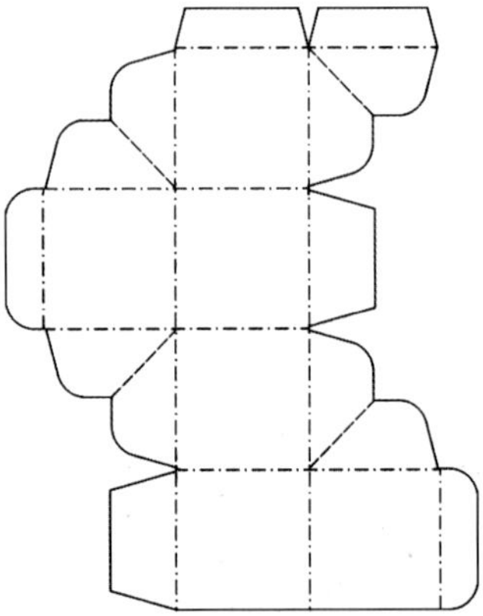

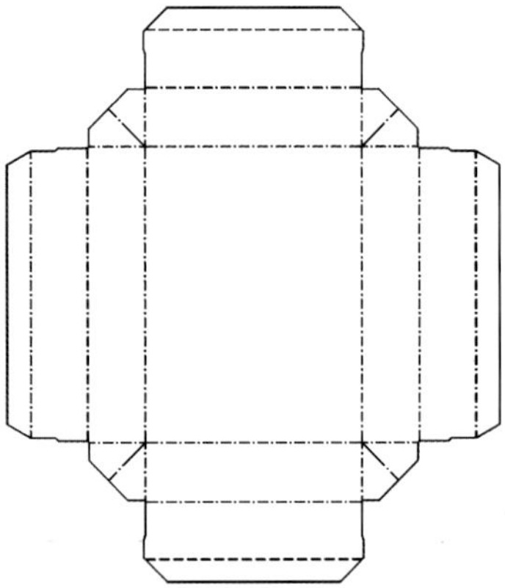

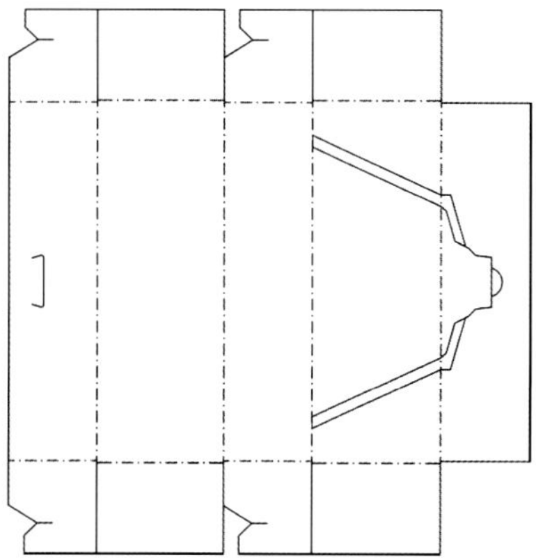

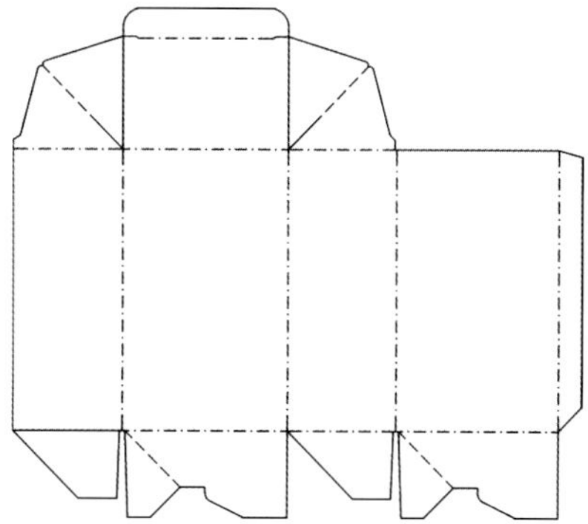

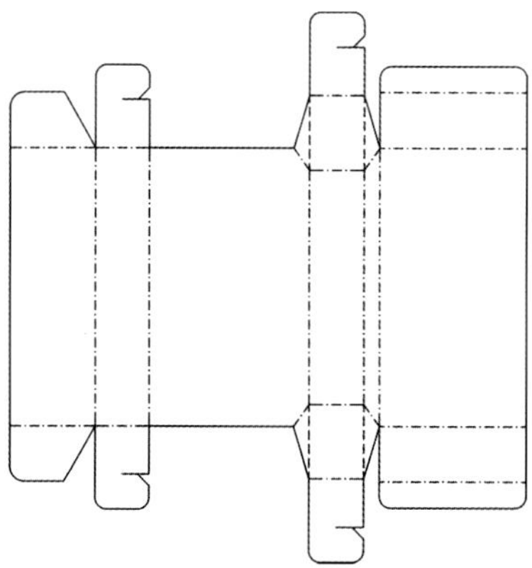

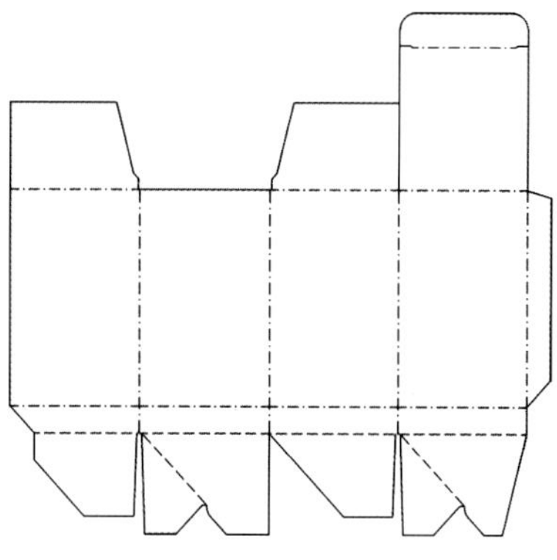

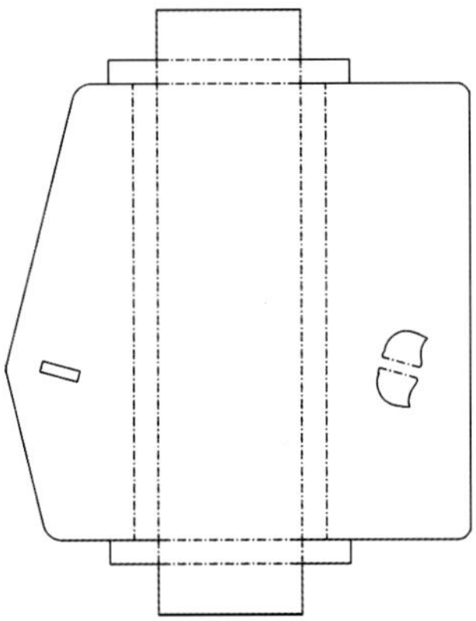

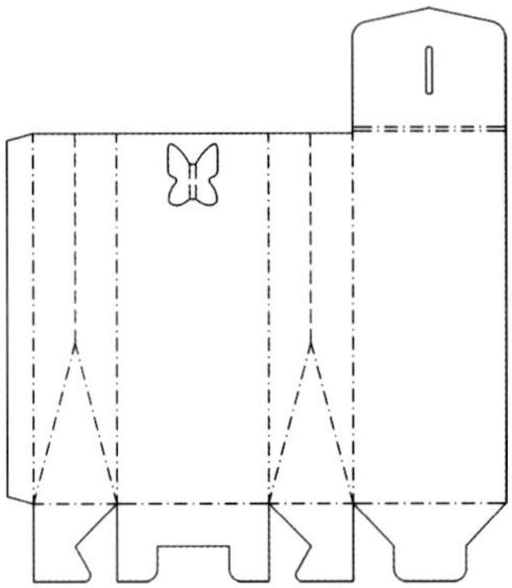

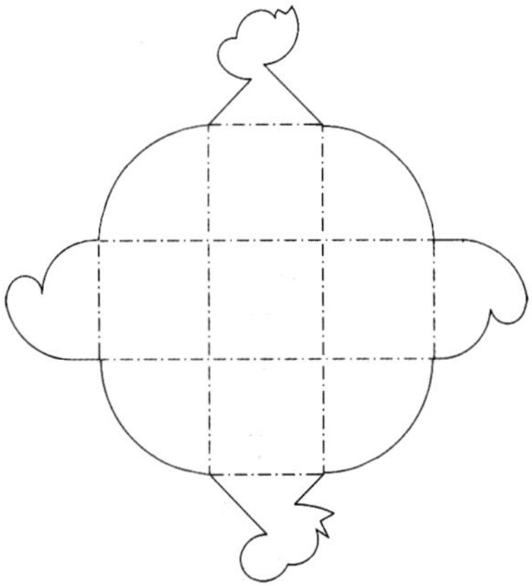

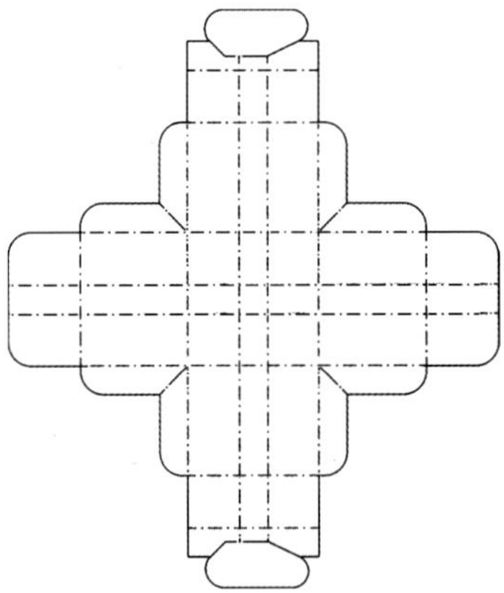

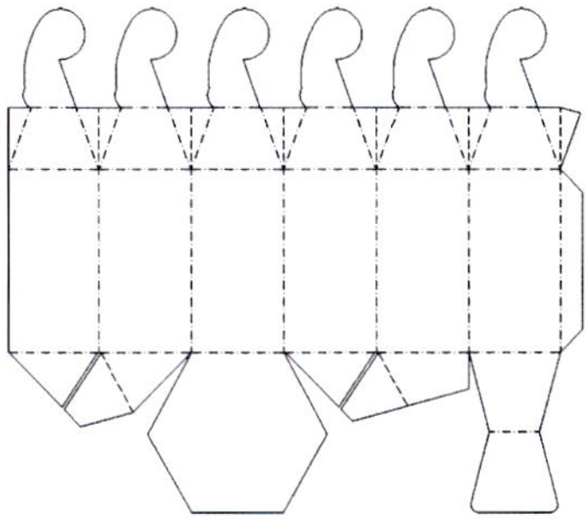

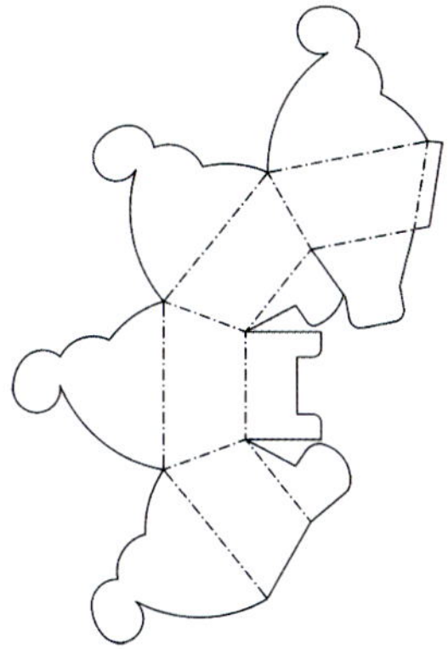

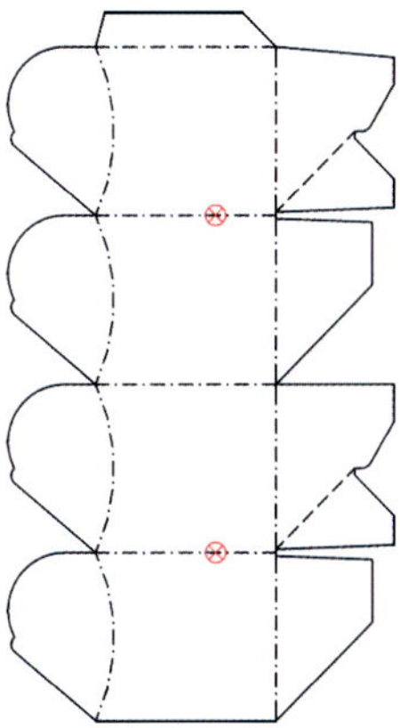

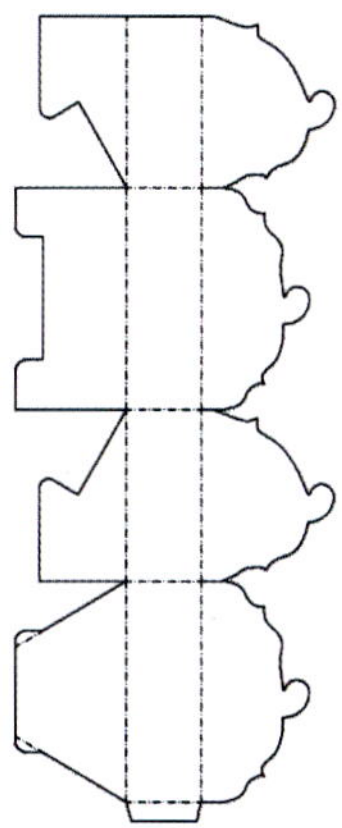

Structures

1 . Universal
2 . Holder
3 . Dispenser
4 . Divider
5 . Combination
6 . Carrier
7 . Window Carton
8 . Display Box
9 . Display Rack
10 . Book-shaped
11 . House-shaped
12 . Diamond
13 . Column Box
14 . Triangular
15 . Trapezoidal Box
16 . Pentagram
17 . Hanging Box
18 . Italic
19 . Lining
20 . Special
21 . Hollow Wall Tray
22 . Double Side Wall
23 . Auto Bottom
24 . Tray
25 . Sealed Ends
26 . Tapered Top
27 . Roof Top
28 . Polygonal Top
29 . Floral Top
30 . Hinged Lid
31 . Flip Top
32 . Dome Top
33 . Perforated Flip Top
34 . Frame-shaped

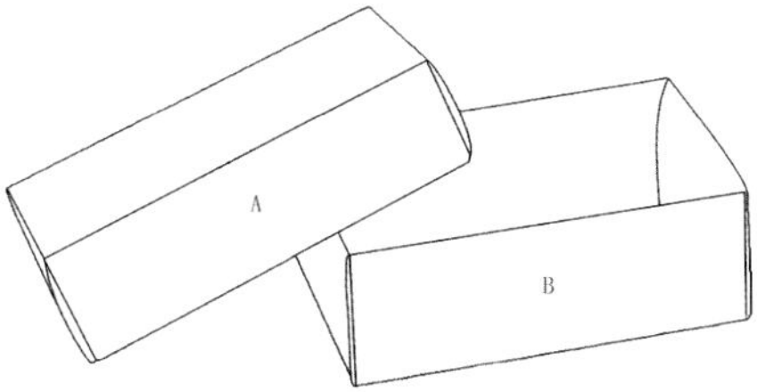

Universal

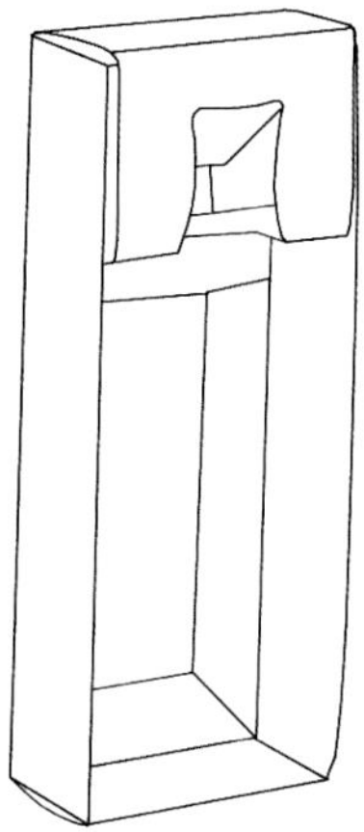

Holder

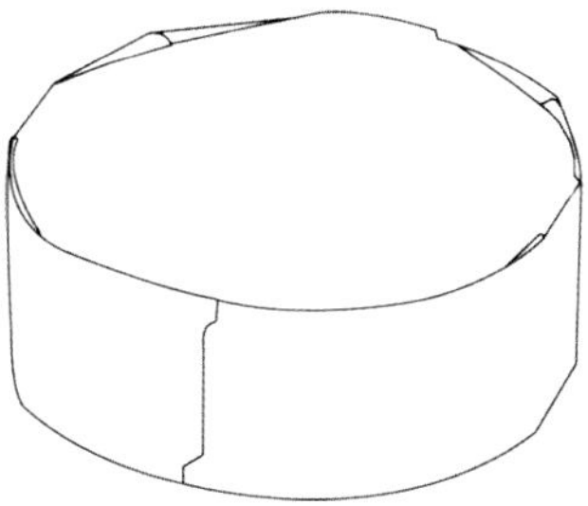

Holder

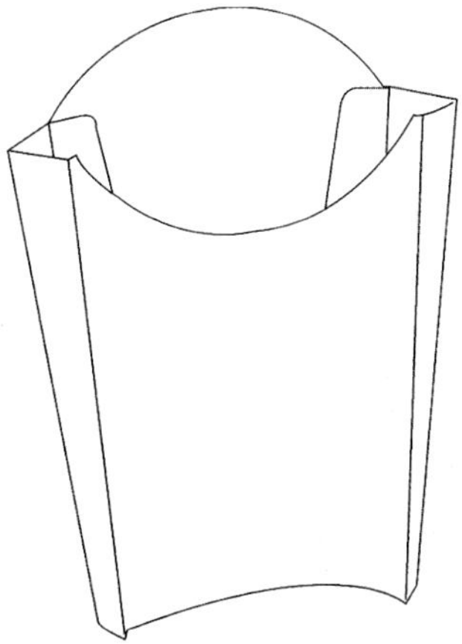

Holder

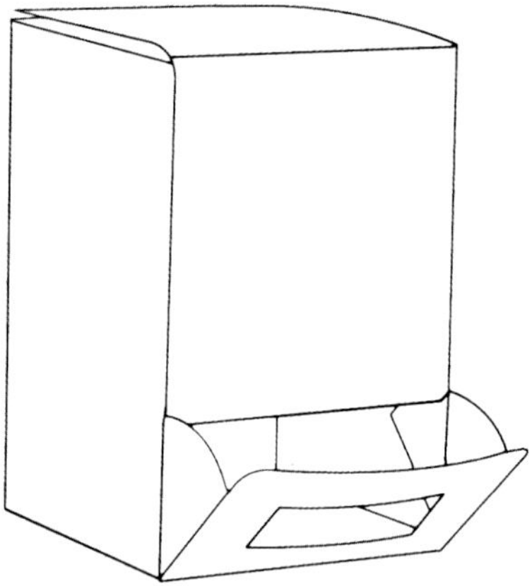

Dispenser

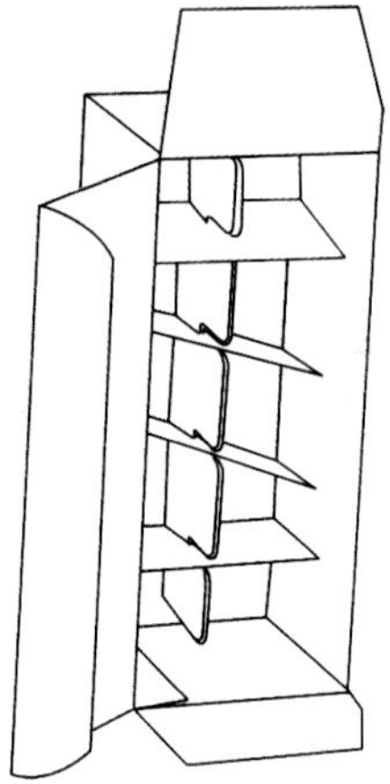

Divider

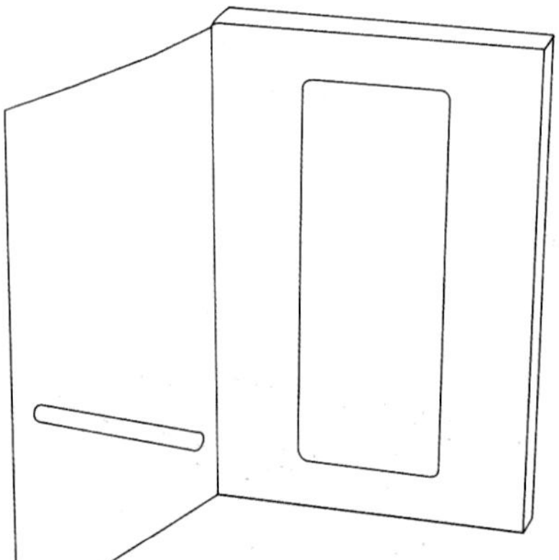

Combination

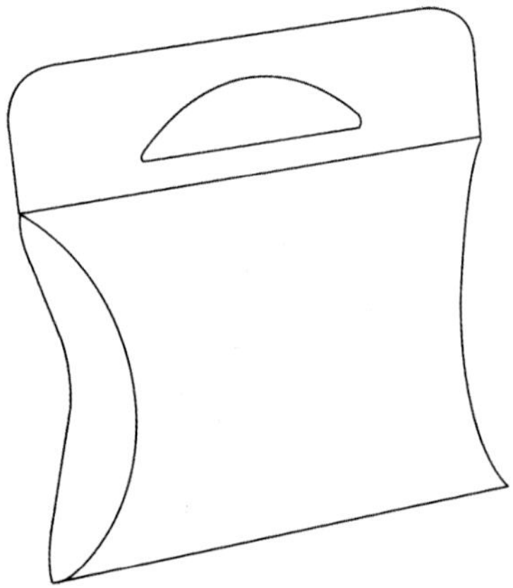

Carrier

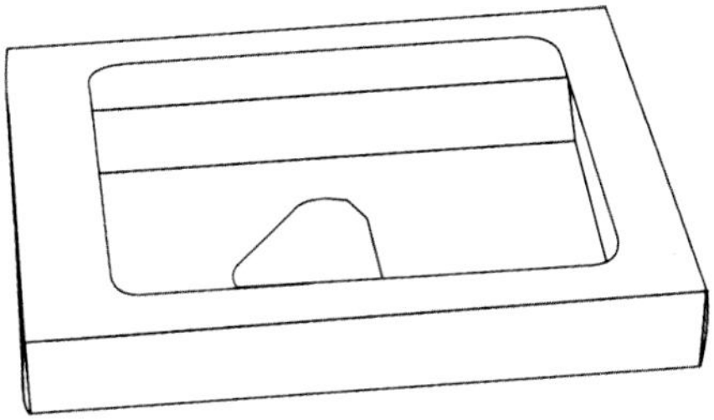

Window Carton

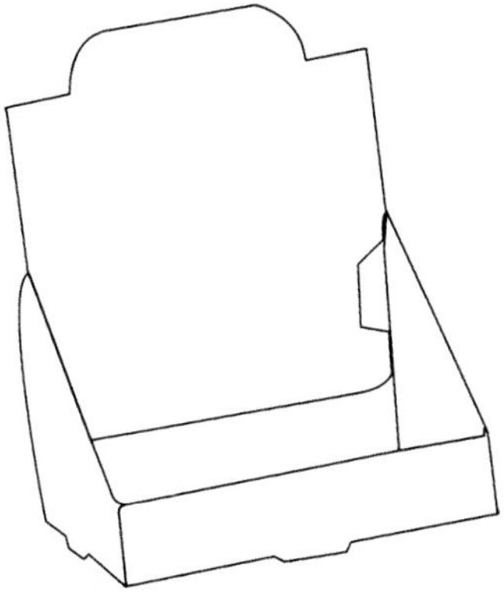

Display Box

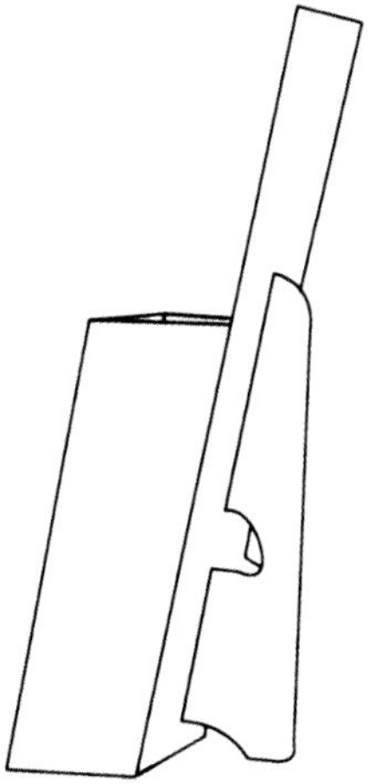

Display Rack

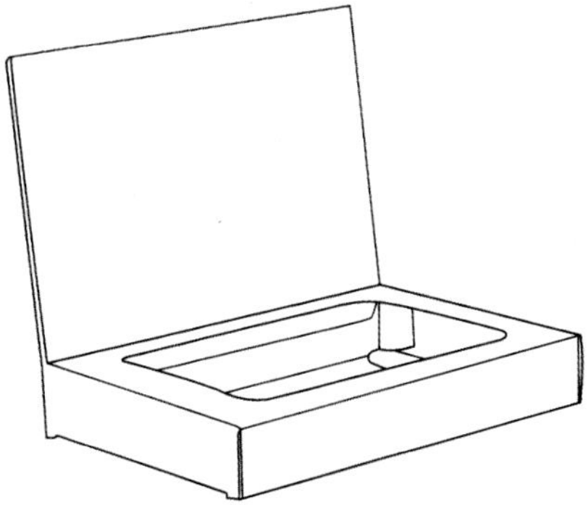

Book-shaped

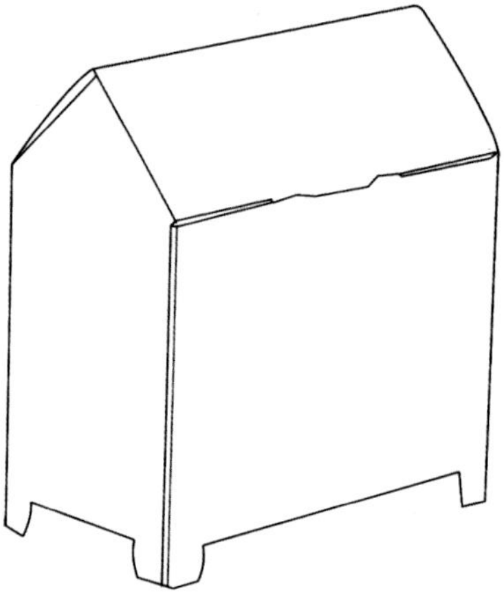

House-shaped

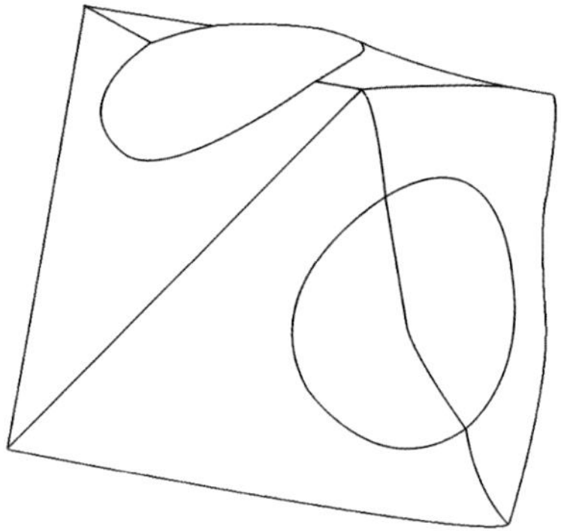

Diamond

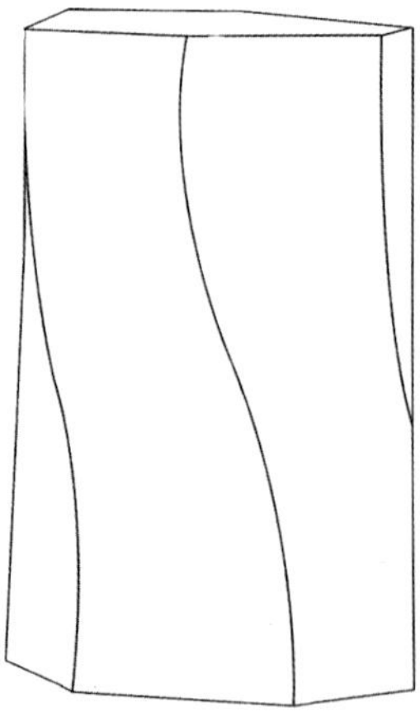

Columnar Box

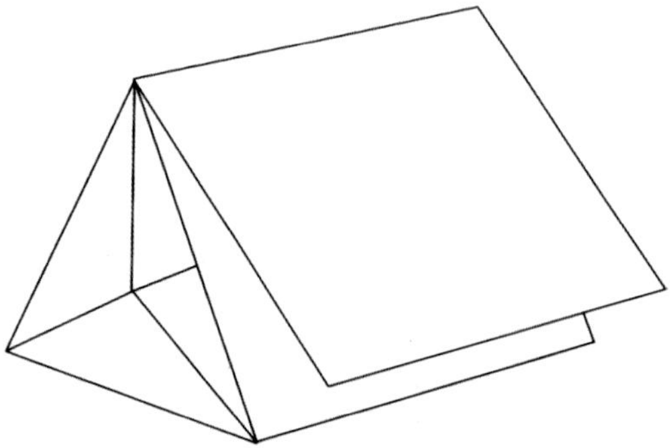

Triangular

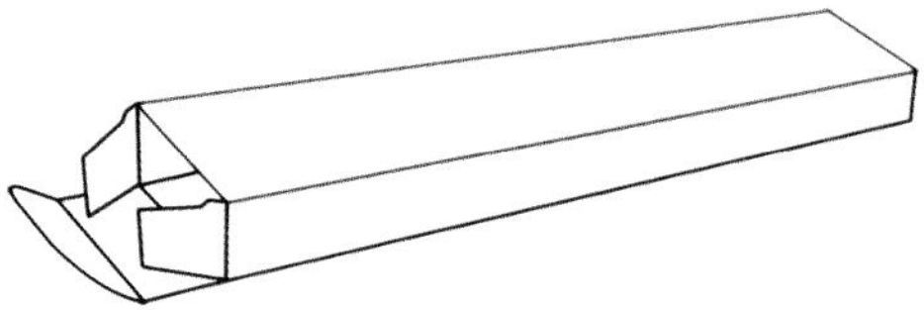

Trapezoidal Box

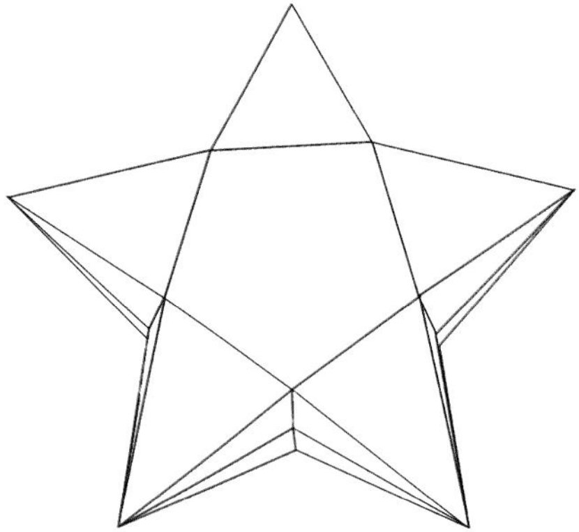

Diamond

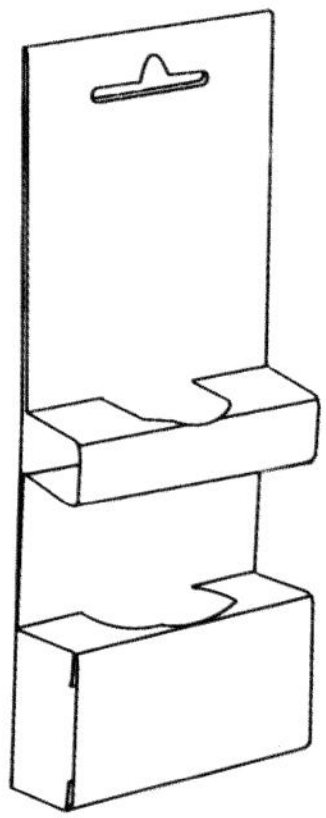

Hanging Box

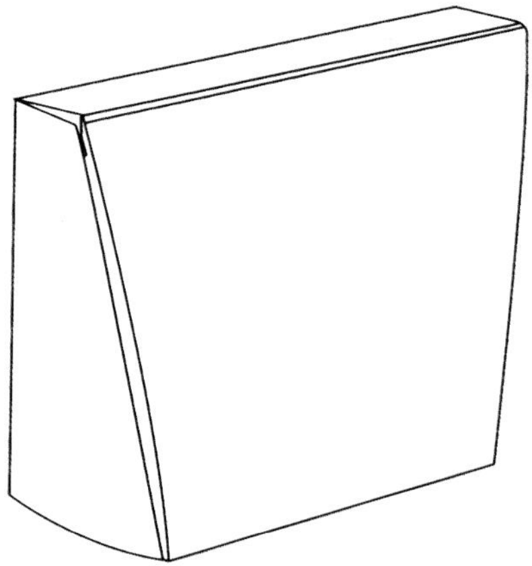

Italic

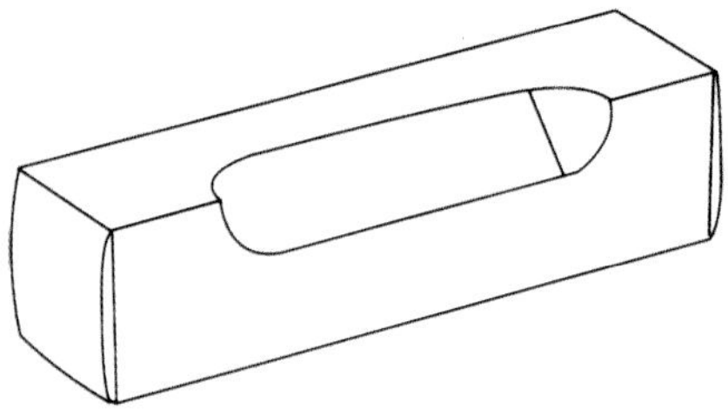

Lining

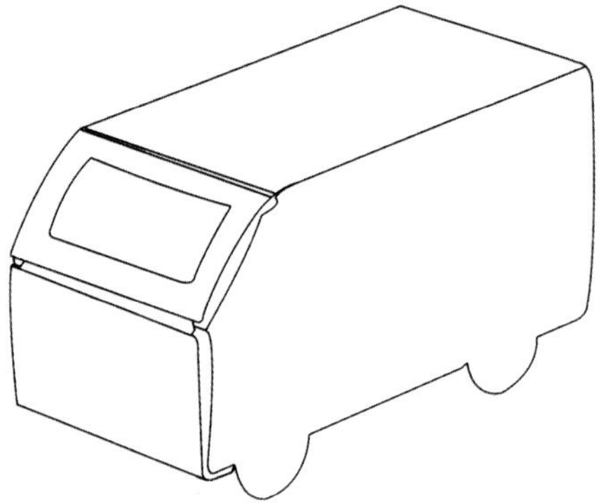

Special

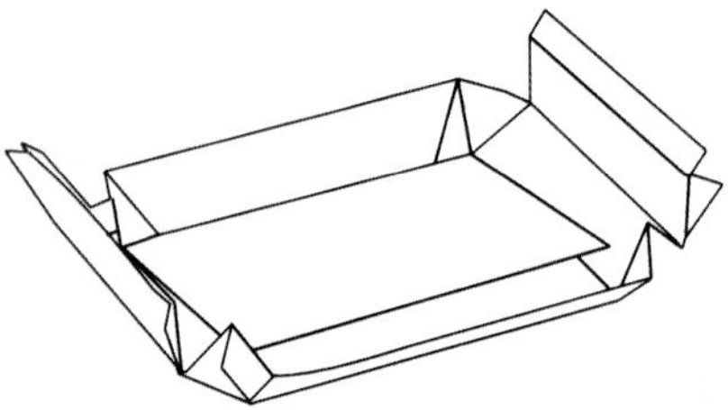

Hollow Wall Tray

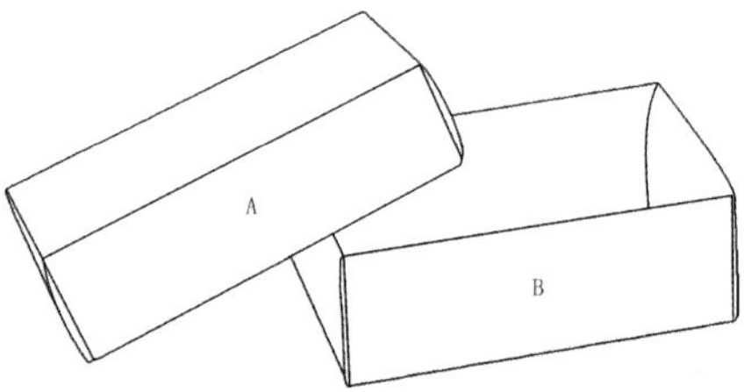

Double Side Wall

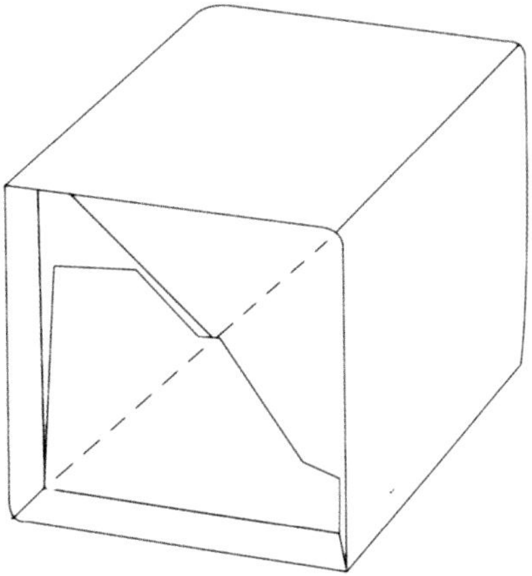

Auto Bottom

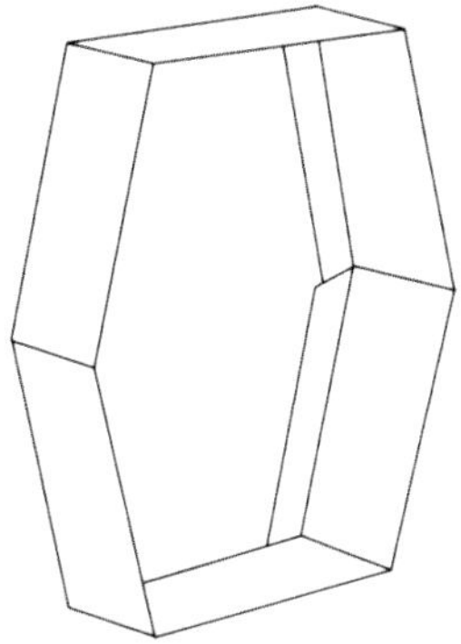

Tray

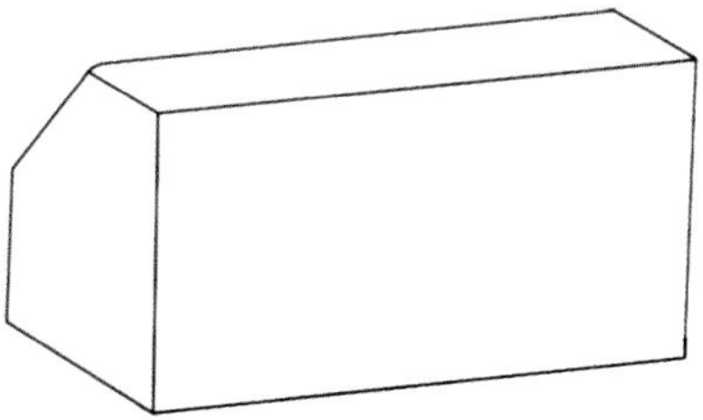

Sealed

Tapered Top

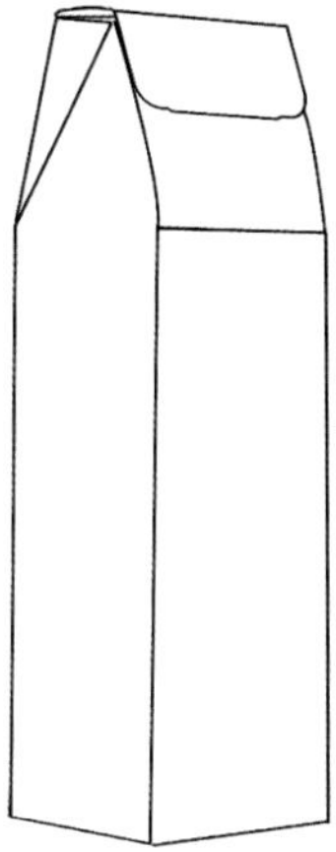

Roof Top

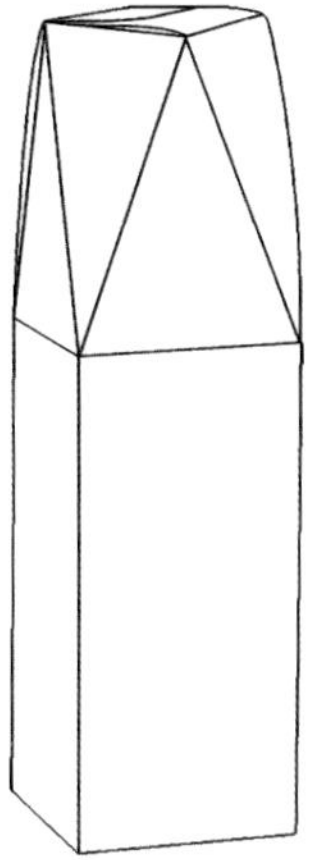

Polygonal Top

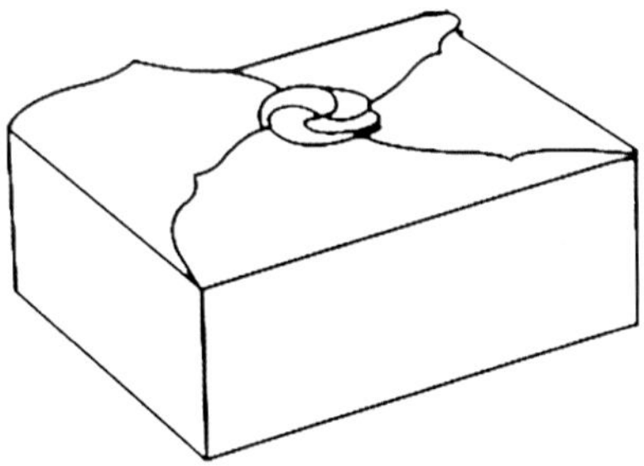

Floral Top

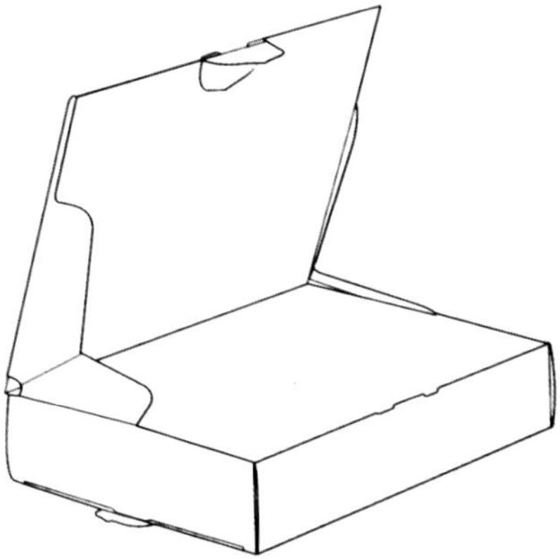

Hinged Lid

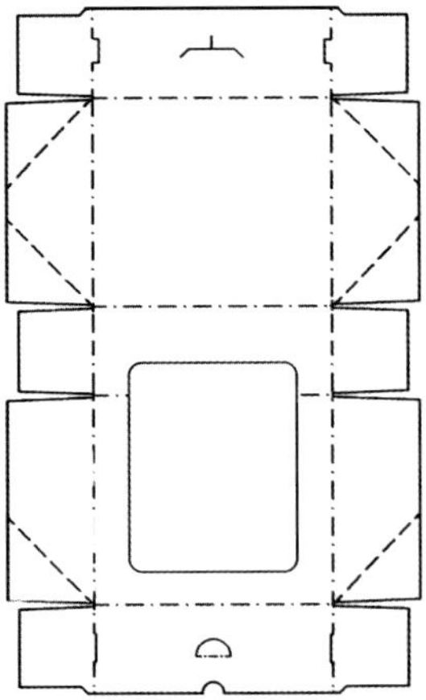

Flip Top

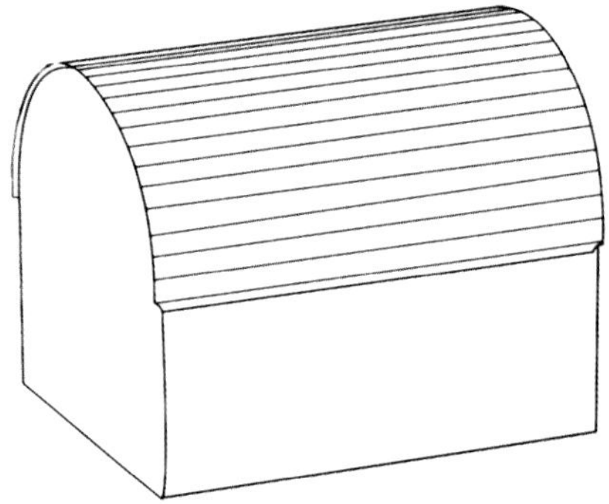

Dome Top

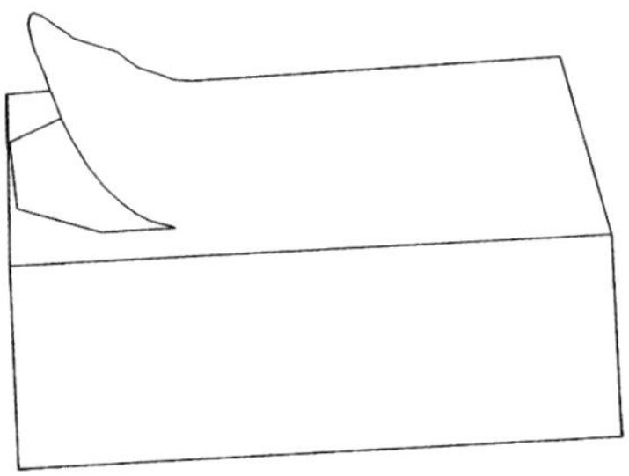

Perforated Flip Top

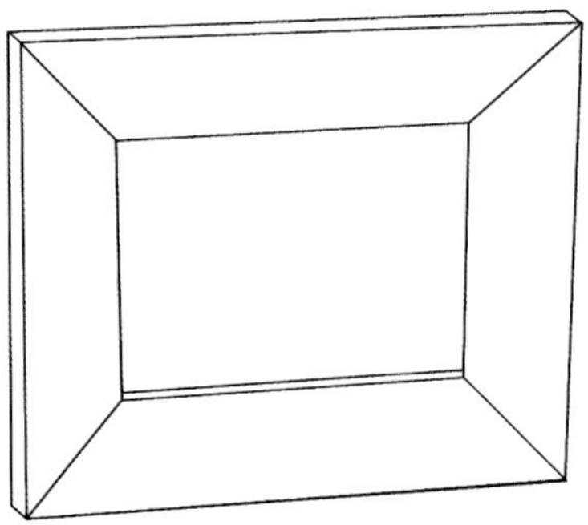

Frame-shaped

Display Packaging

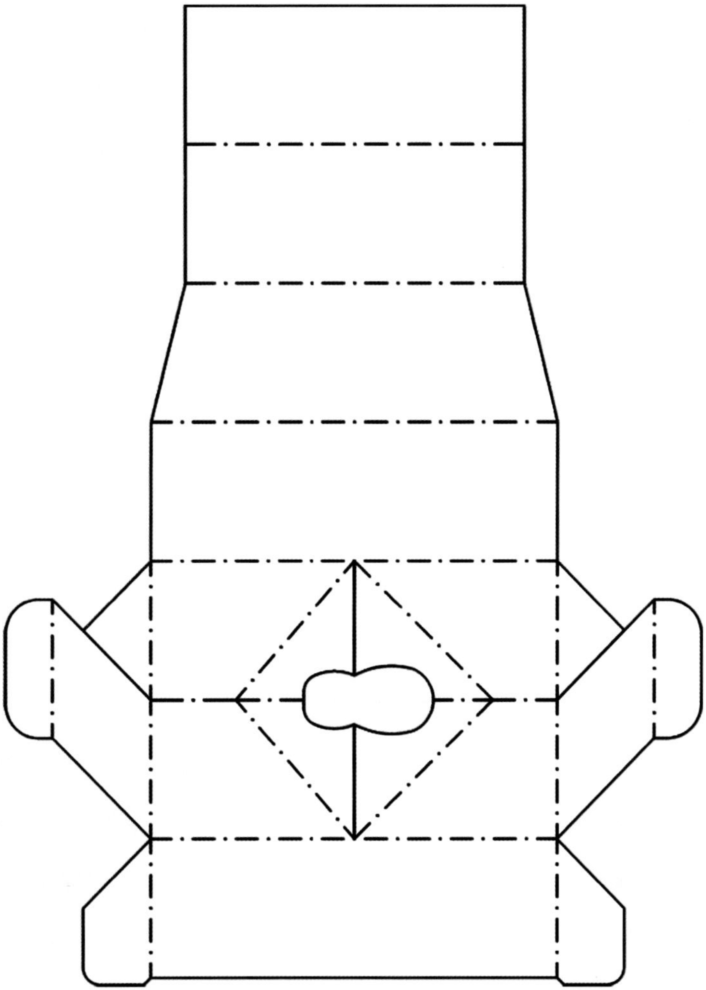

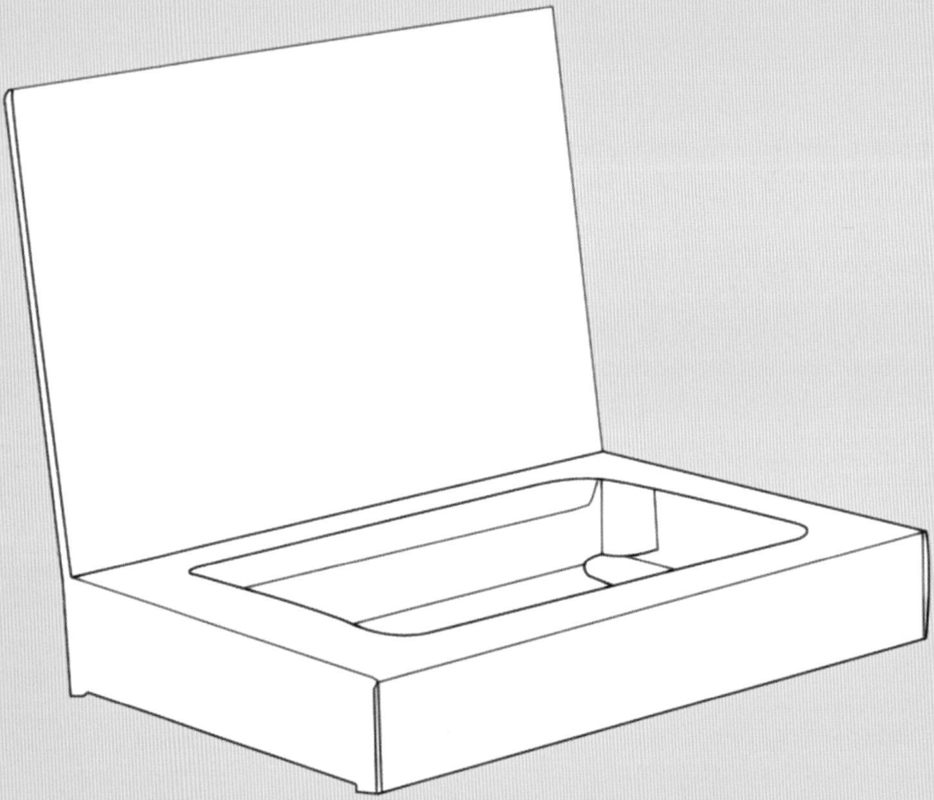

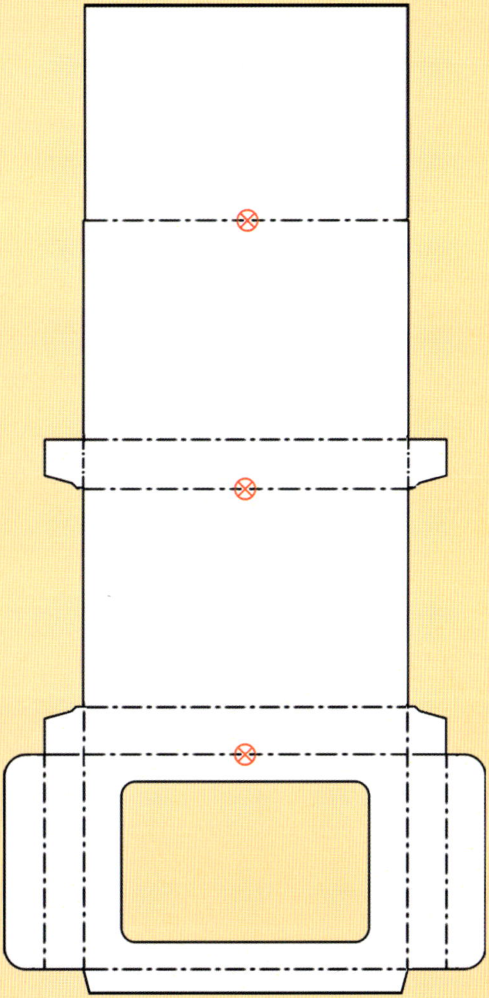

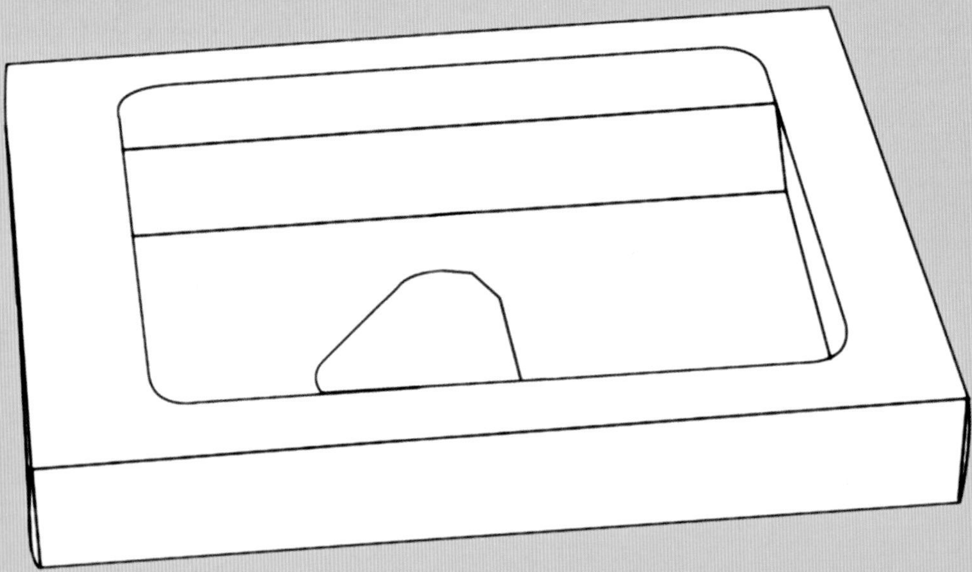

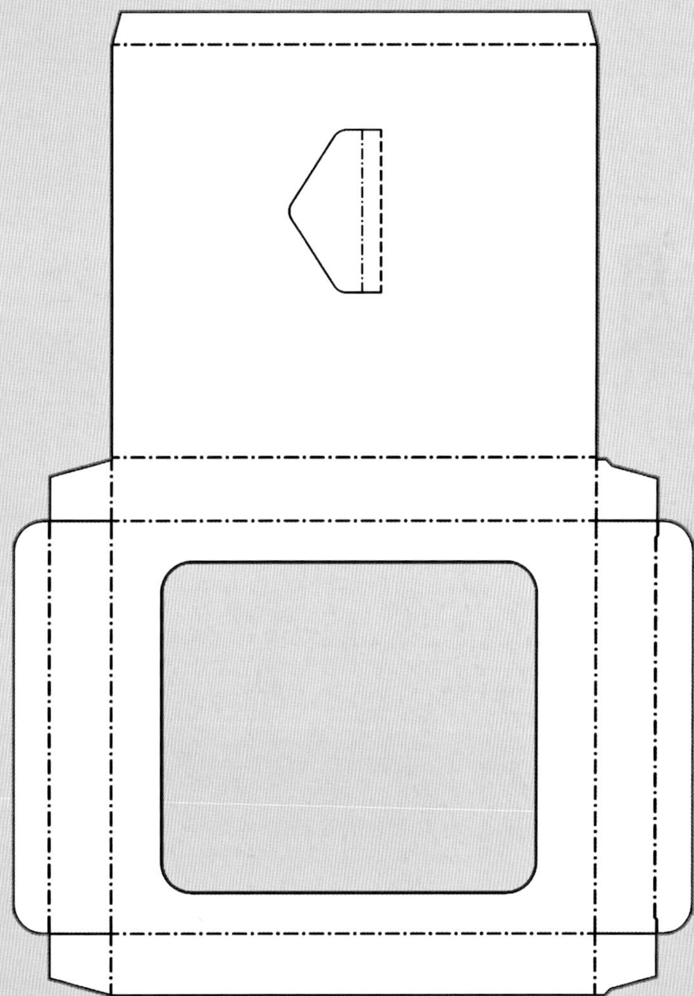

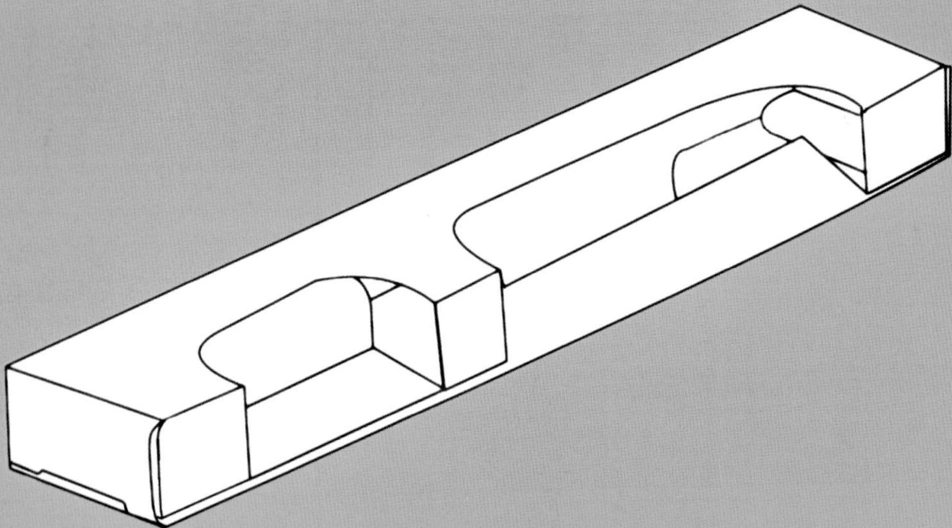

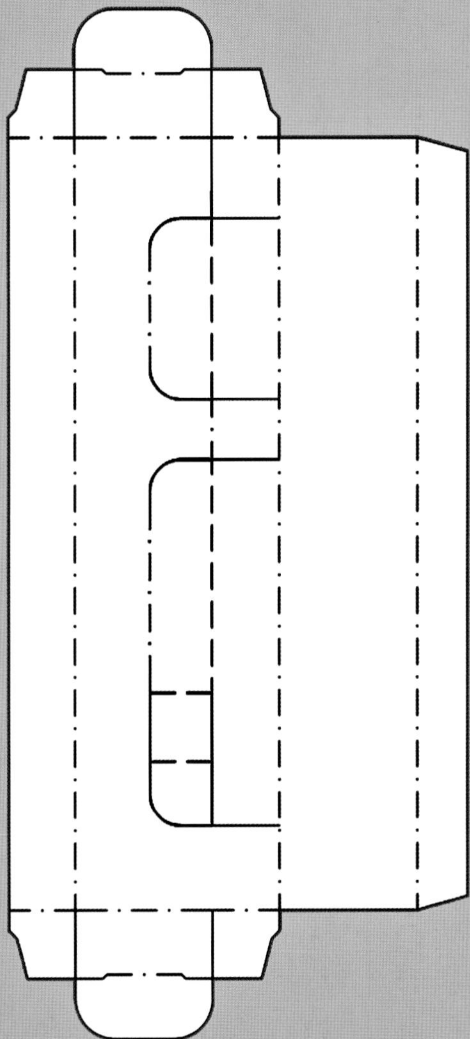

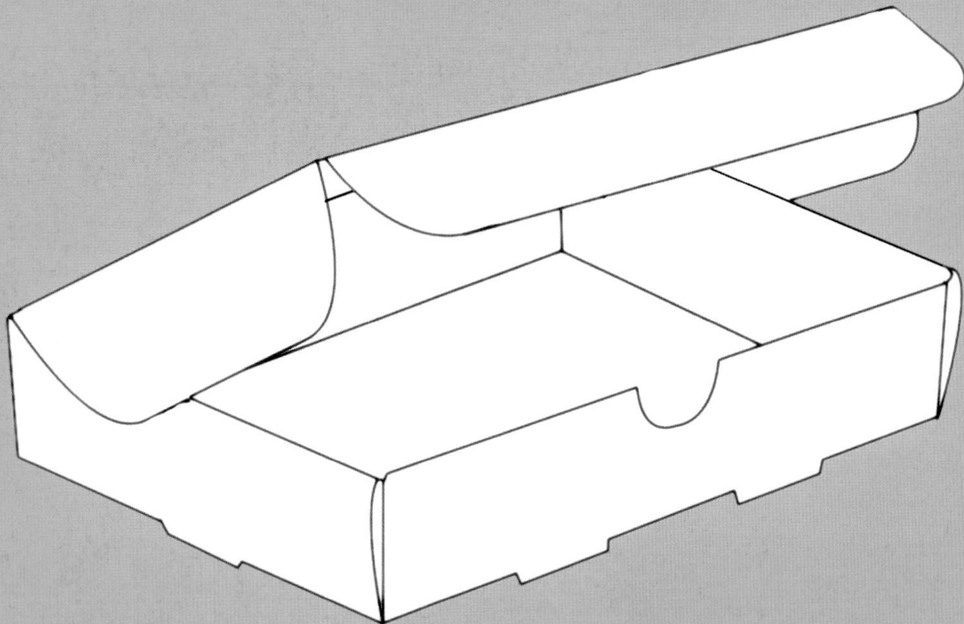

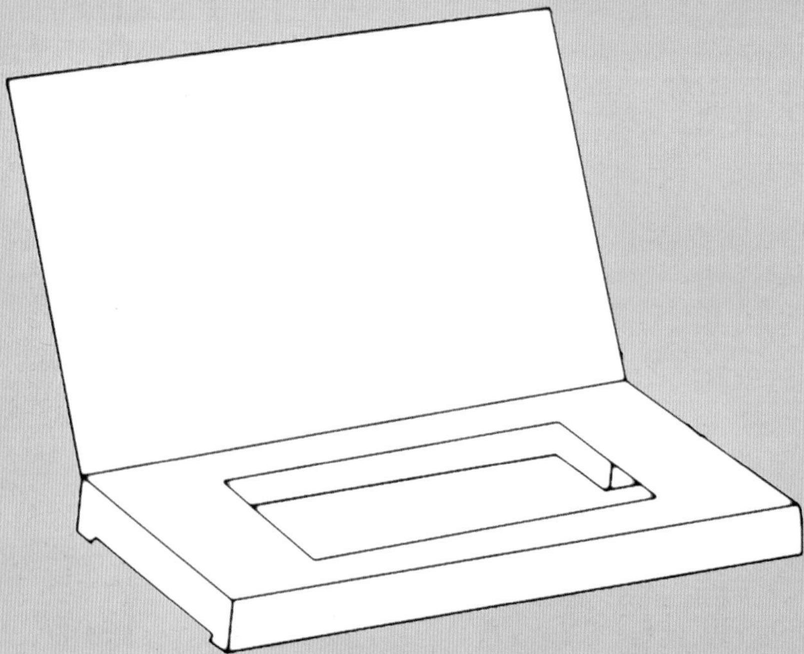

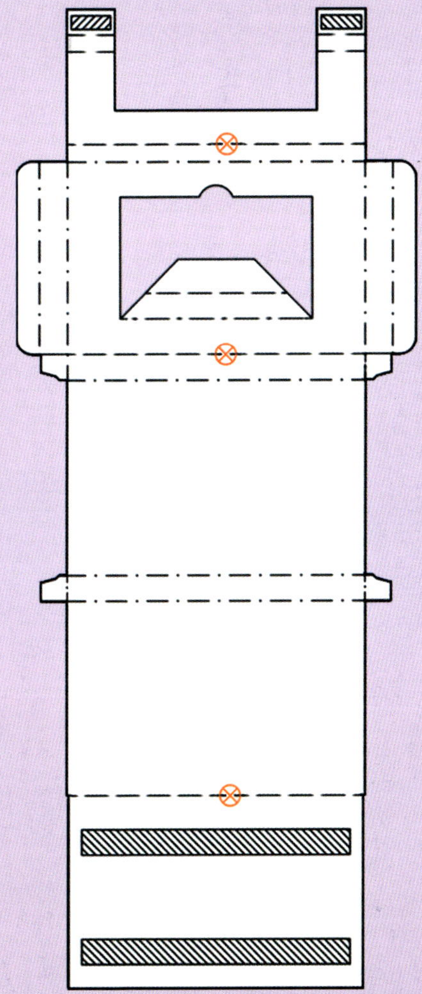

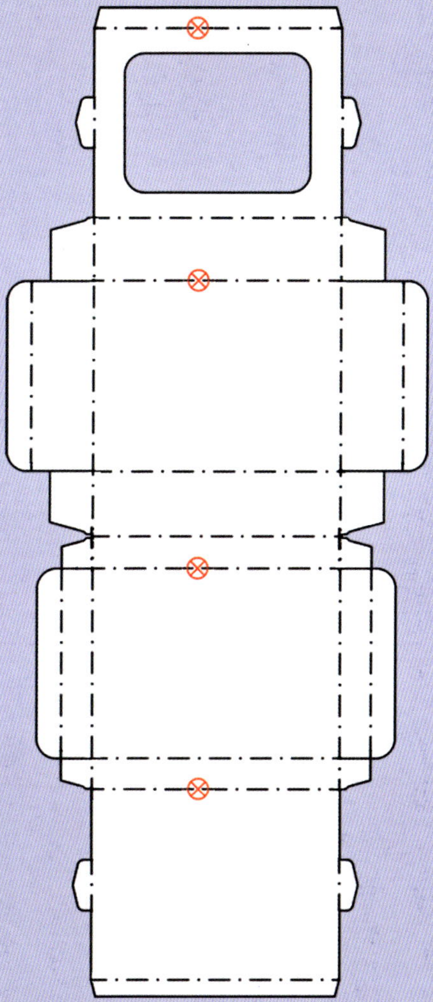

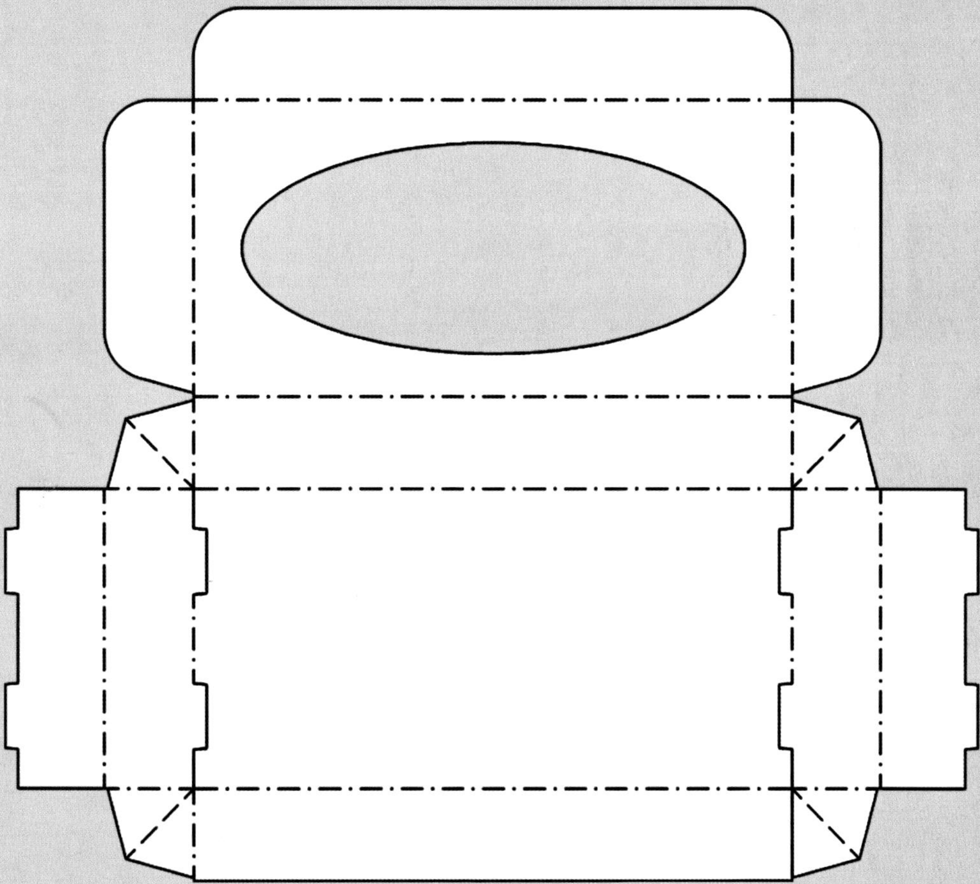

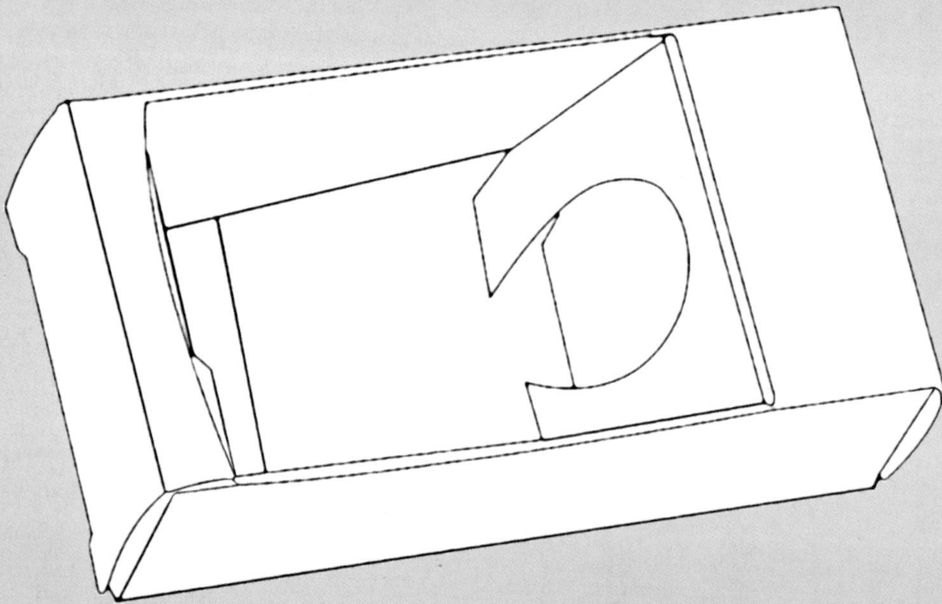

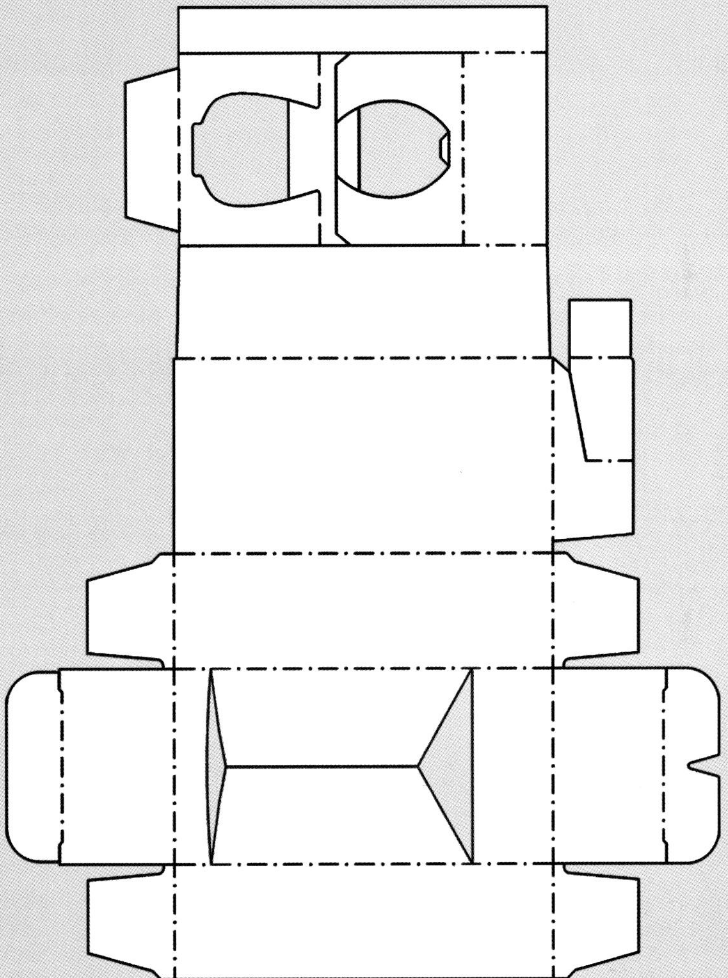

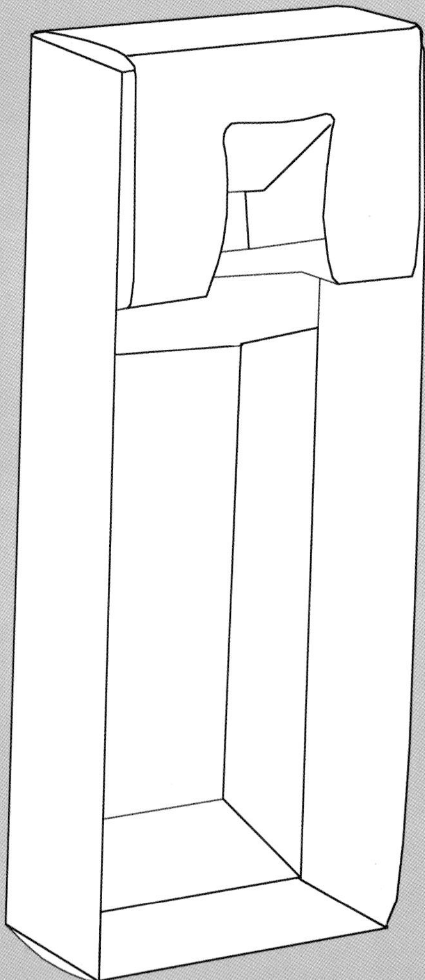

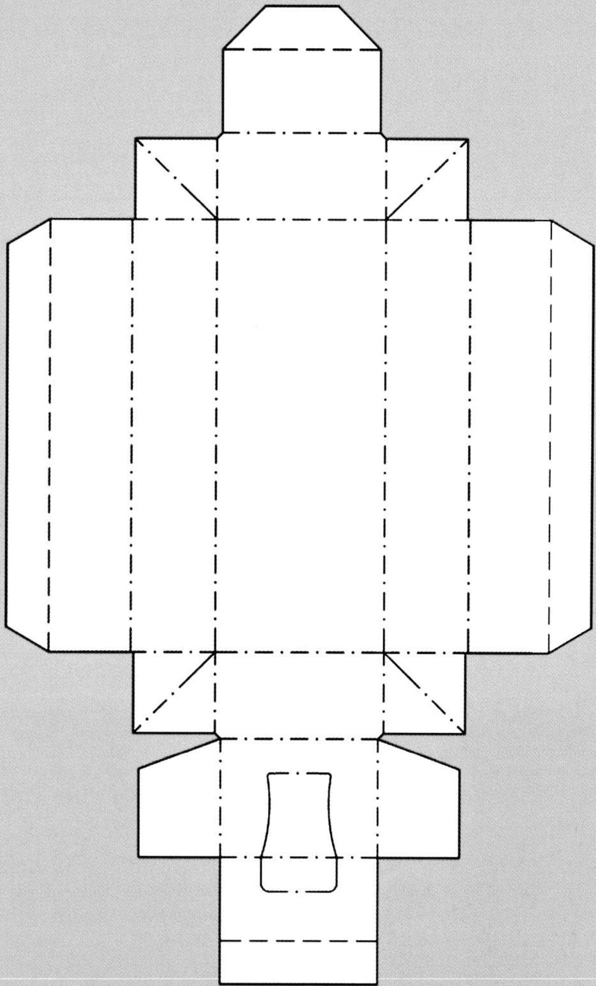

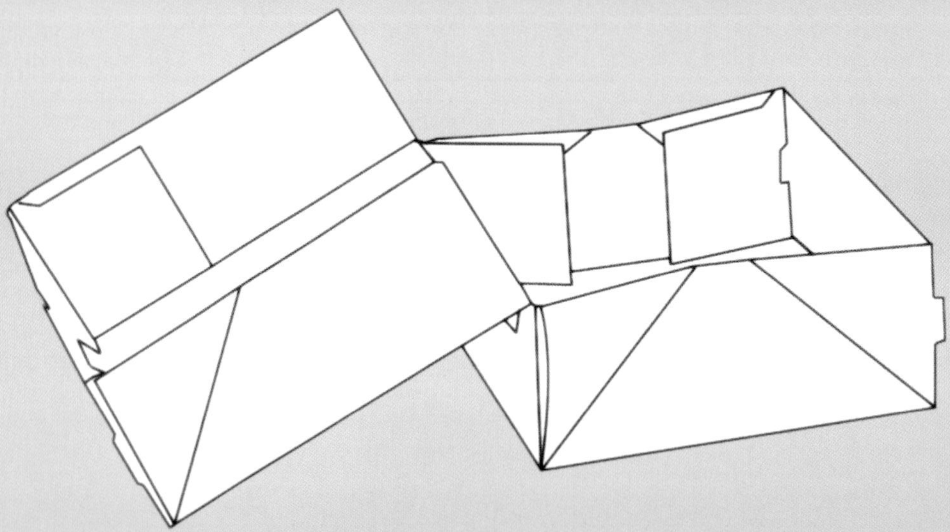

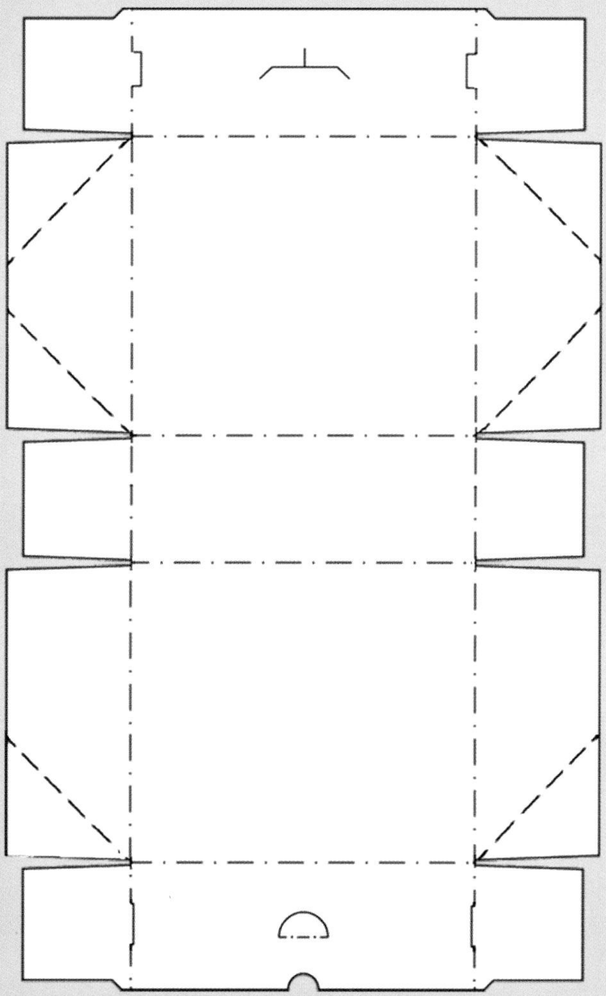

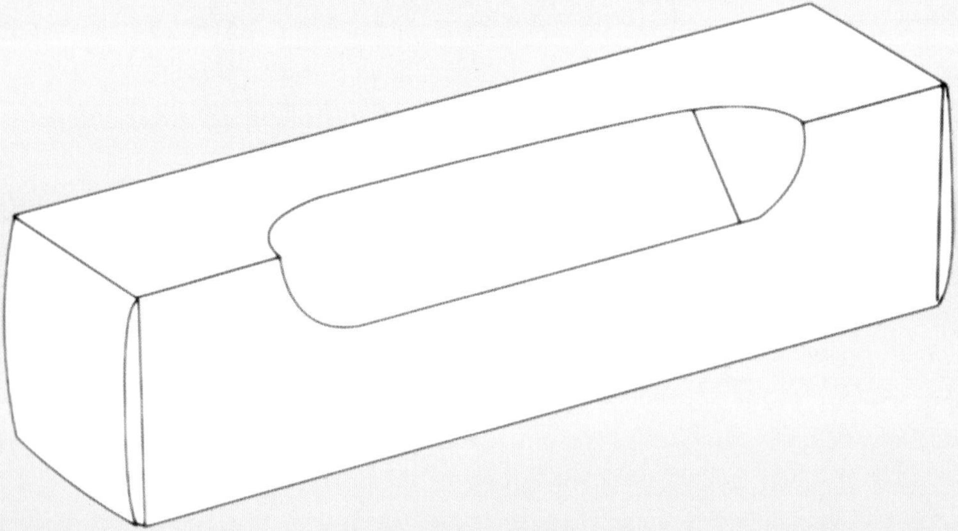

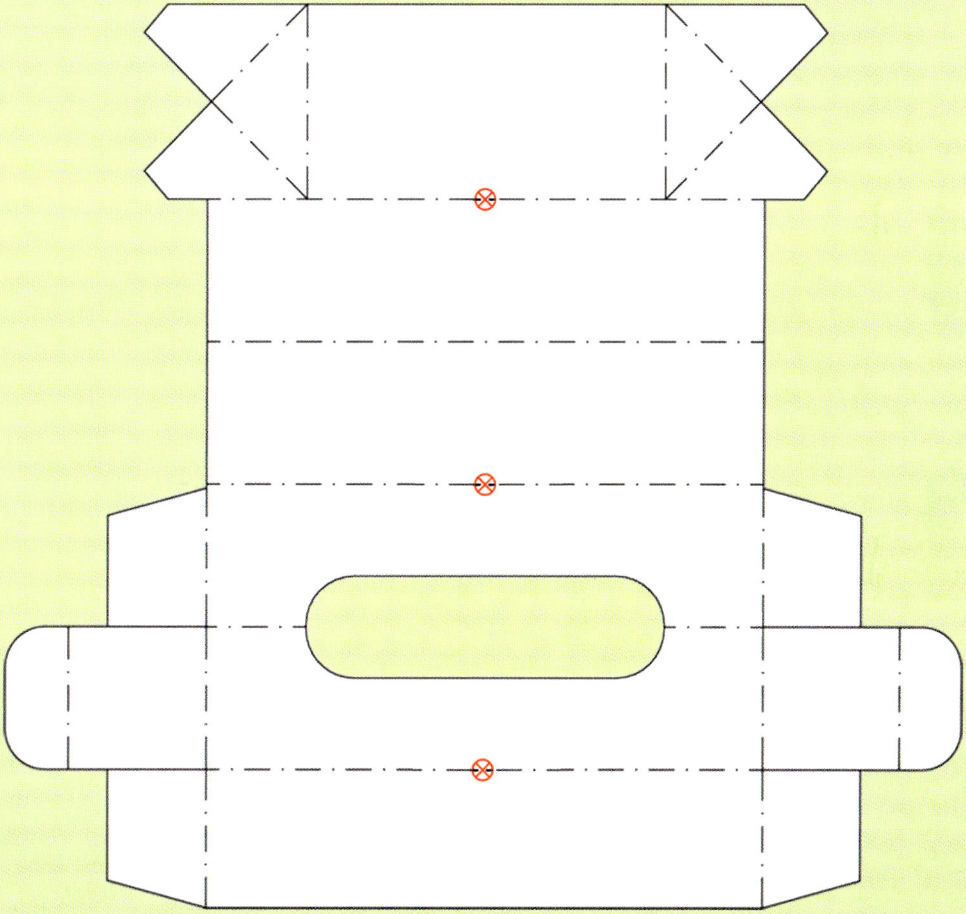

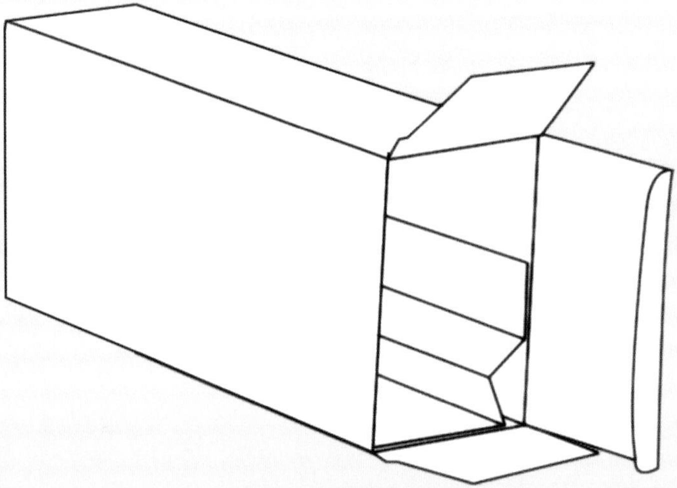

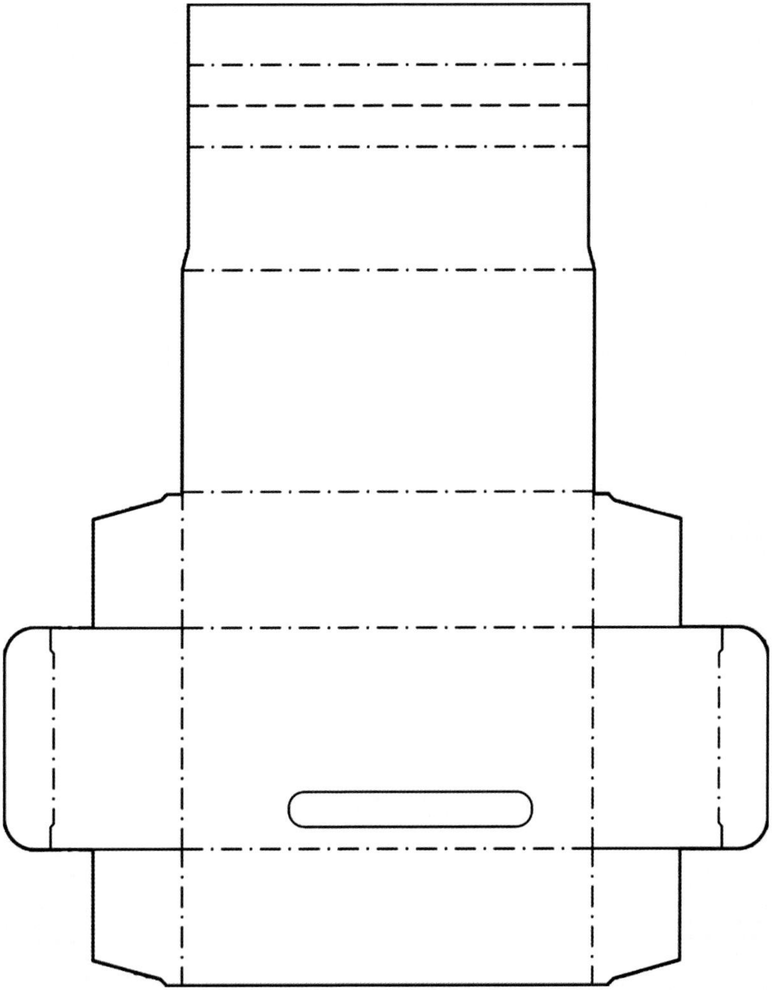

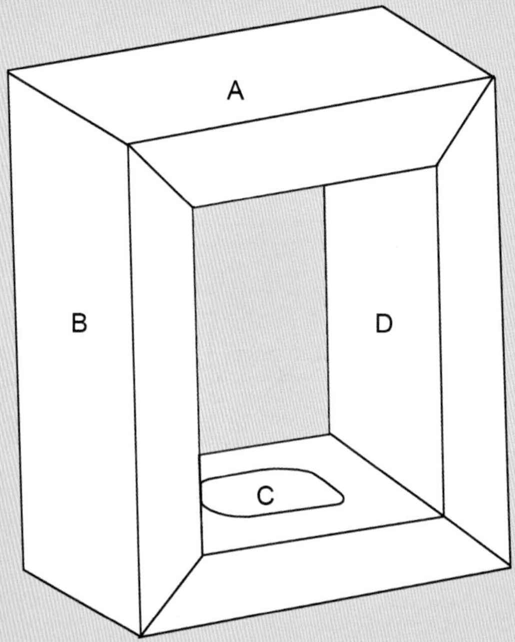
A
B
D
C

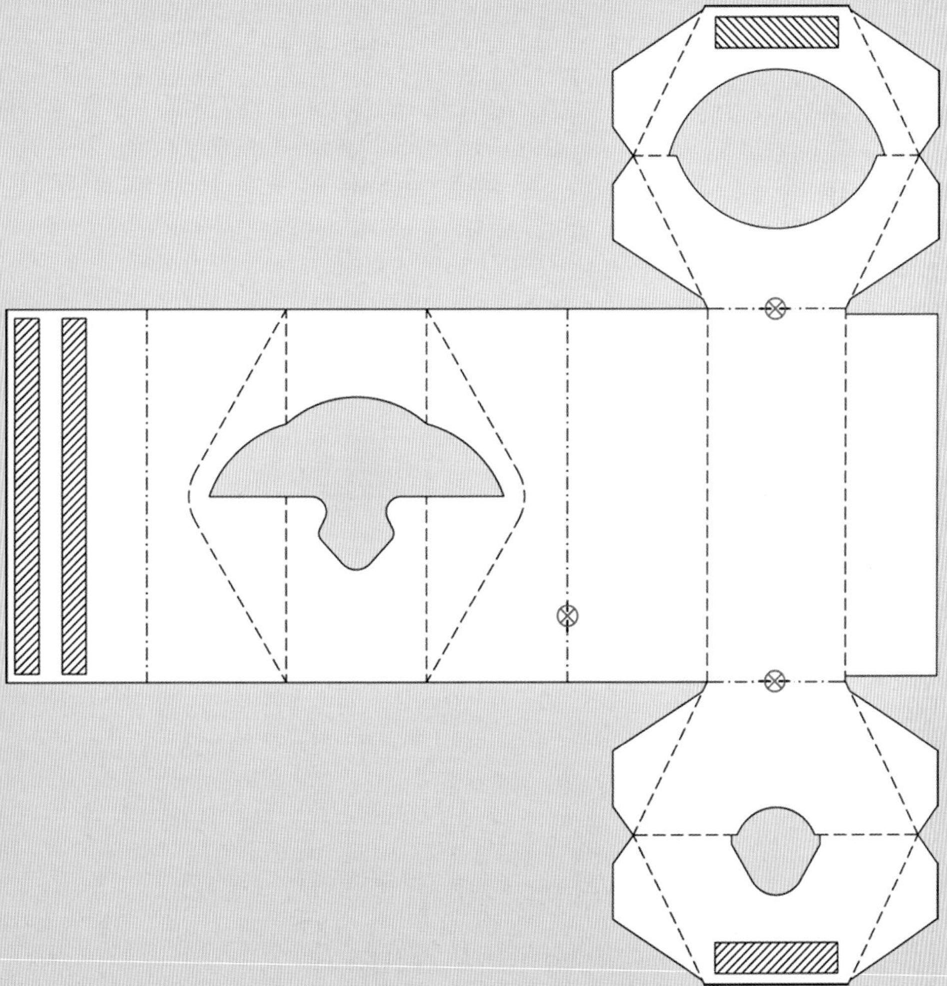

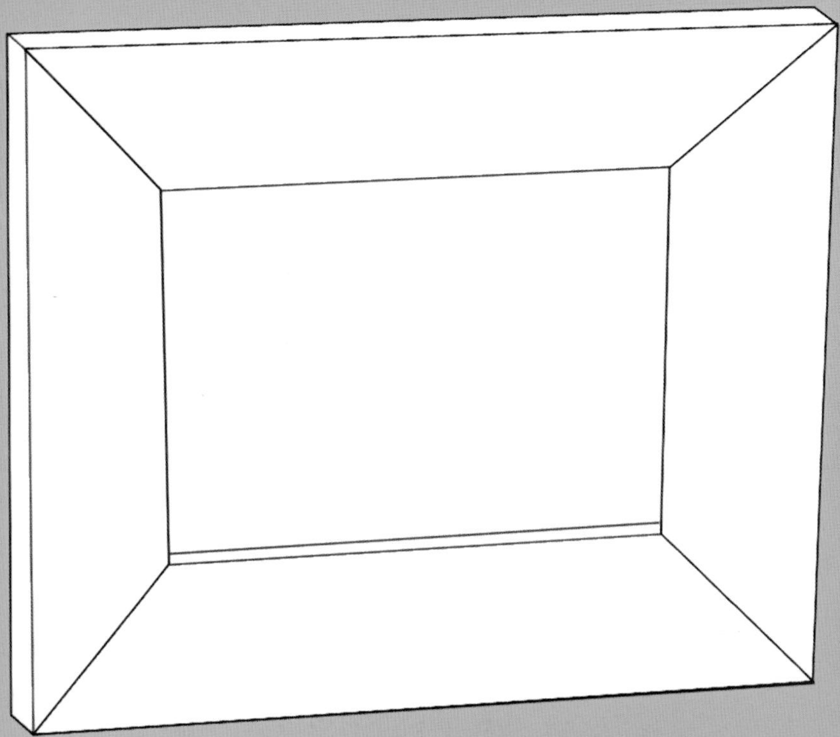

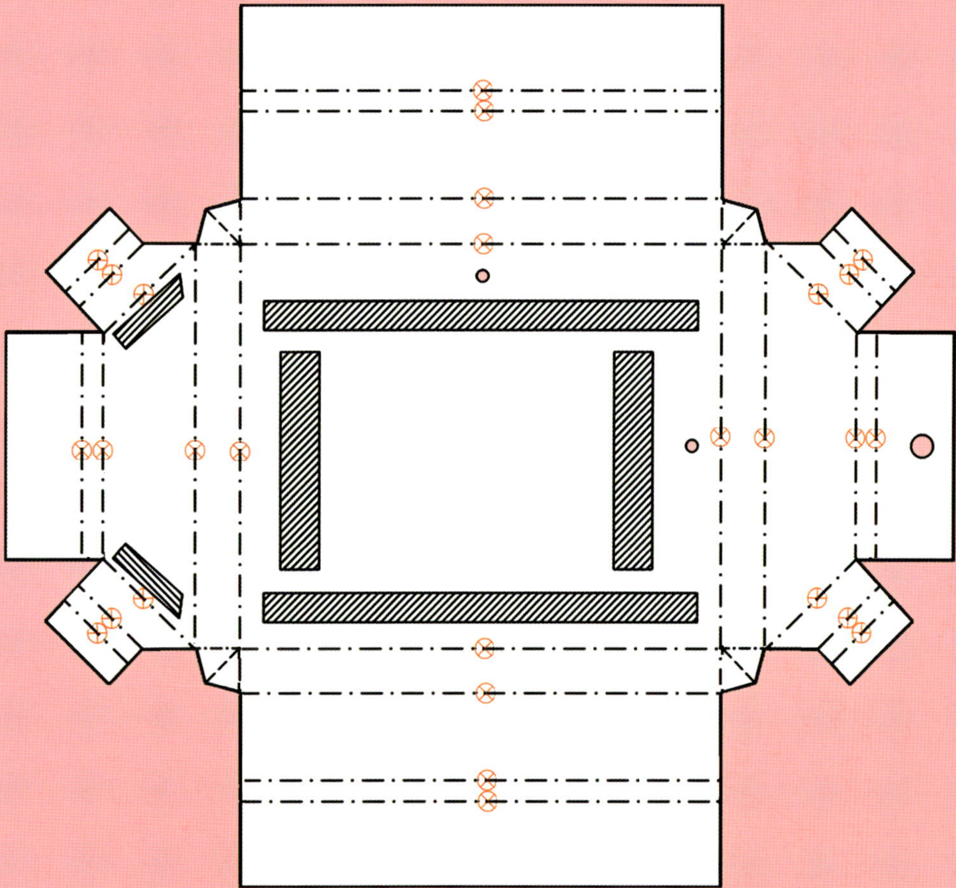

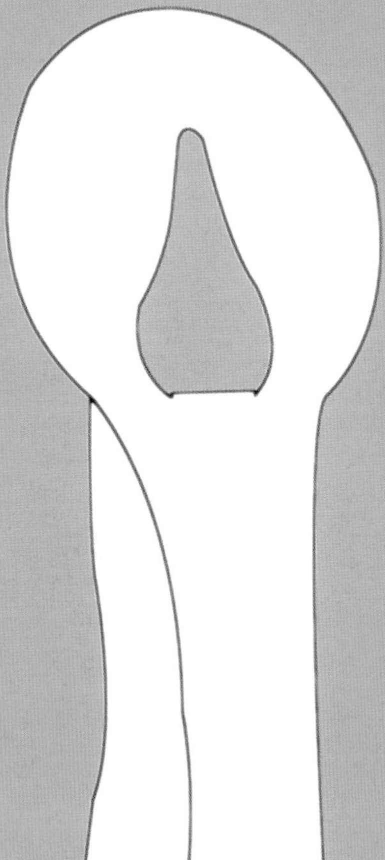

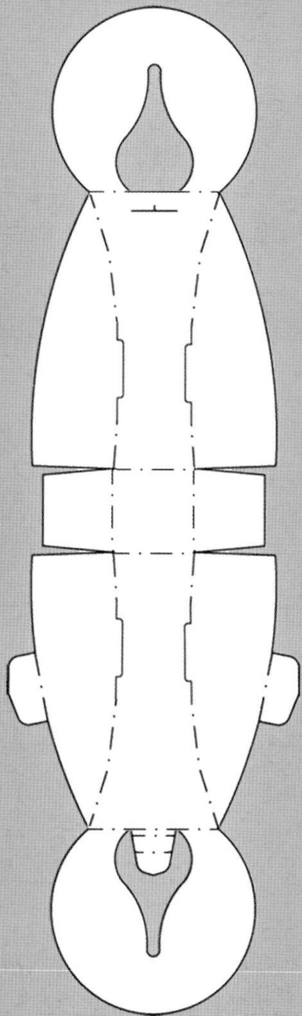

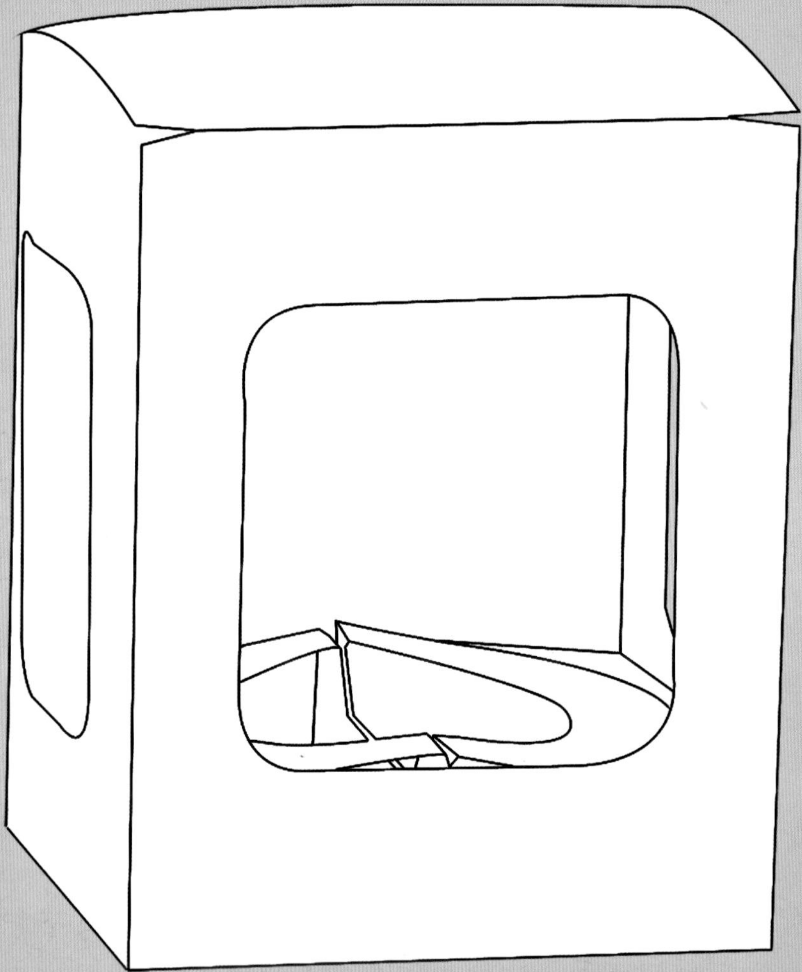

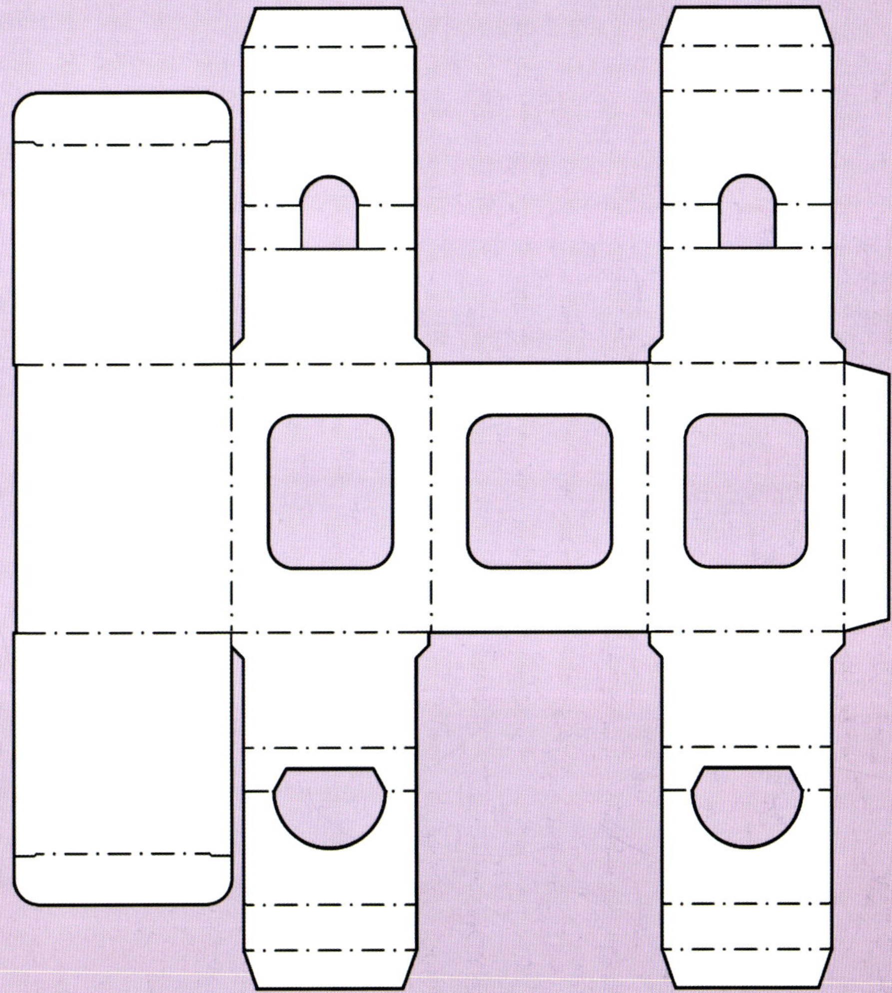

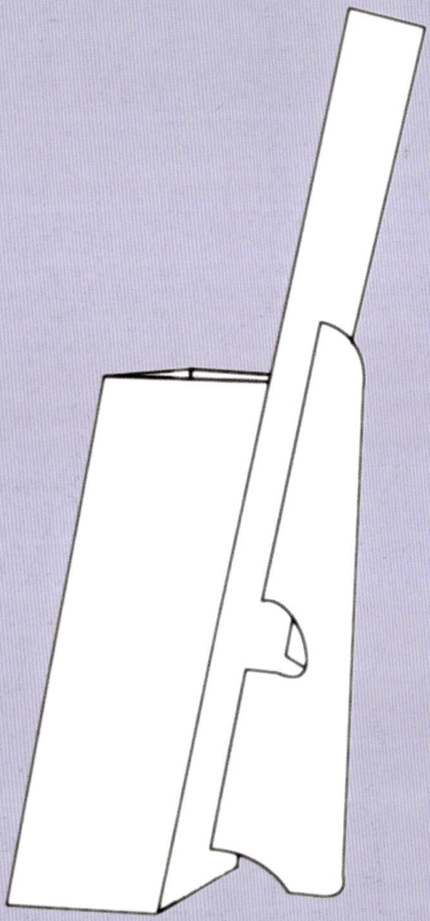

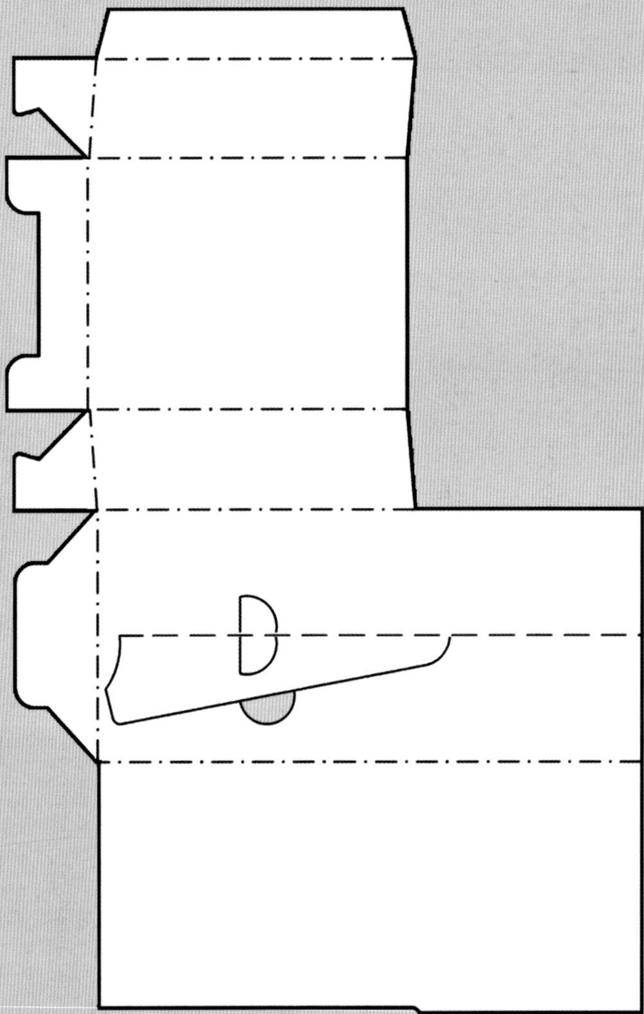

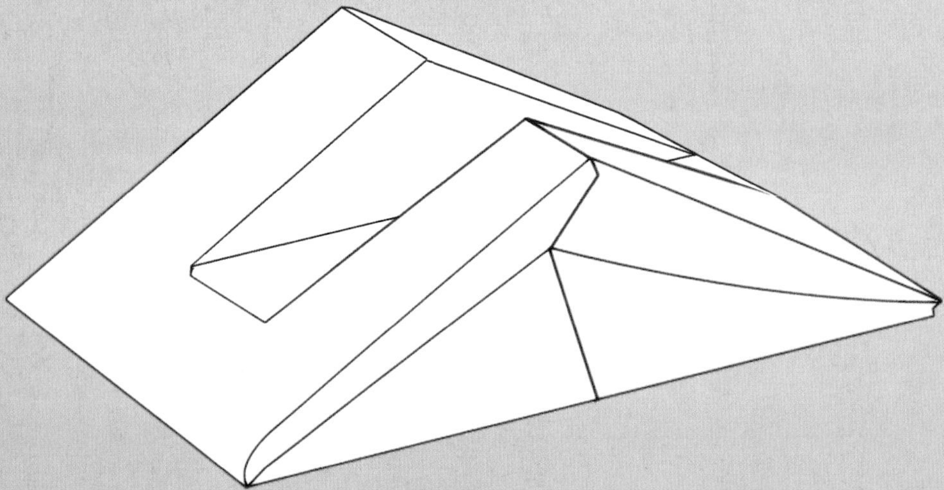

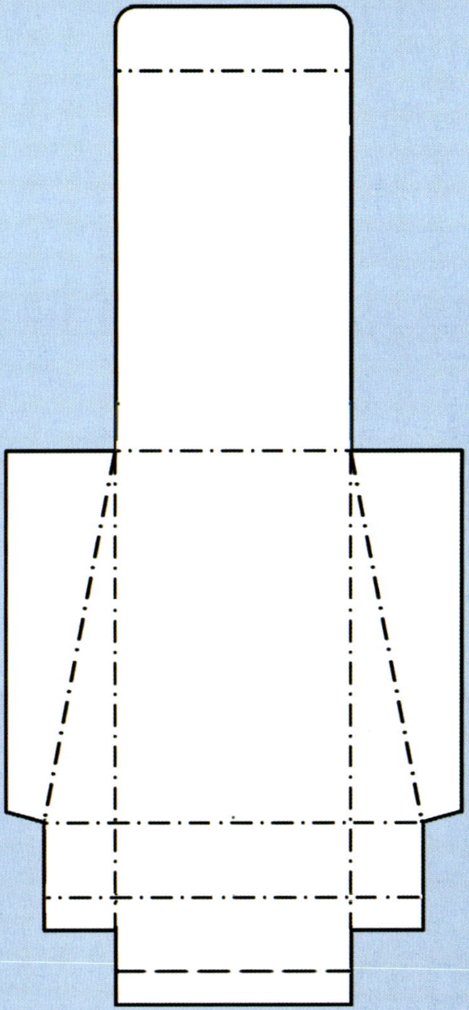

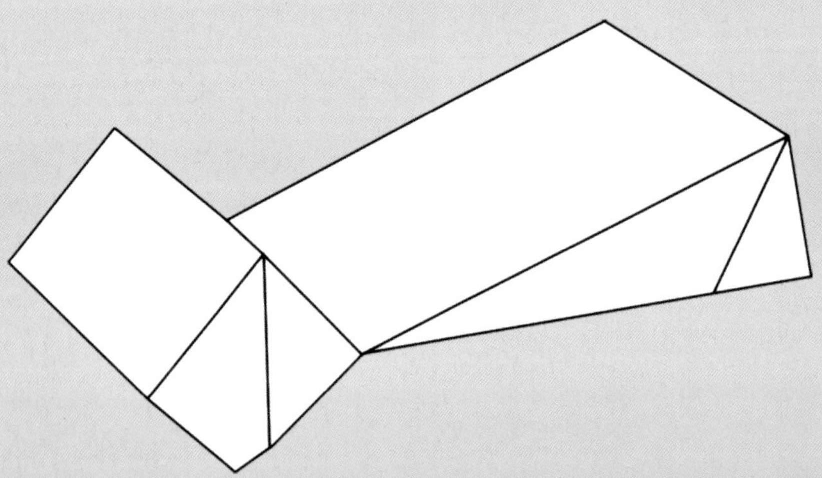

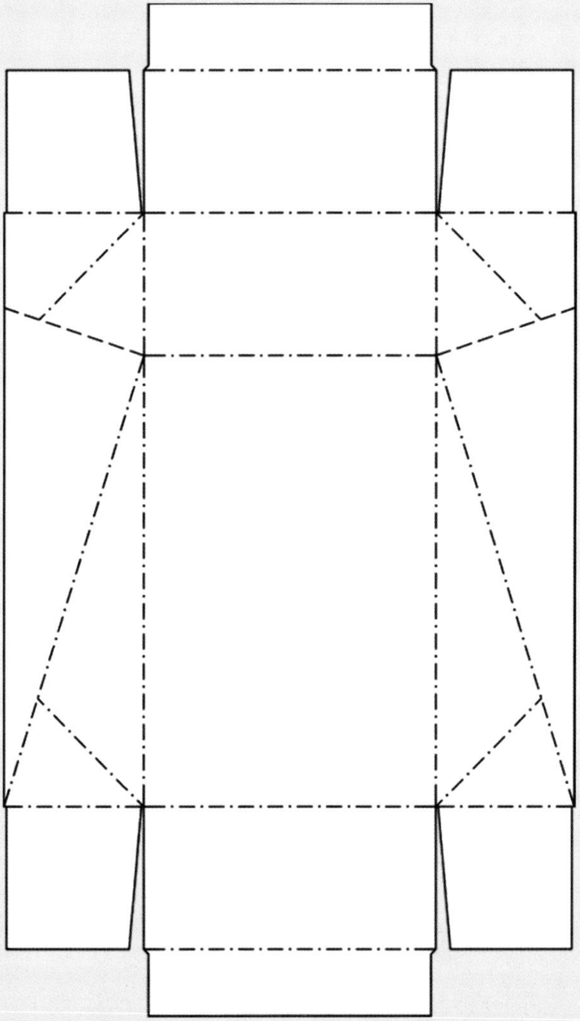

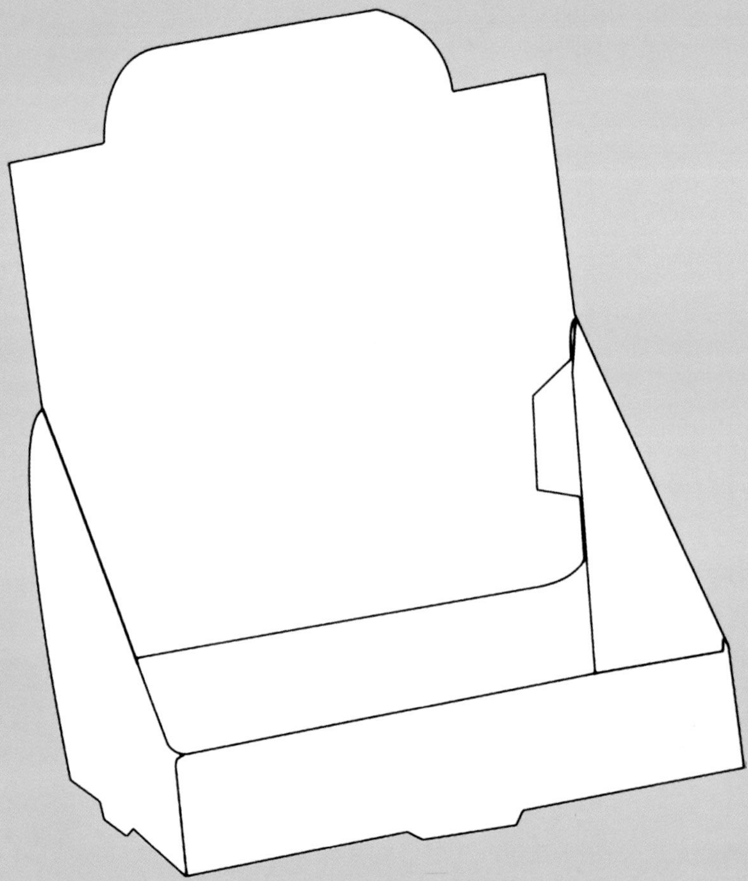

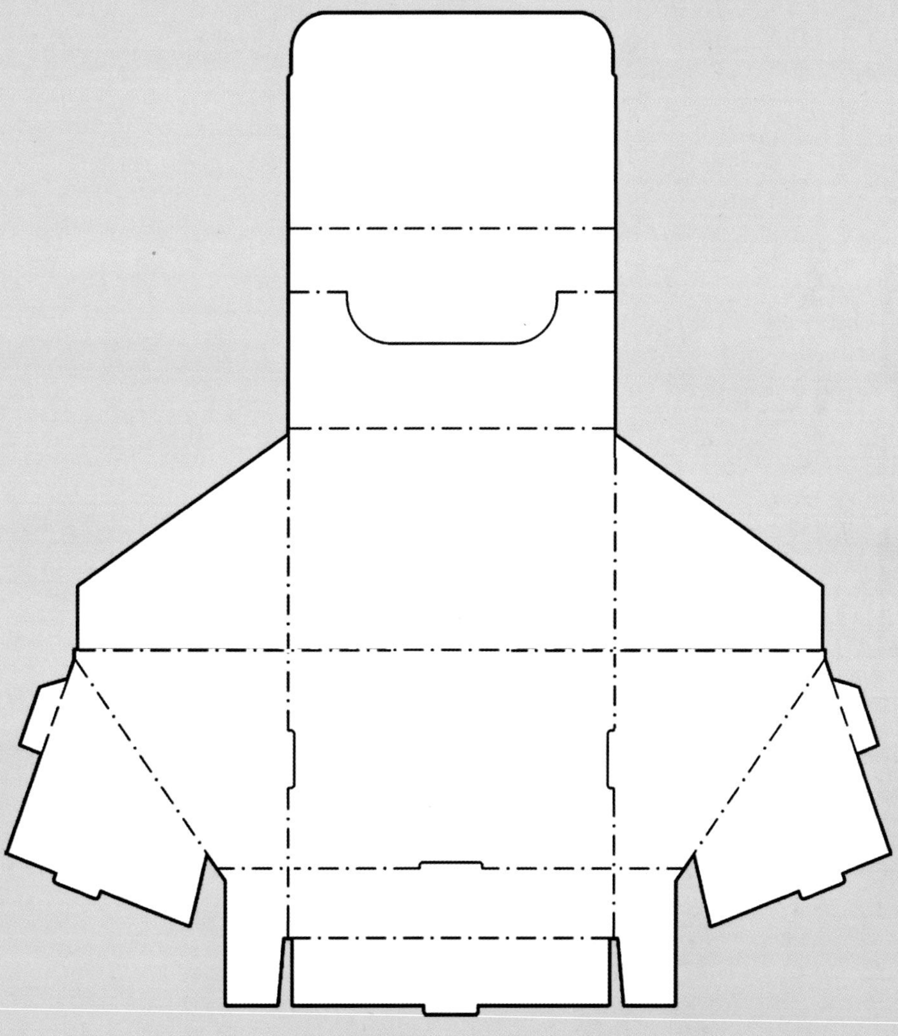

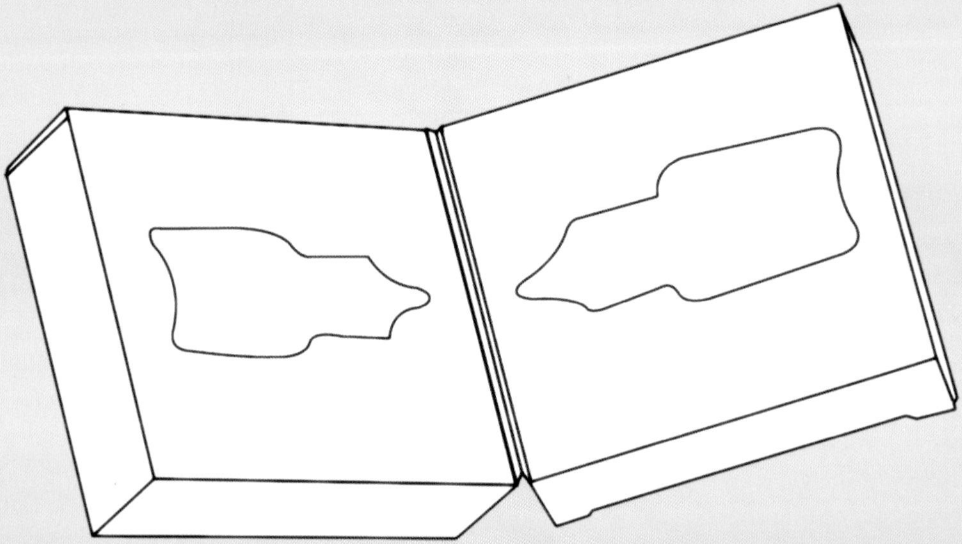

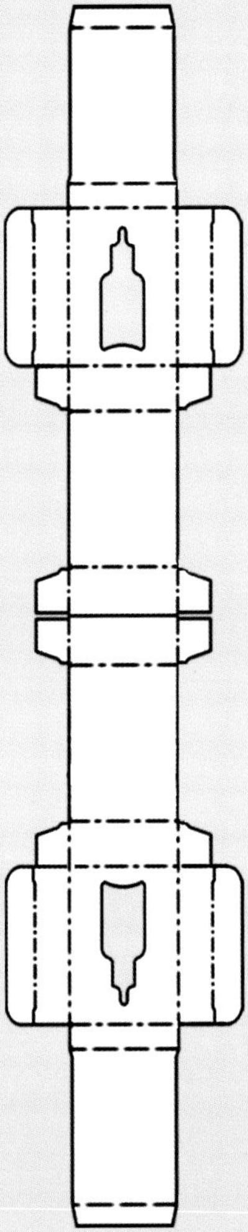

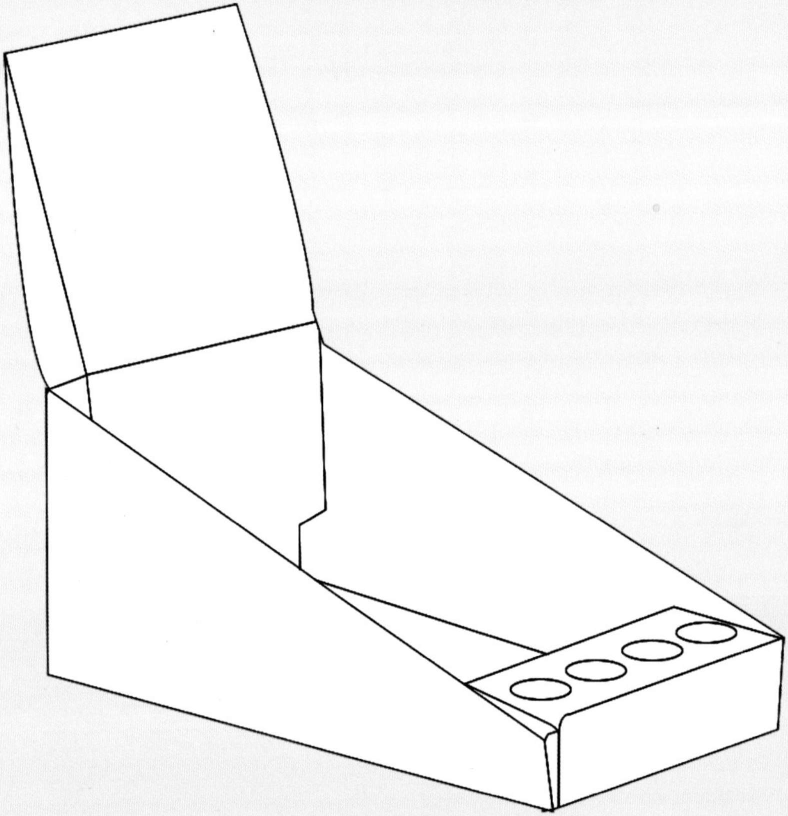

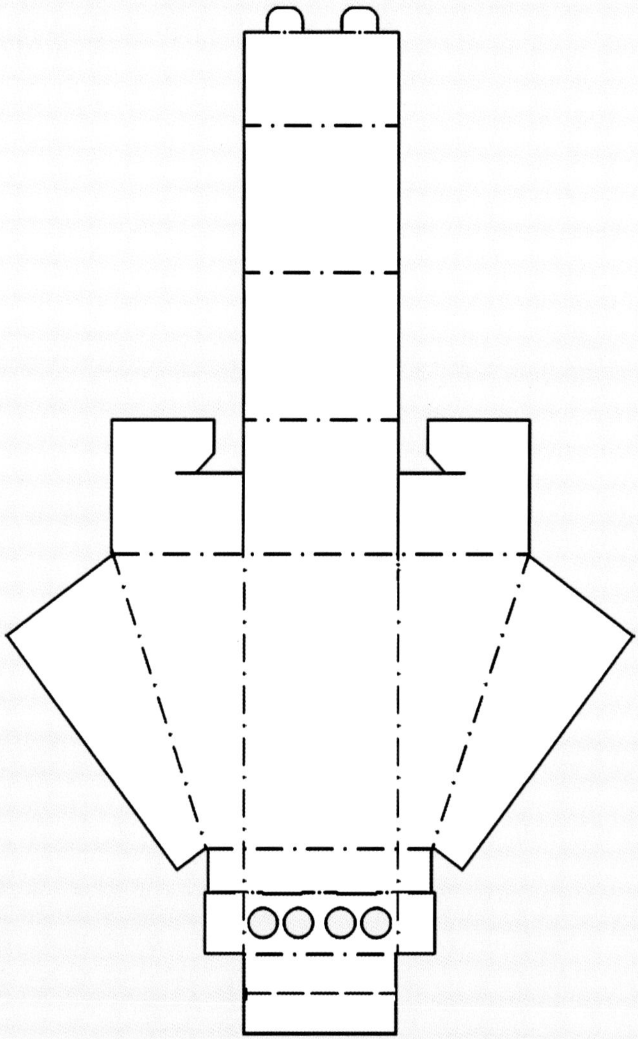

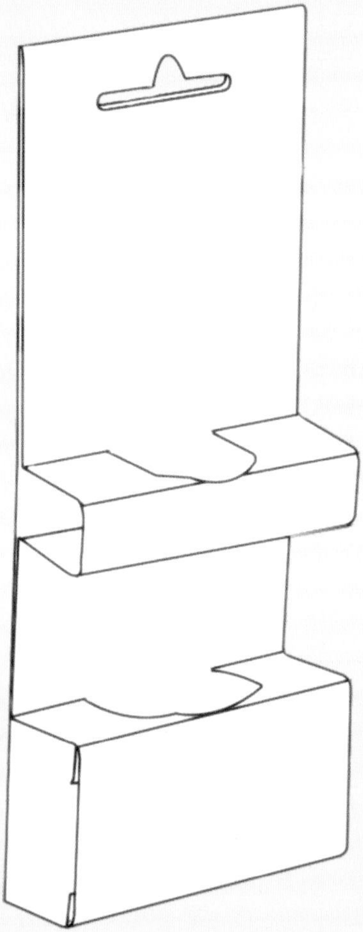

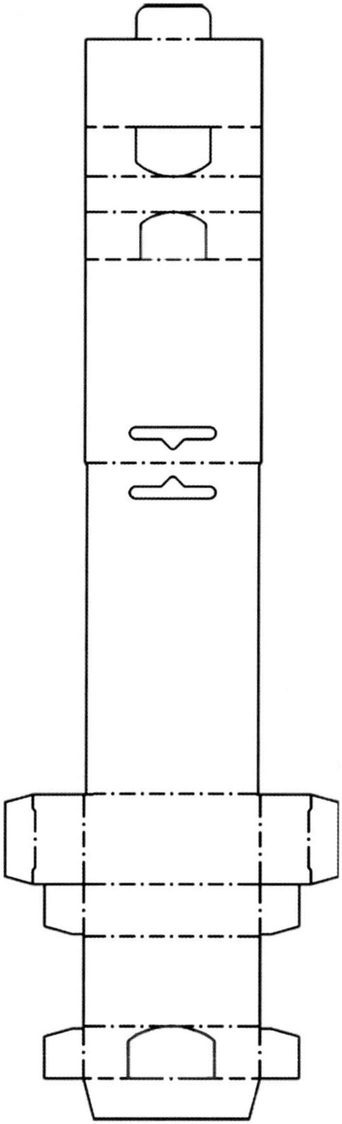

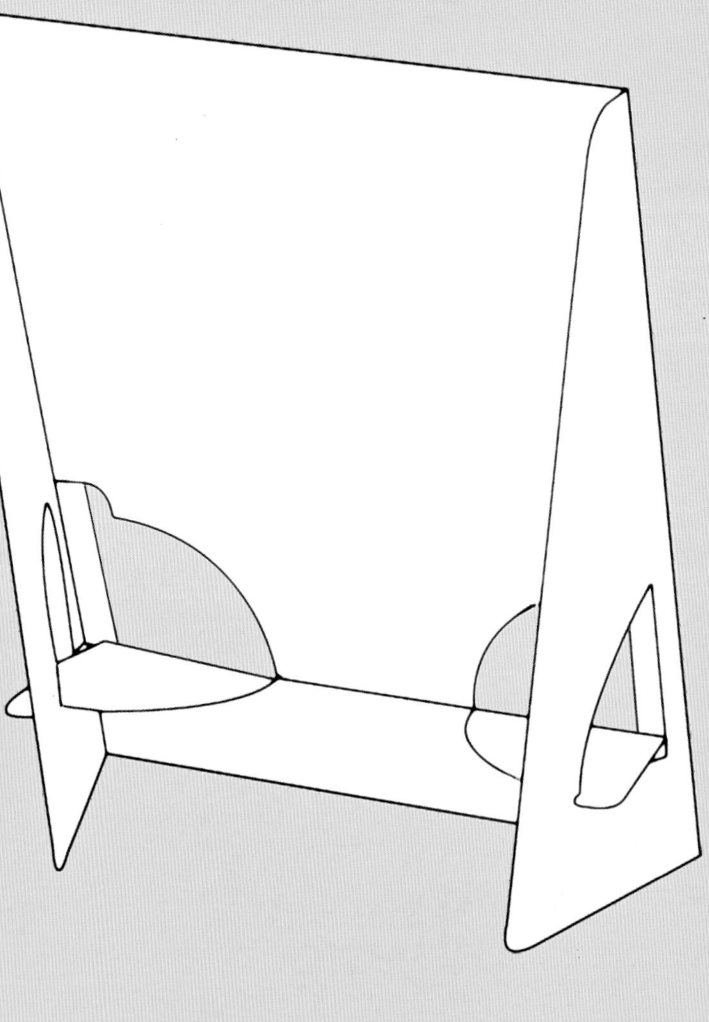

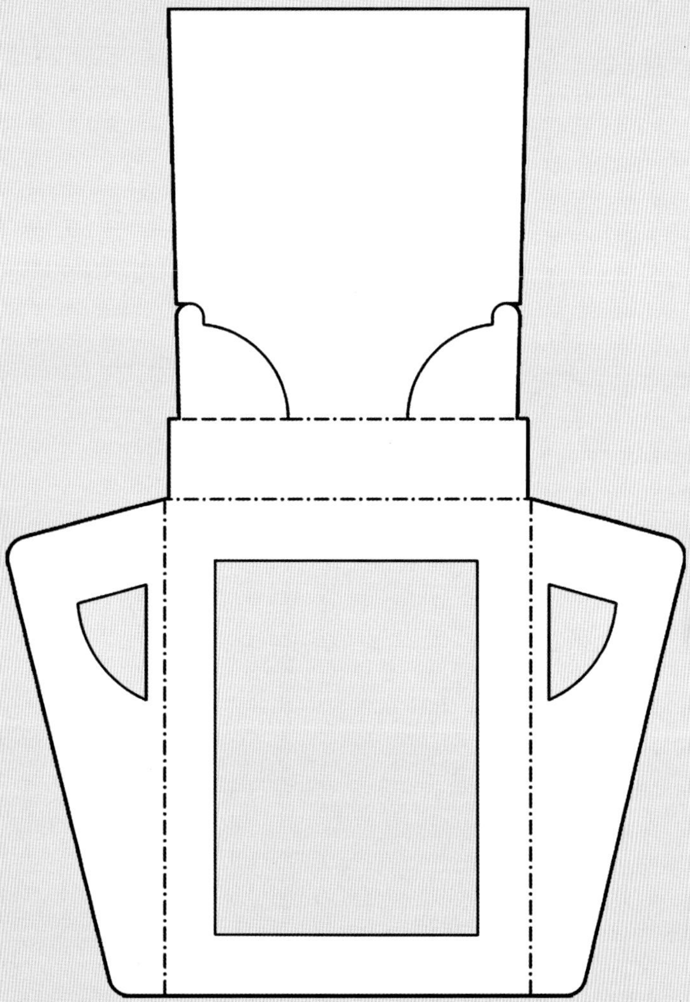

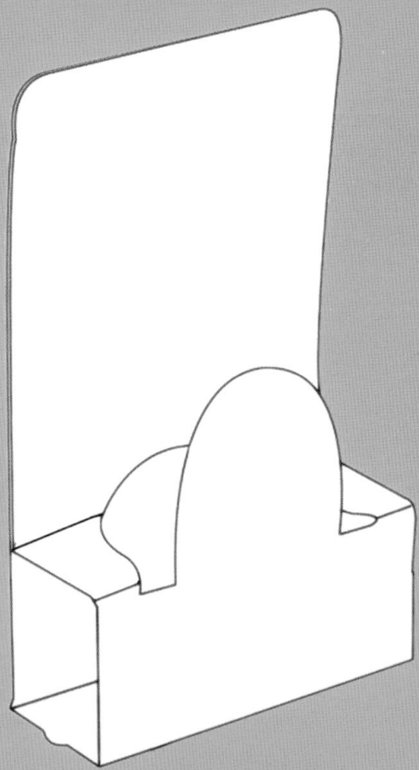

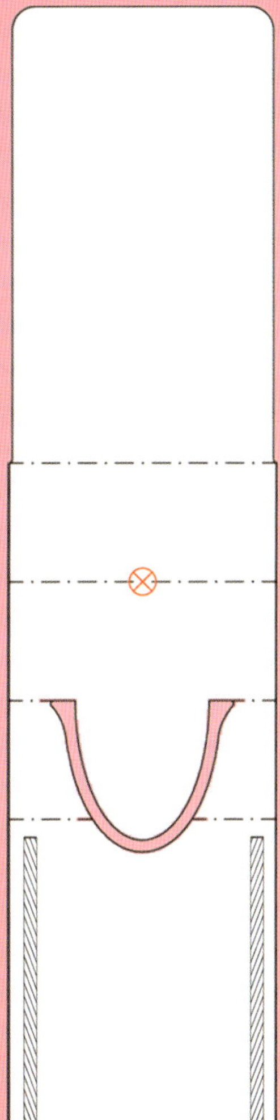

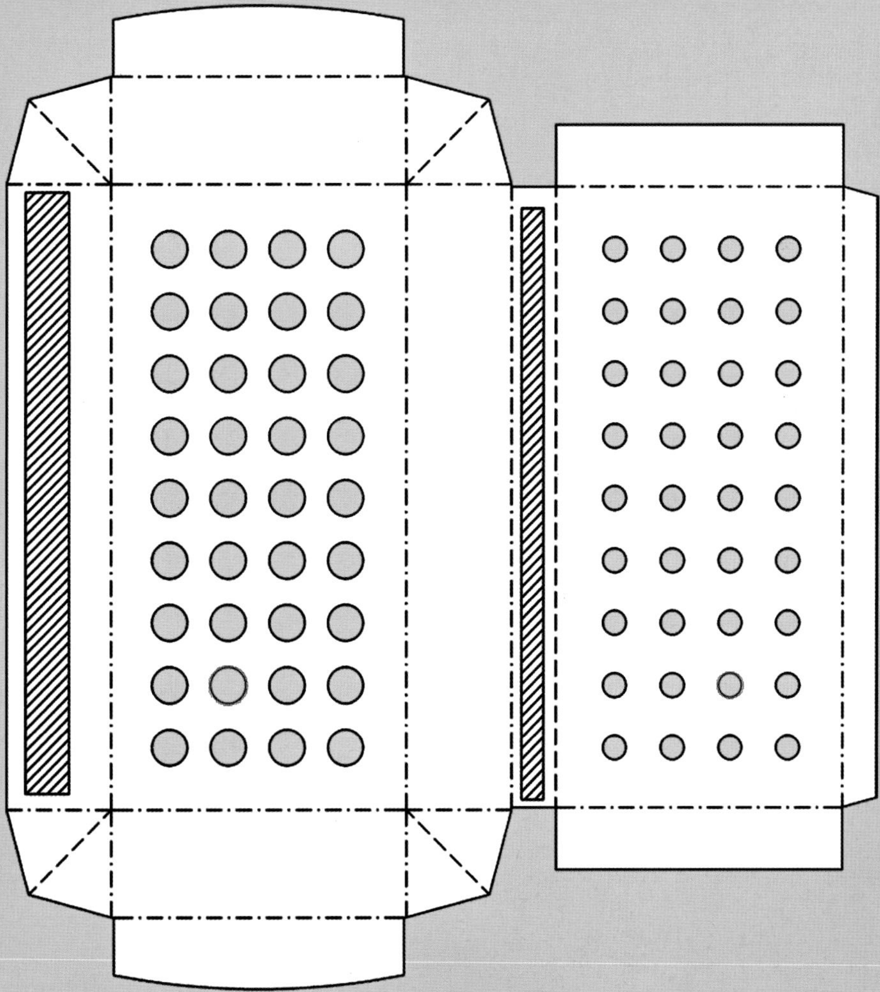

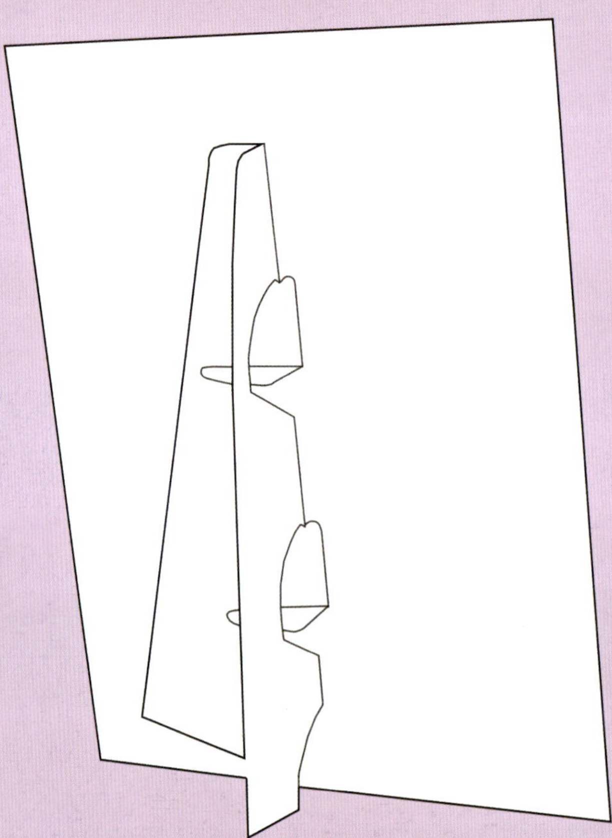

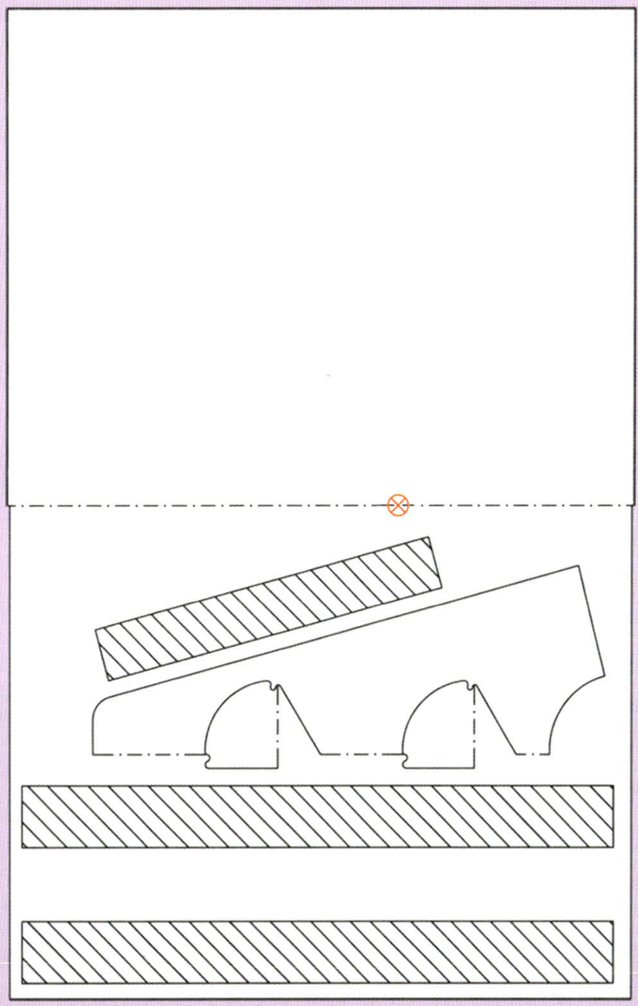

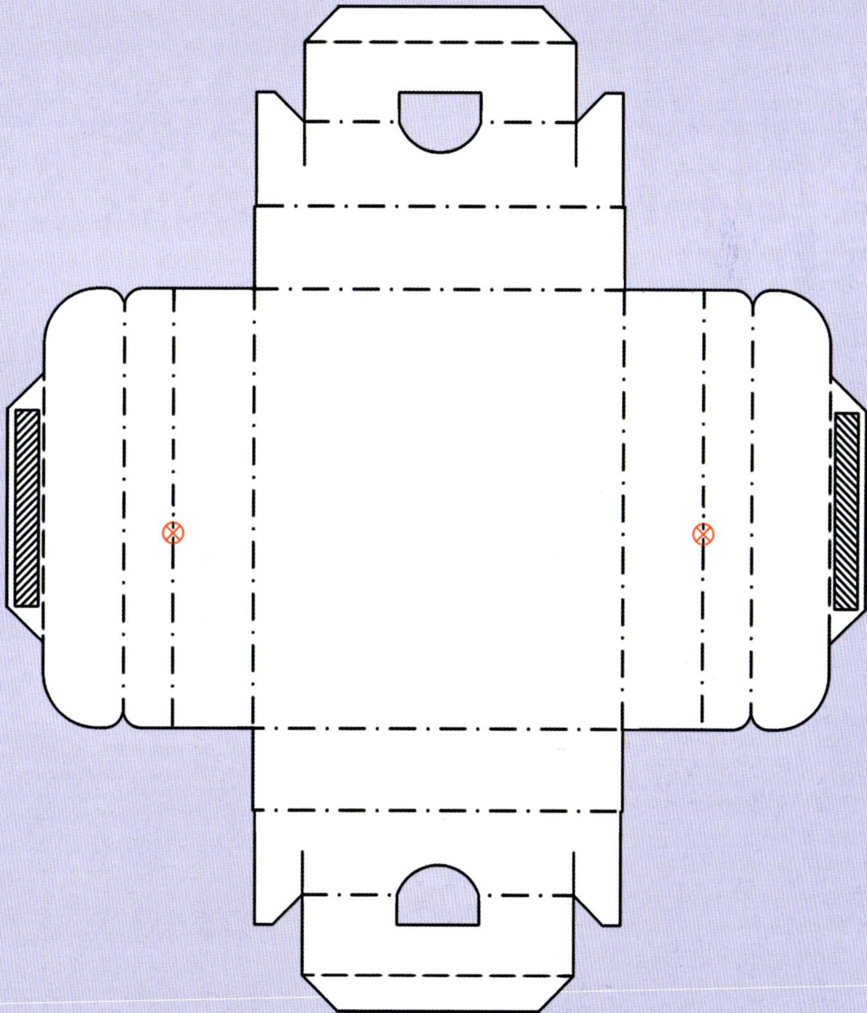

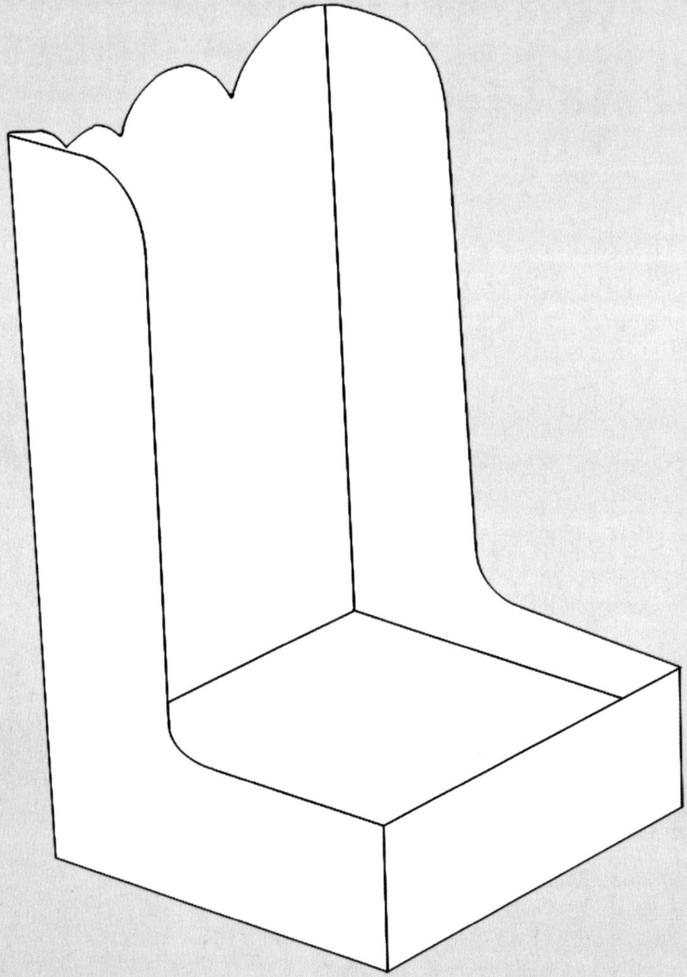

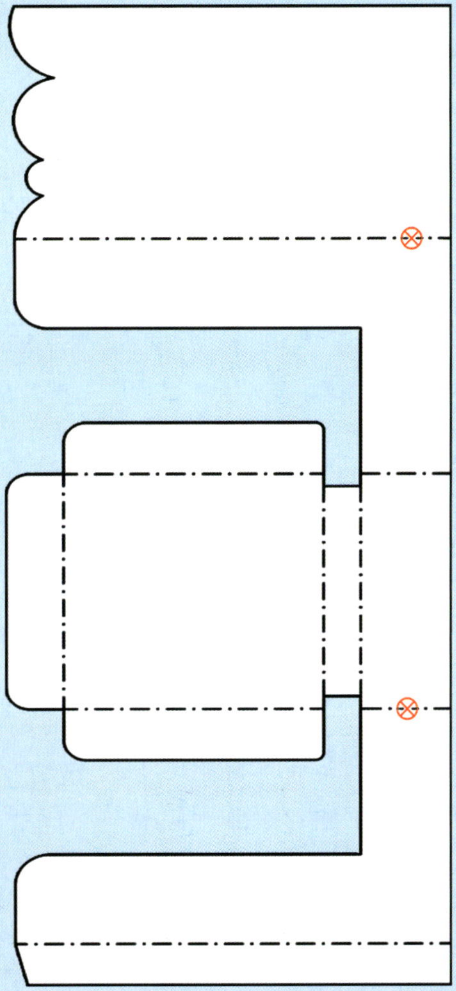

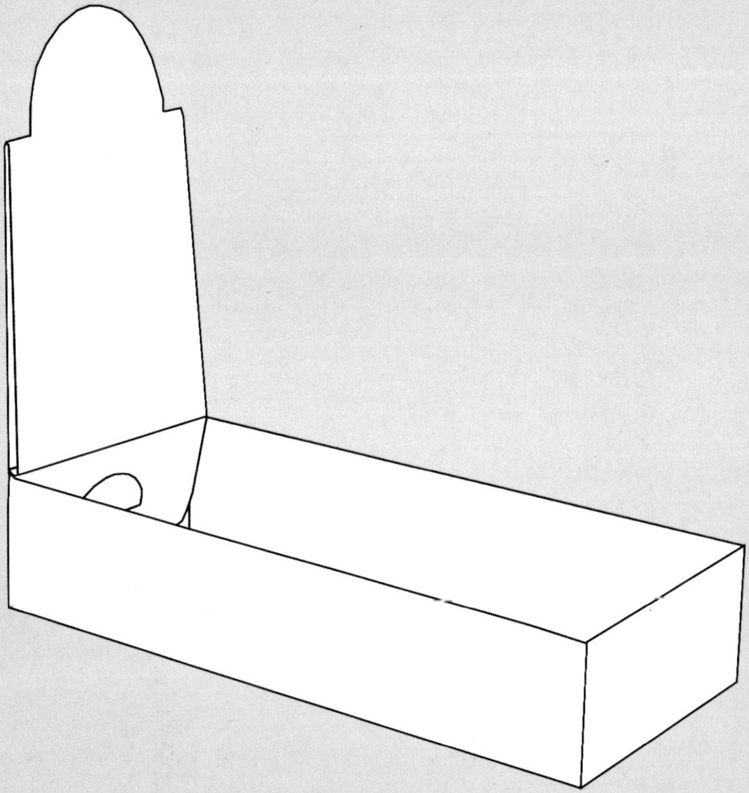

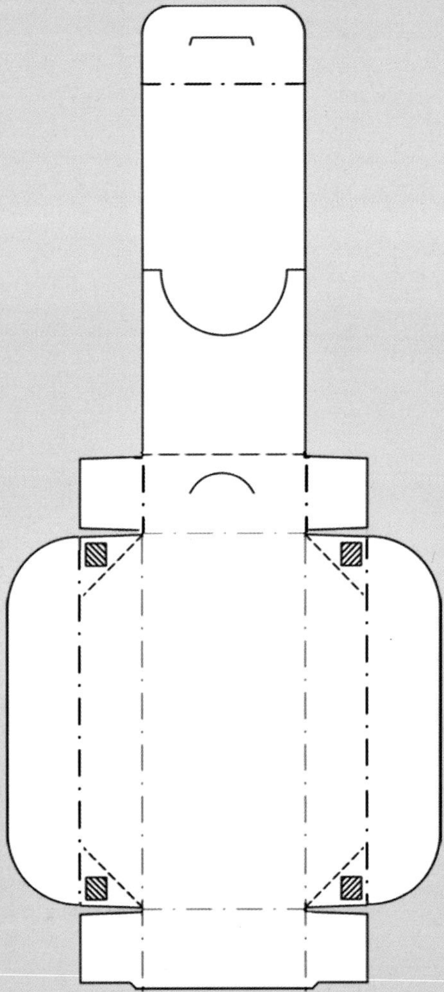

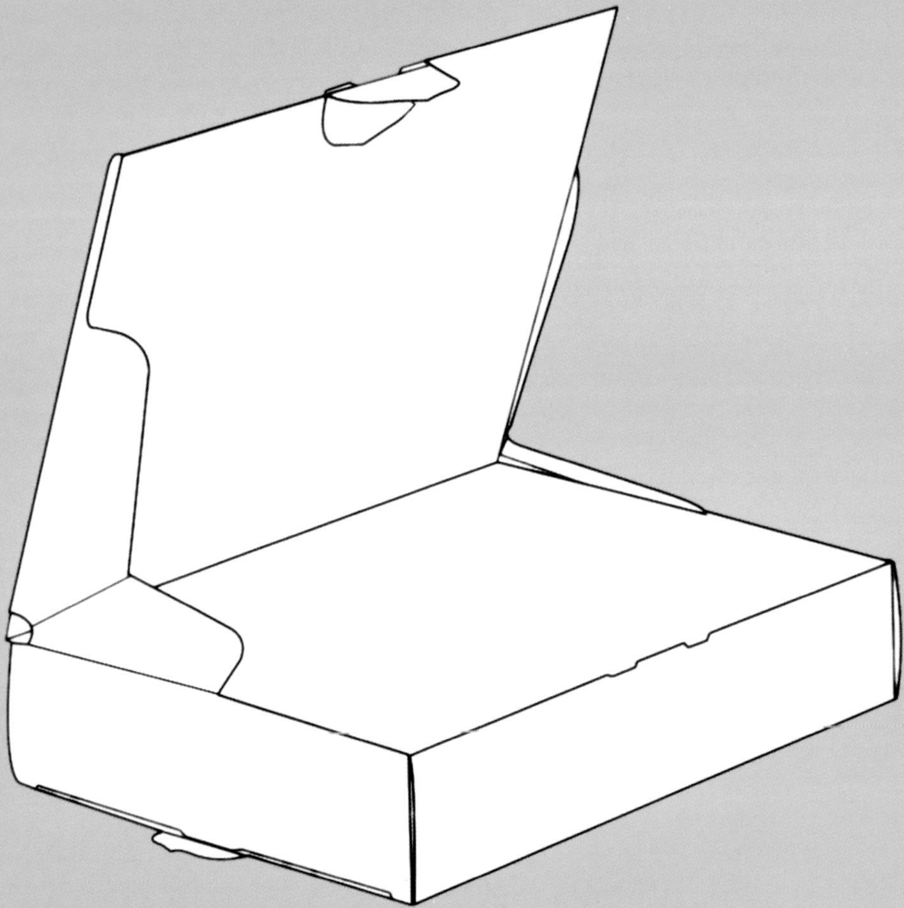

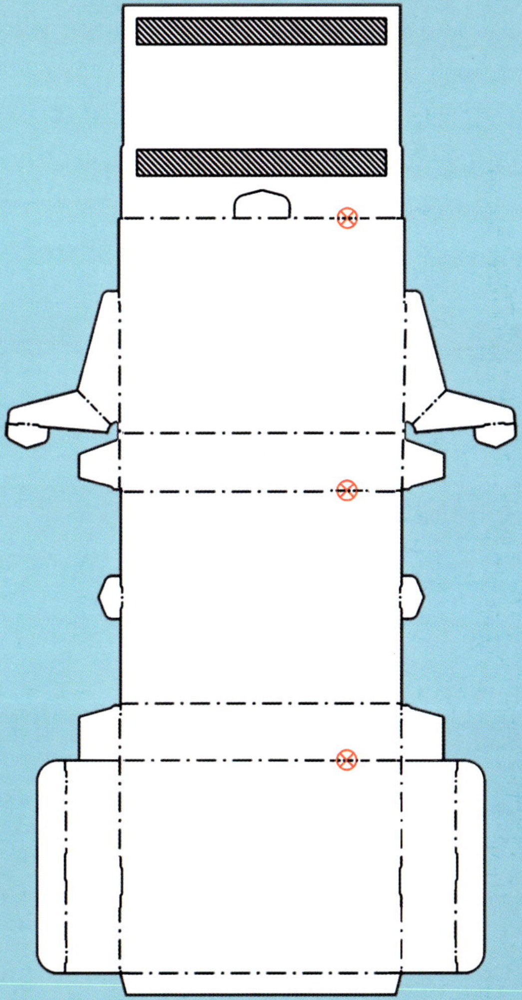

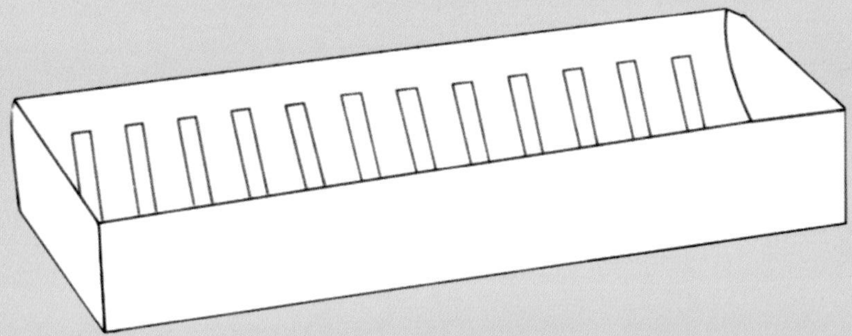

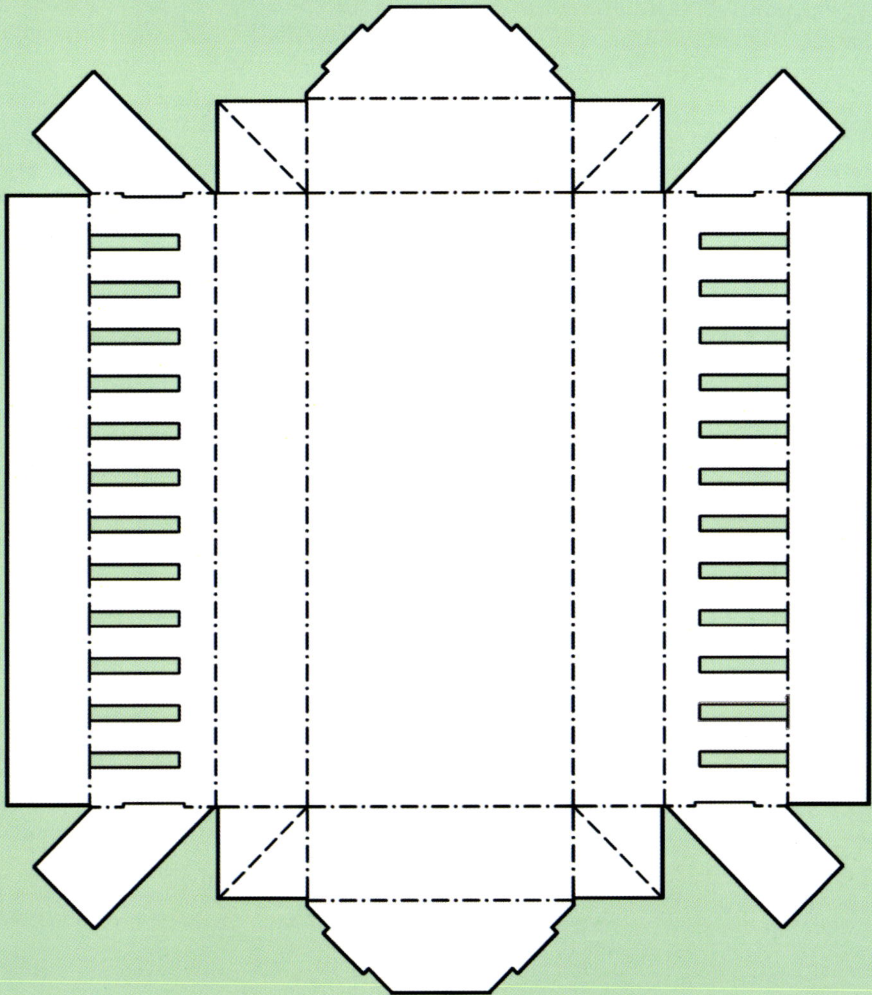

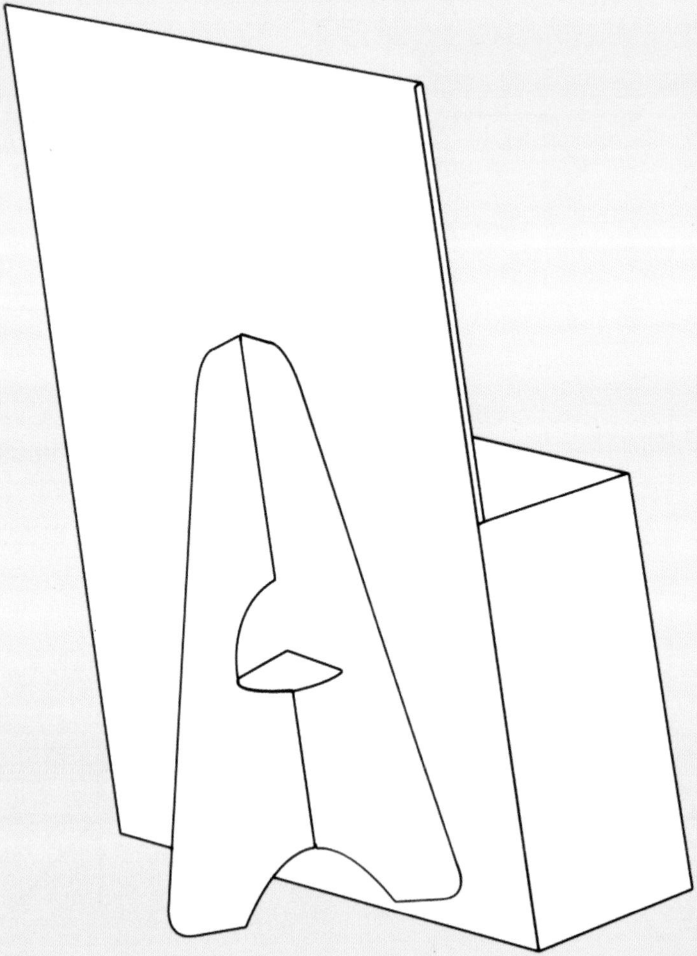

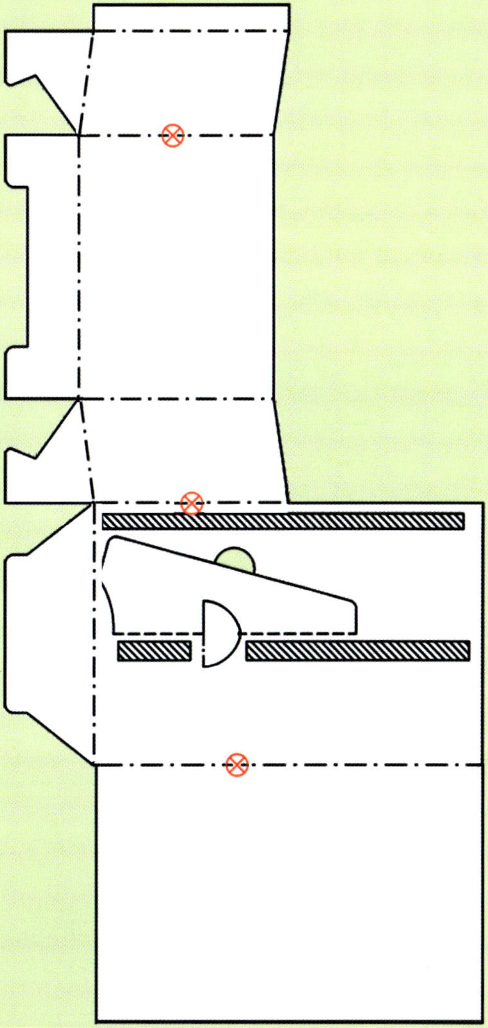

Regular Packaging

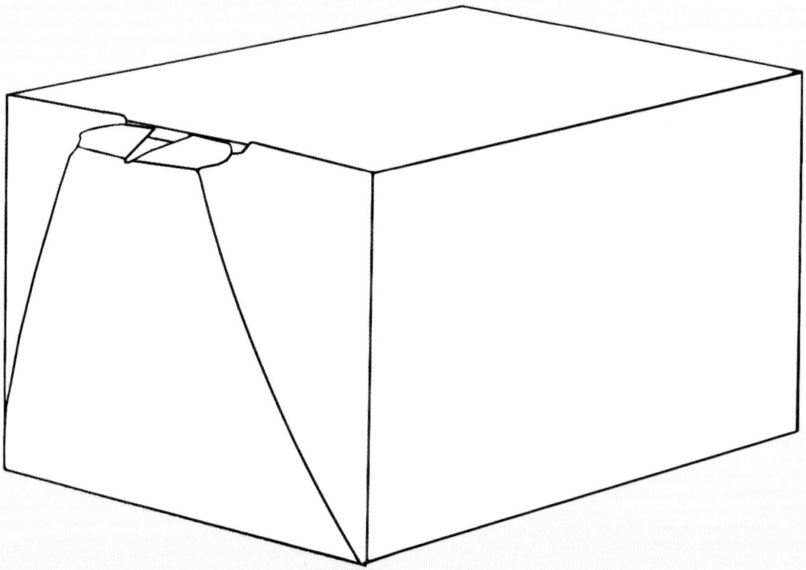

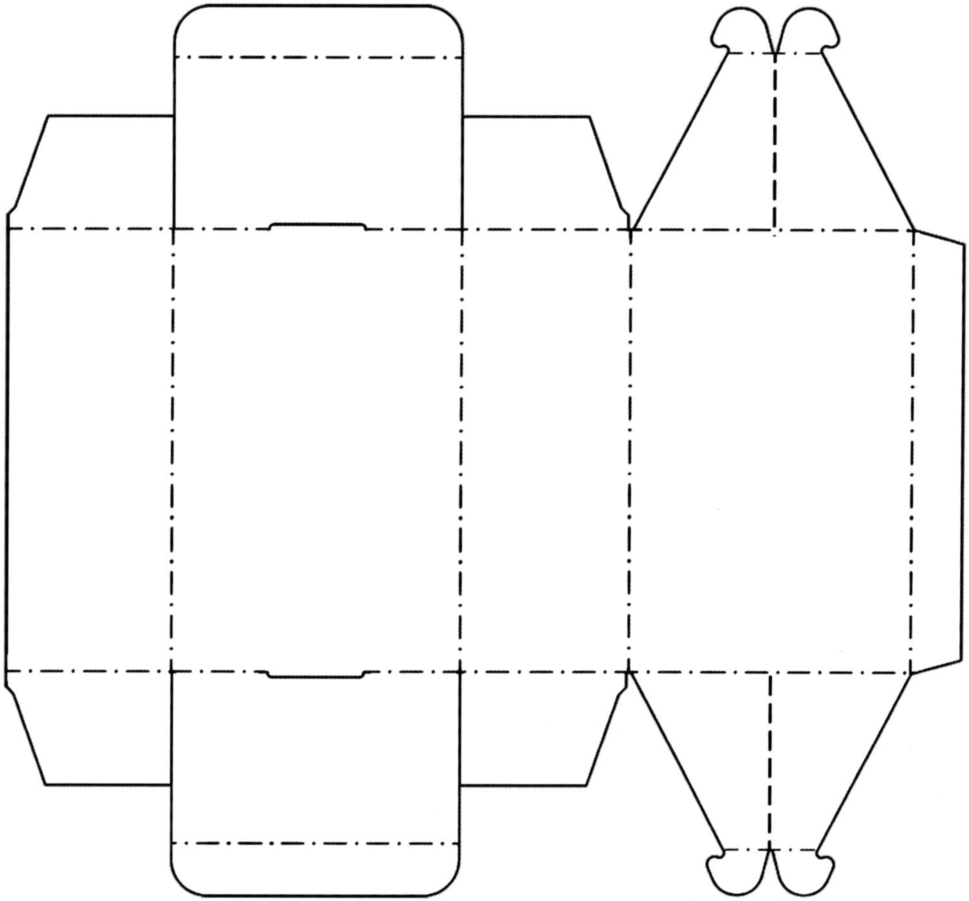

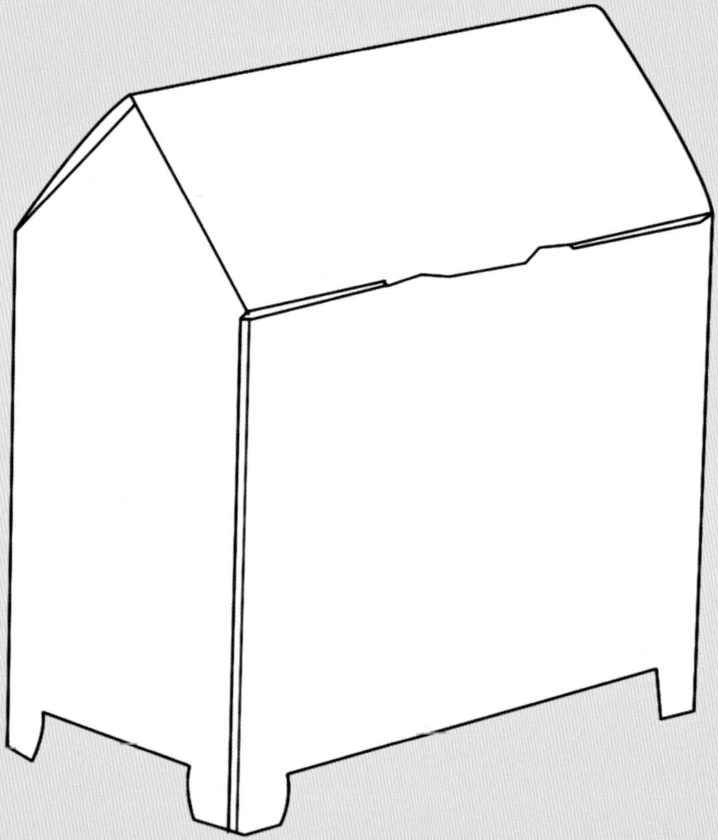

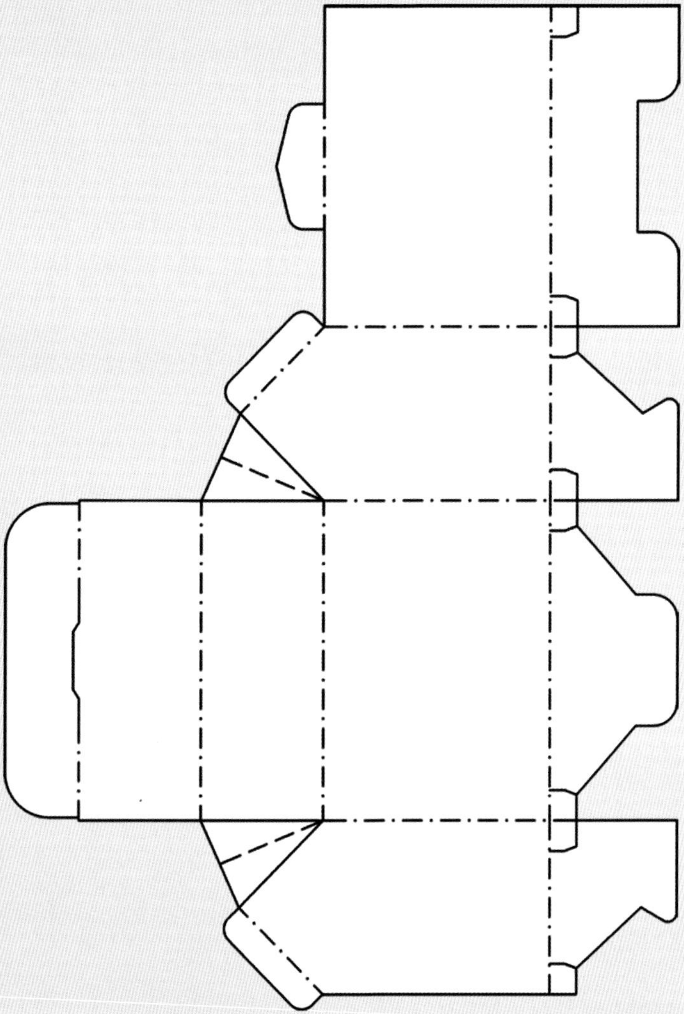

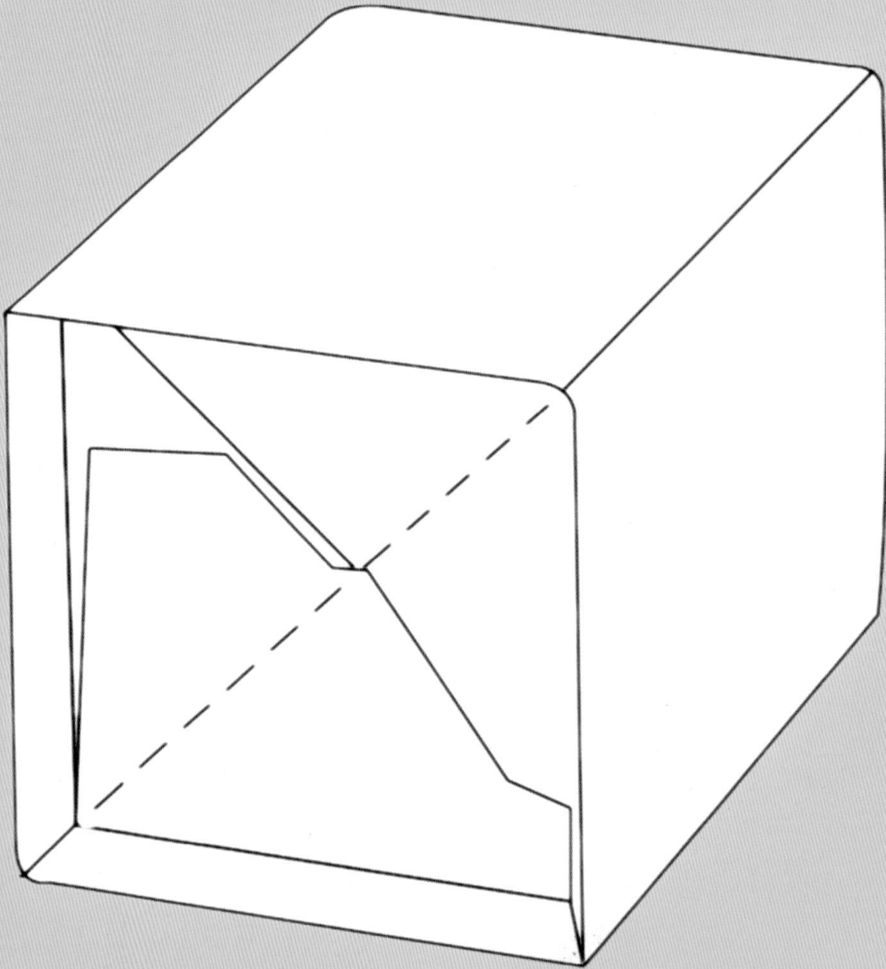

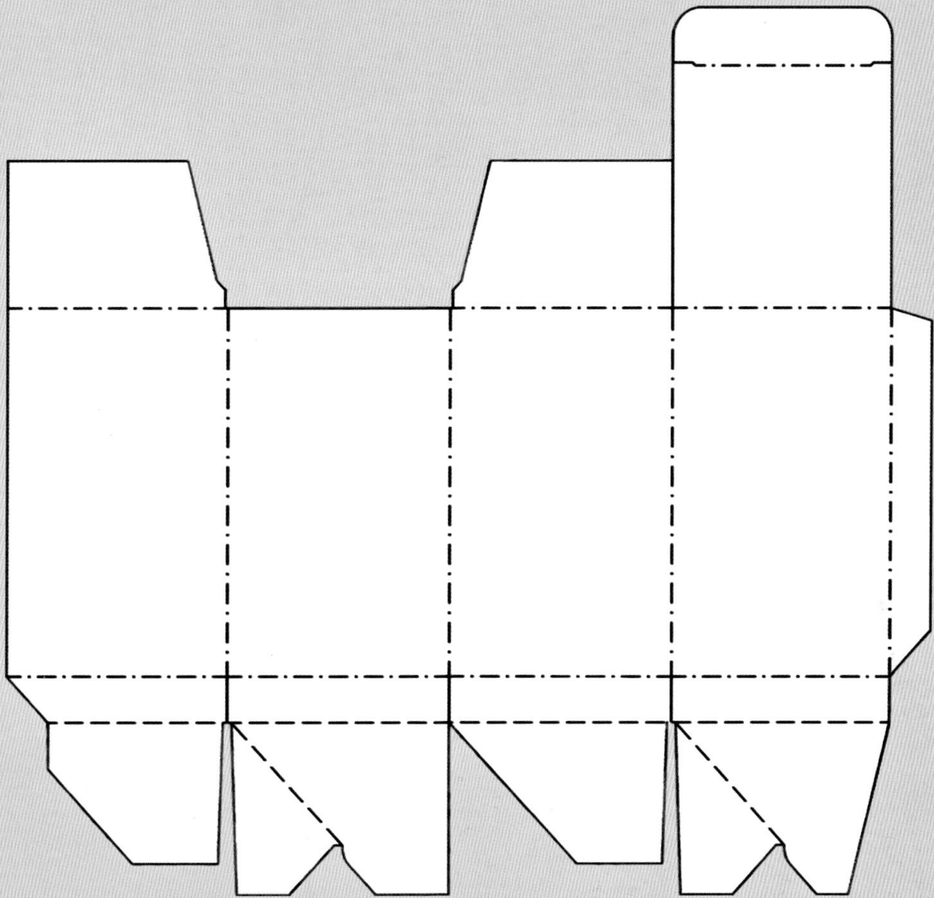

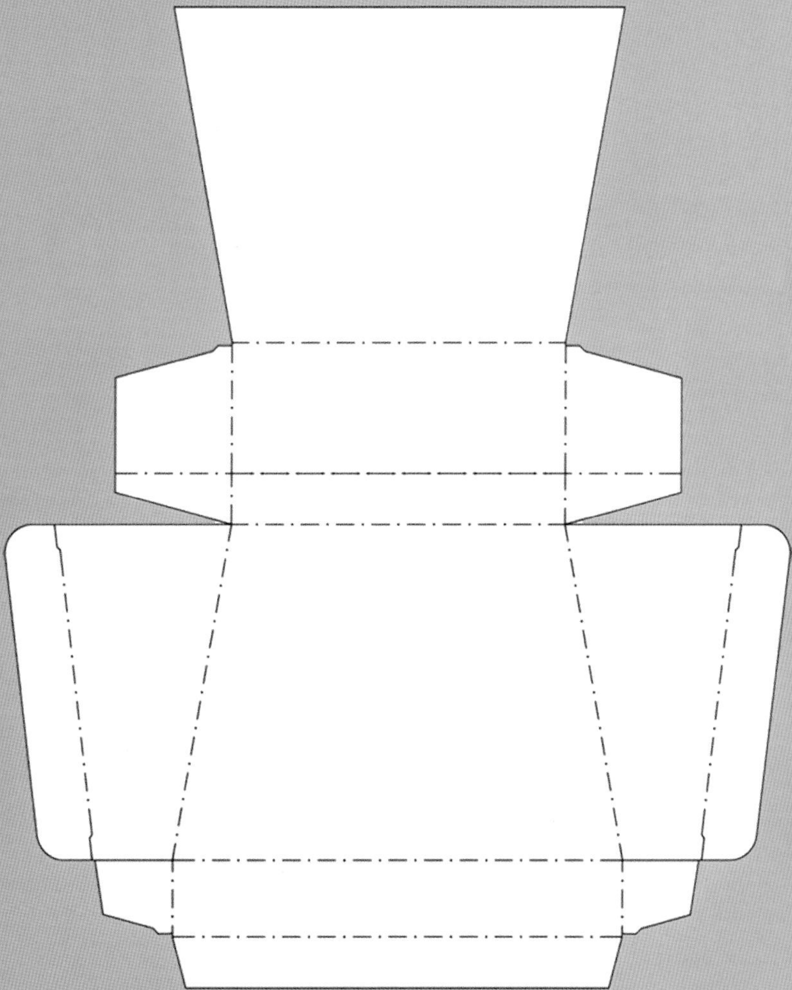

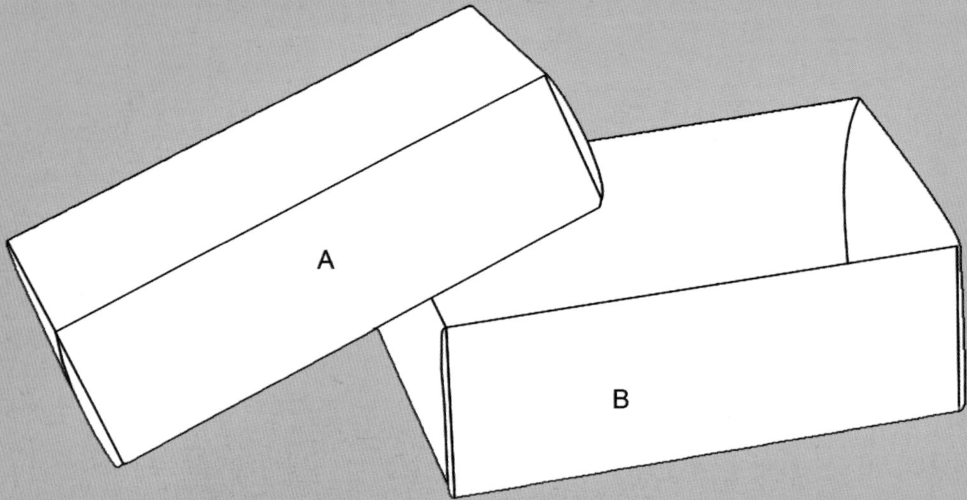
A
B

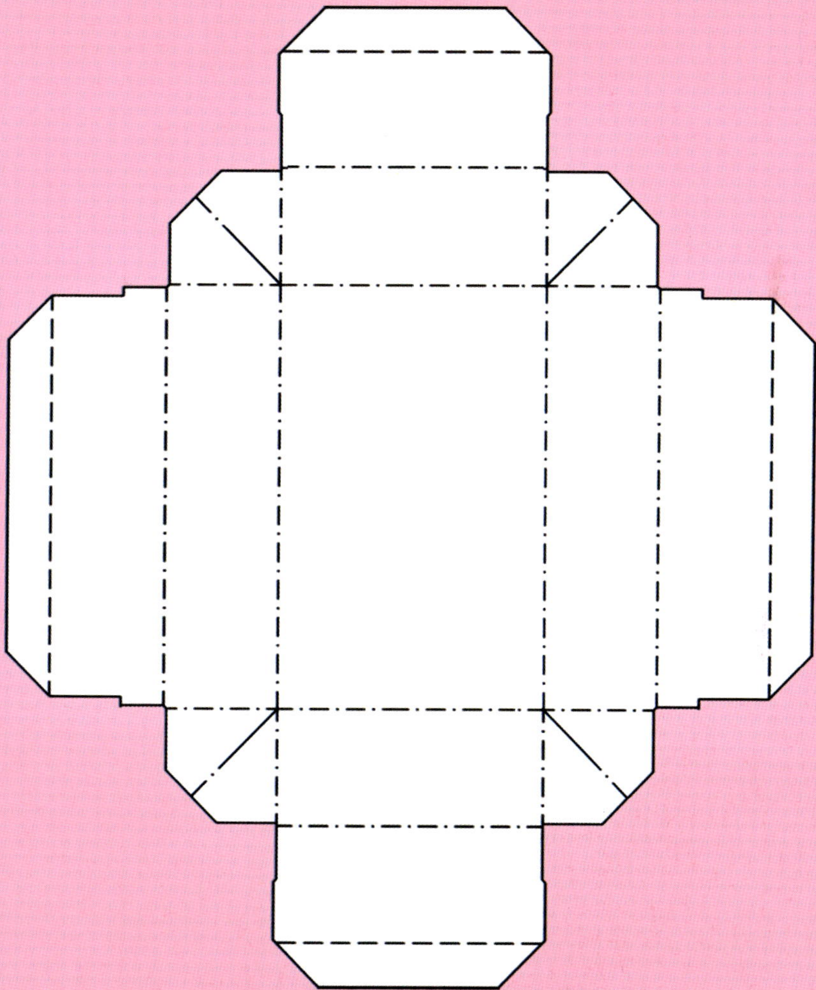

A

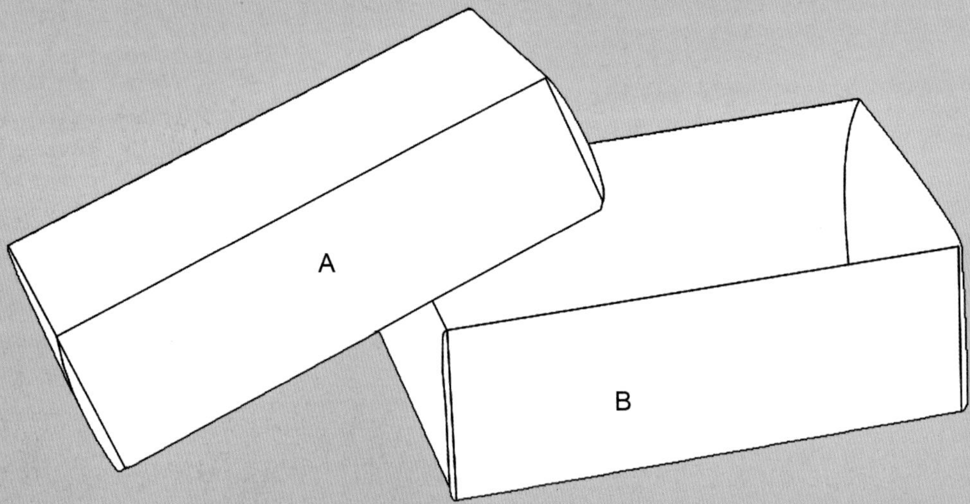
A
B

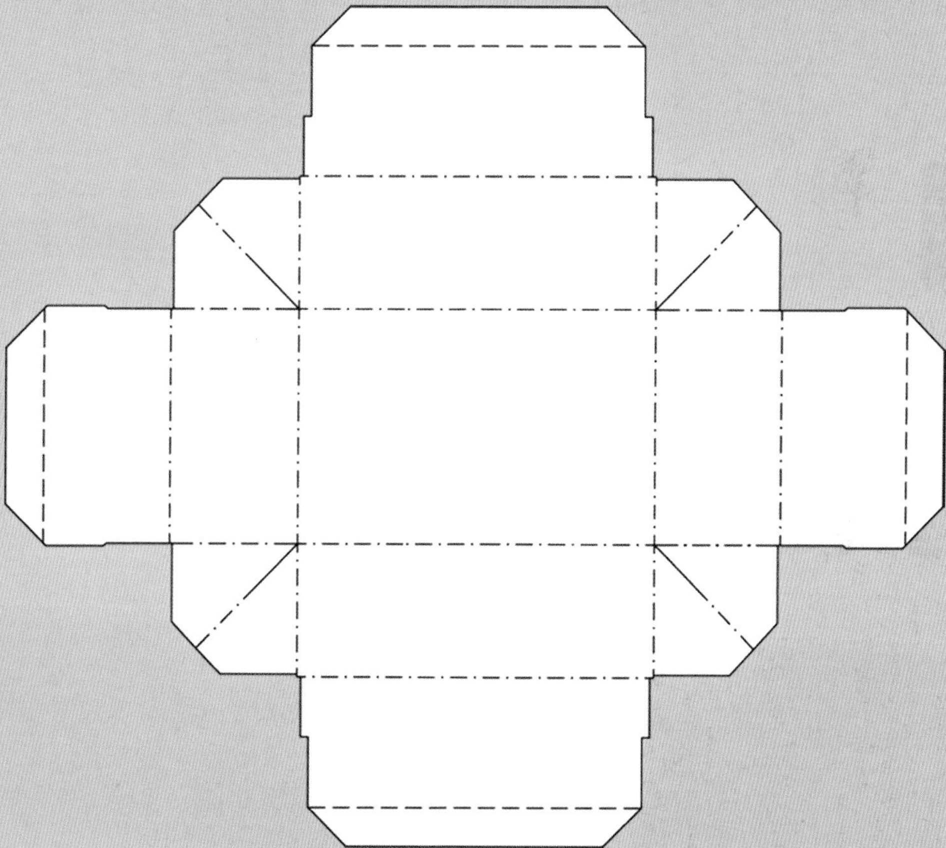

B

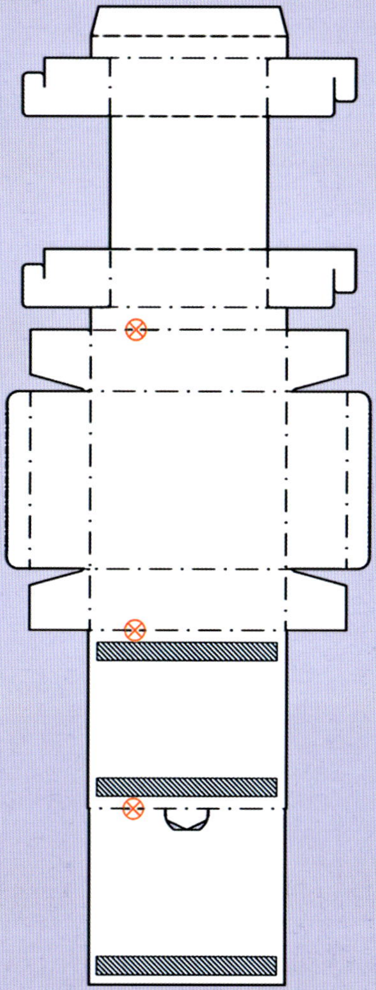

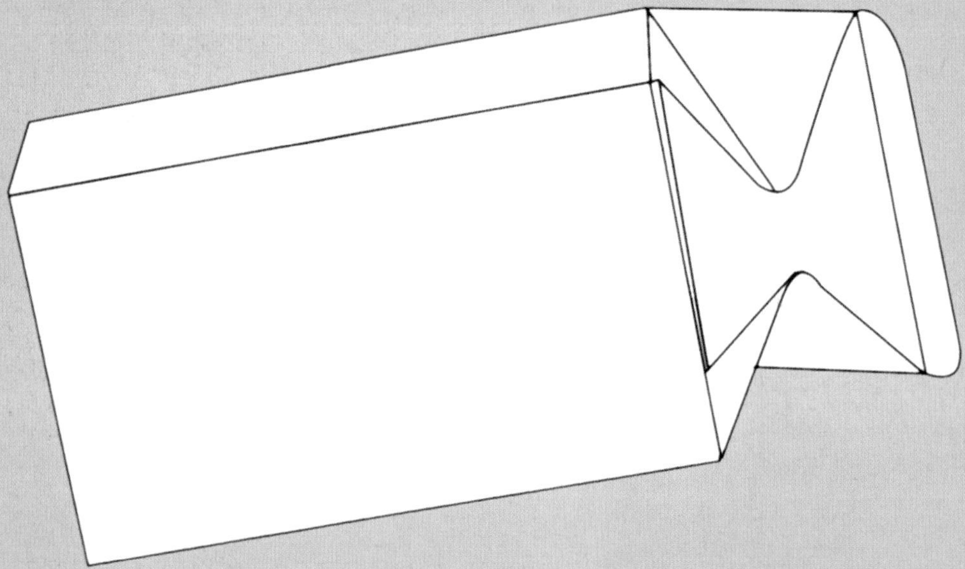

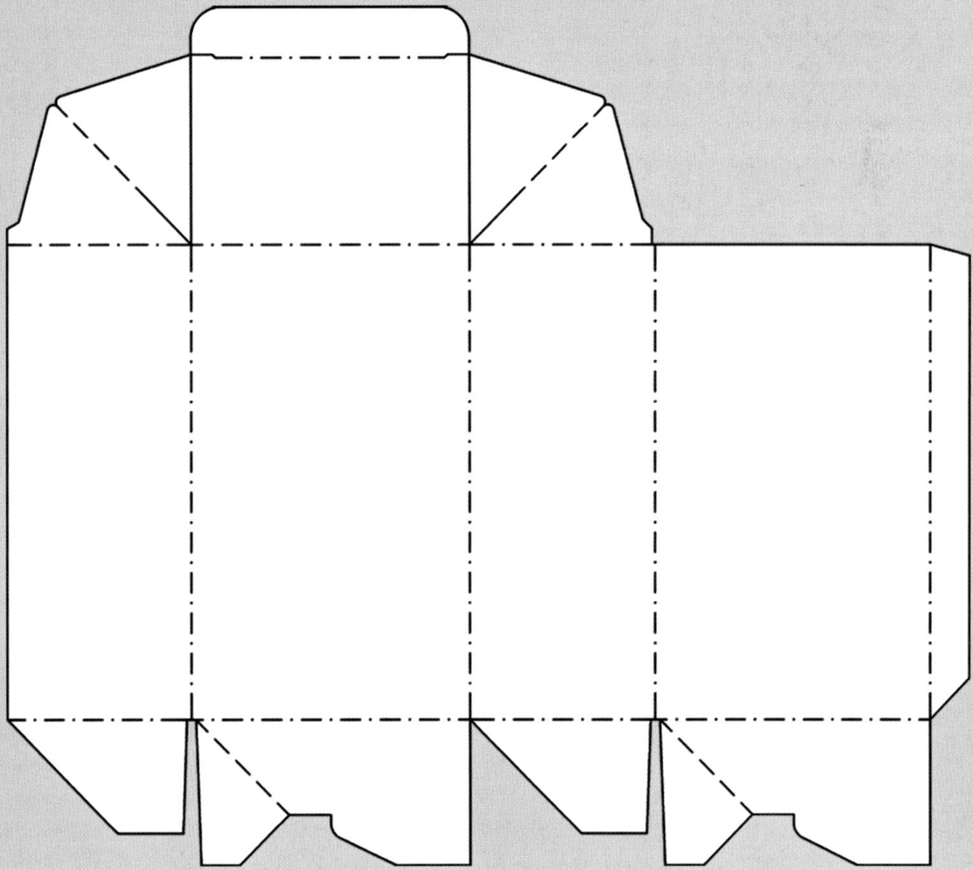

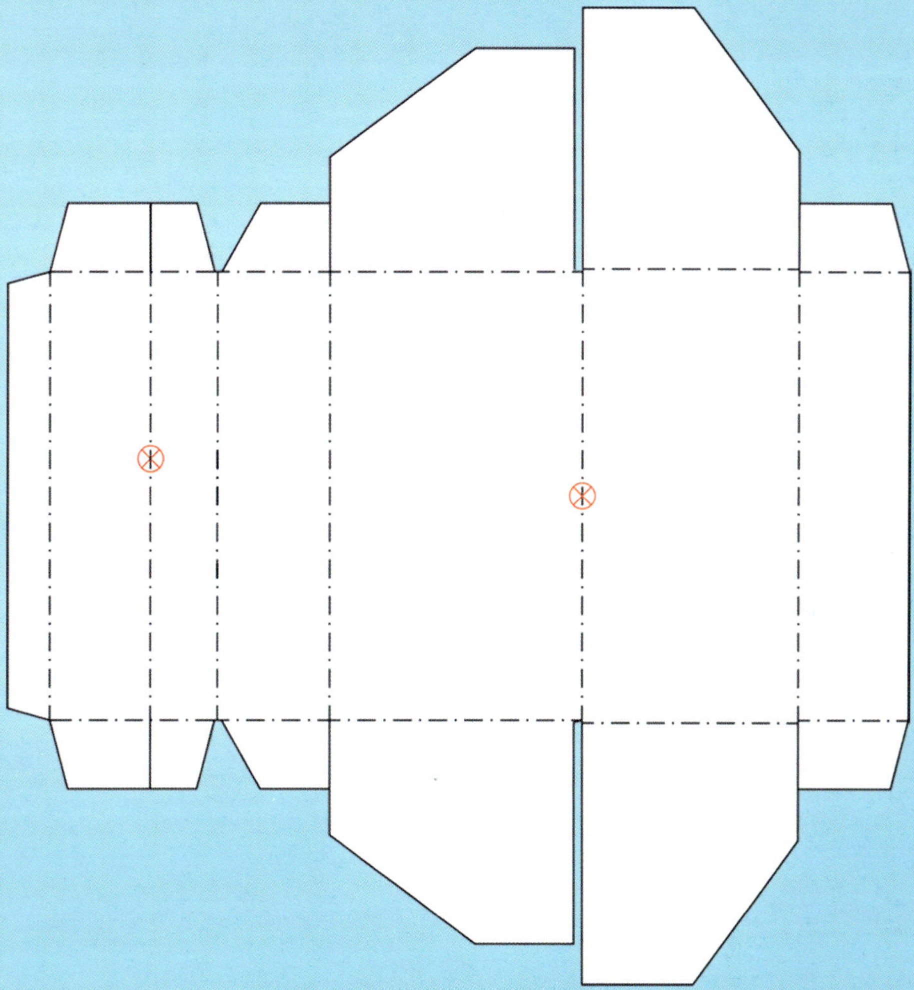

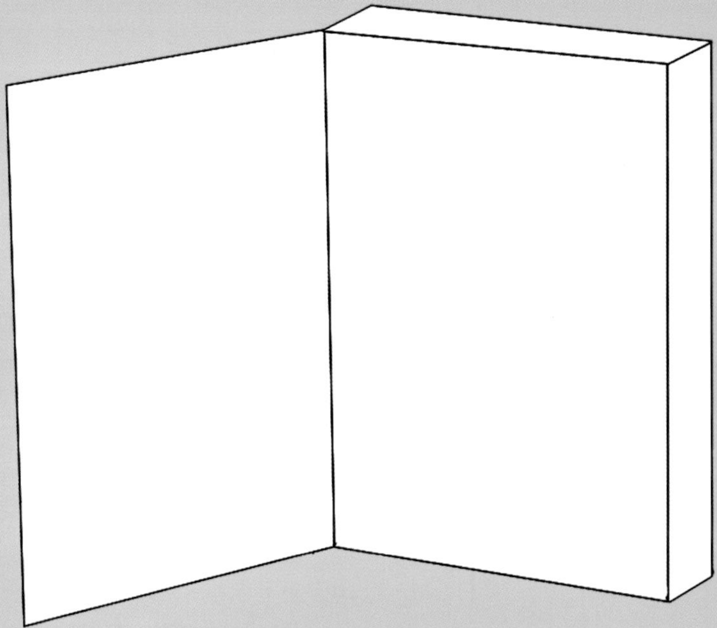

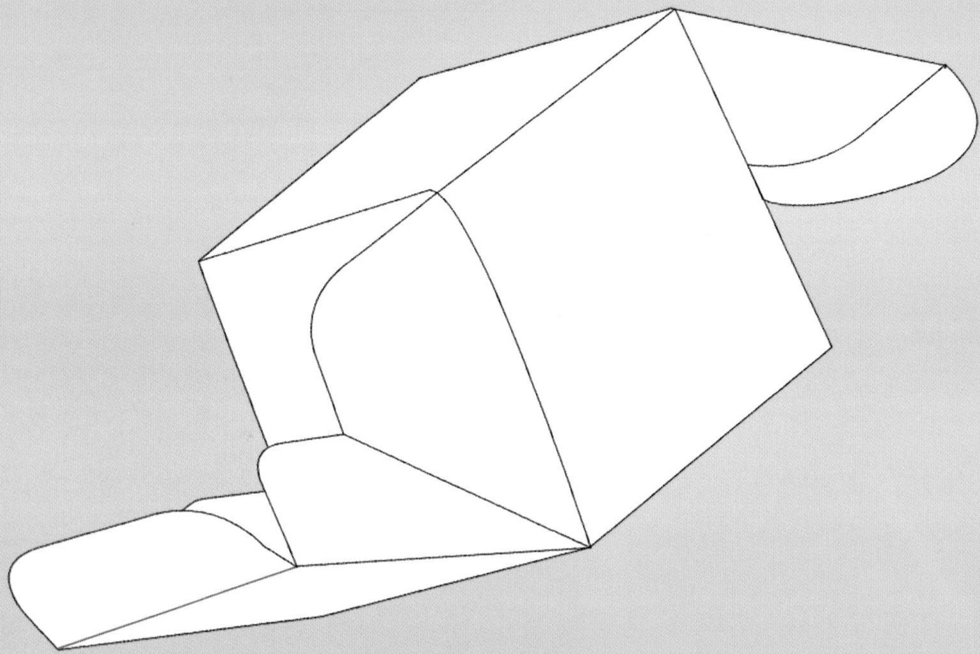

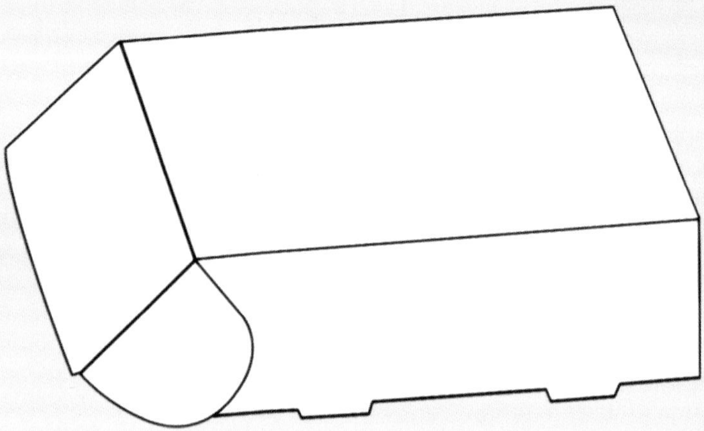

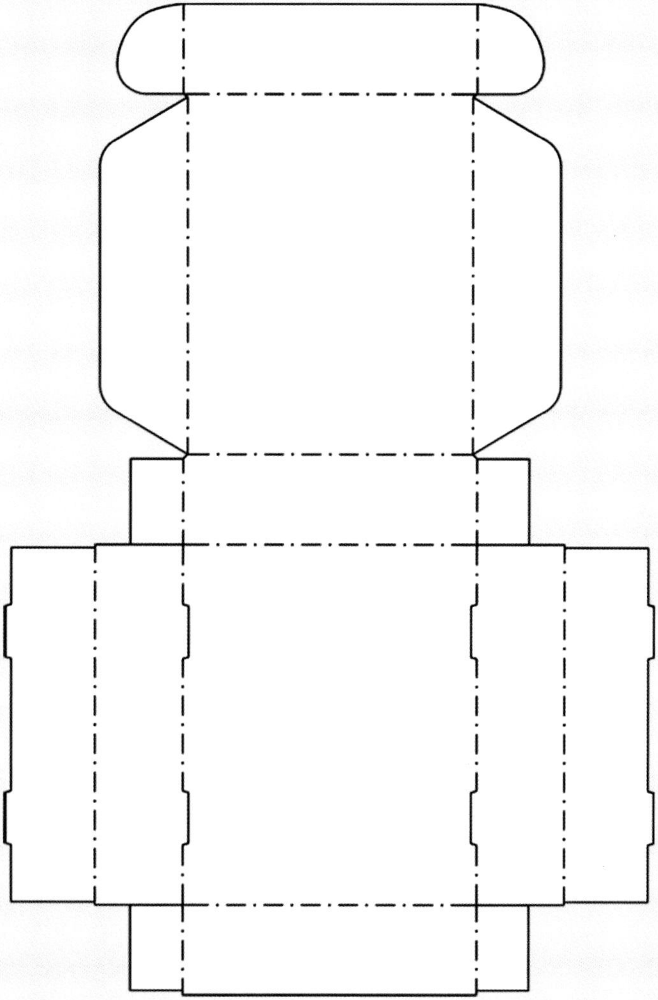

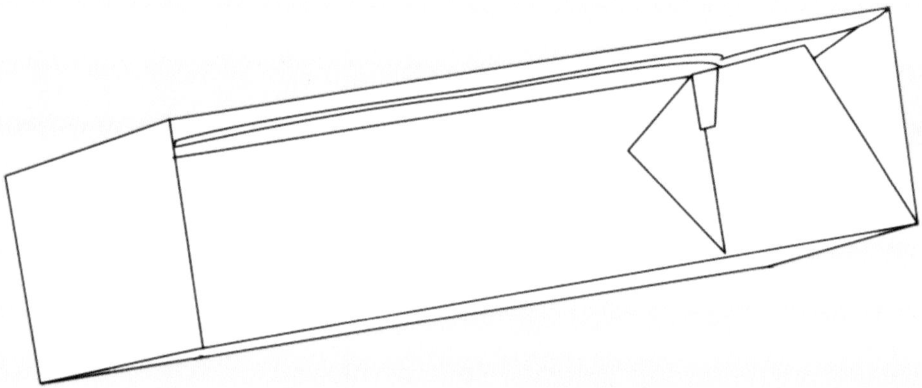

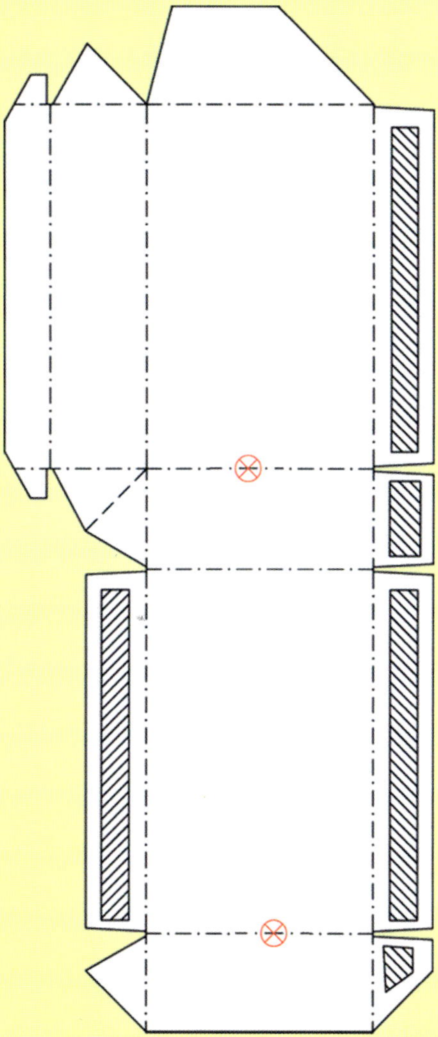

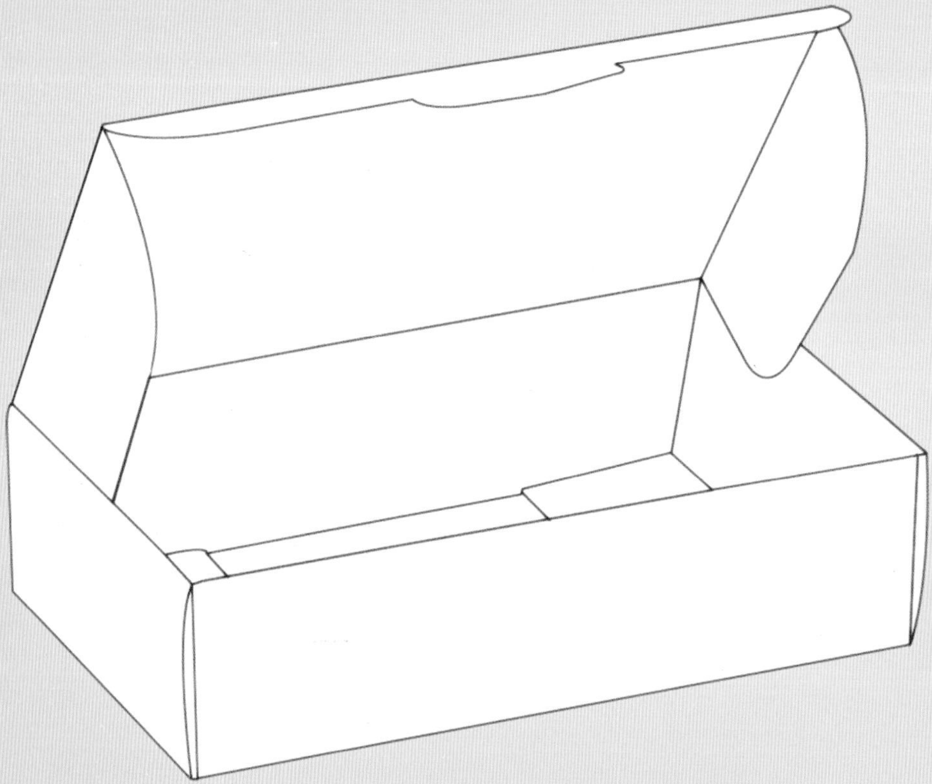

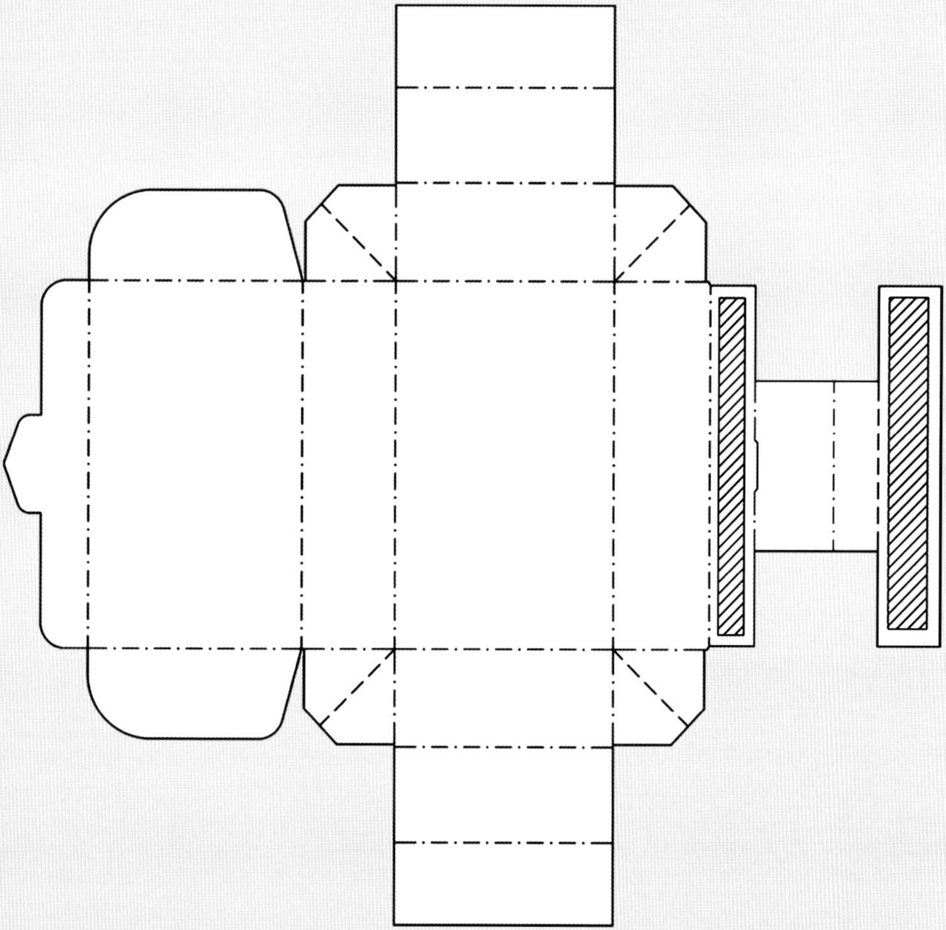

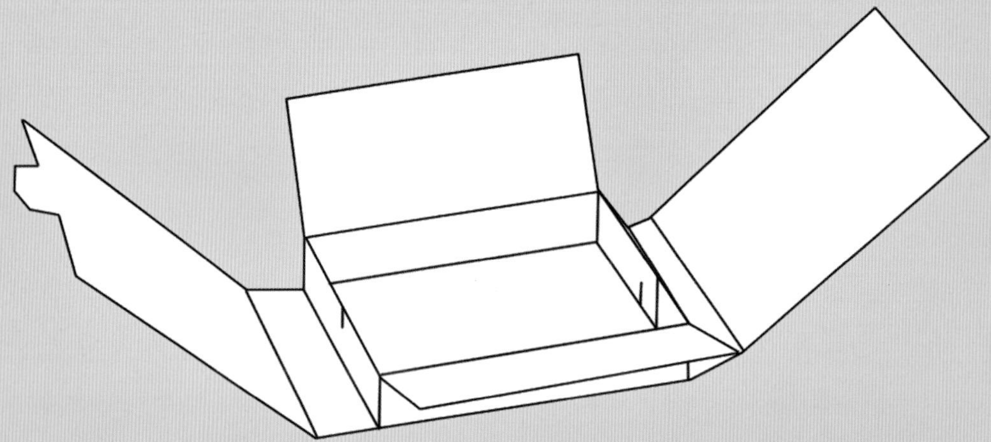

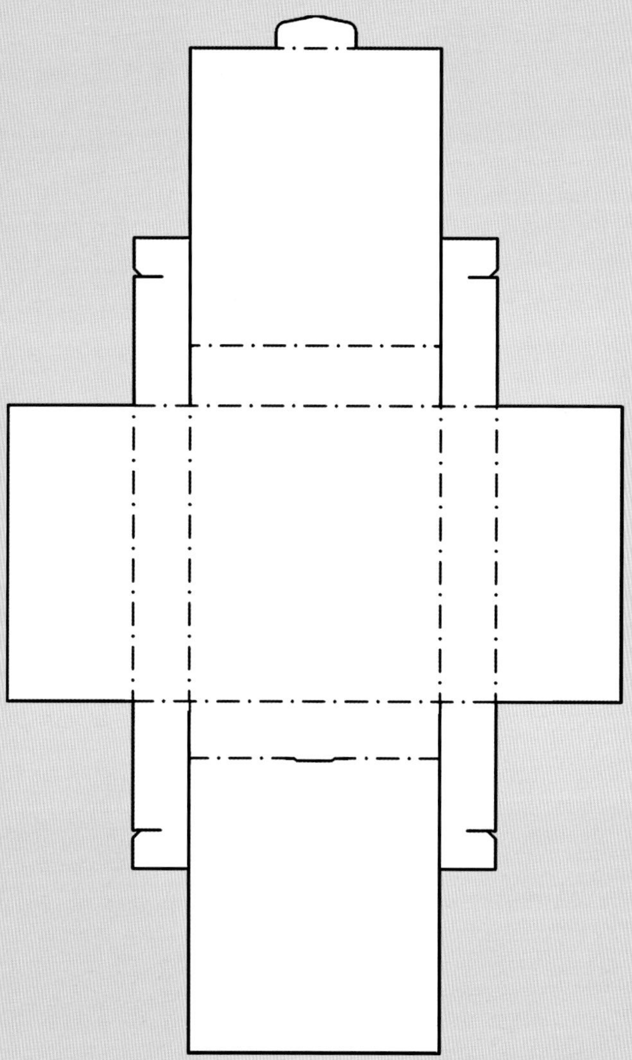

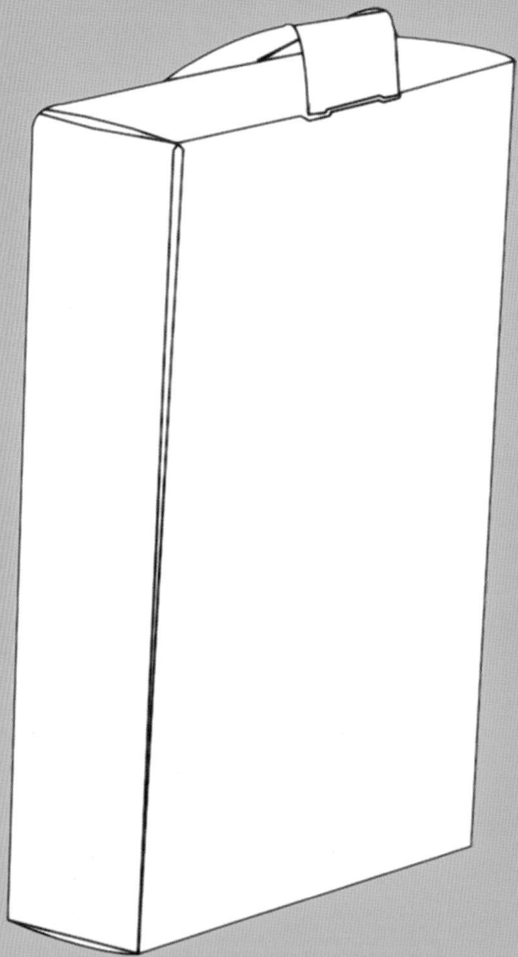

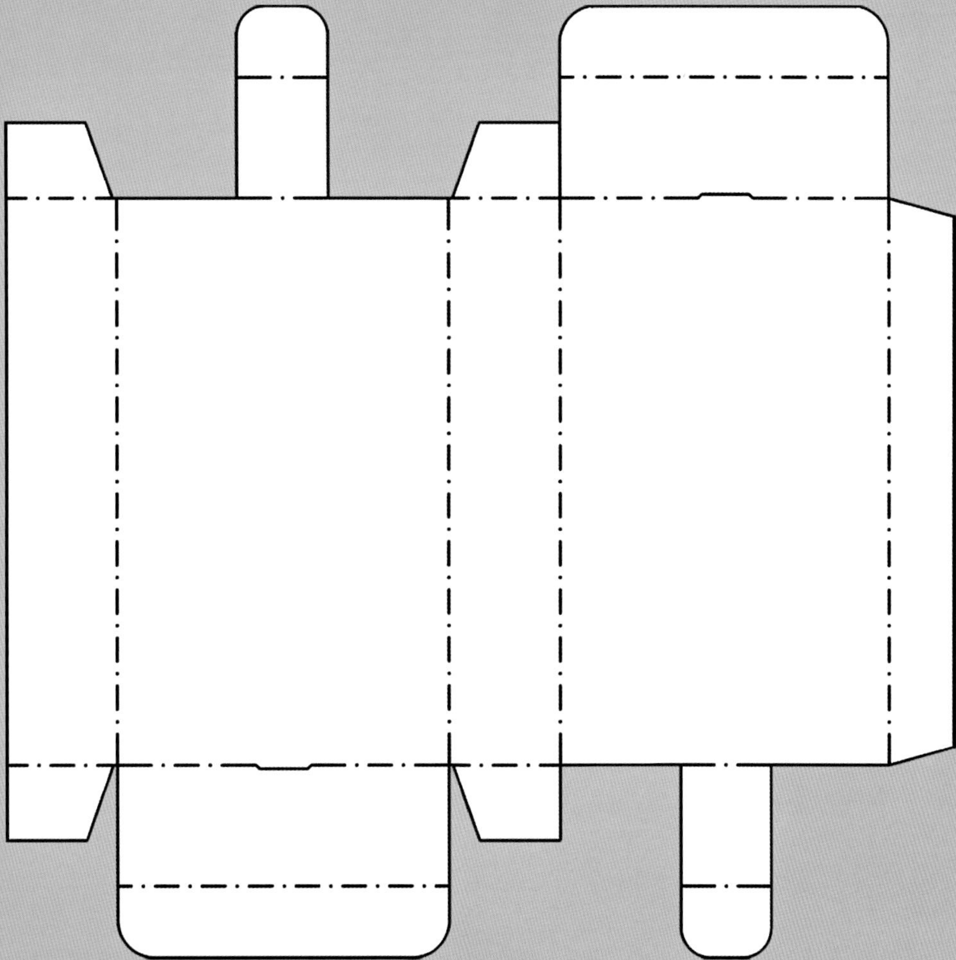

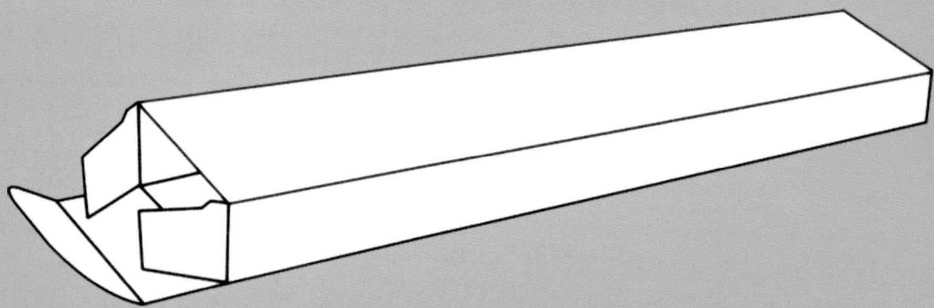

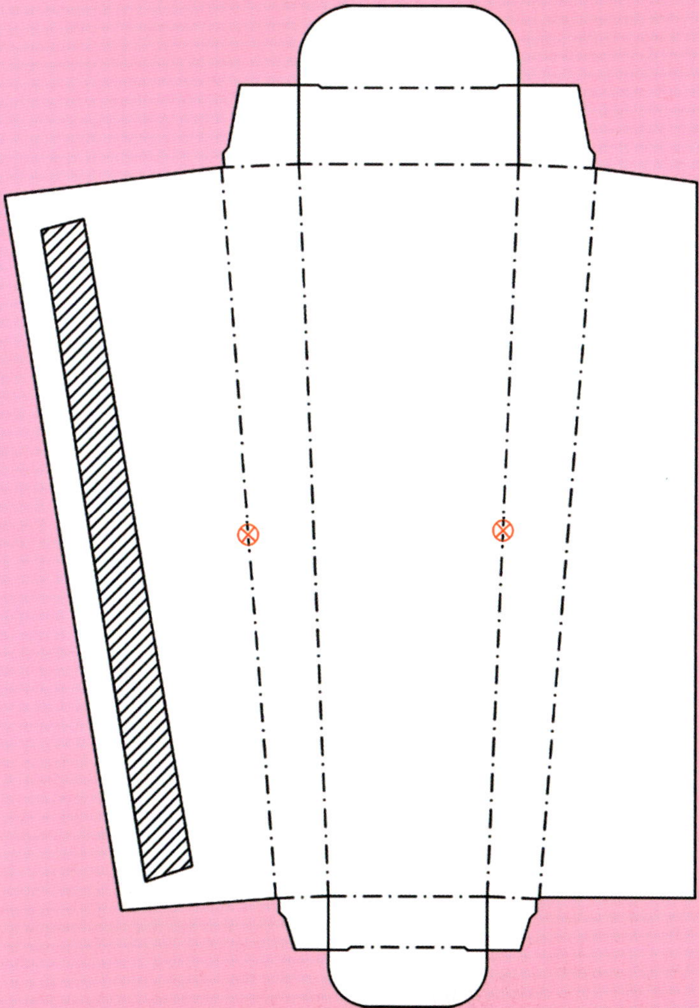

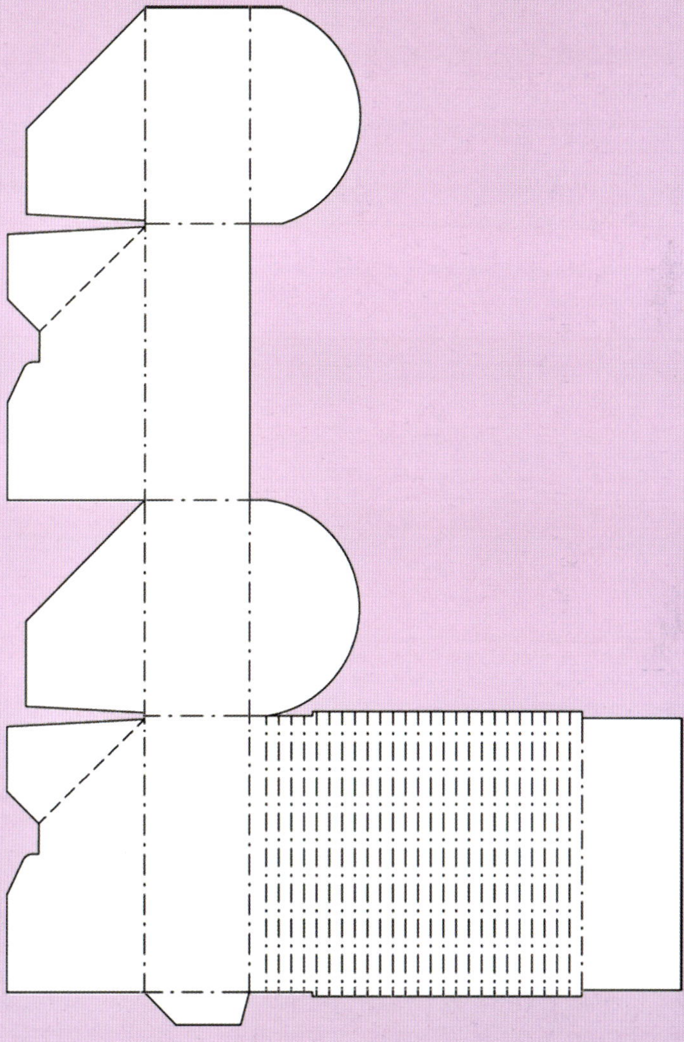

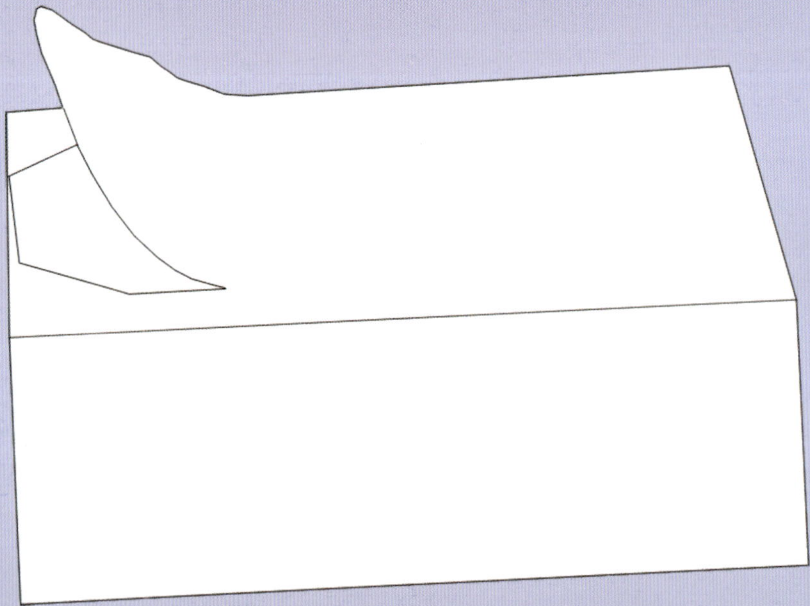

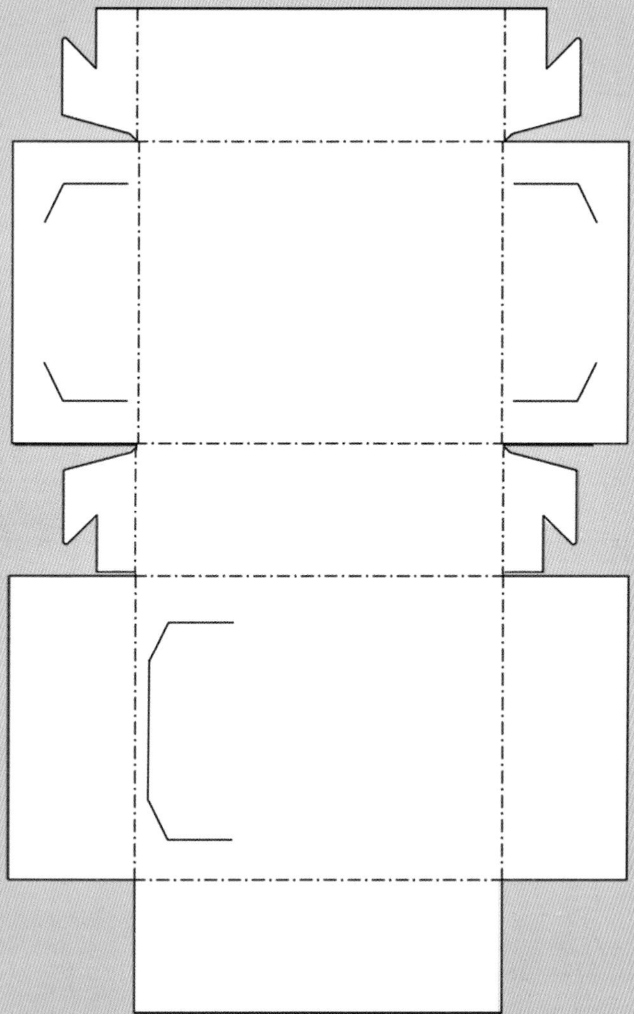

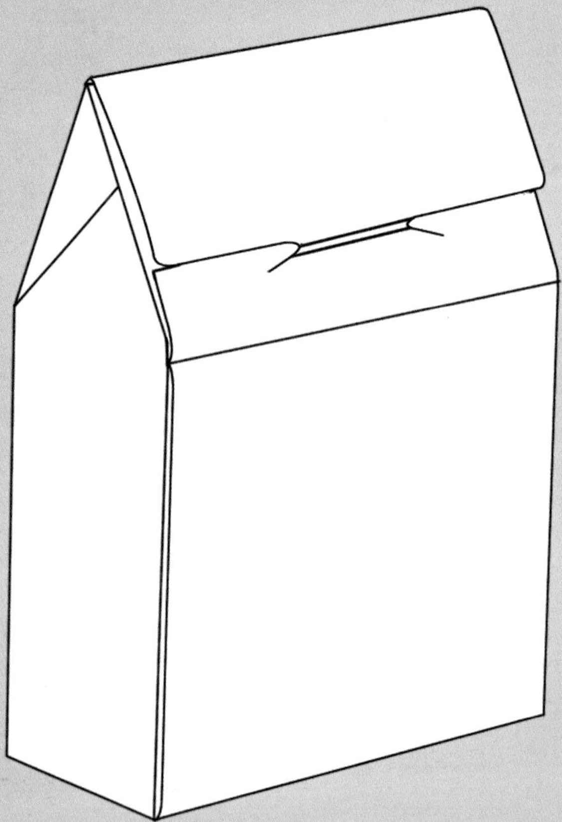

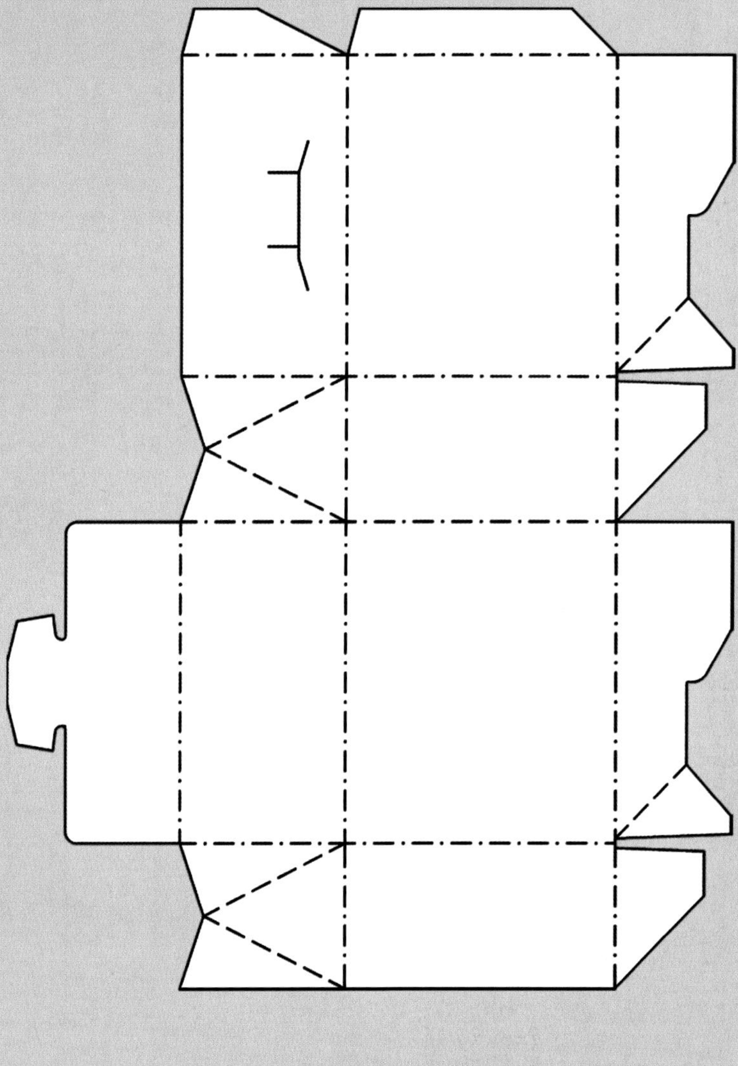

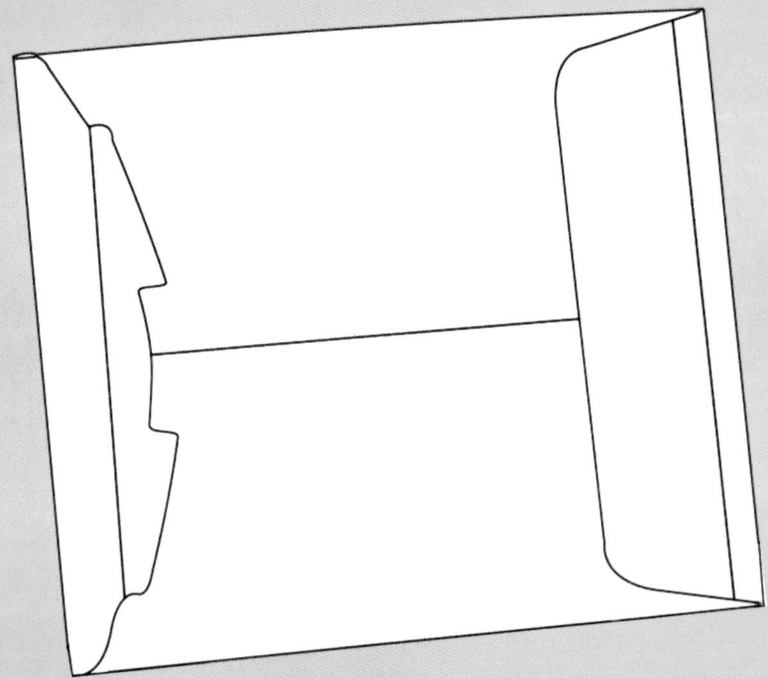

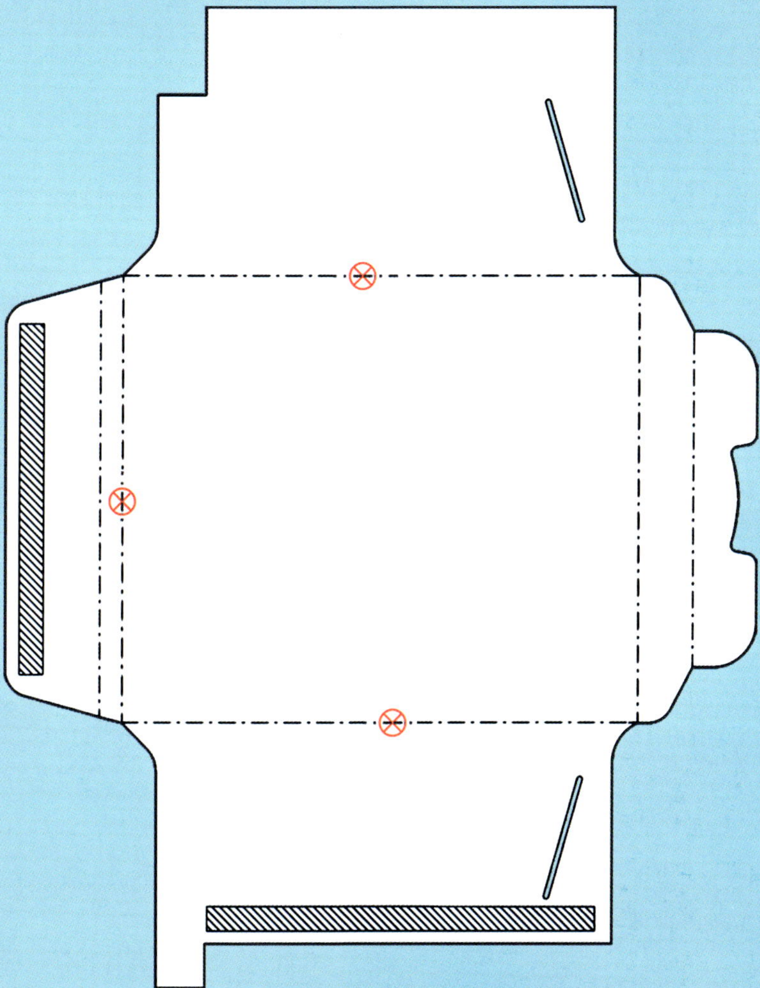

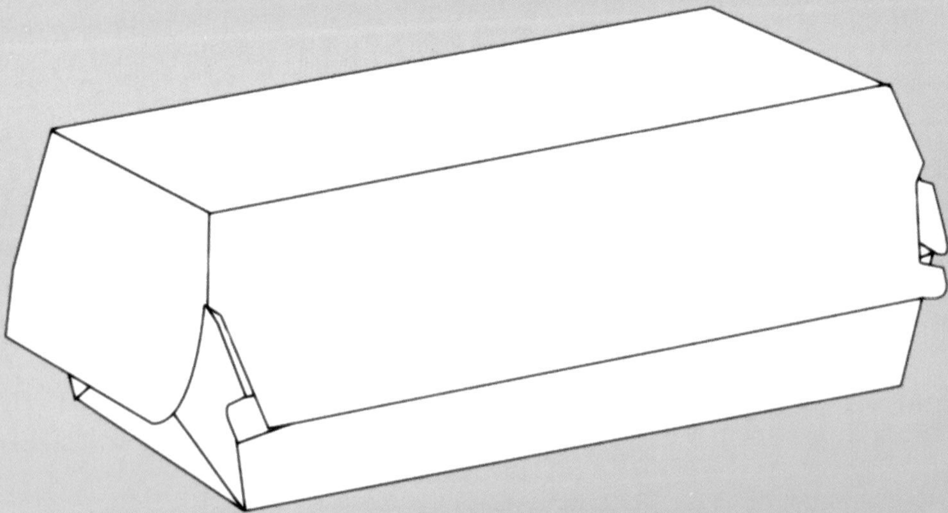

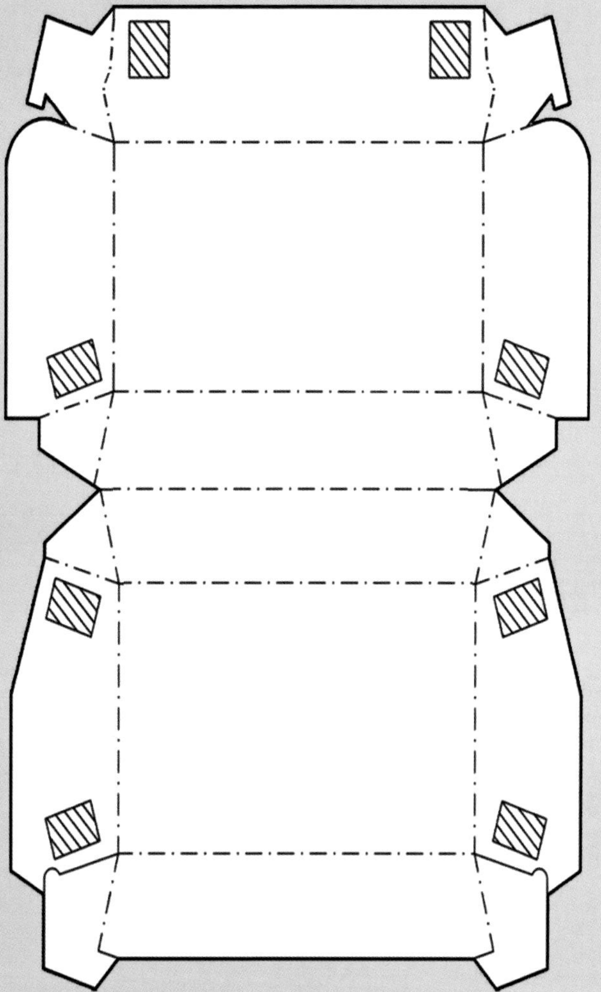

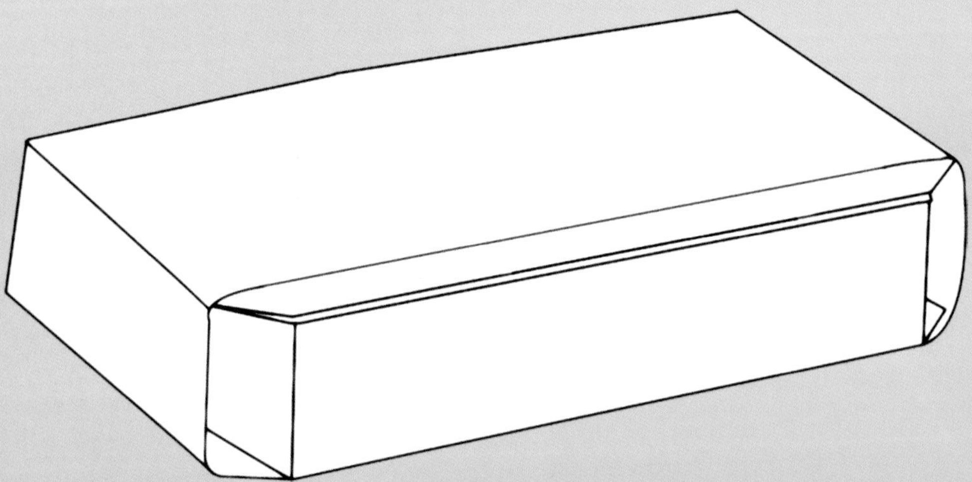

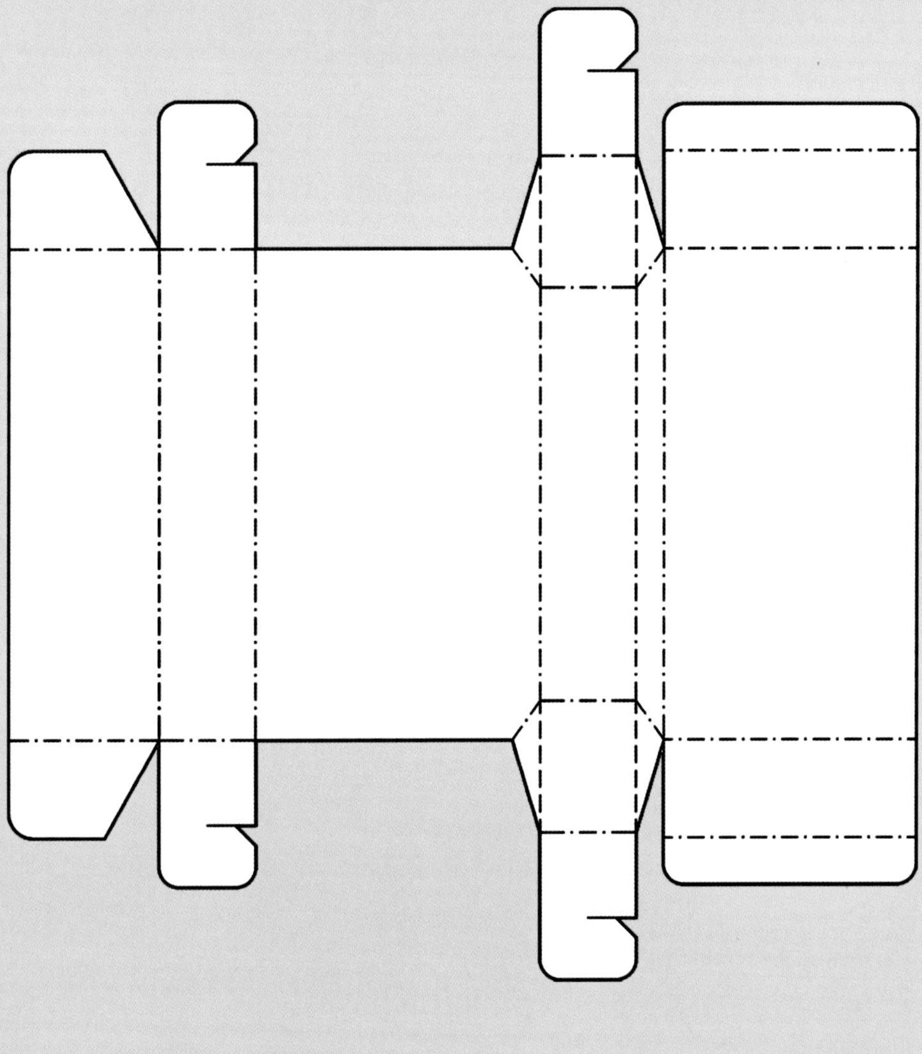

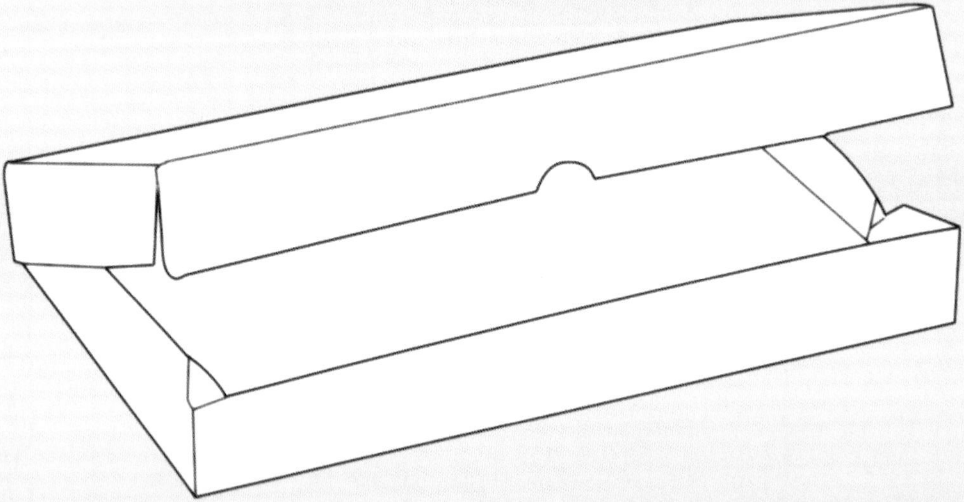

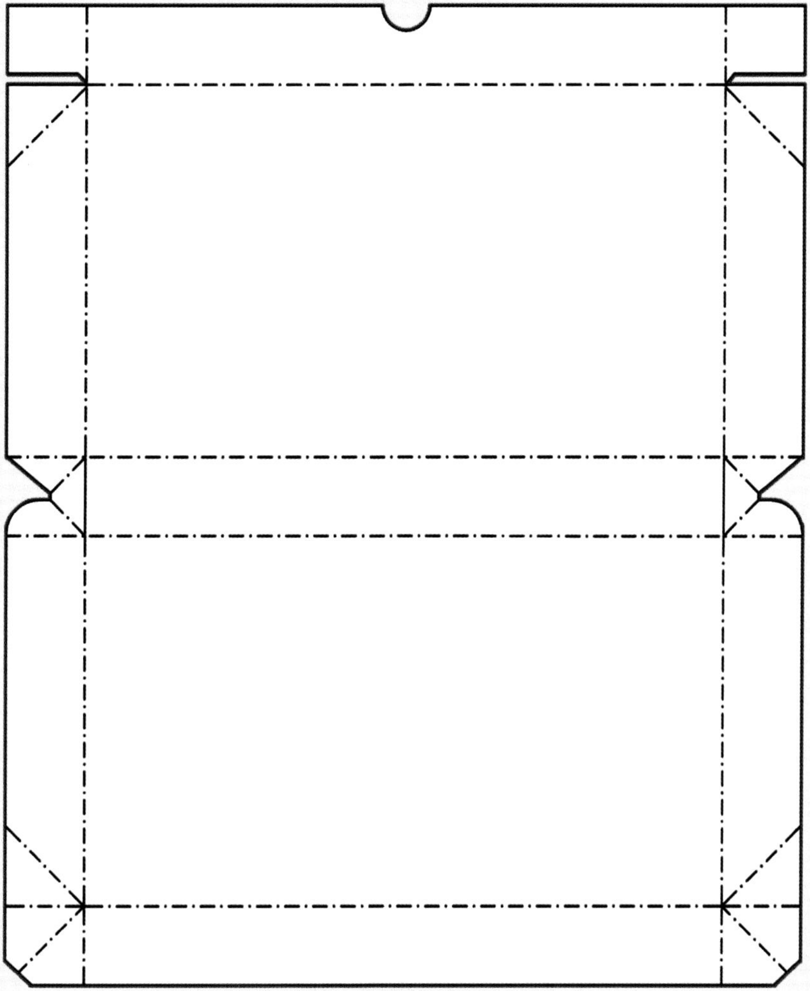

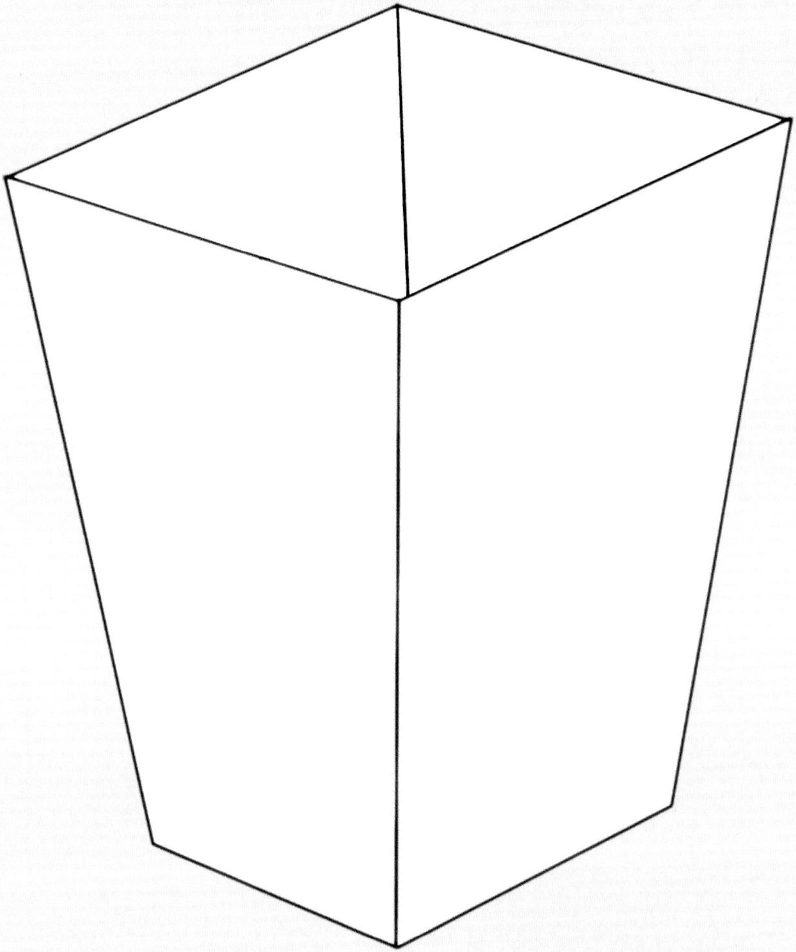

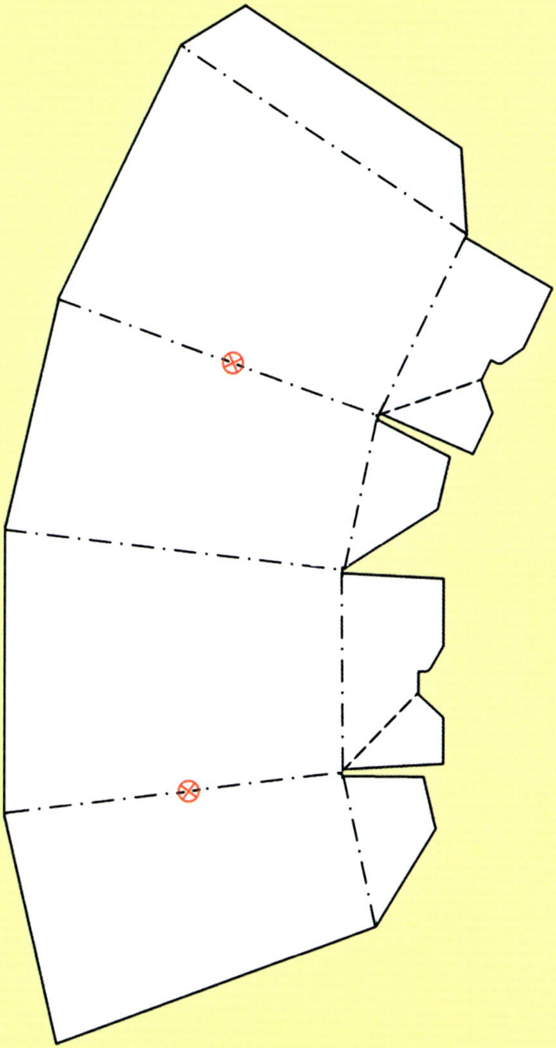

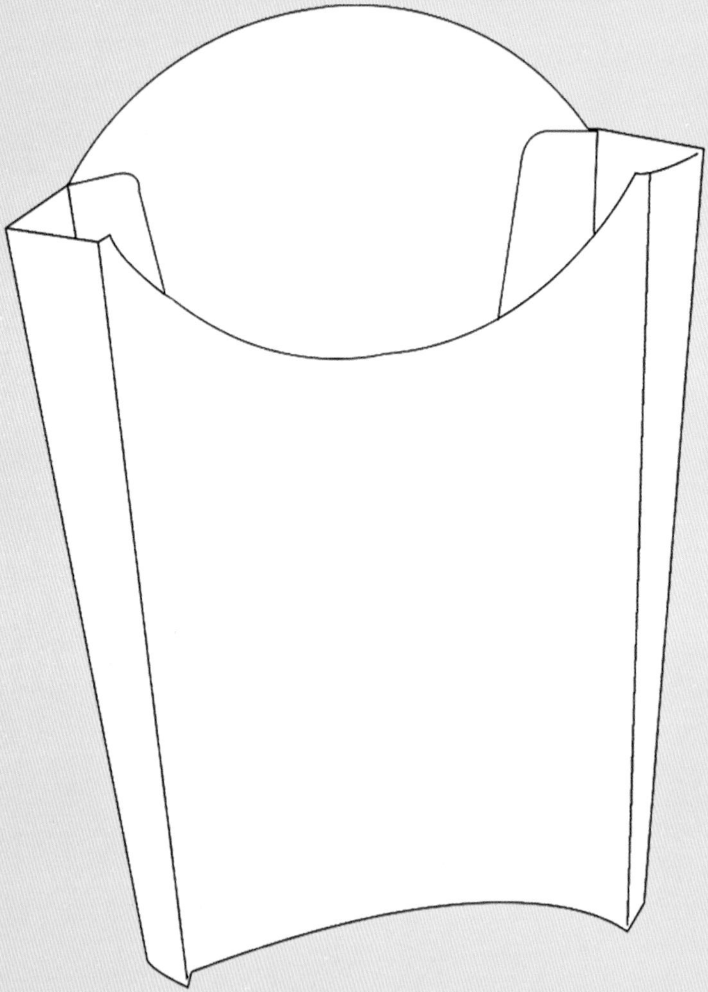

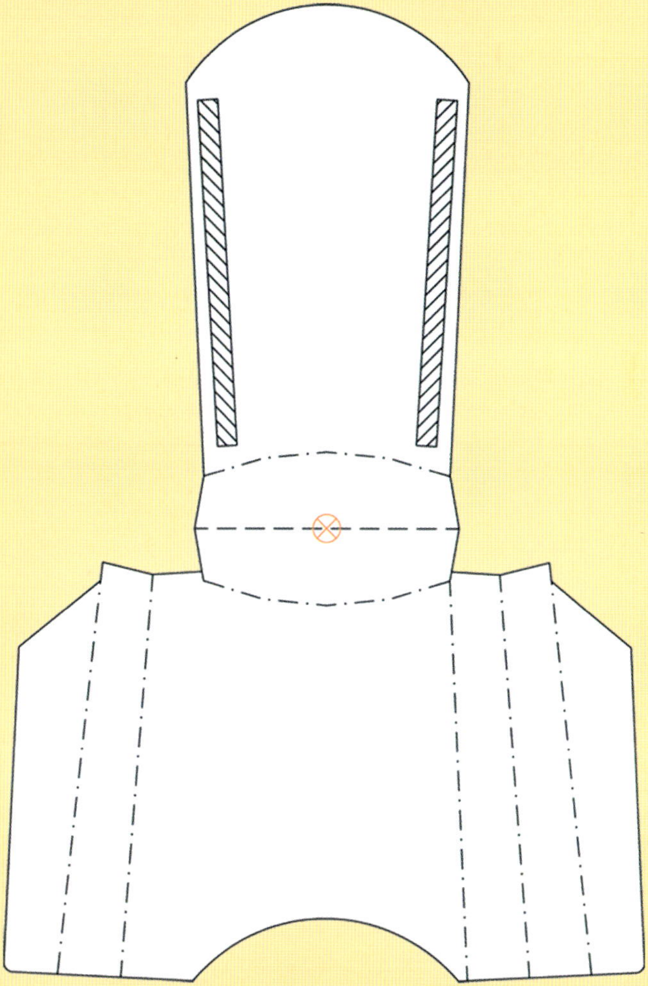

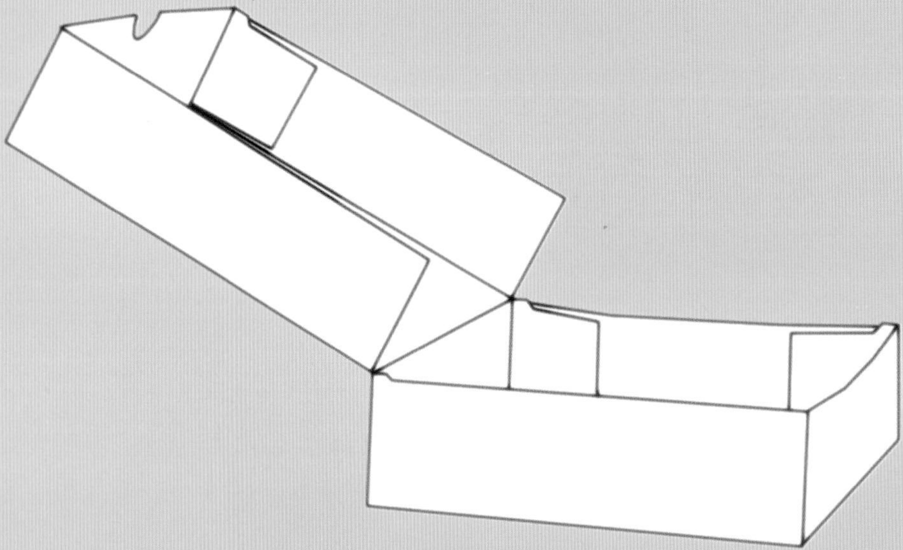

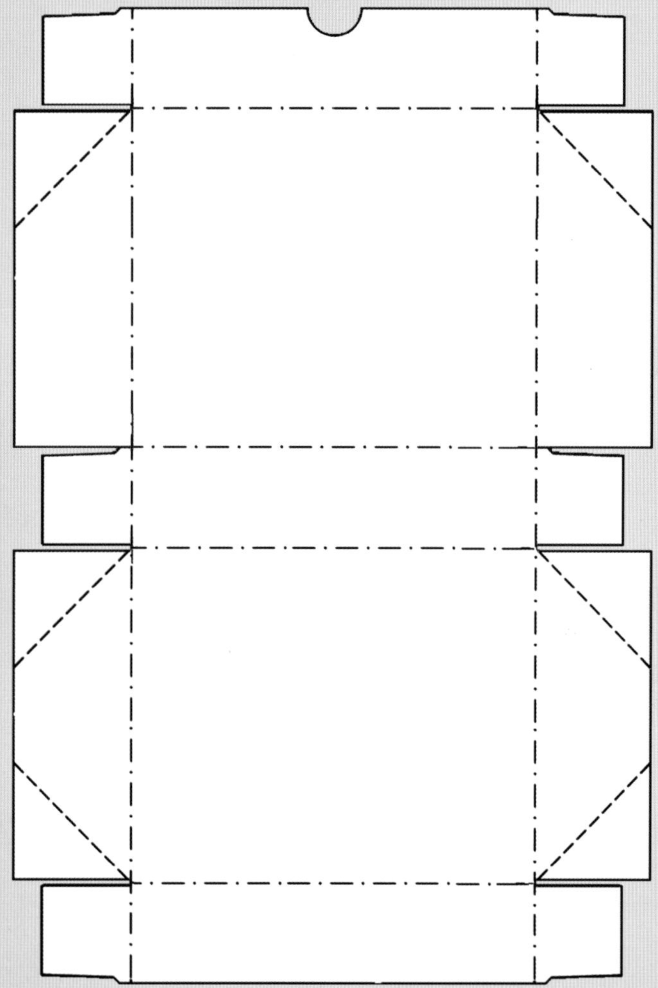

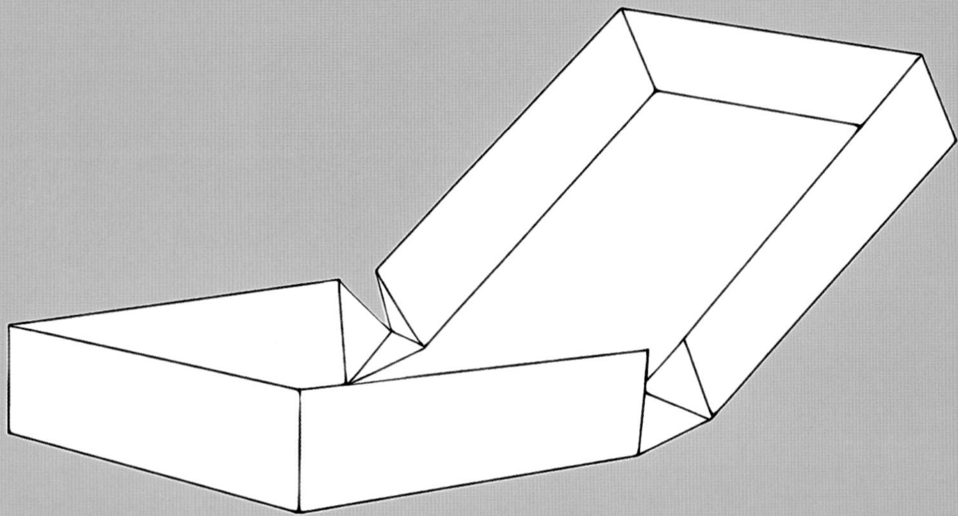

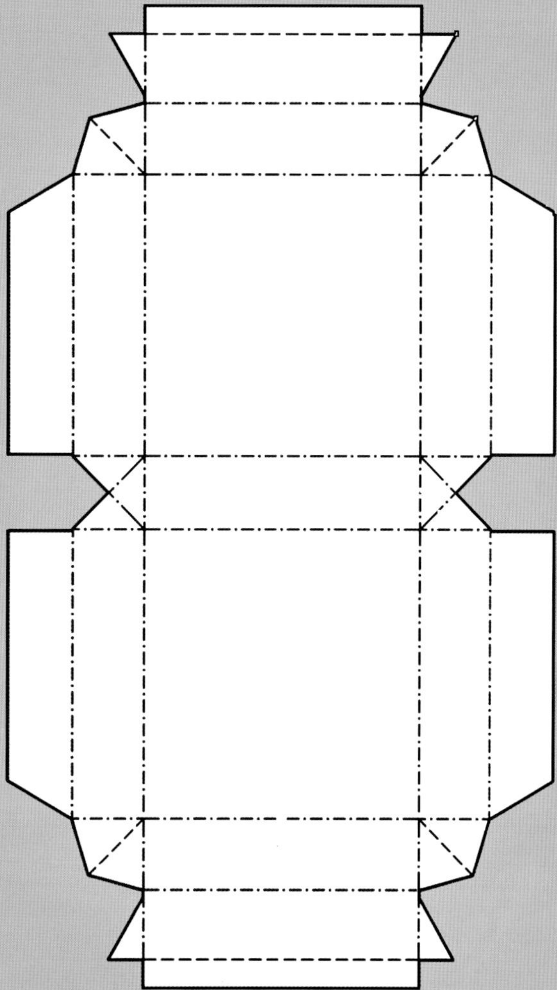

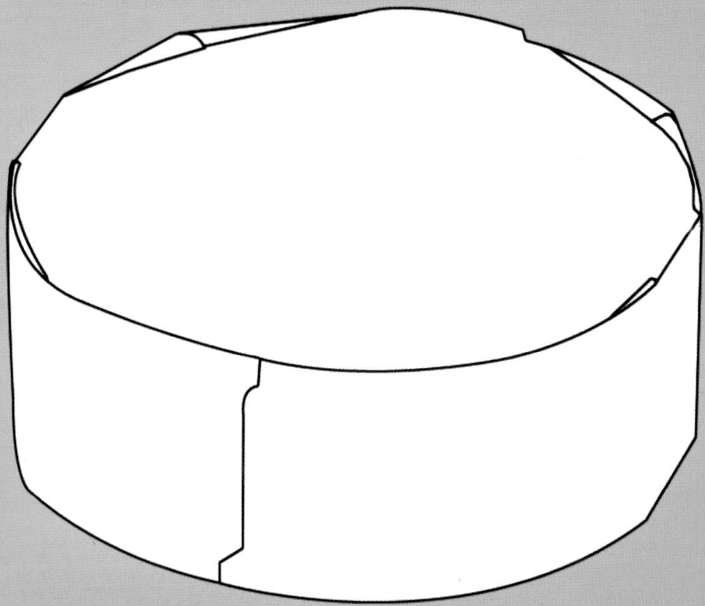

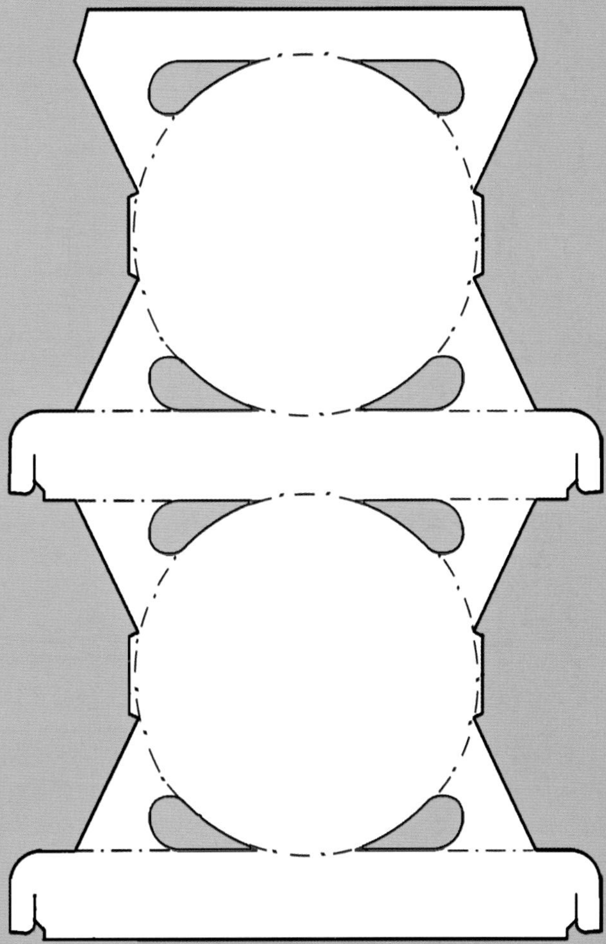

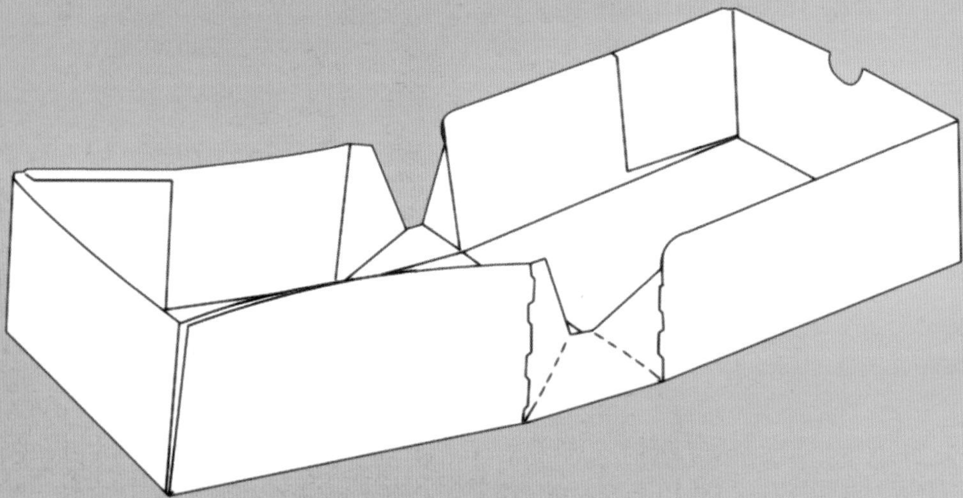

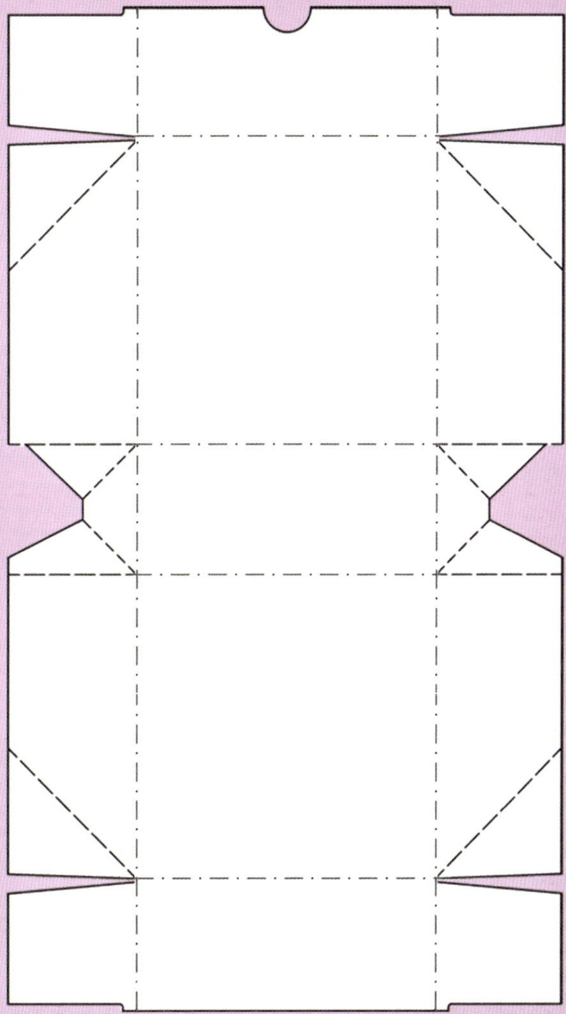

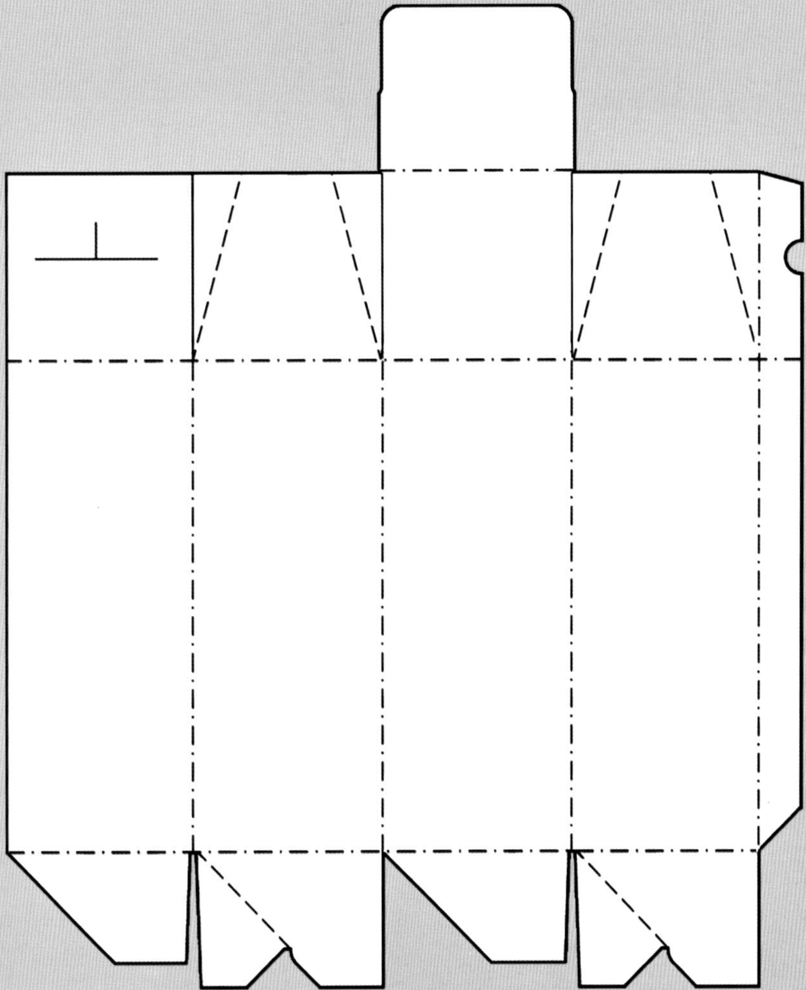

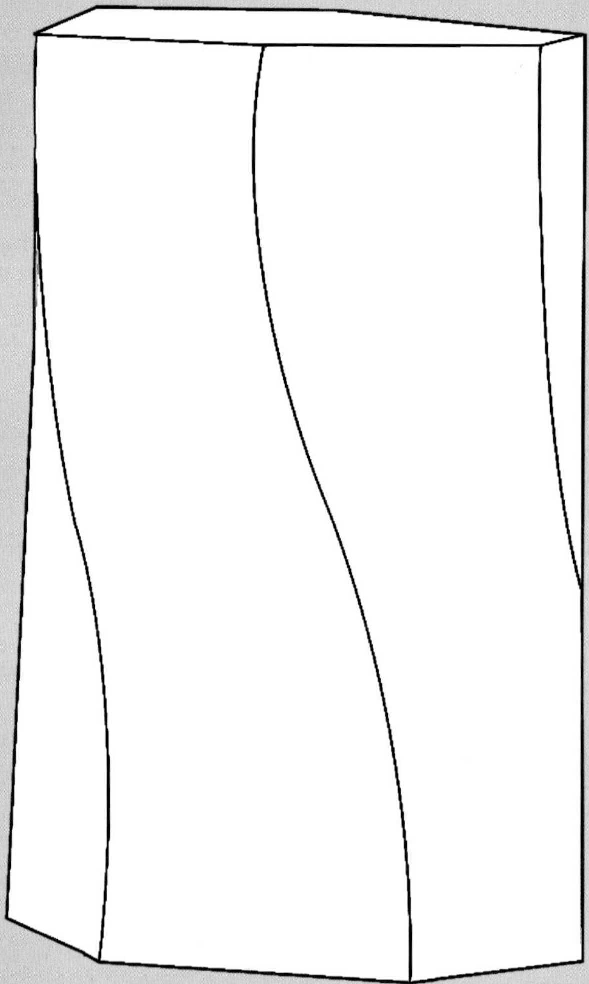

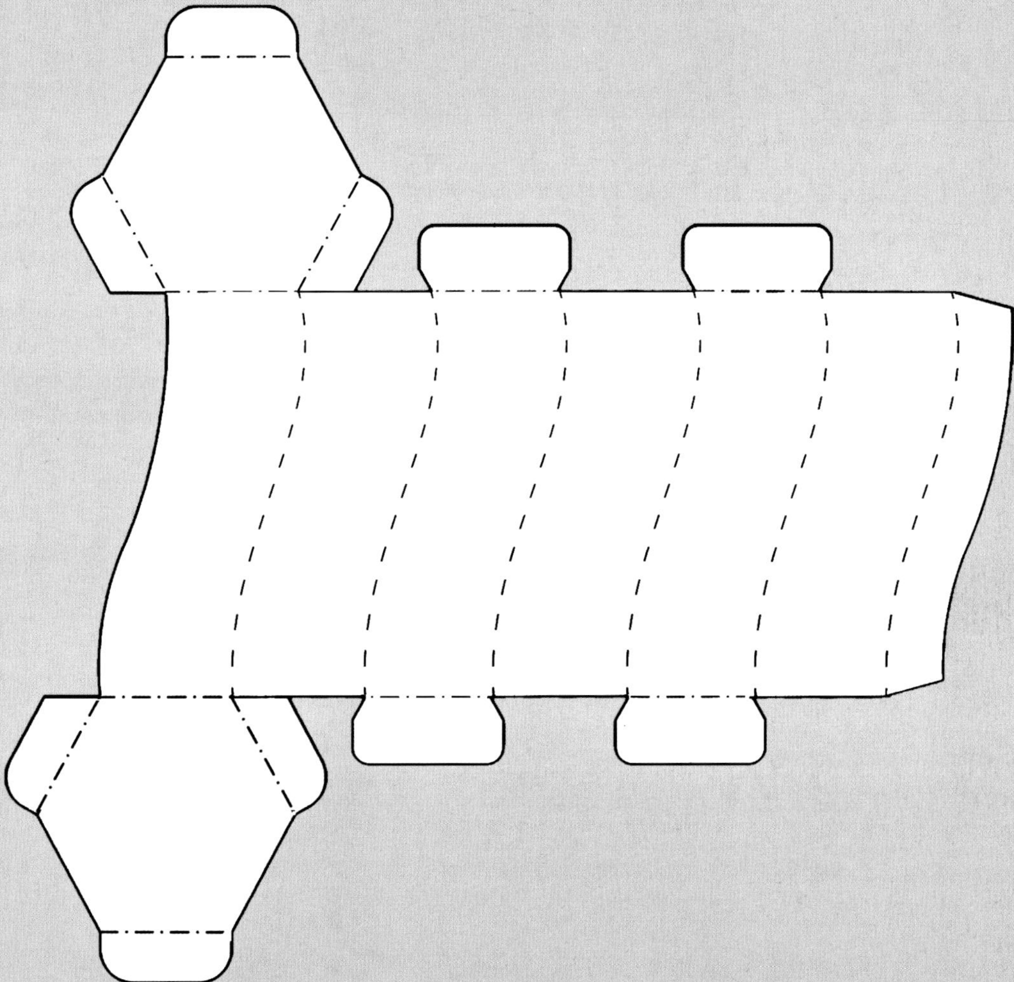

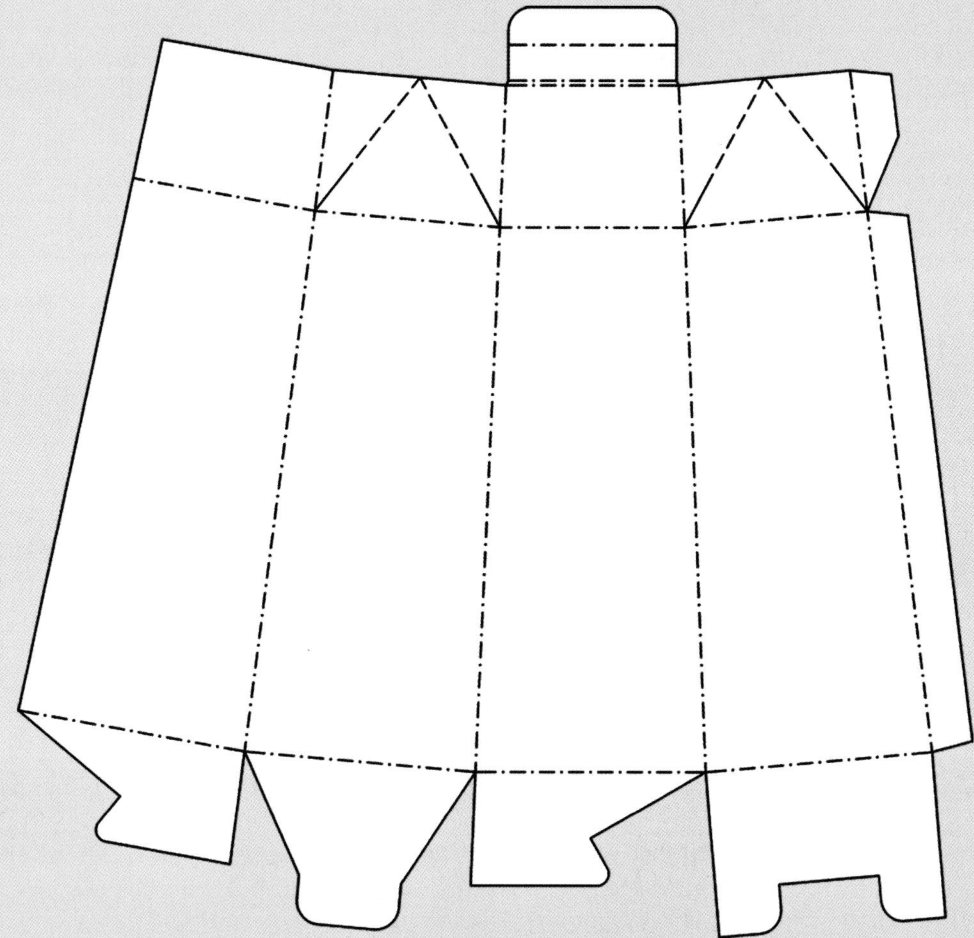

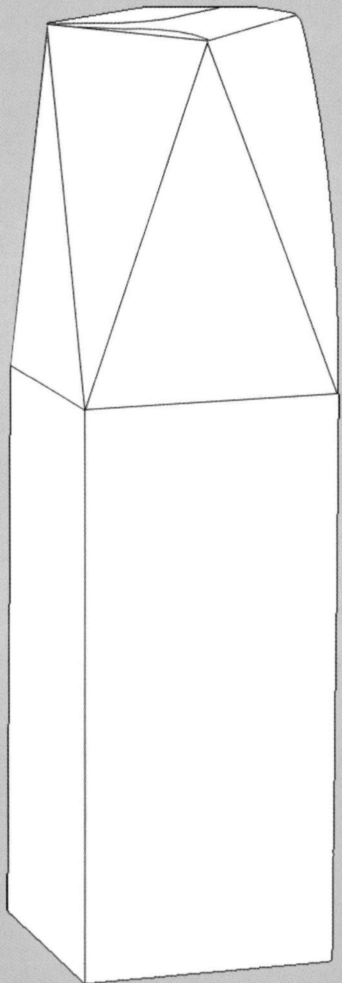

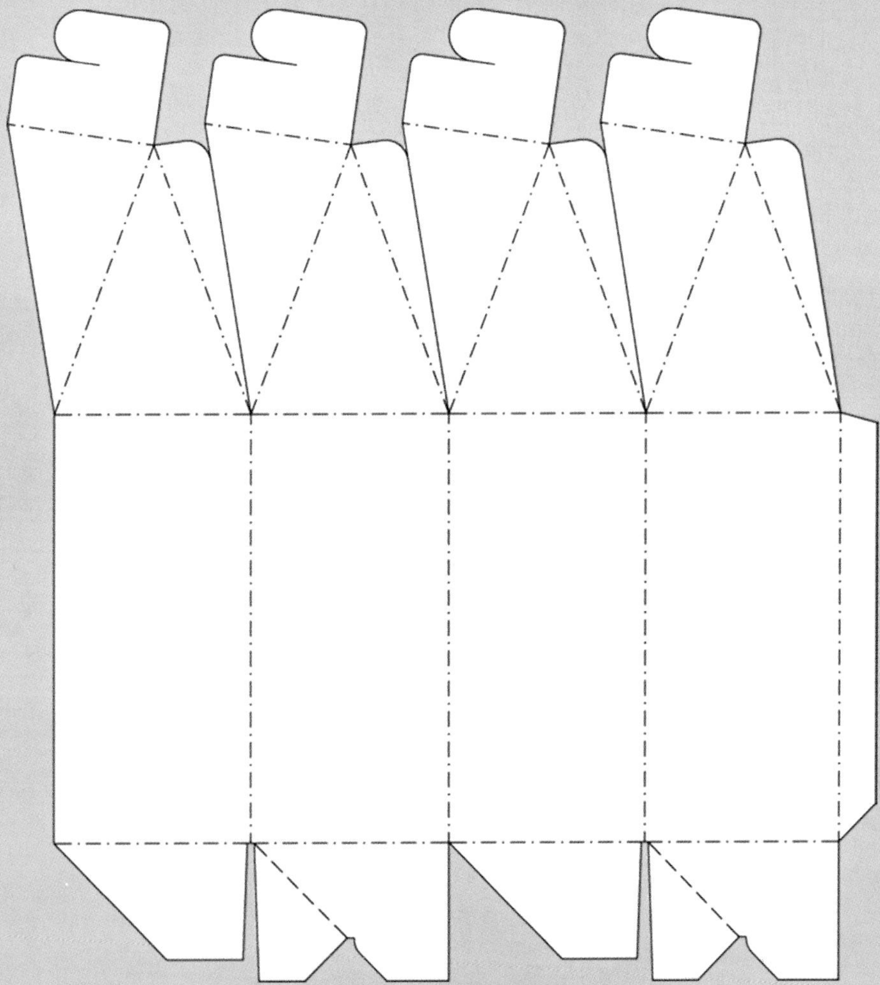

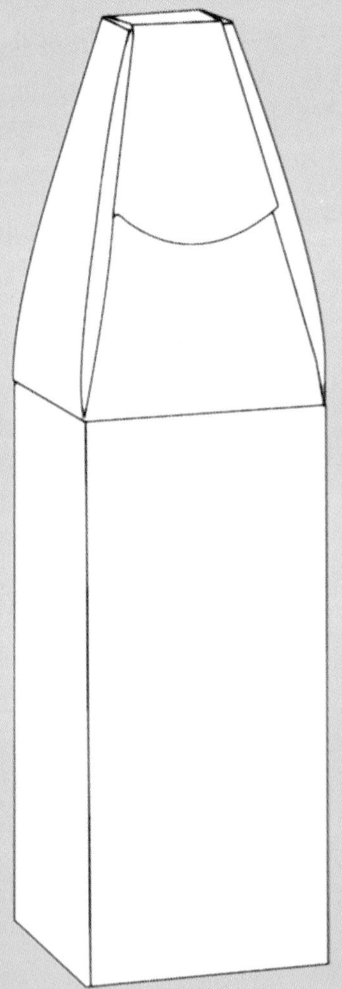

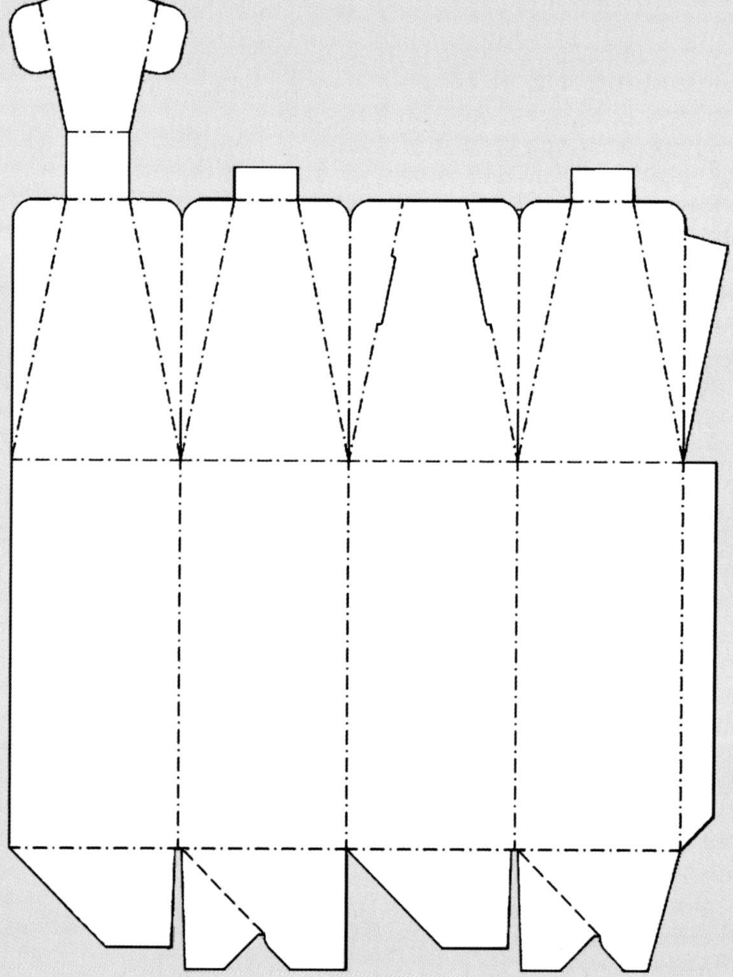

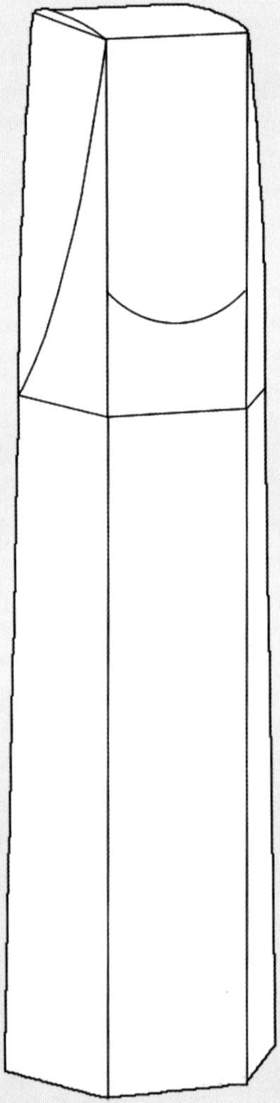

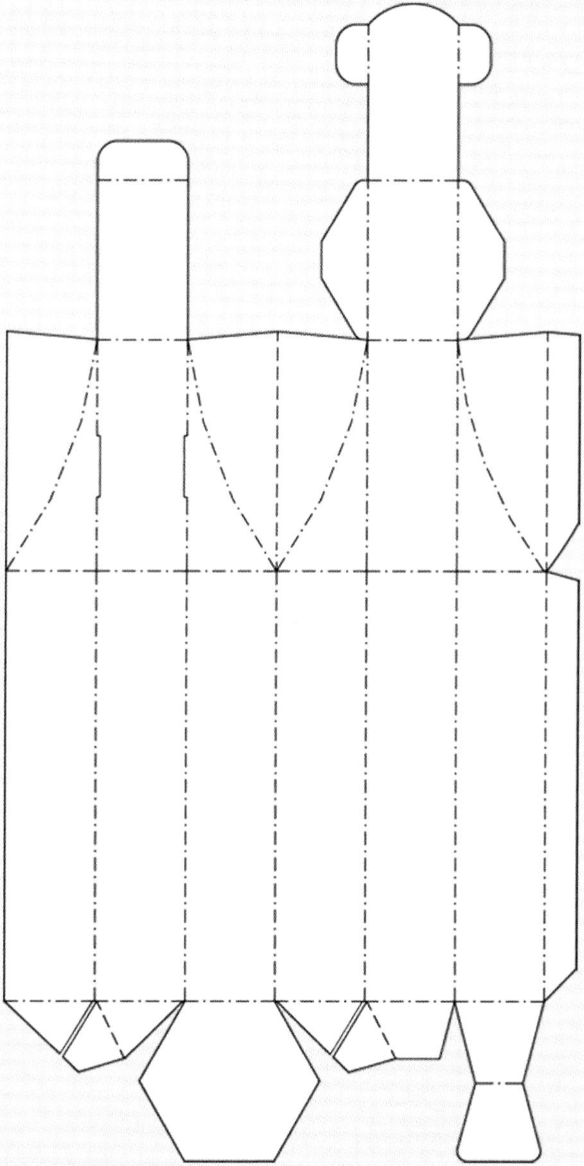

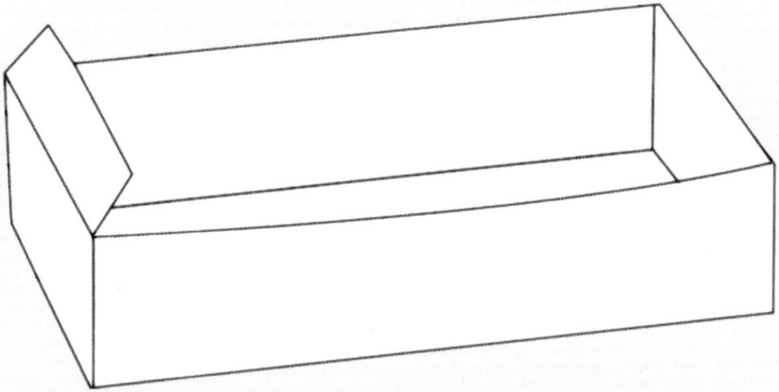

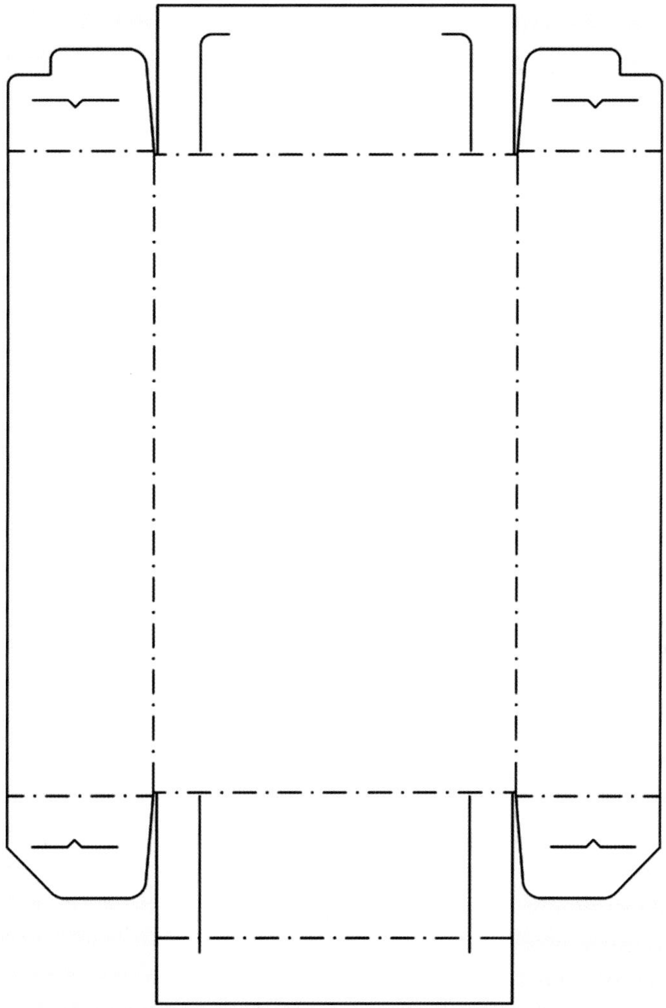

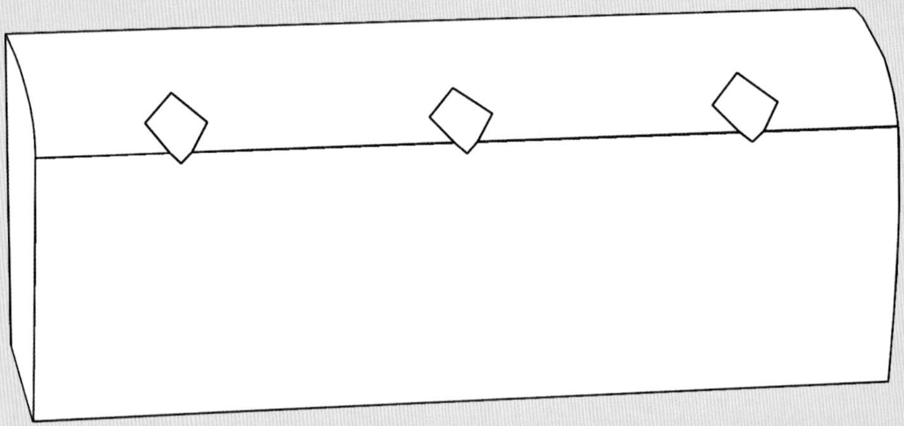

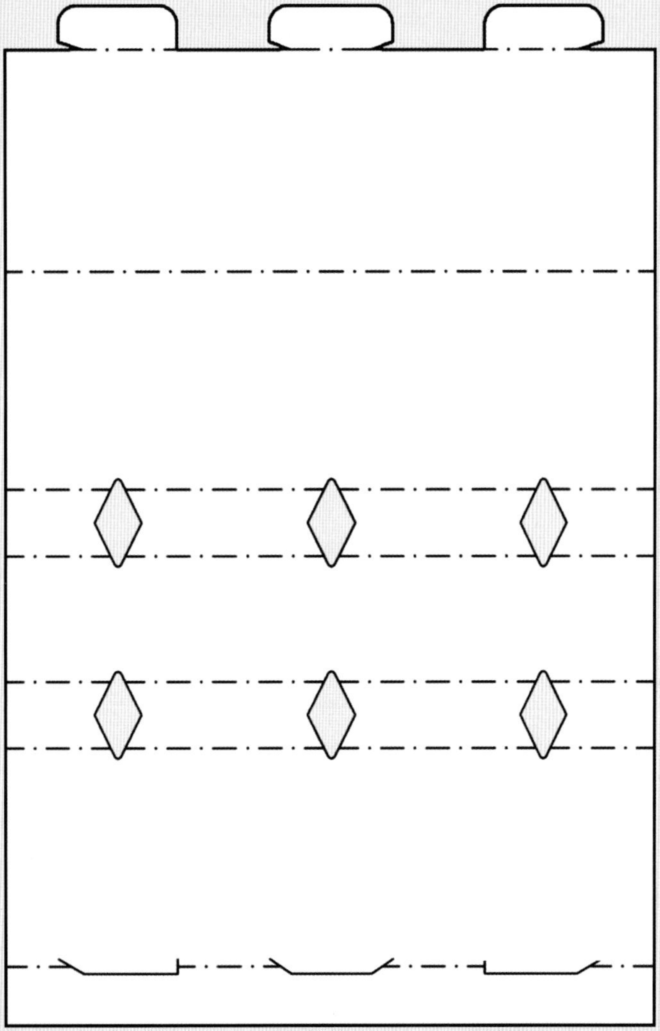

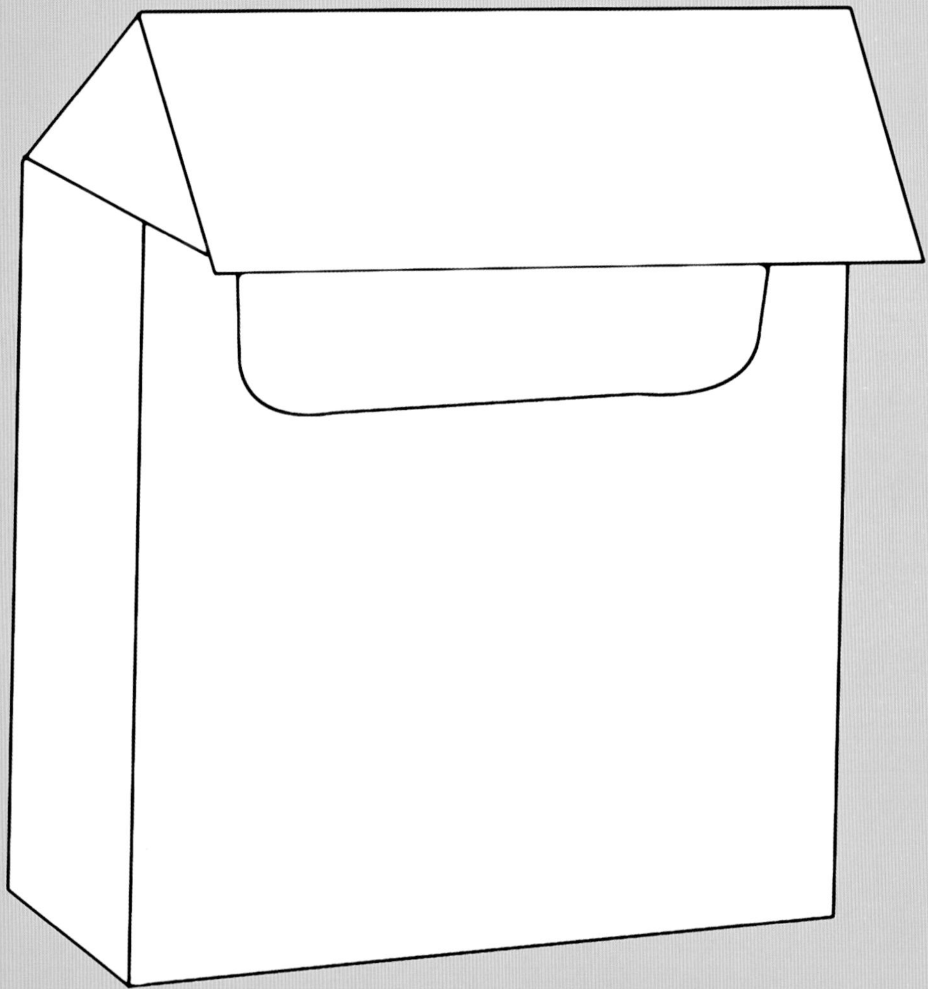

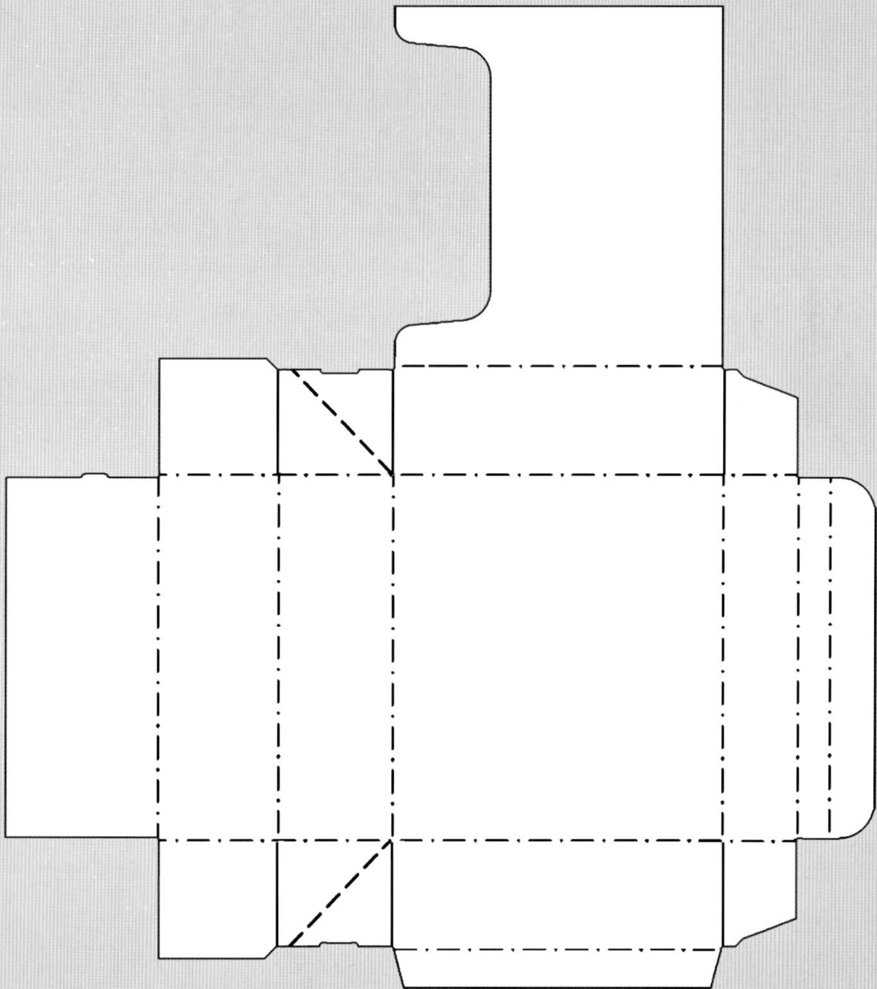

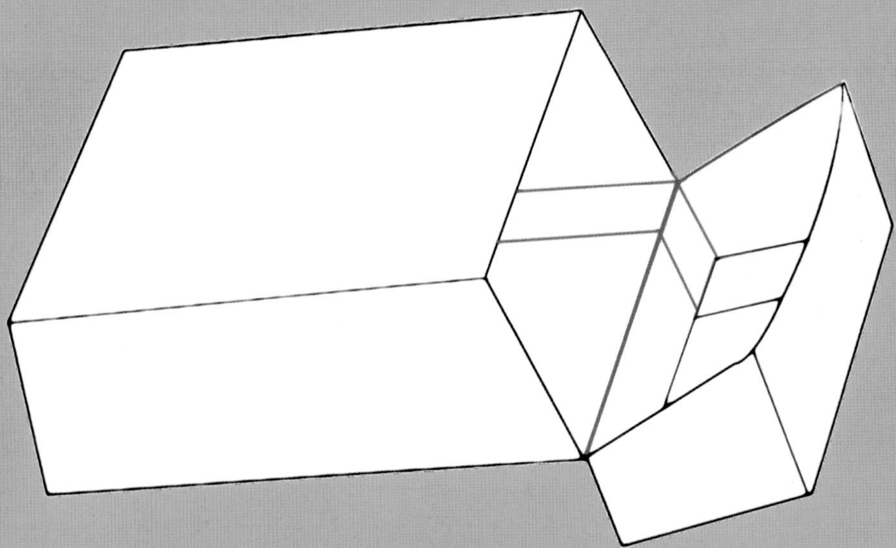

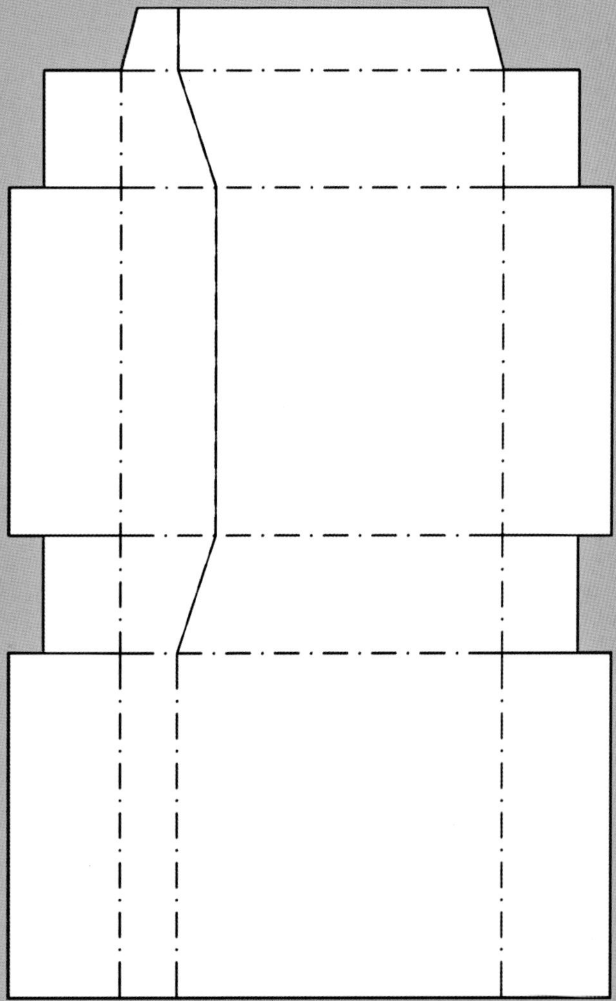

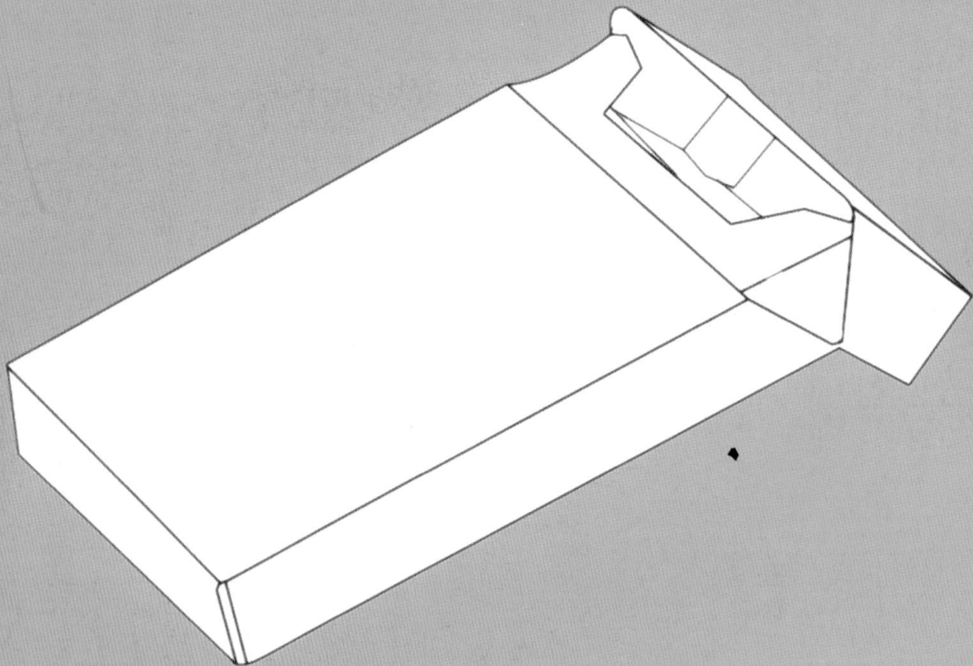

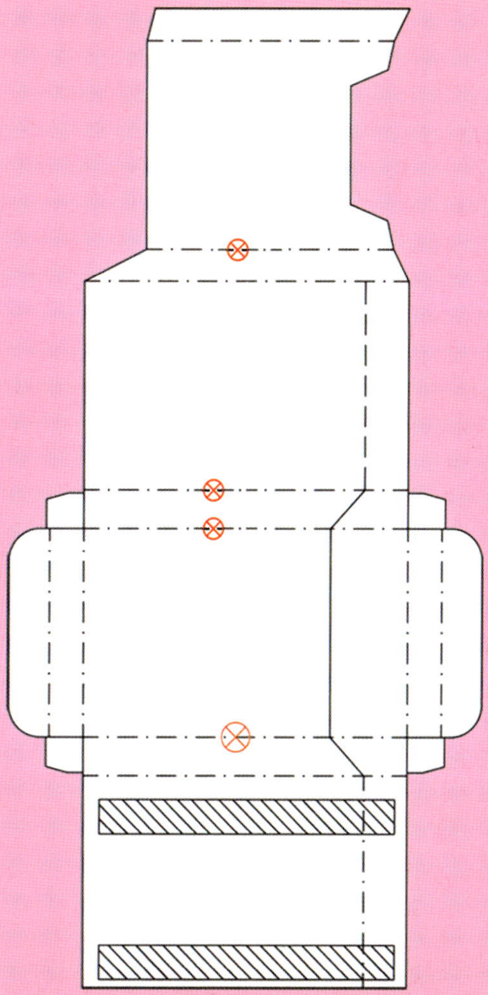

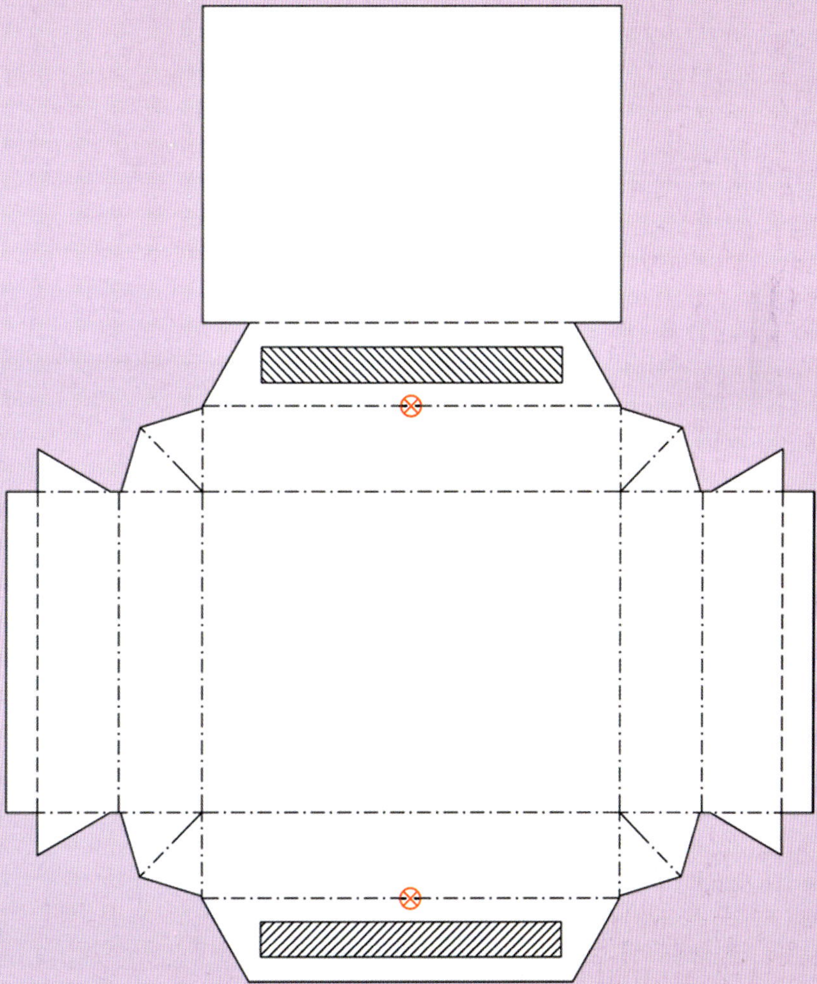

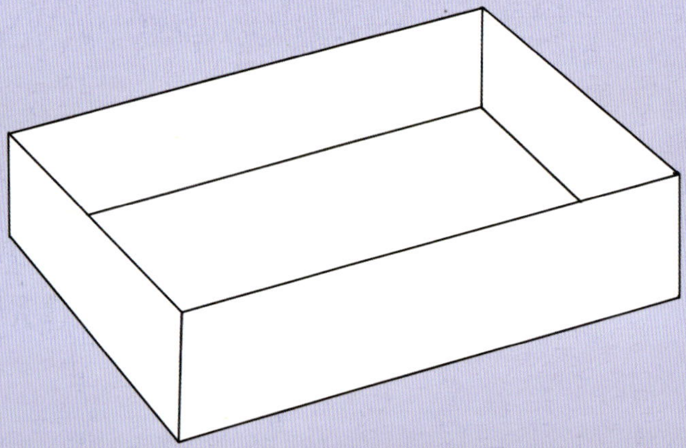

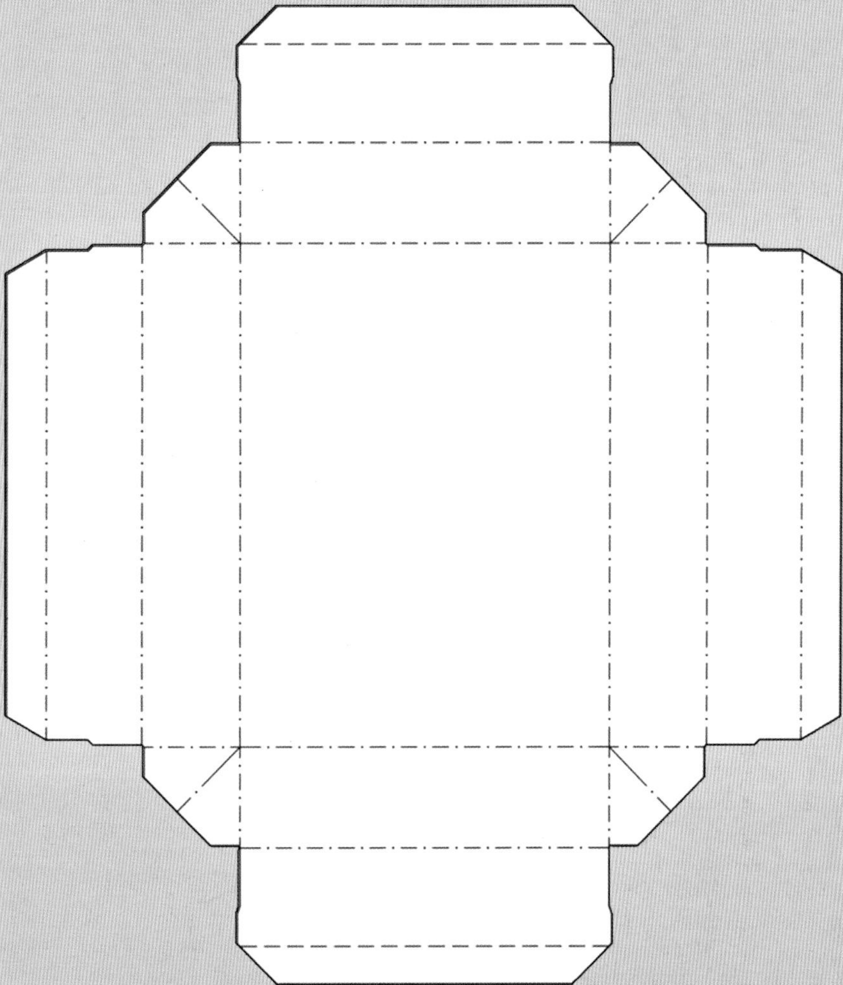

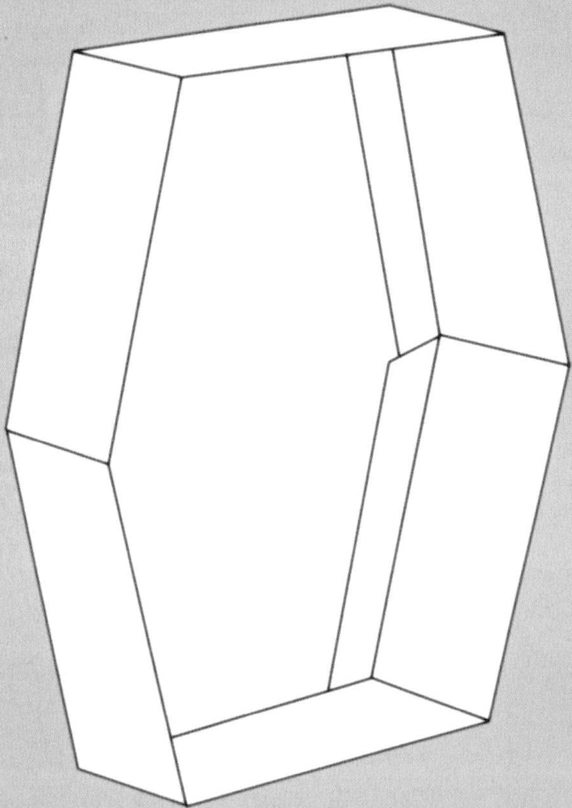

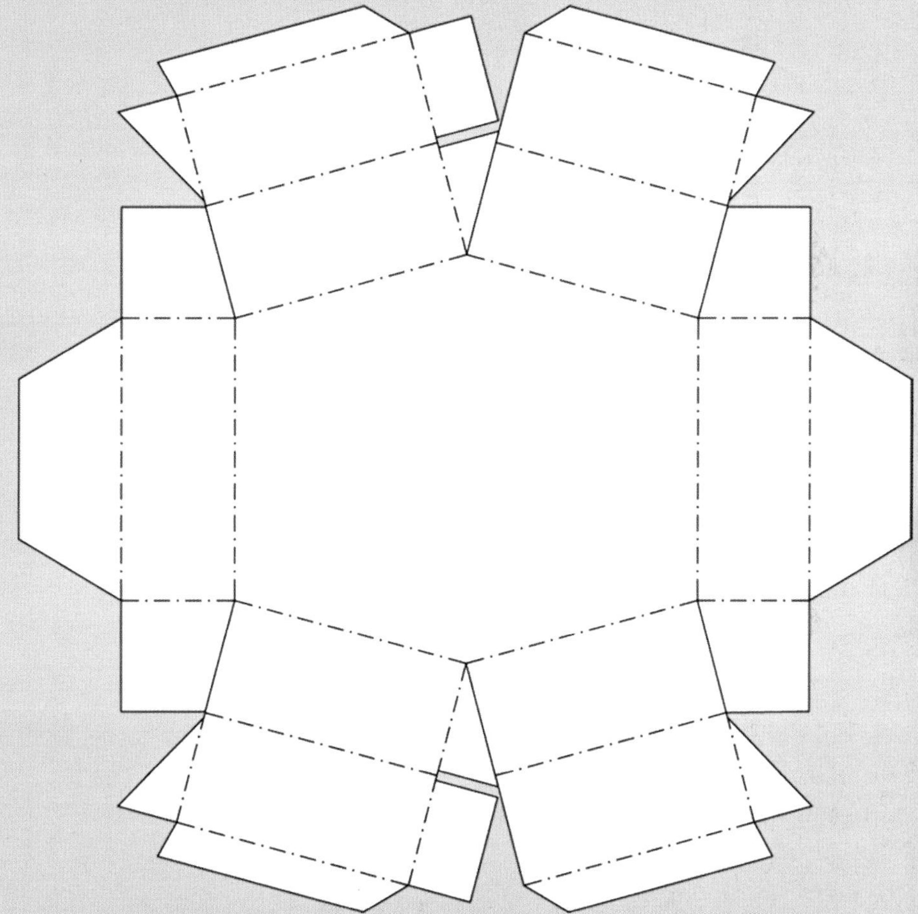

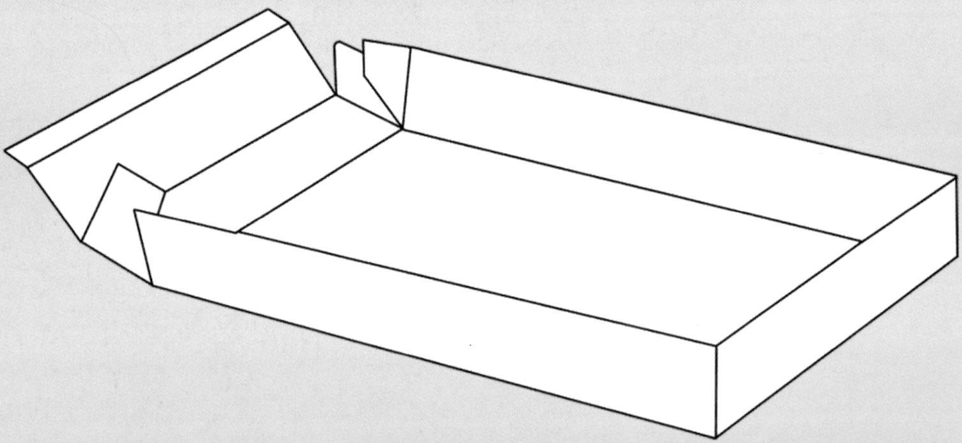

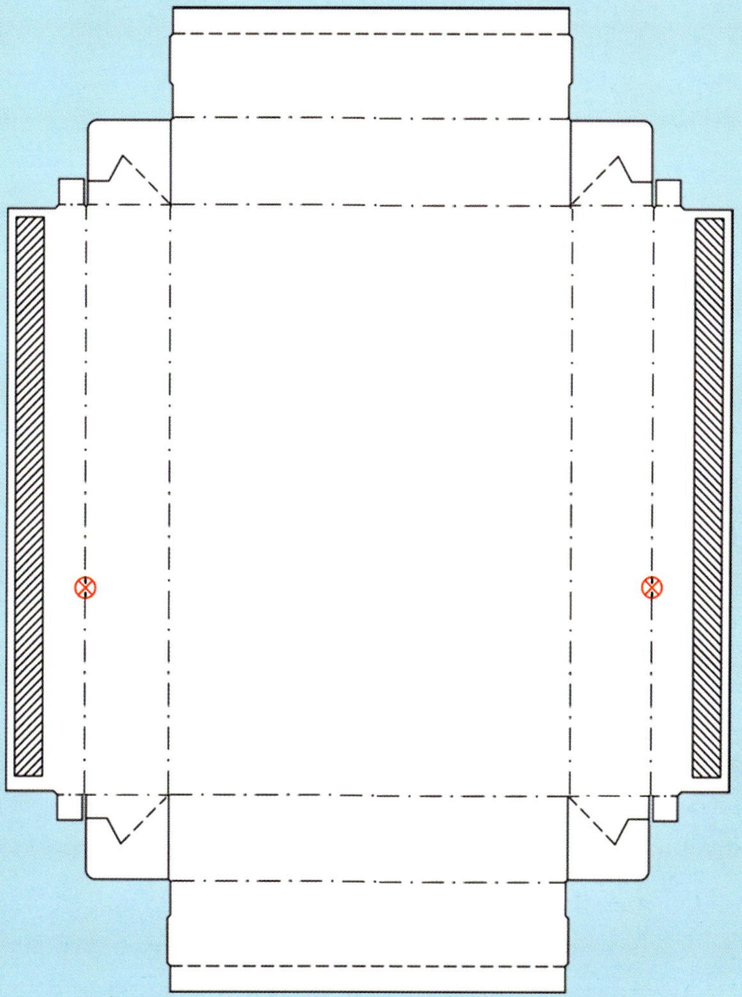

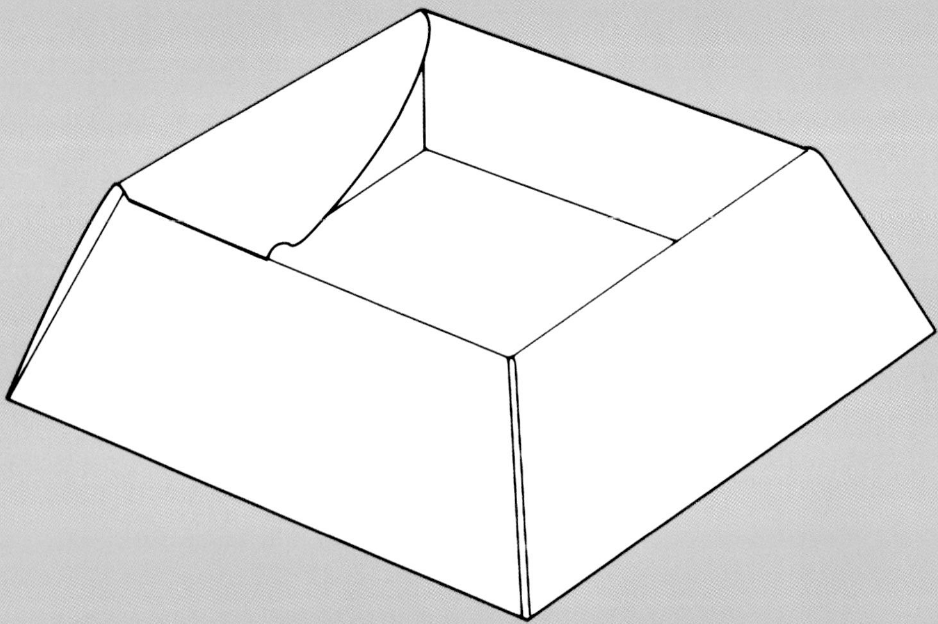

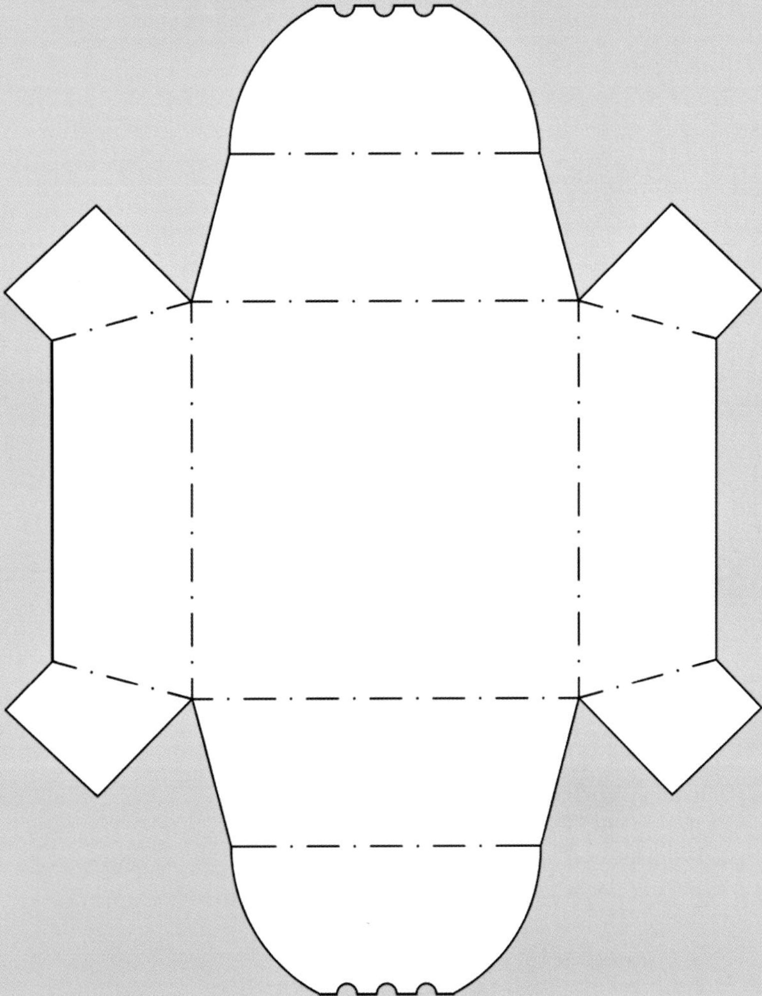

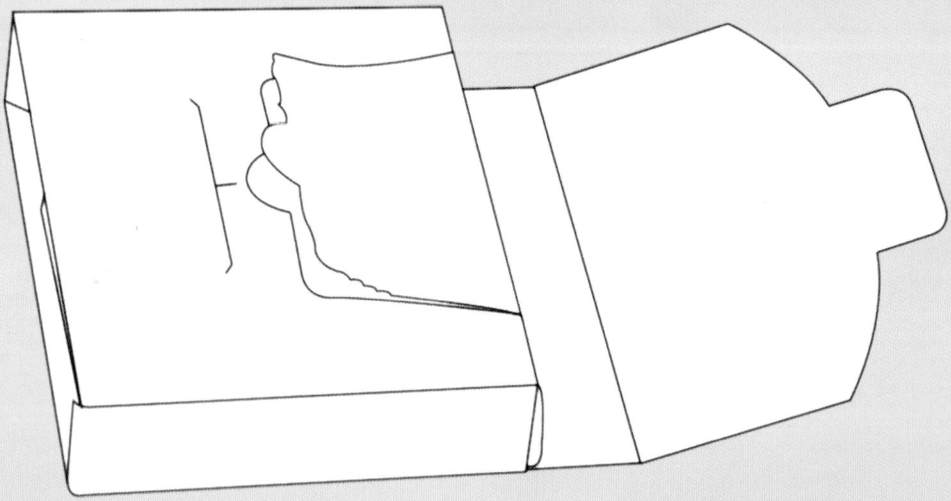

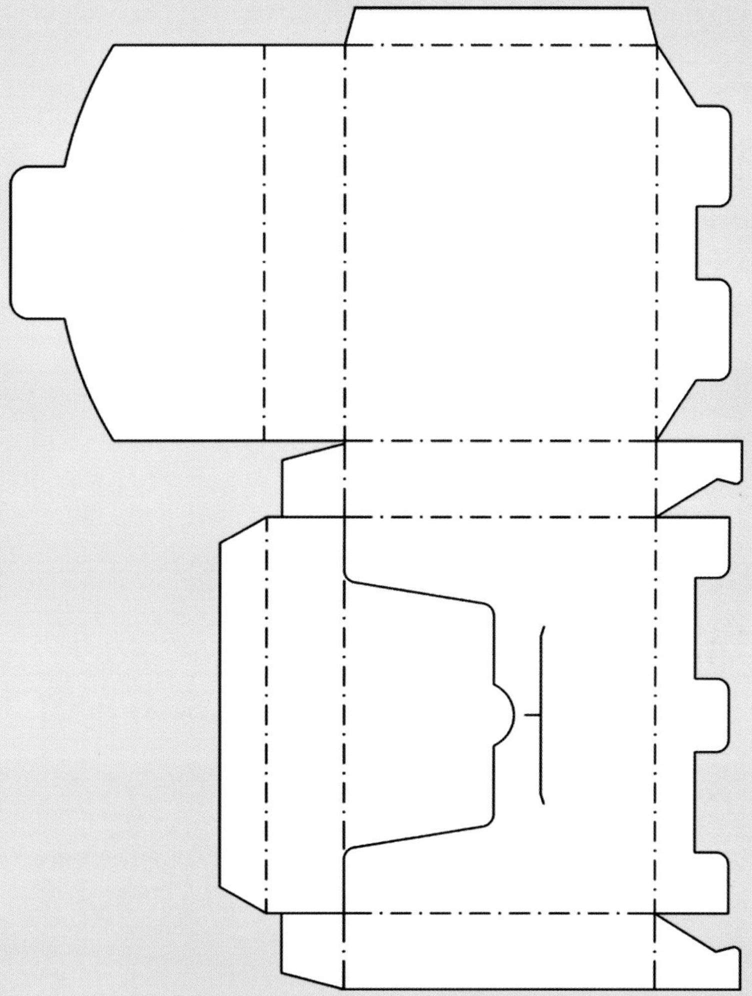

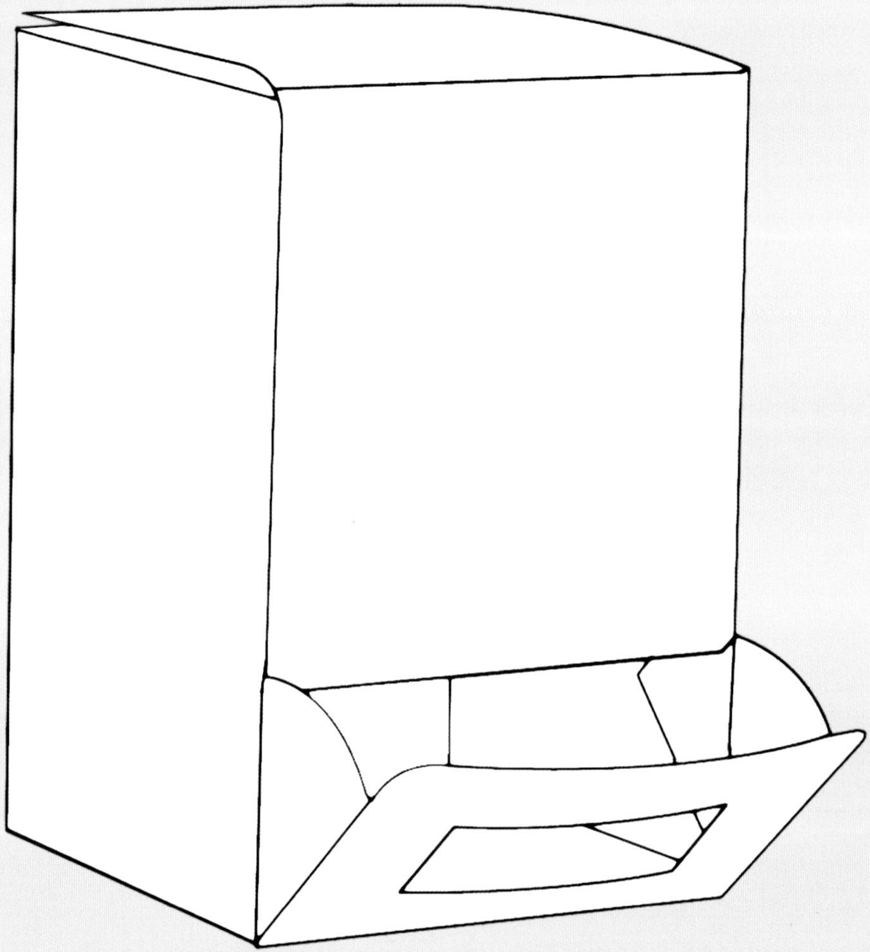

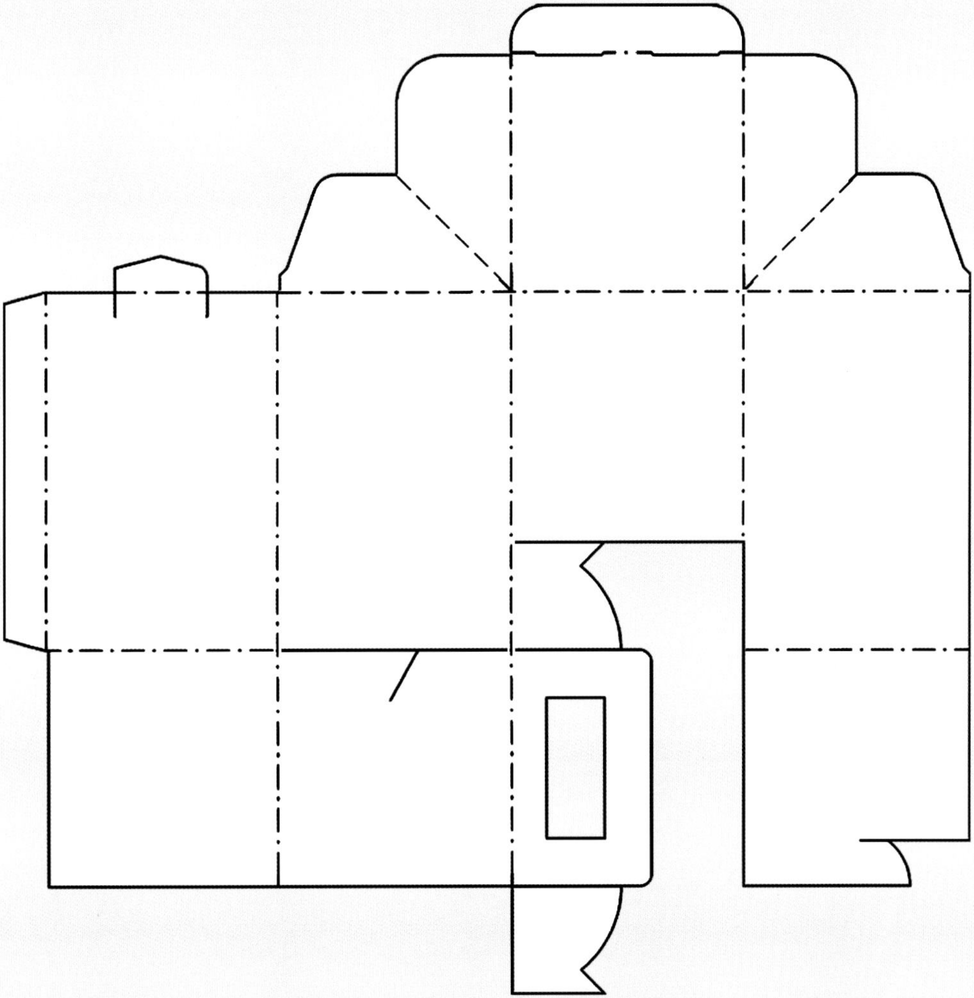

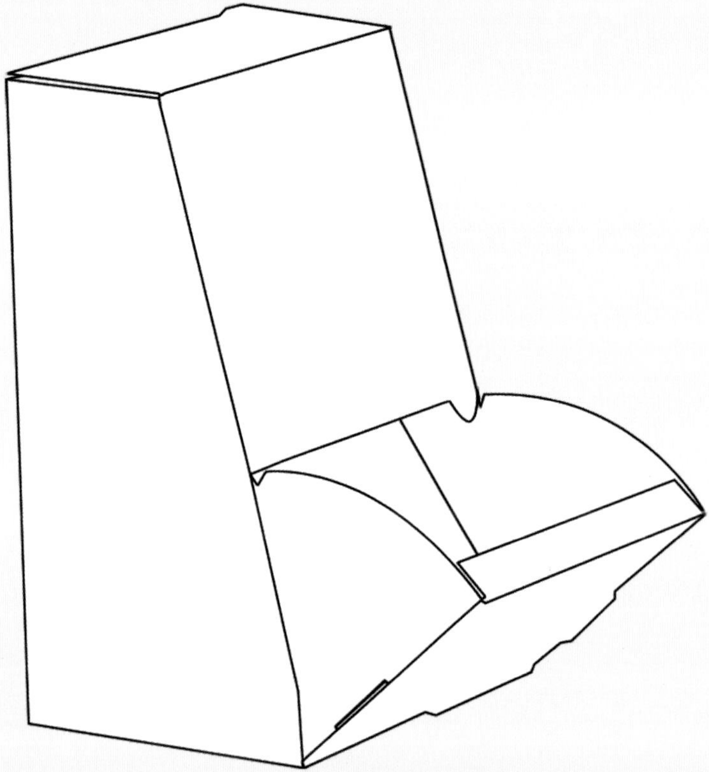

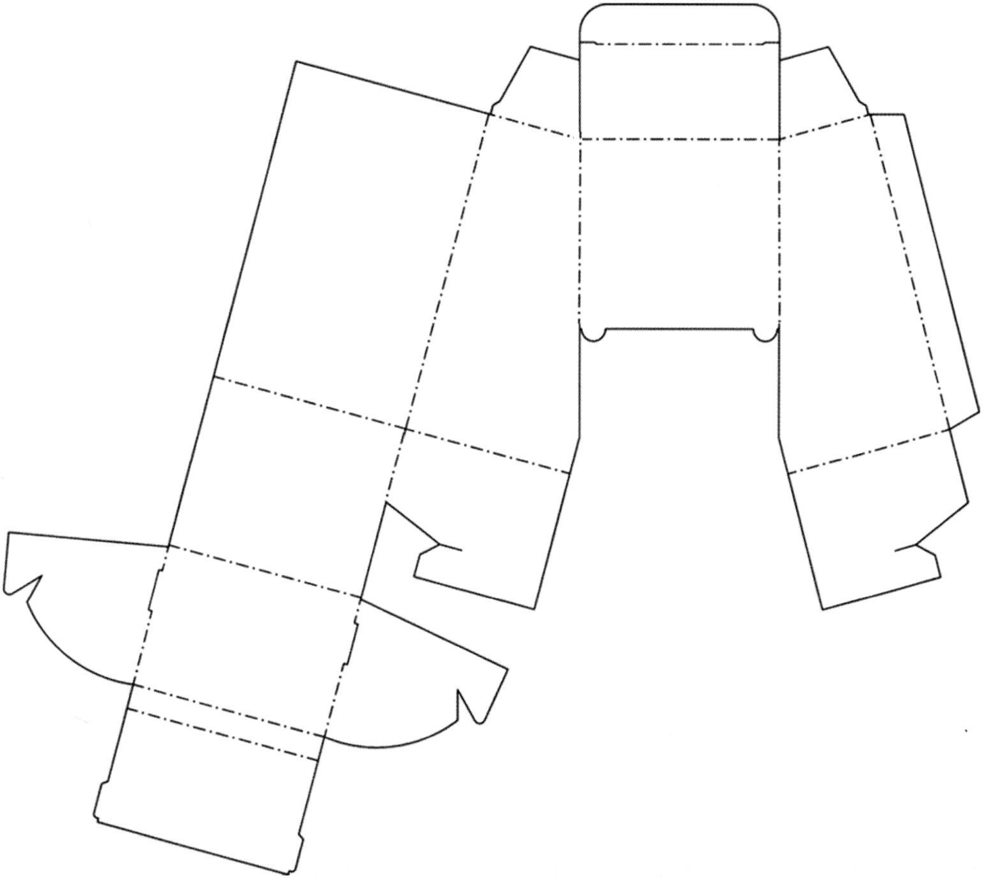

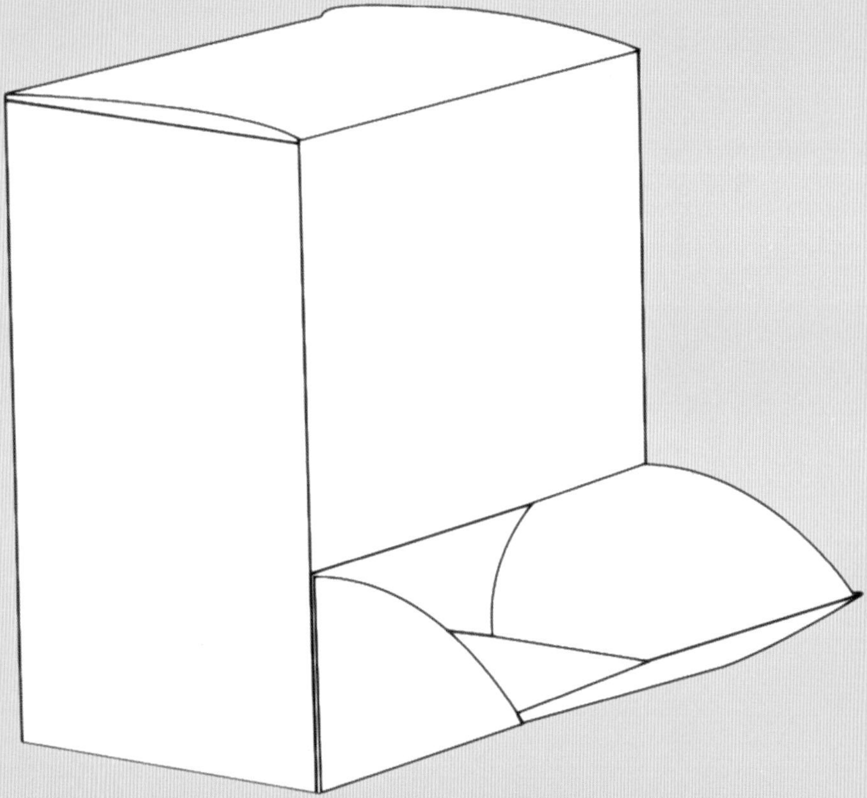

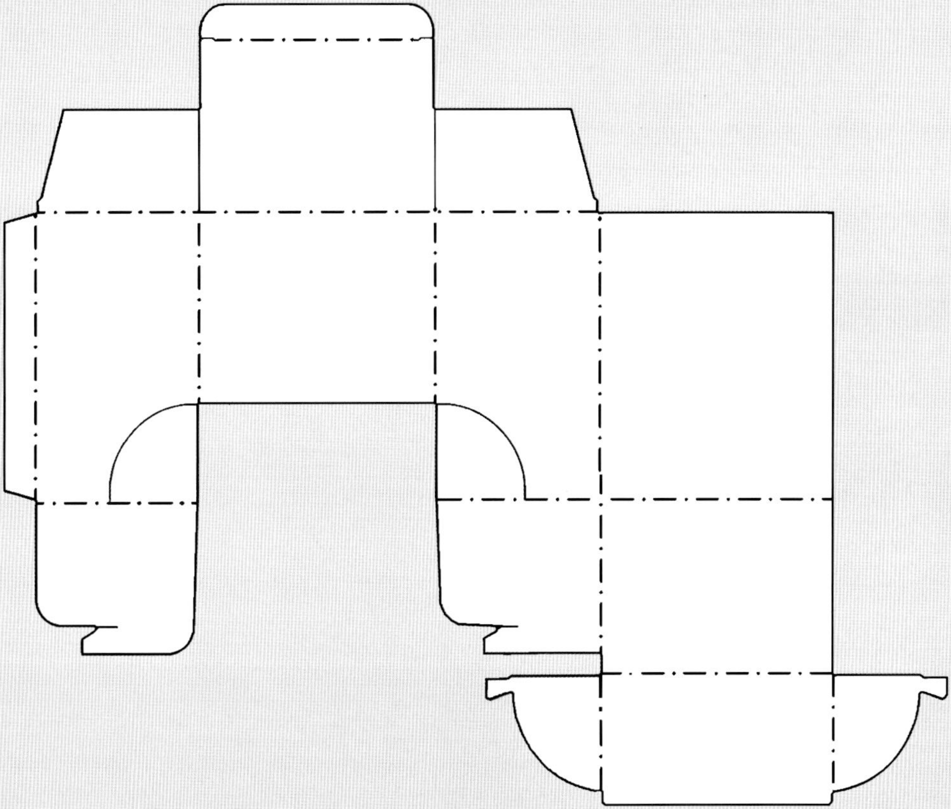

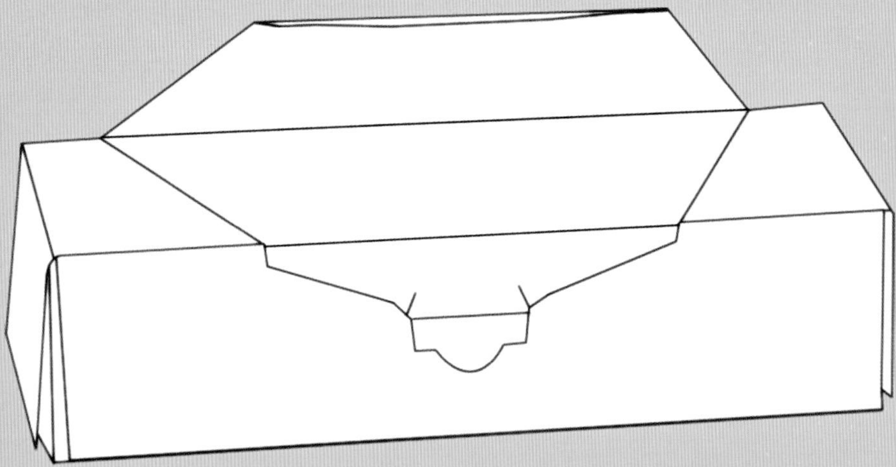

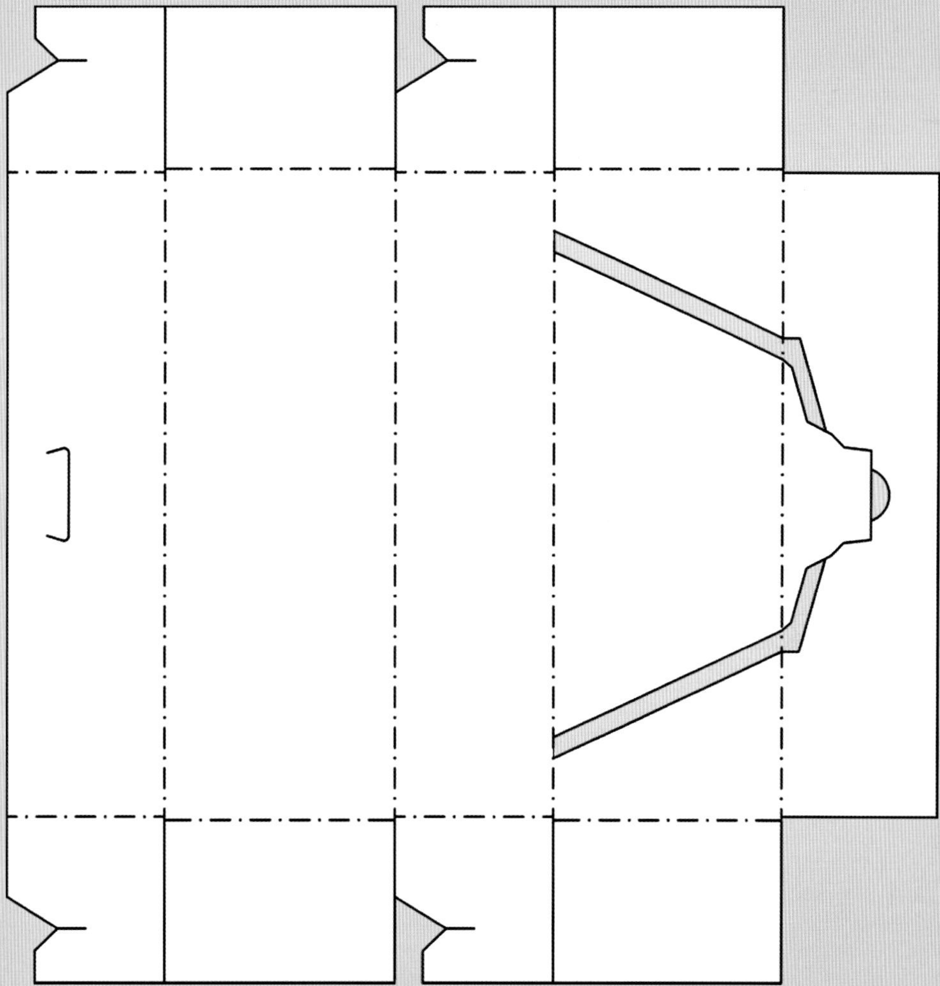

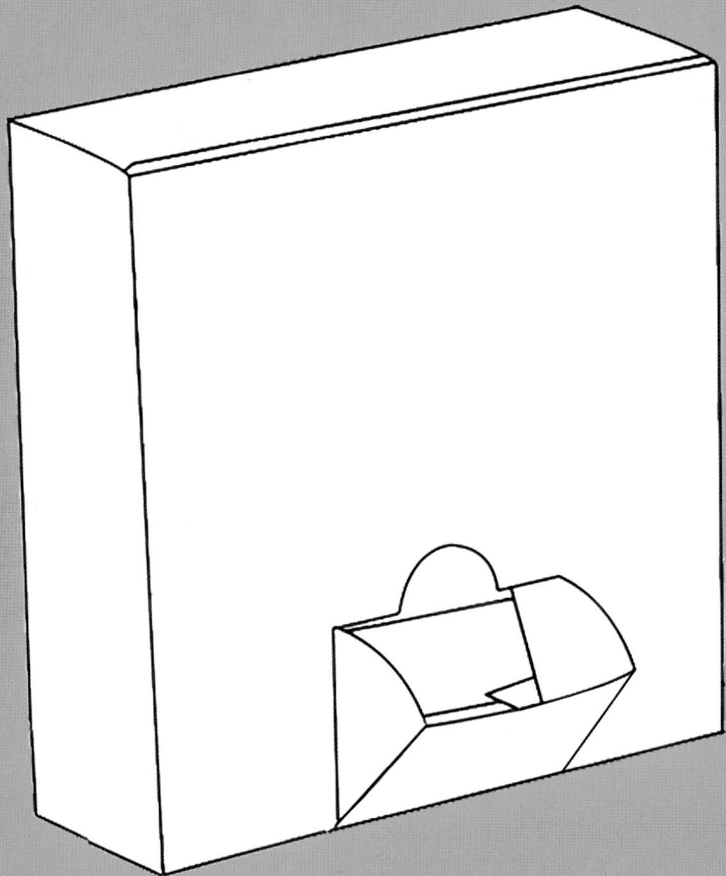

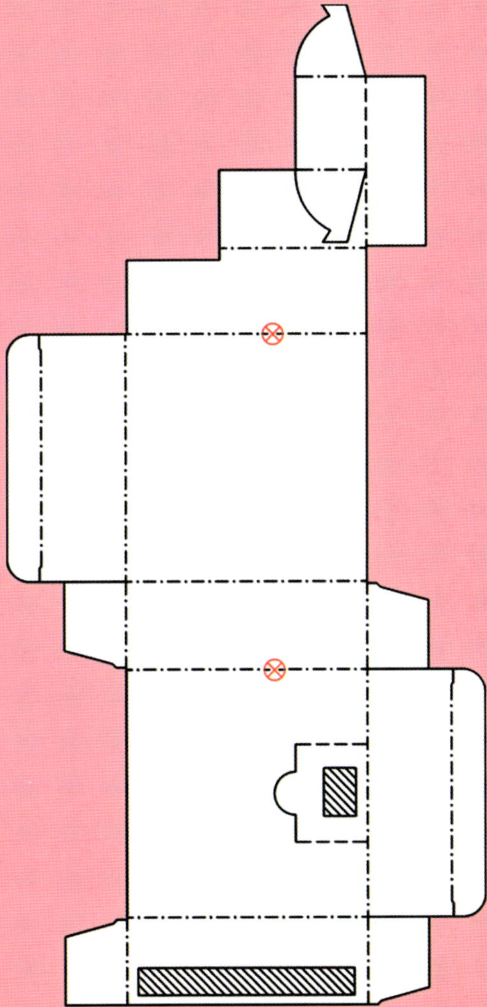

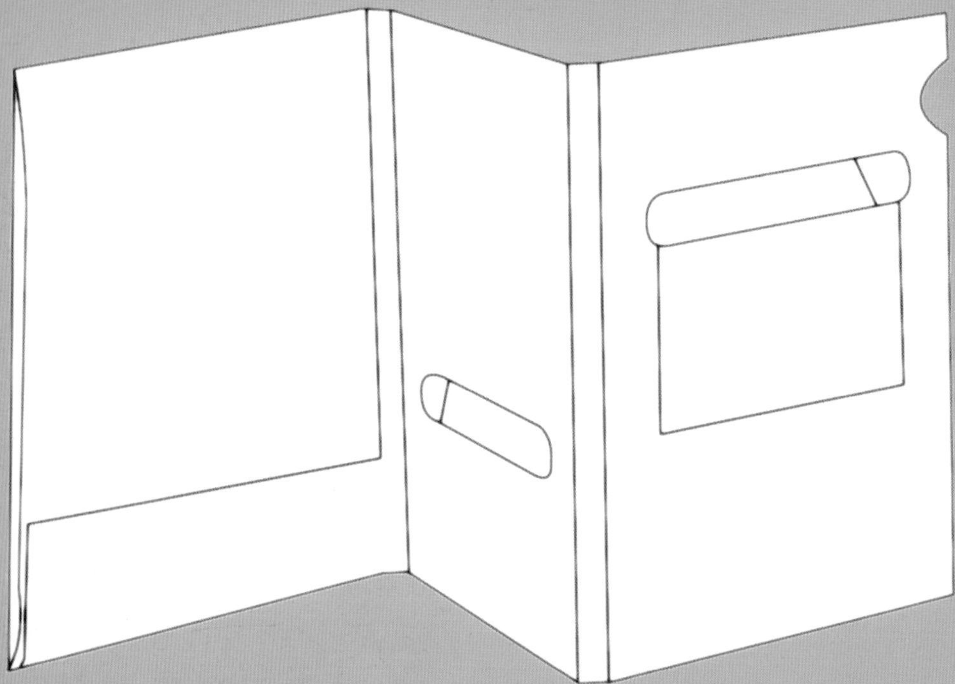

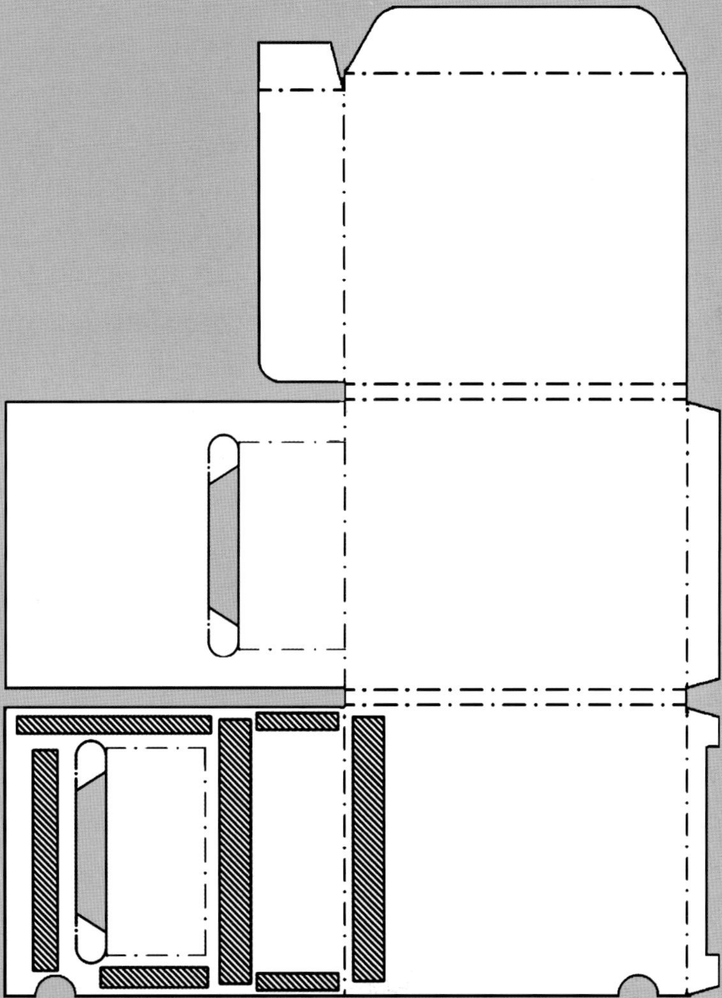

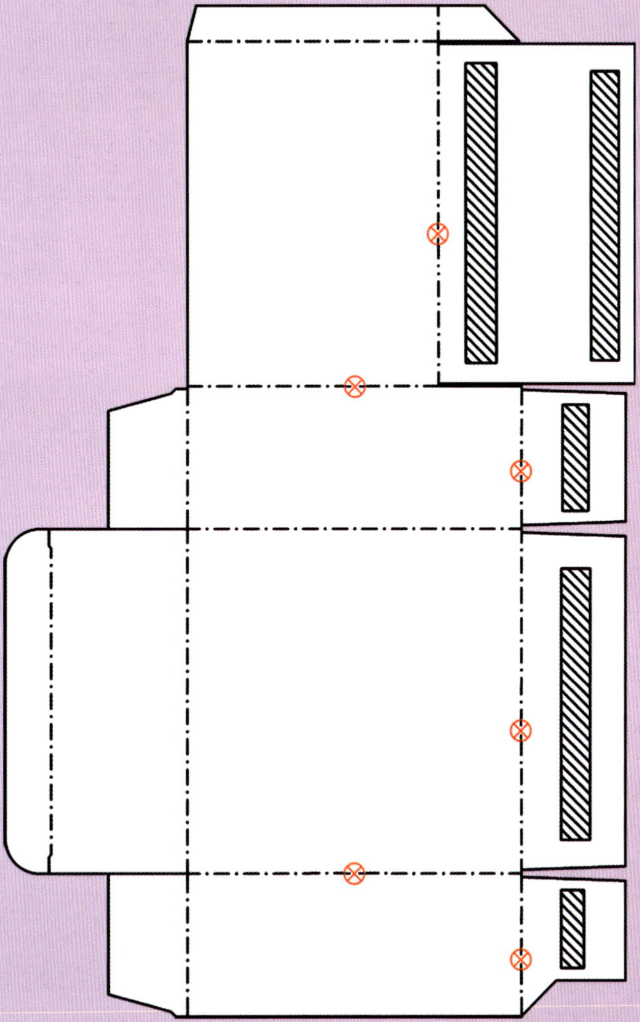

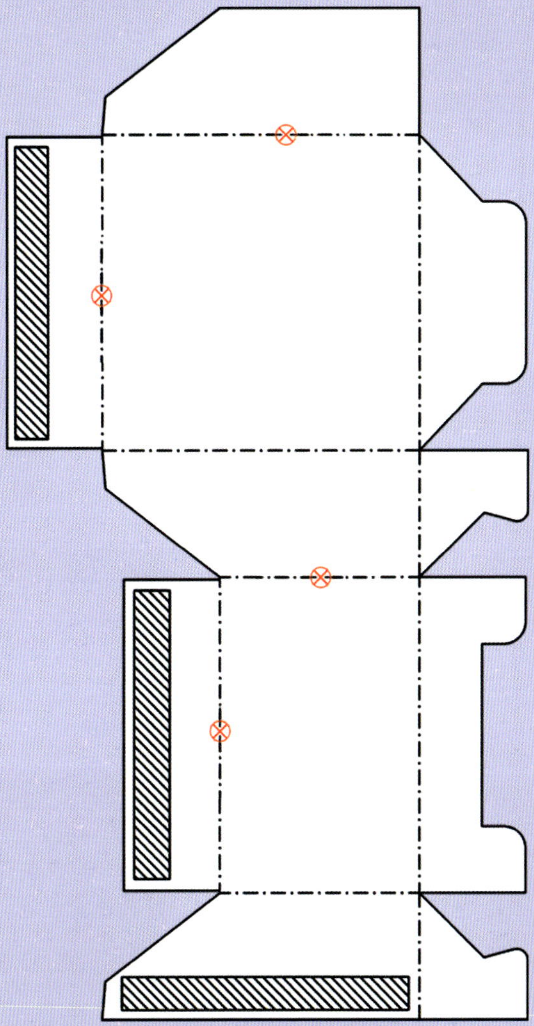

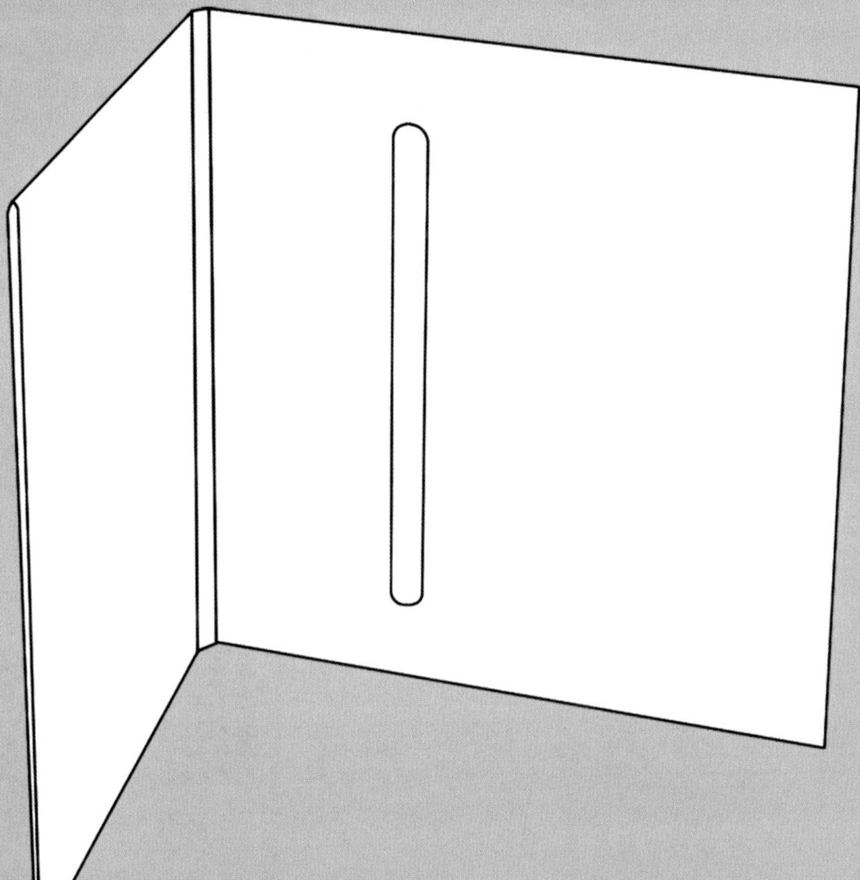

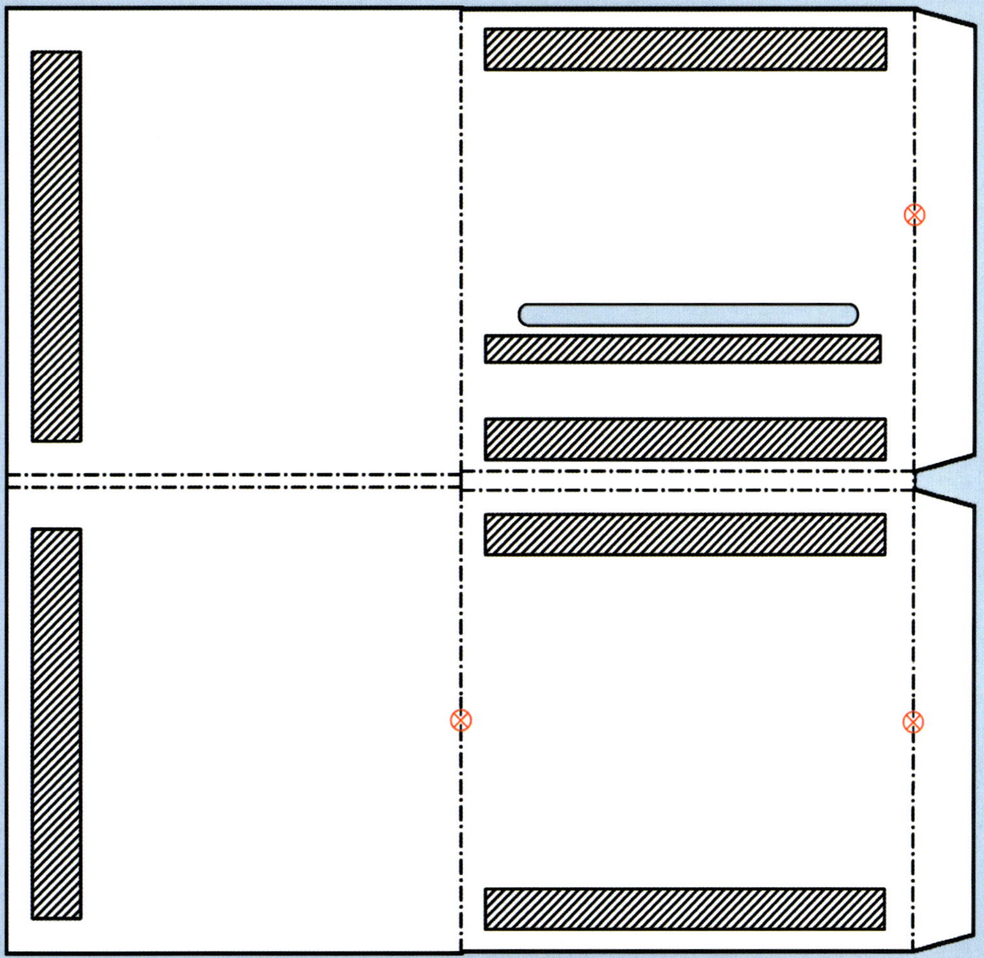

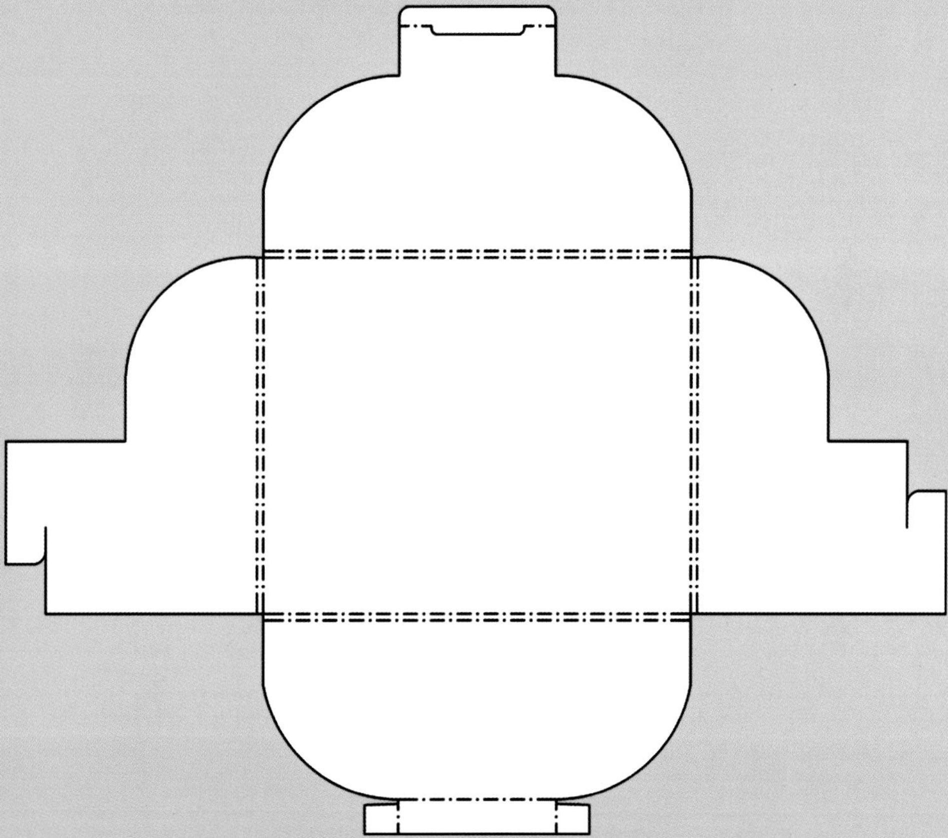

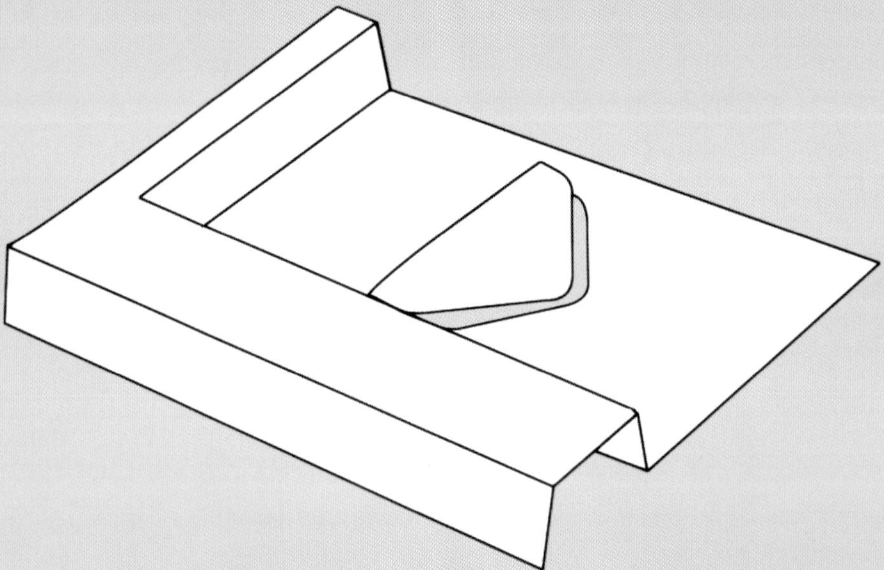

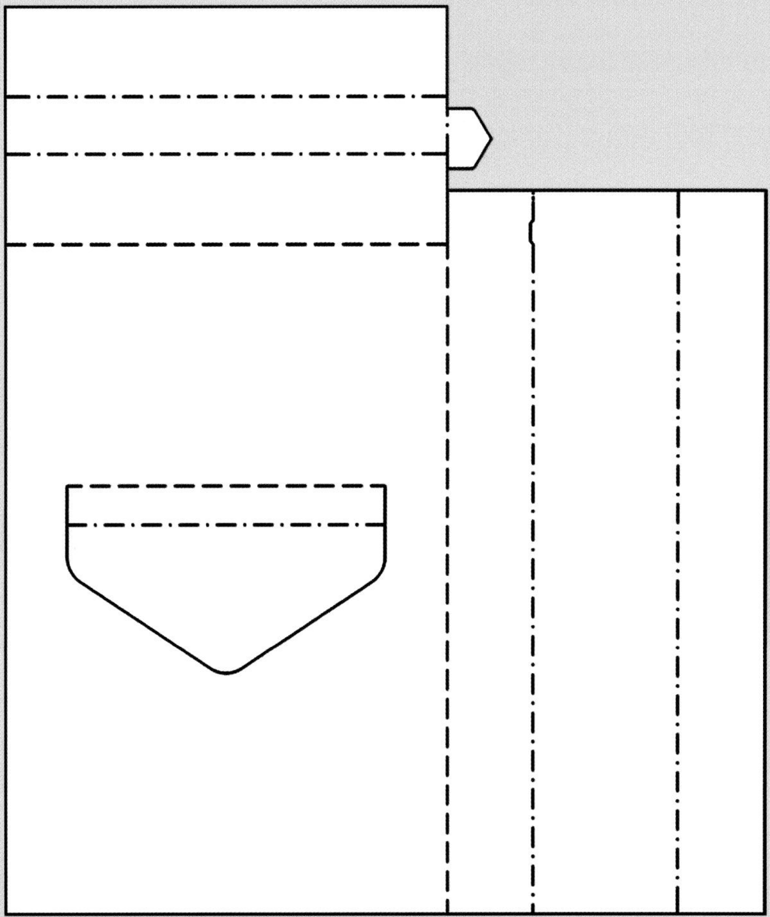

Dividers

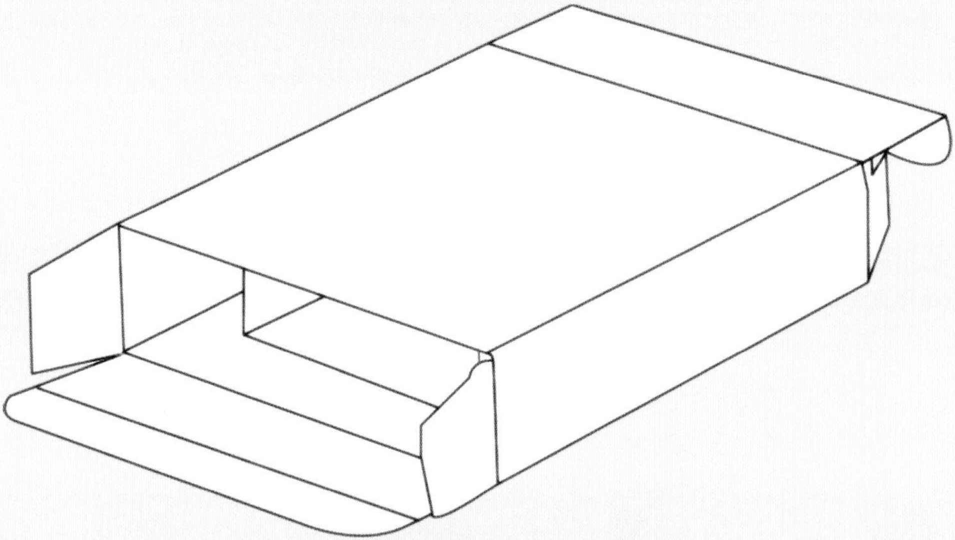

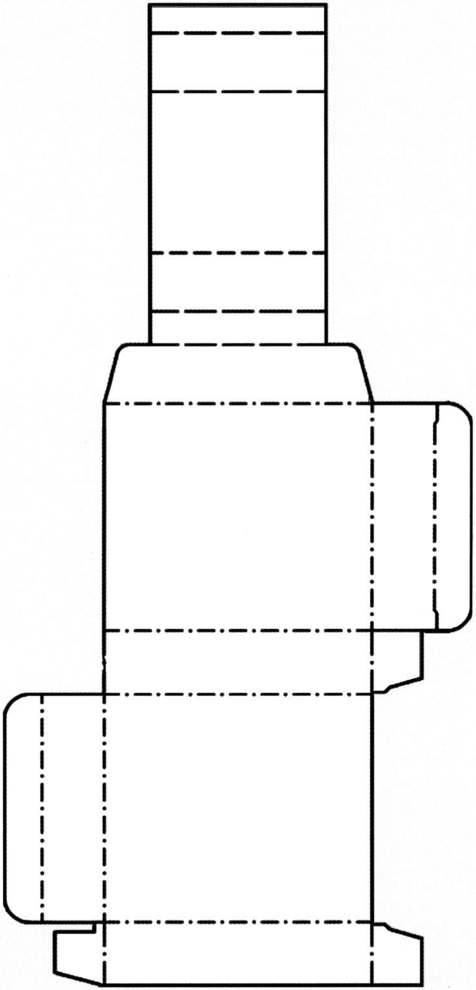

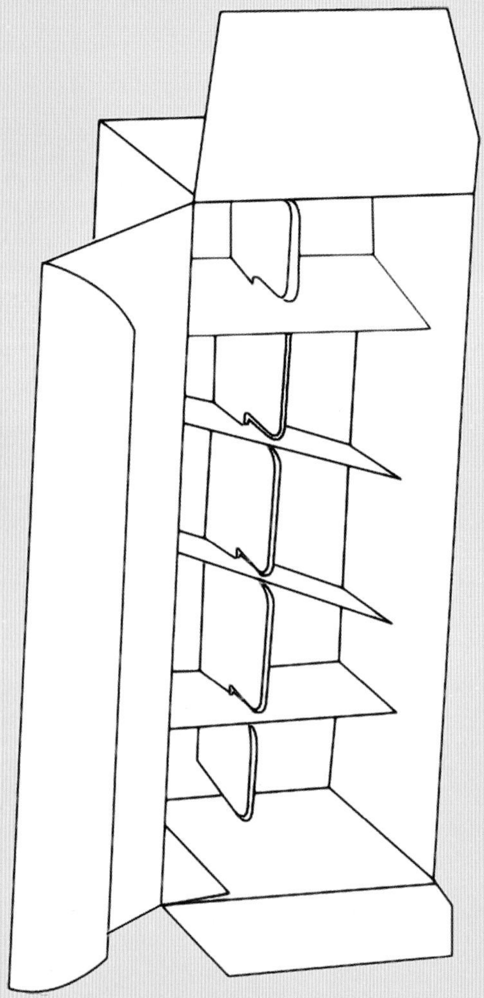

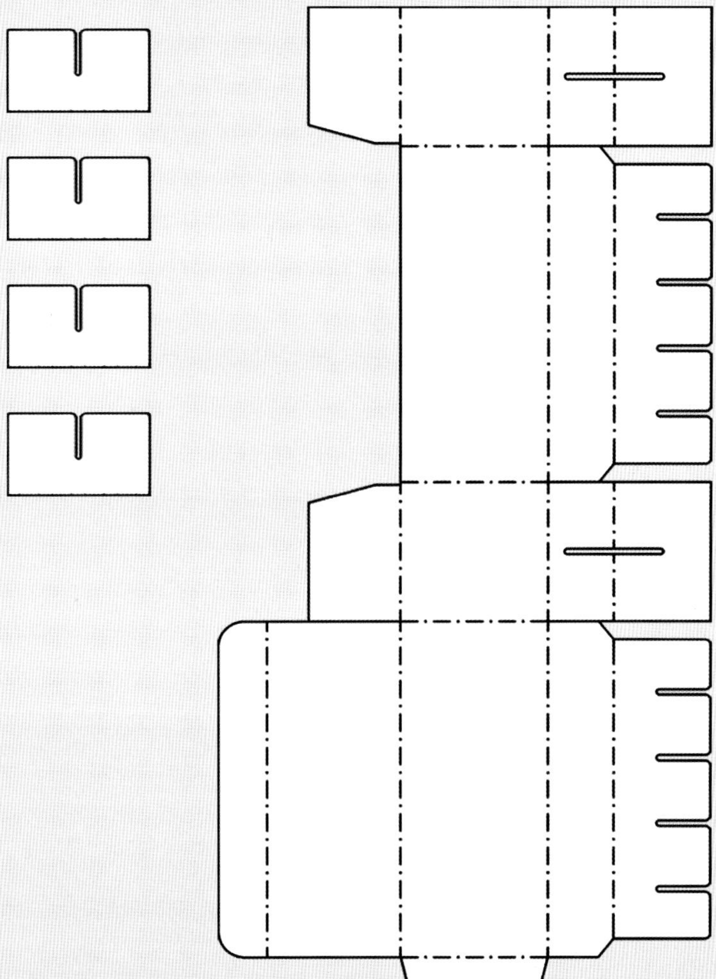

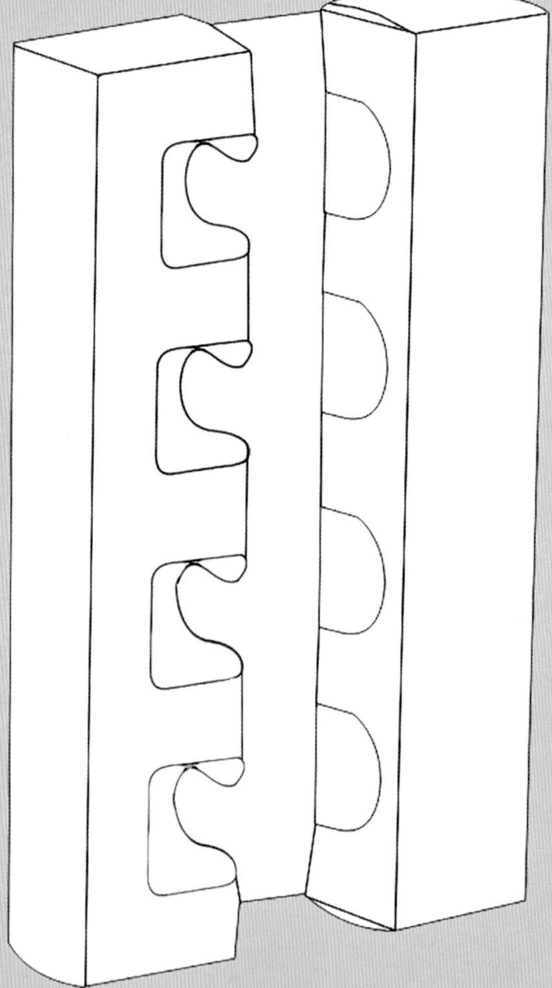

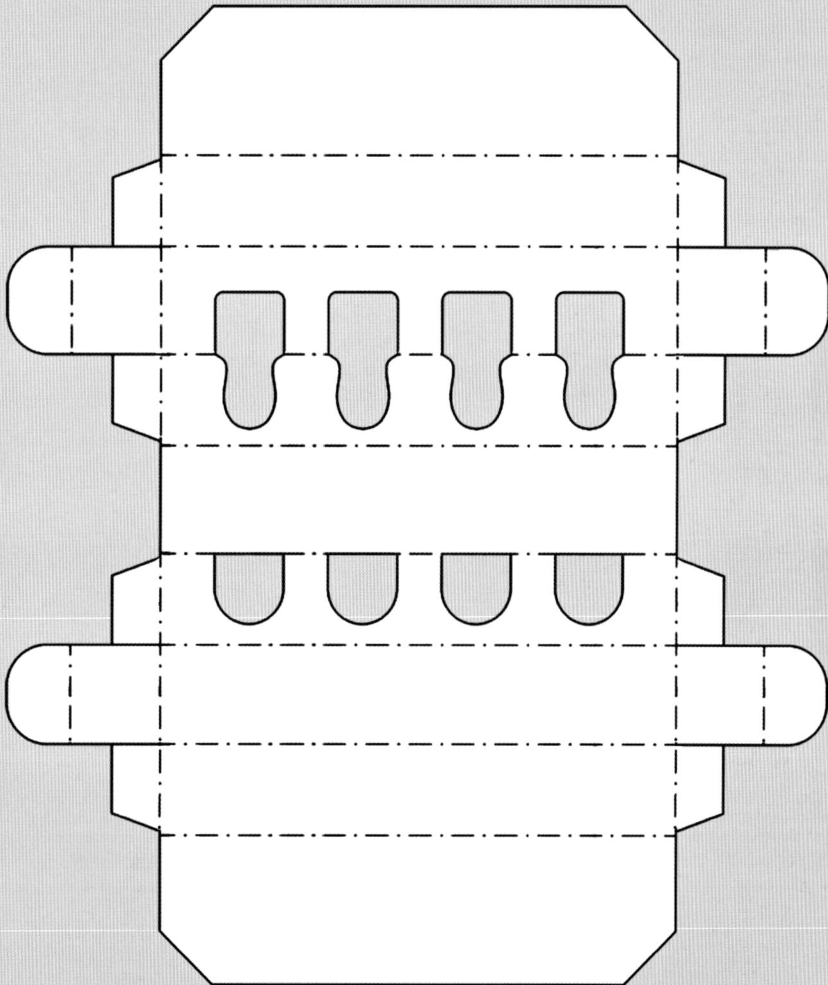

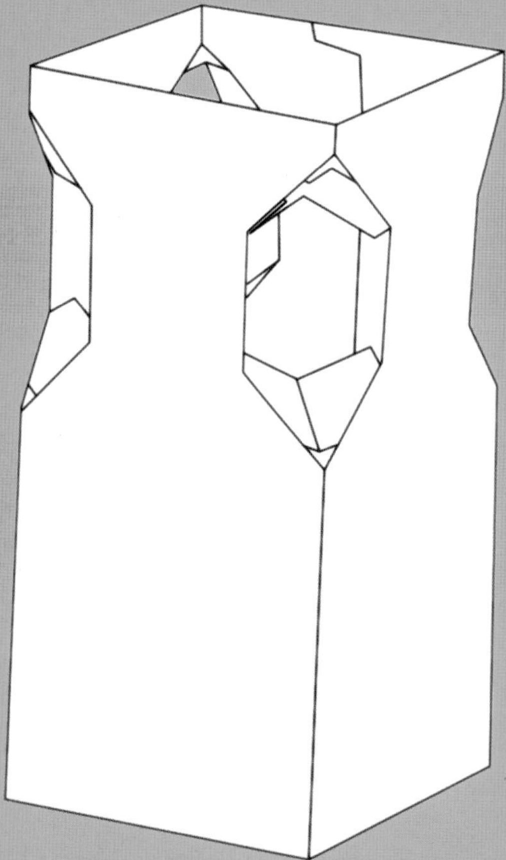

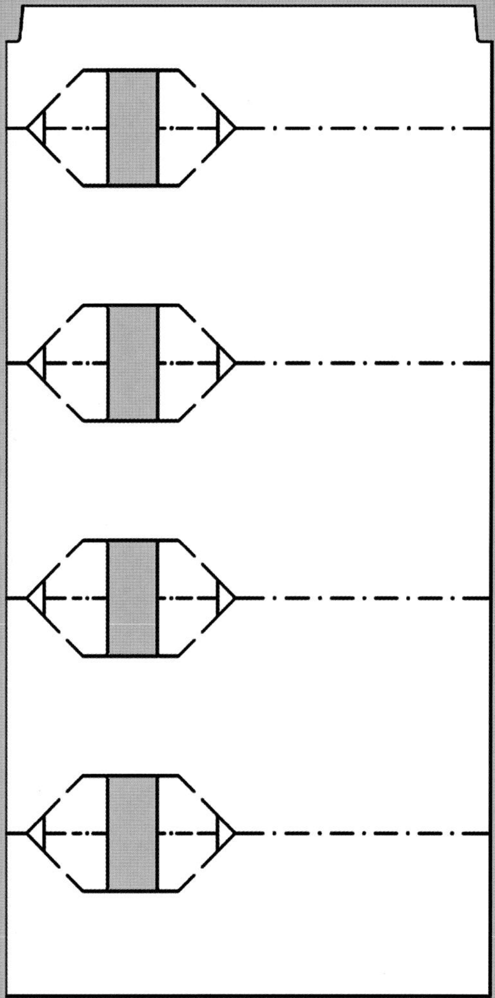

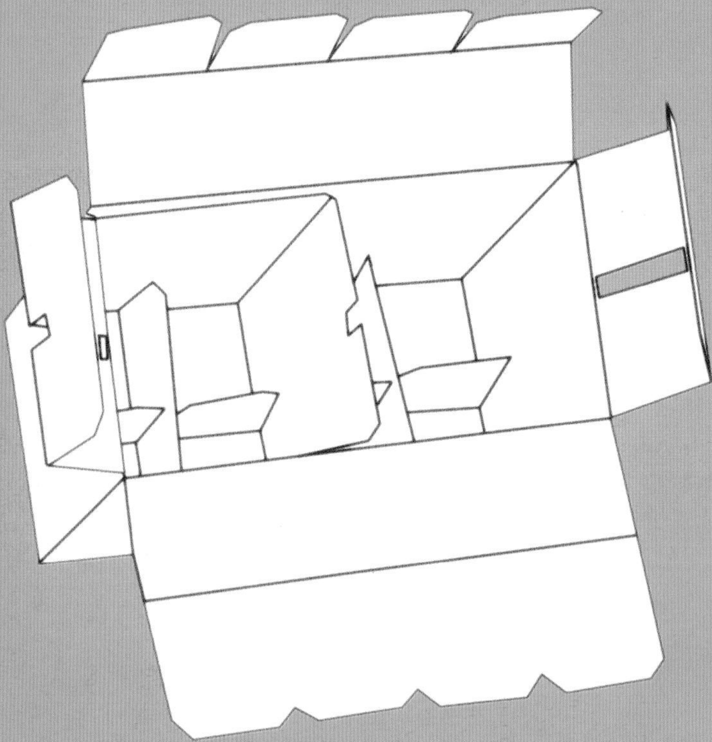

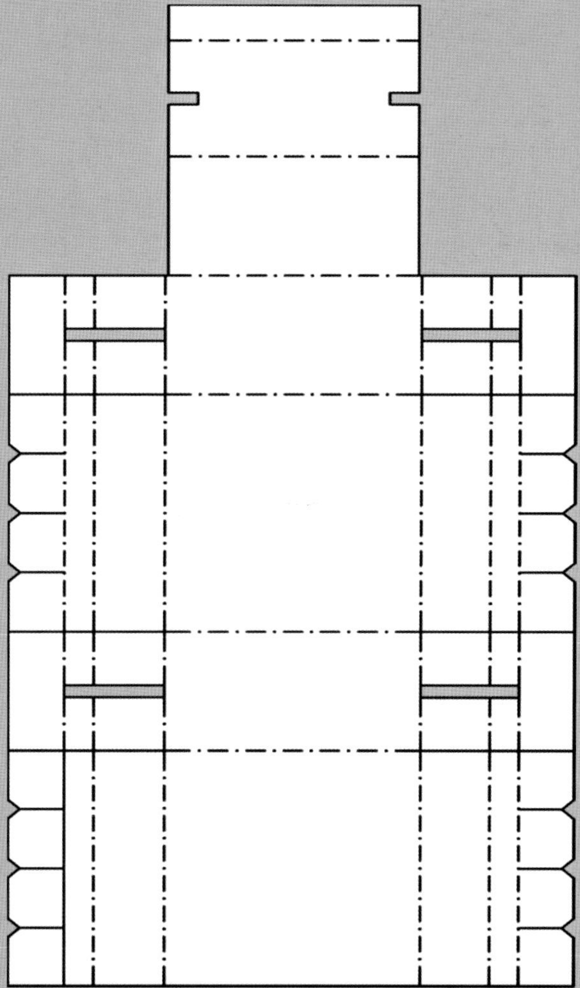

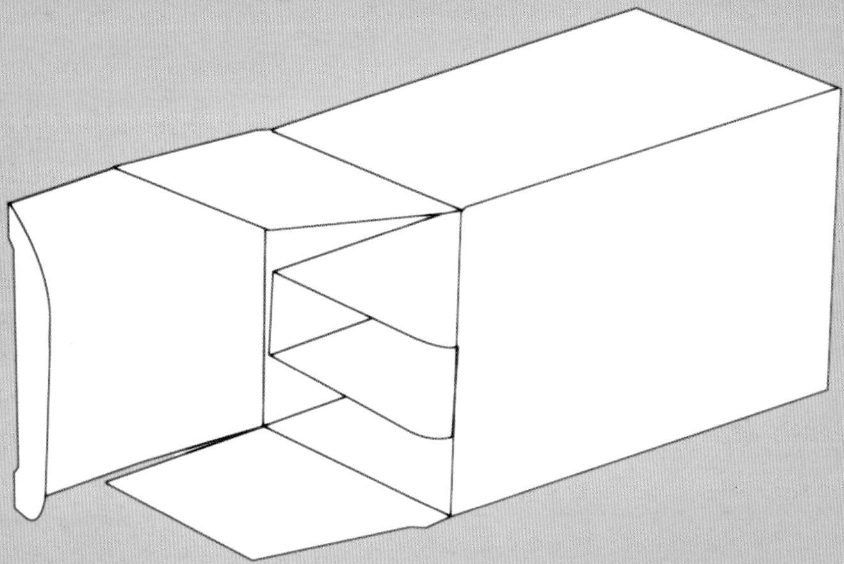

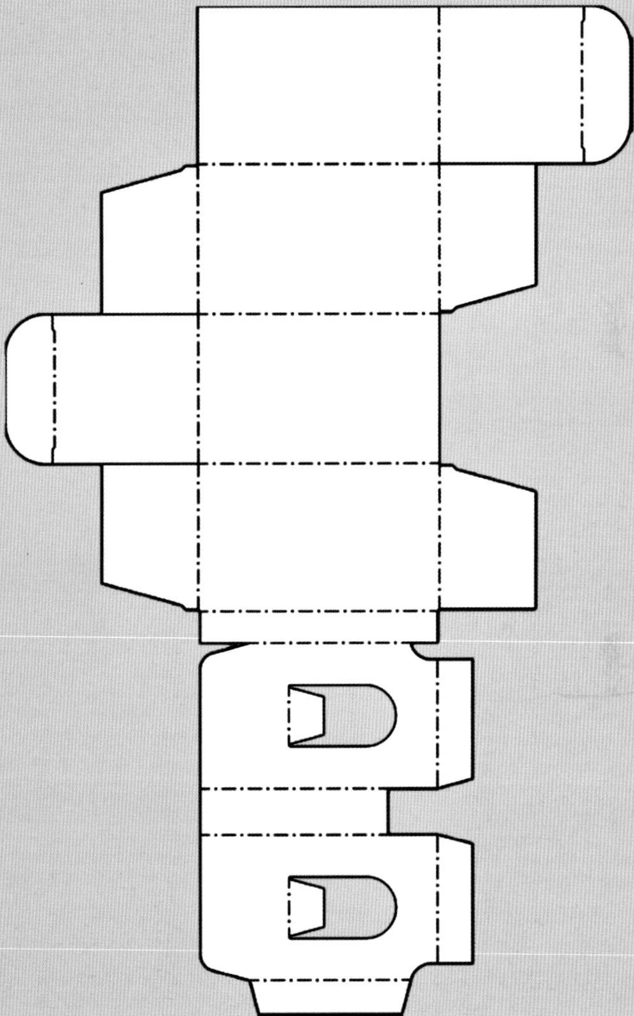

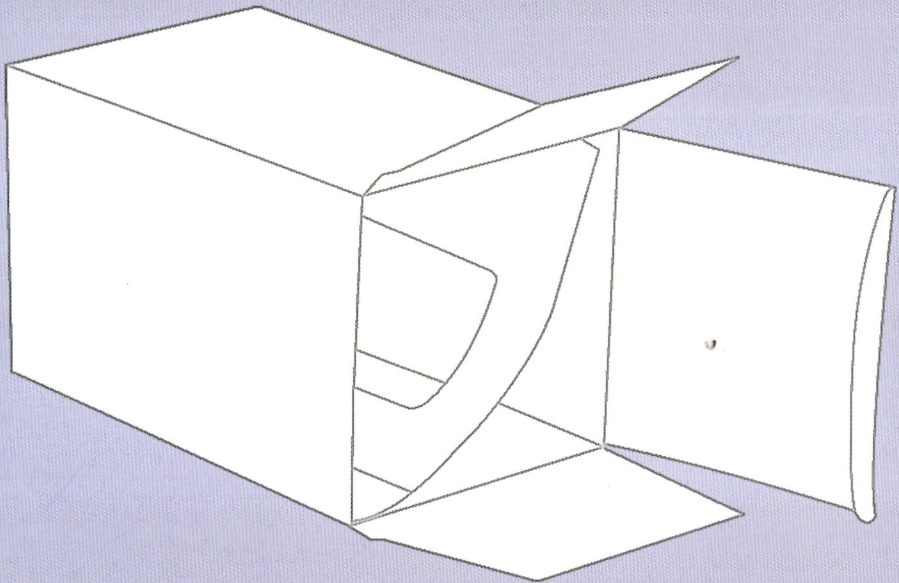

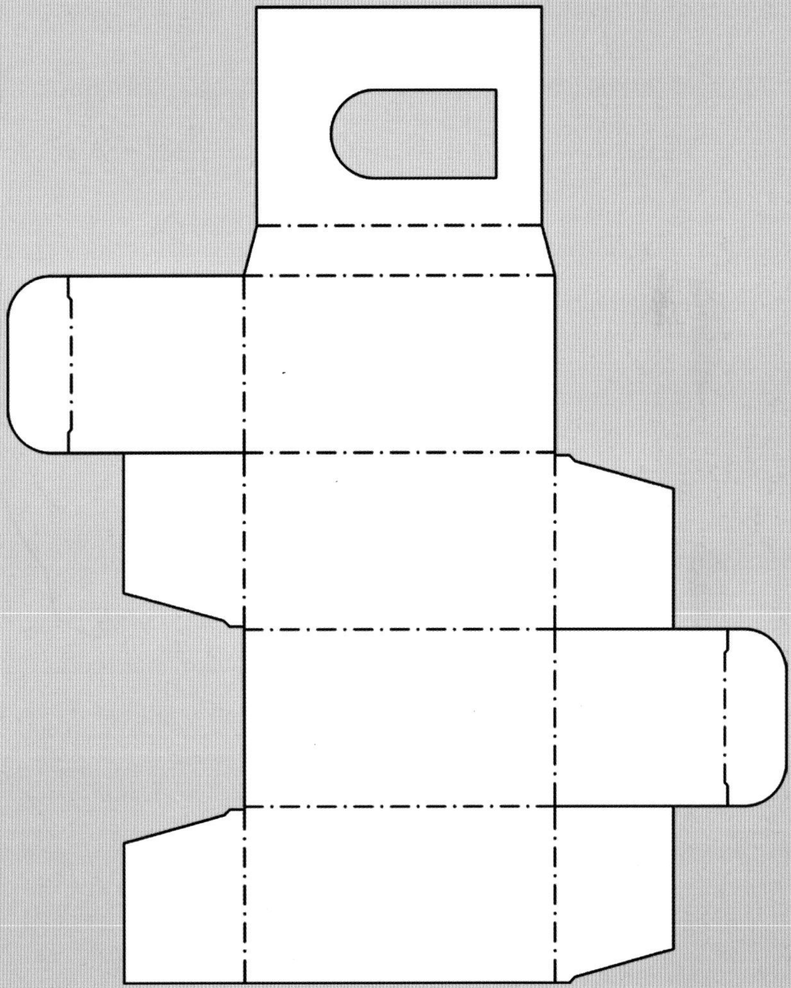

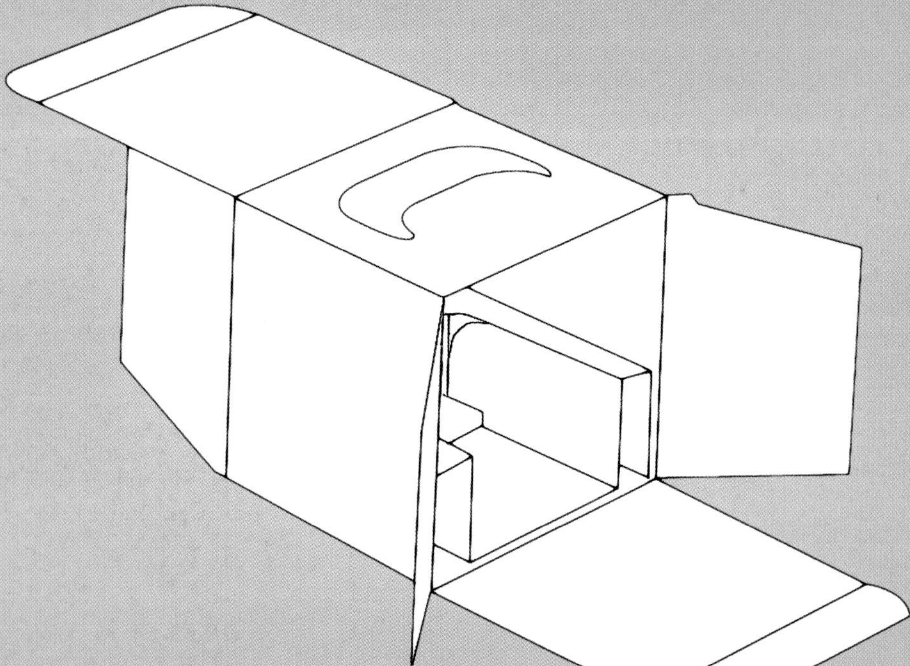

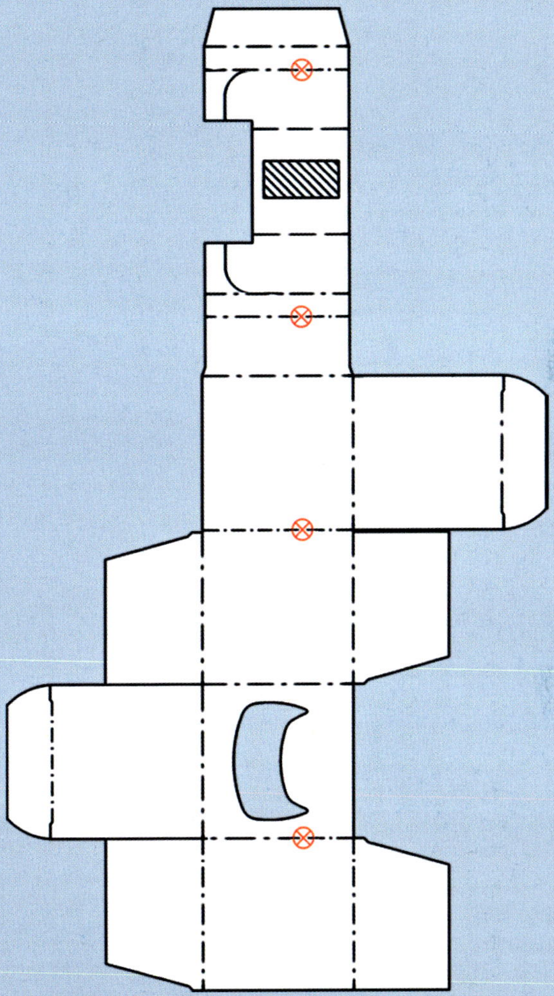

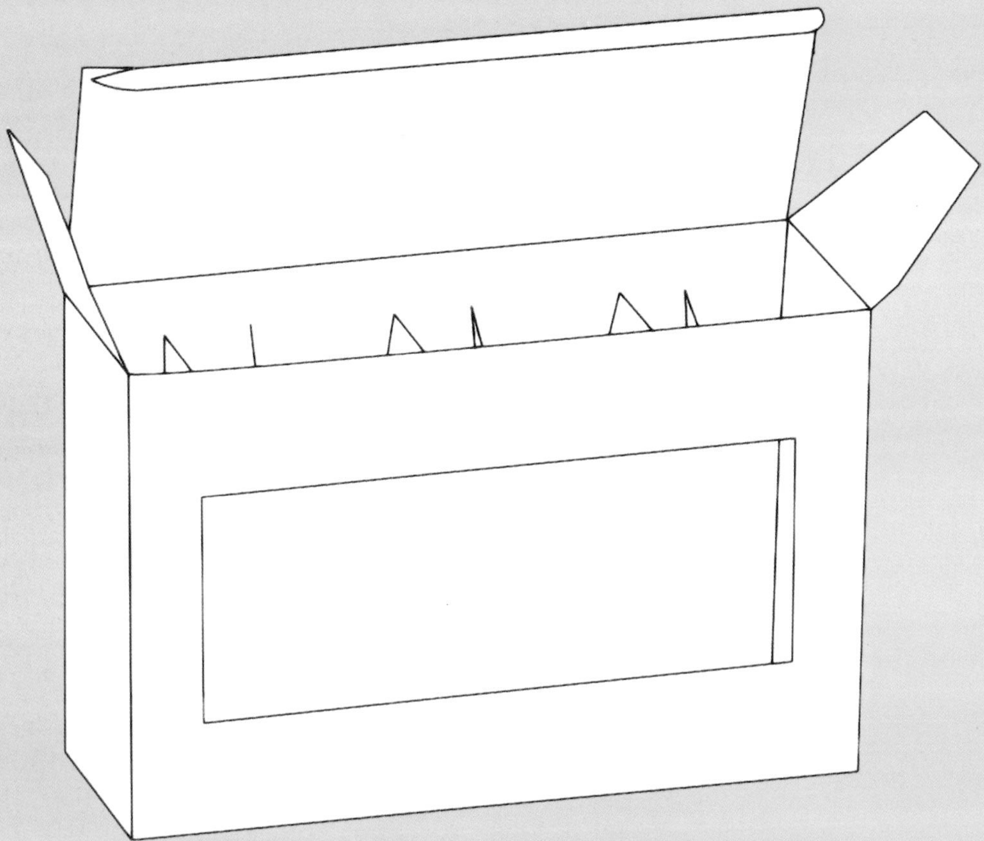

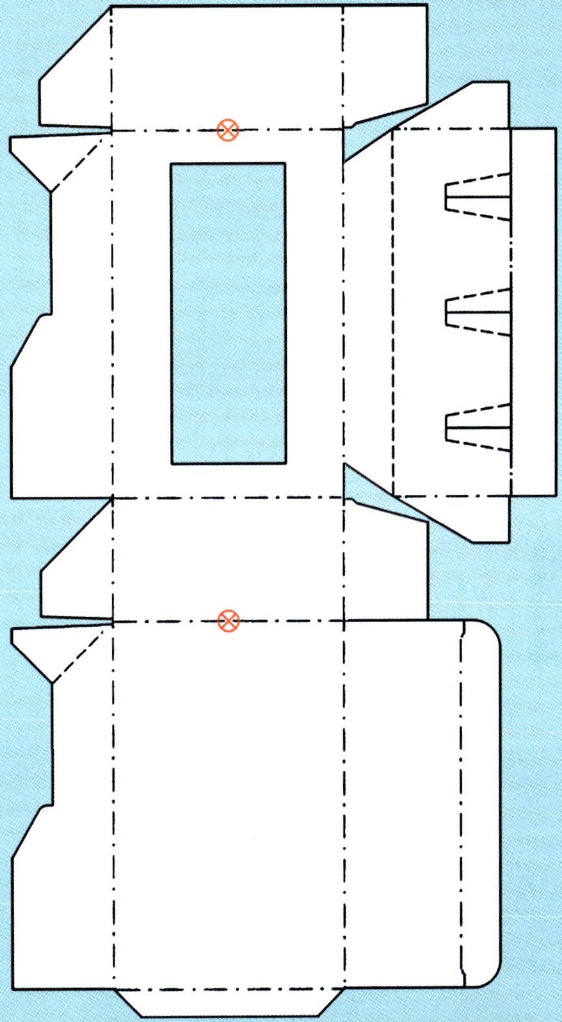

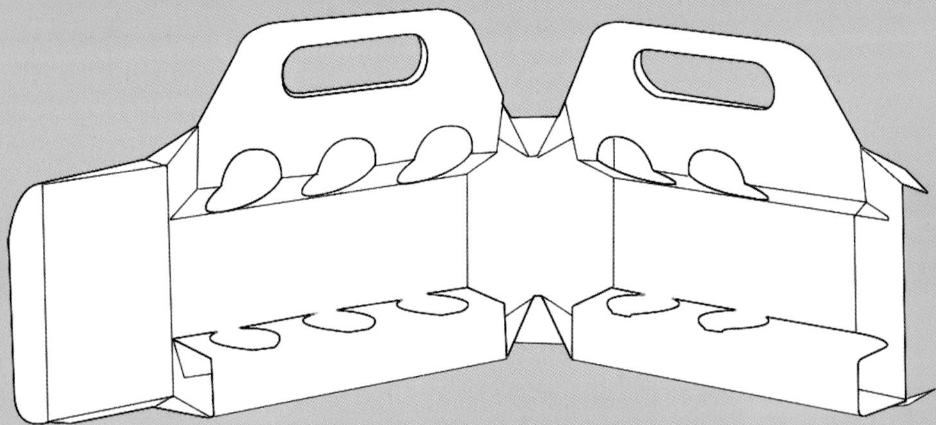

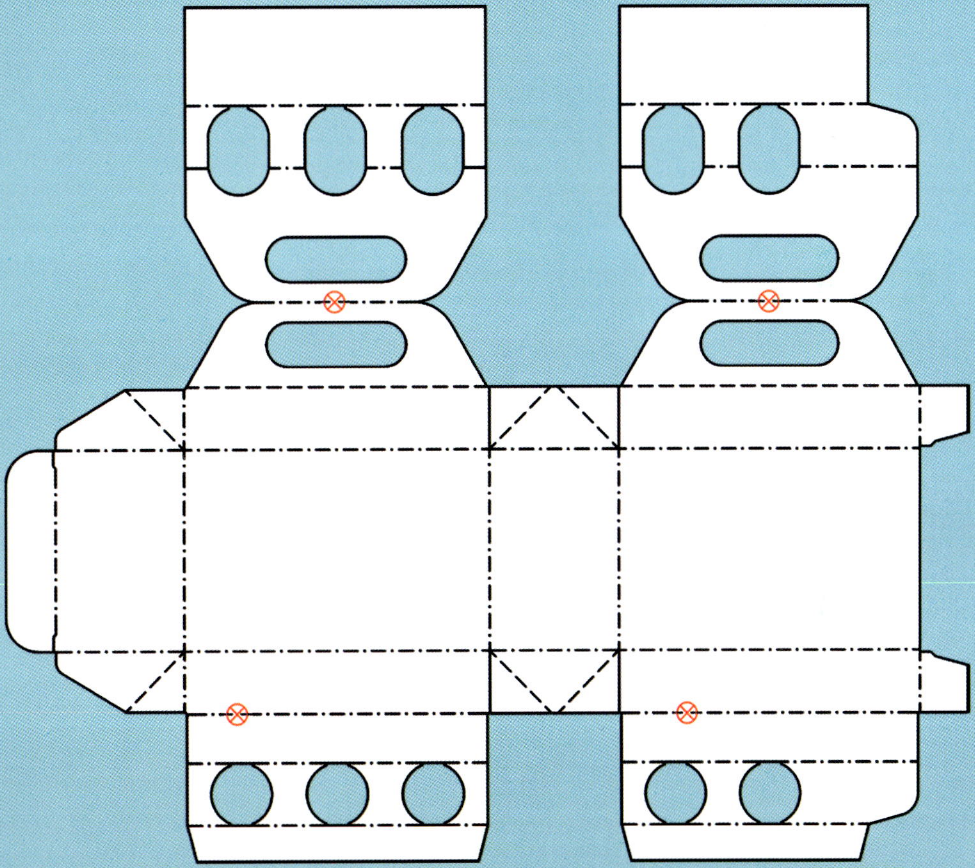

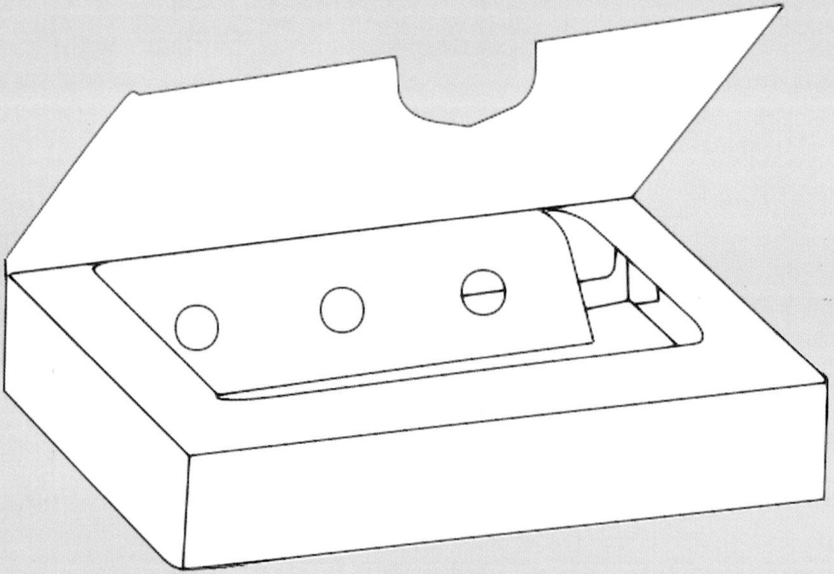

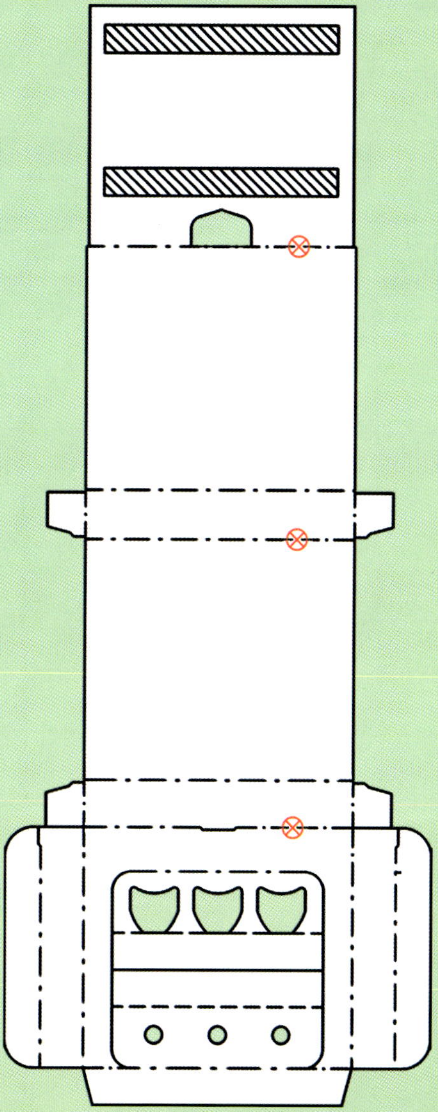

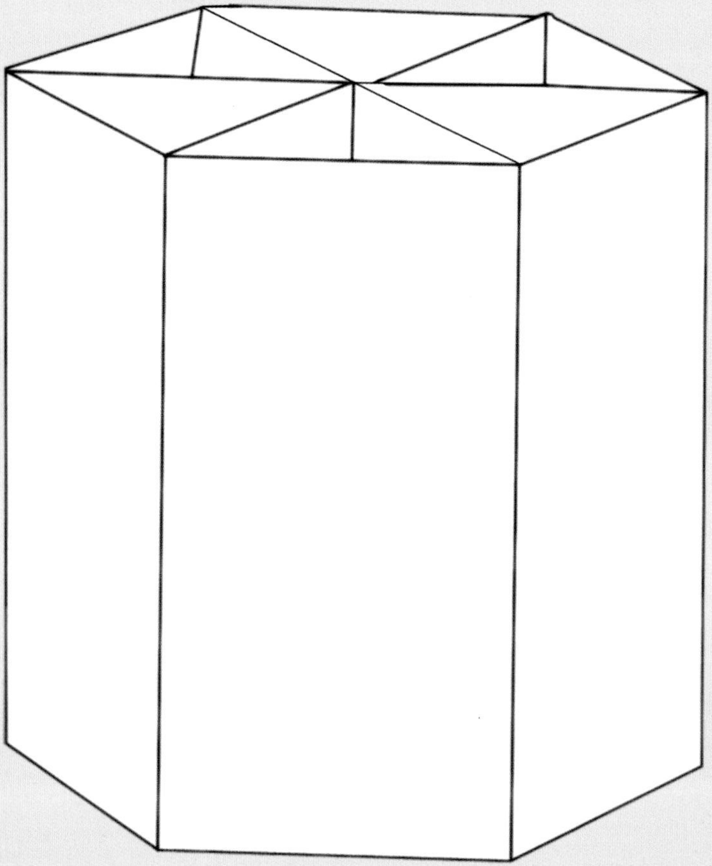

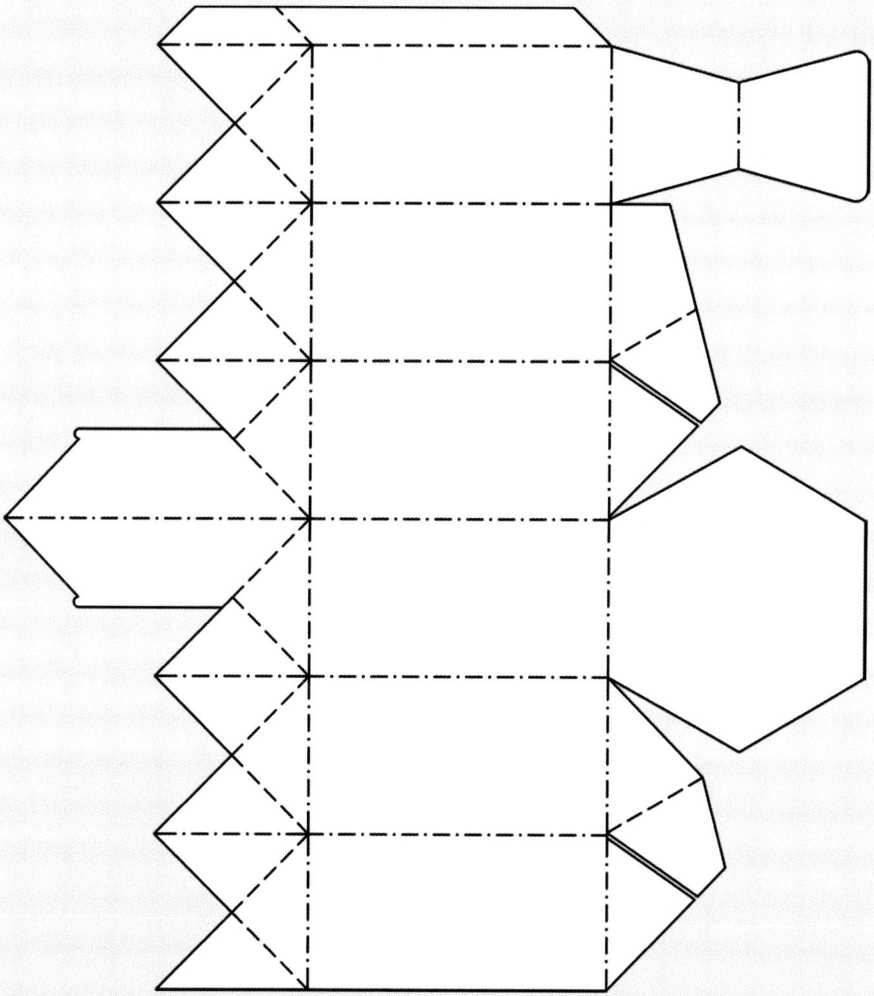

Special Shapes

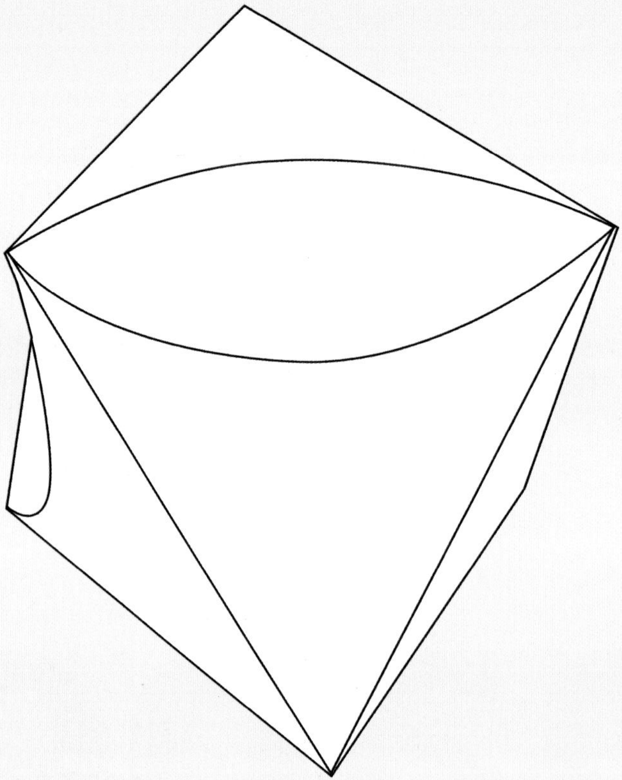

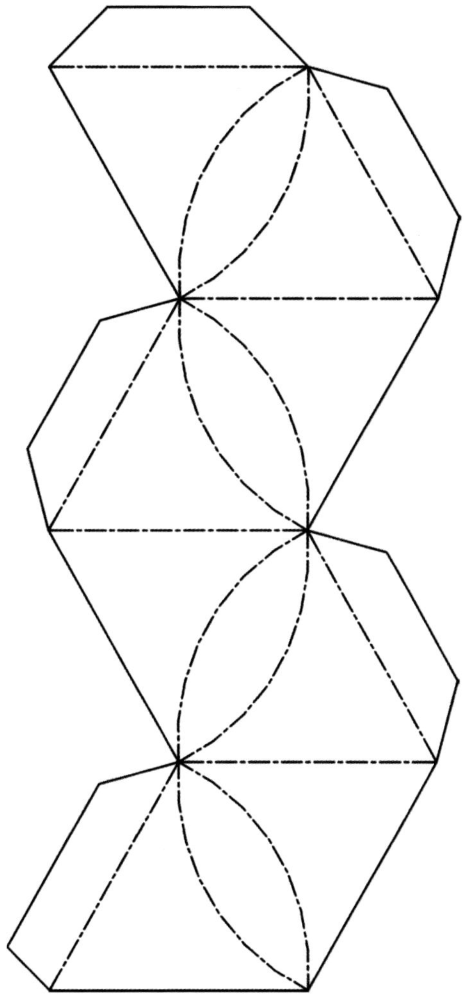

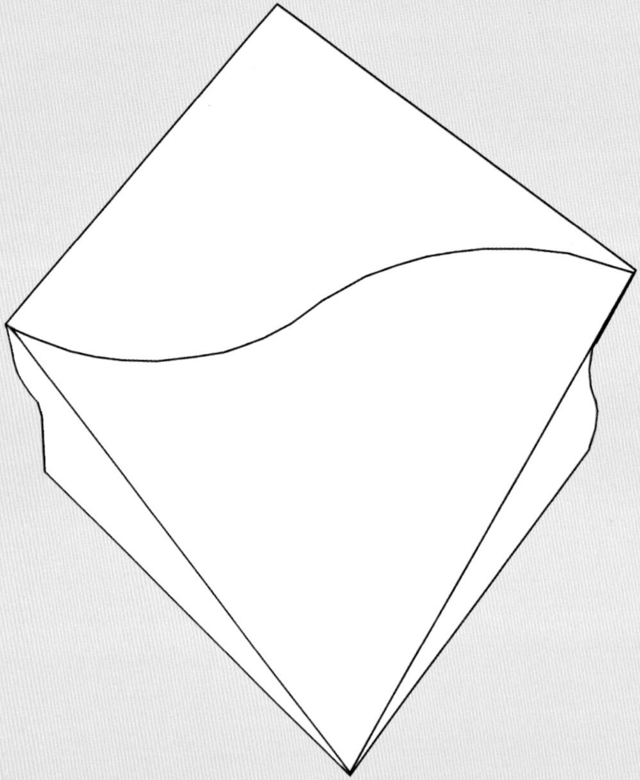

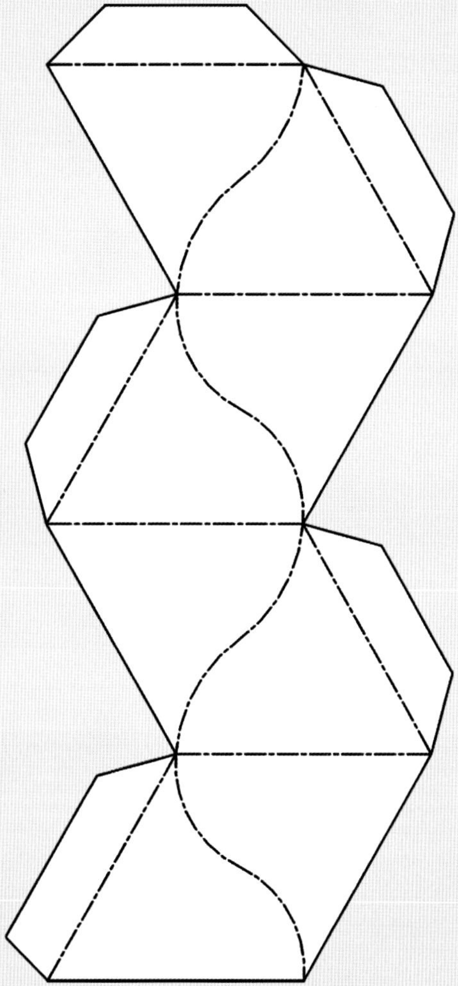

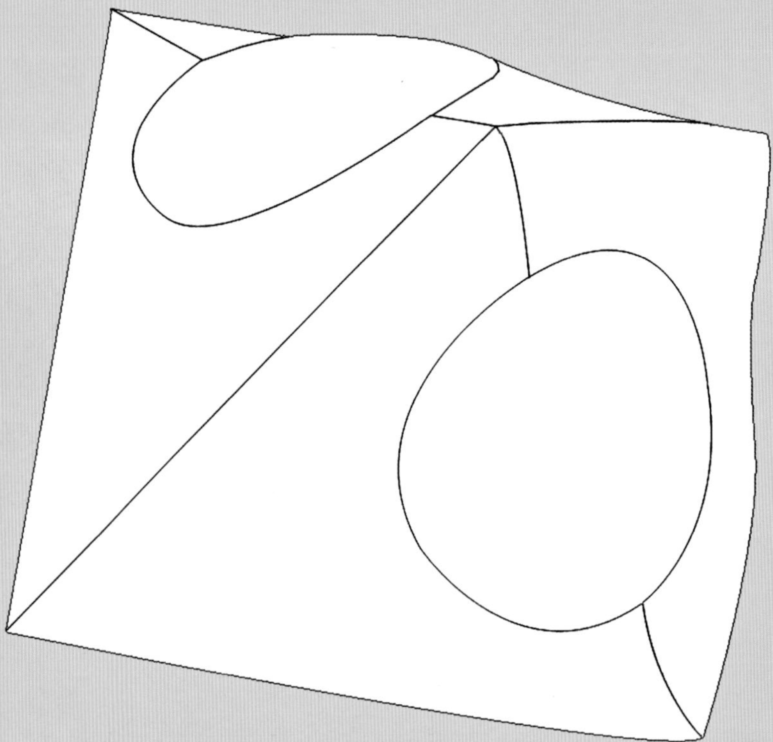

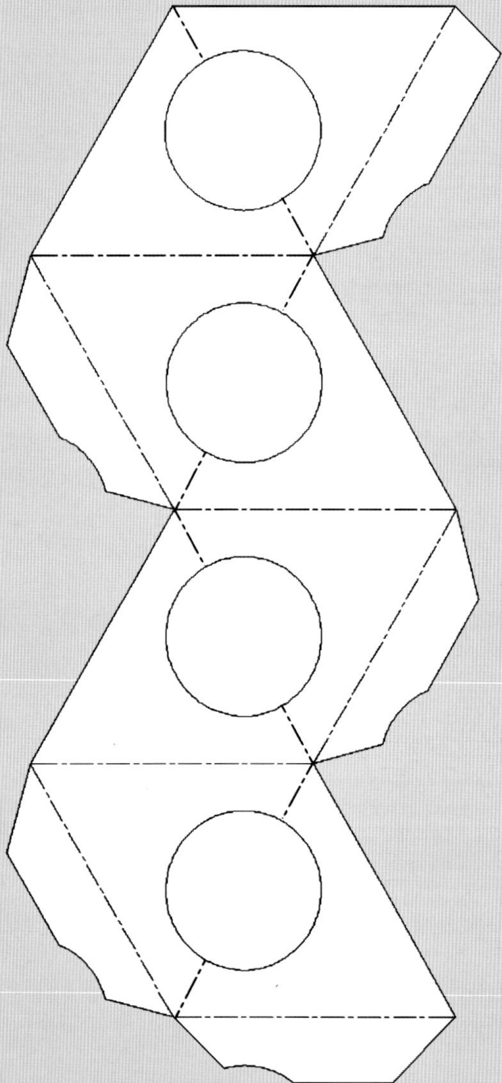

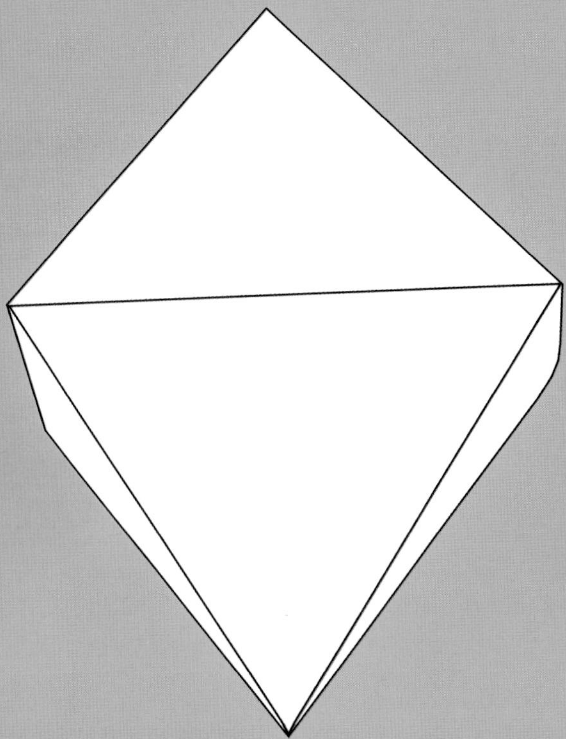

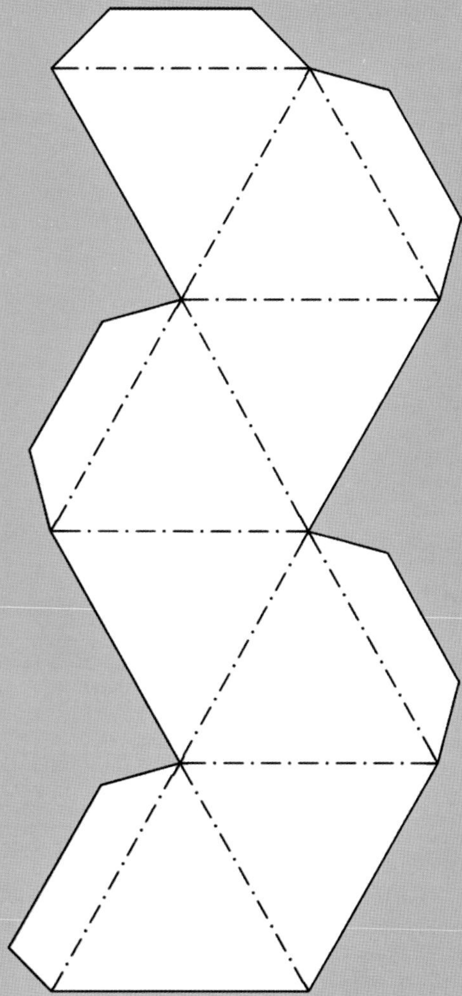

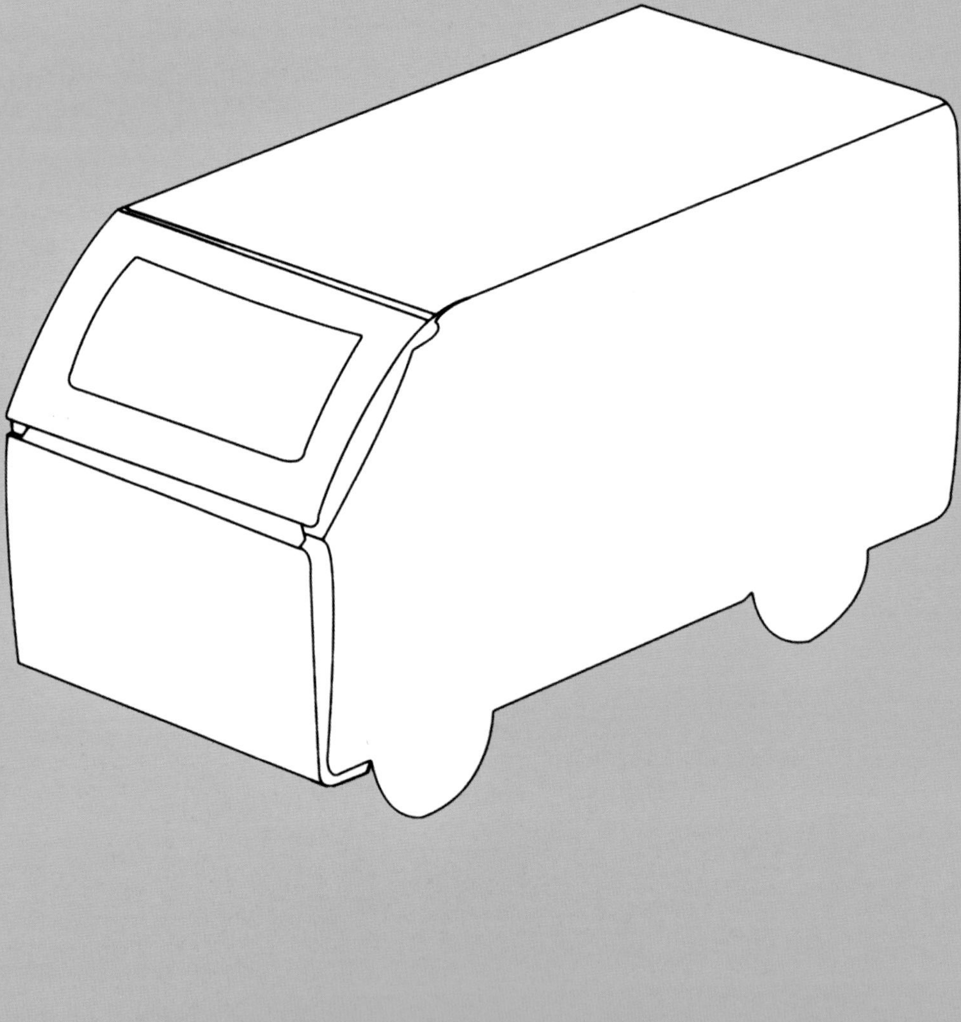

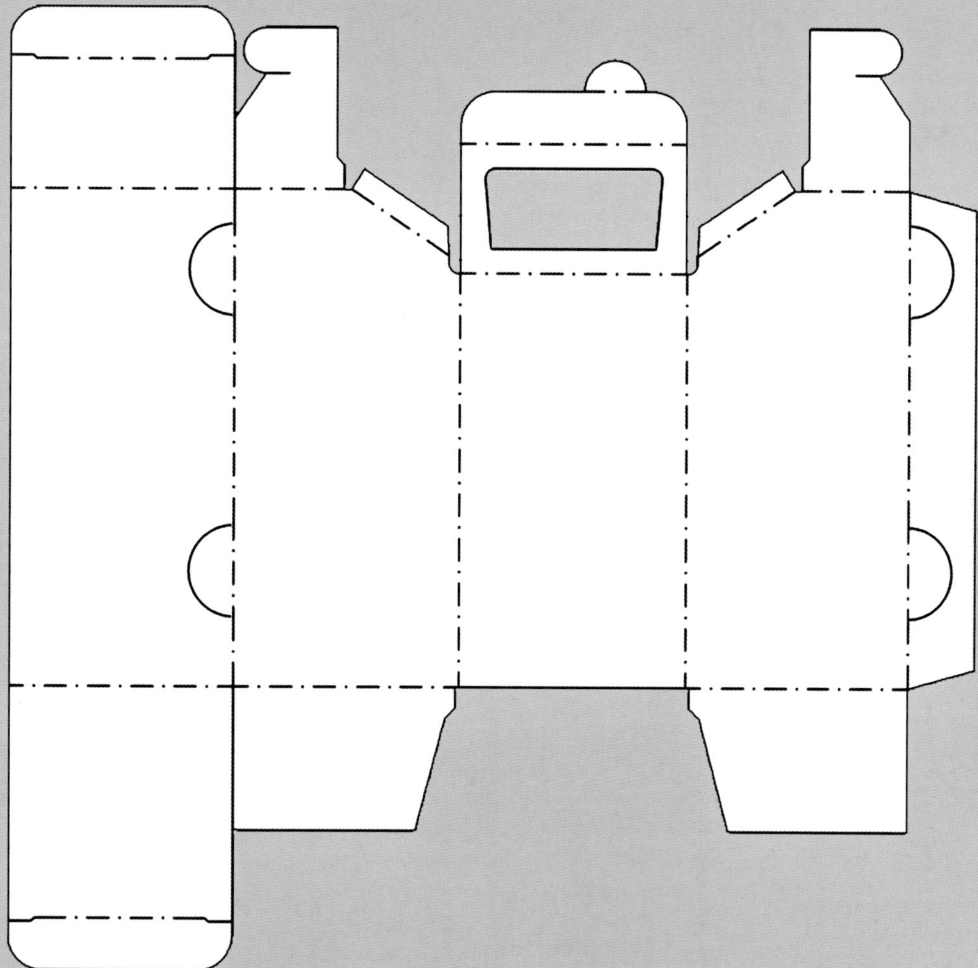

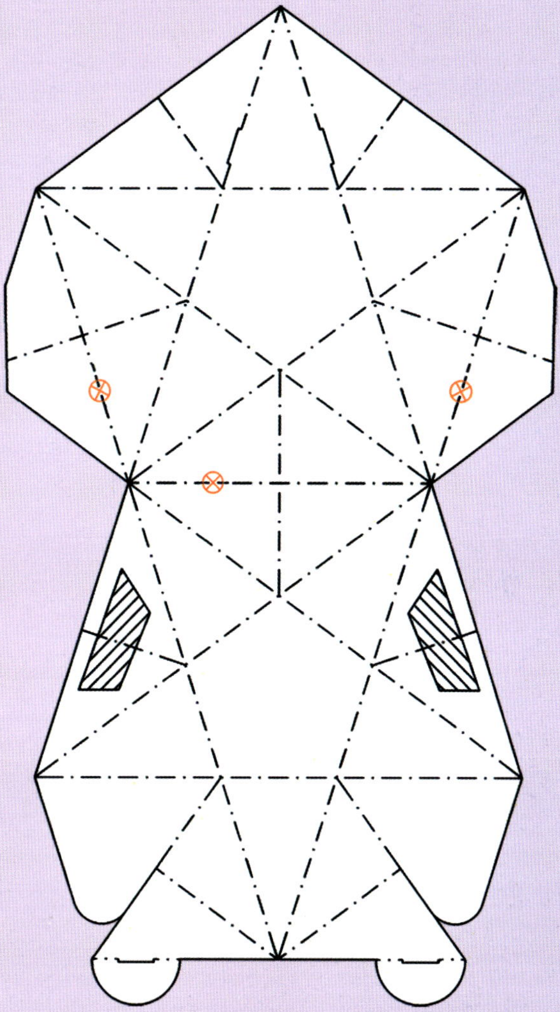

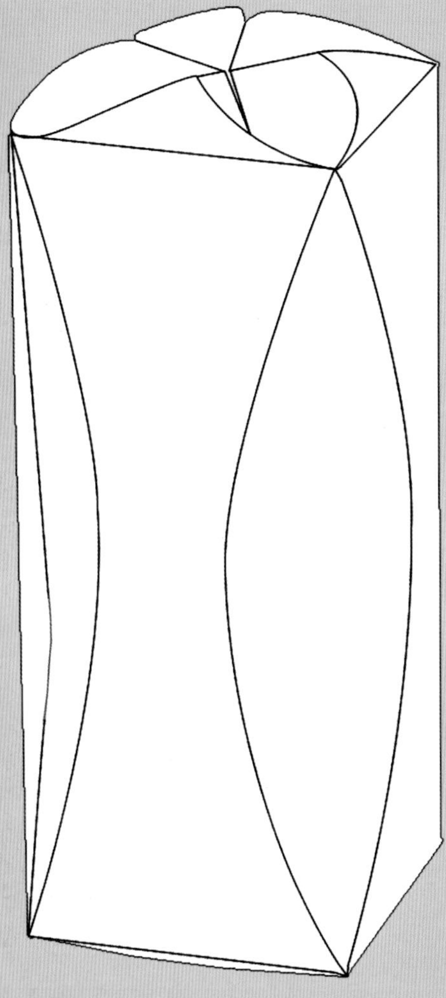

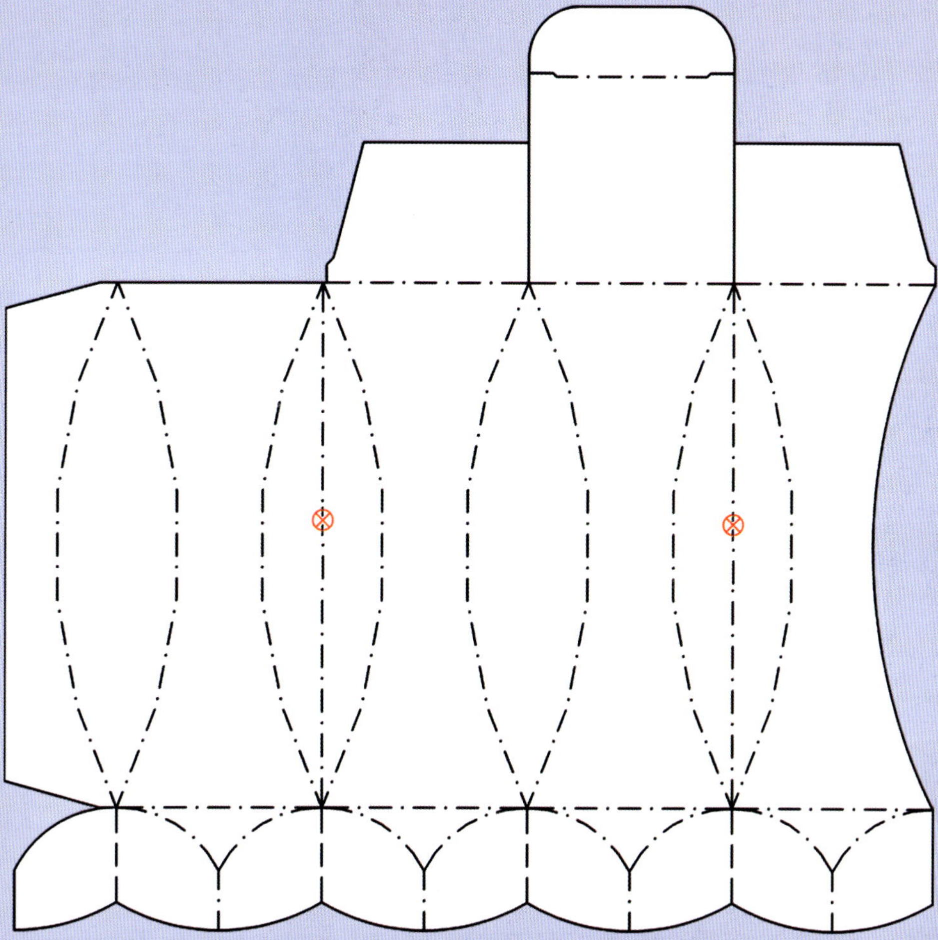

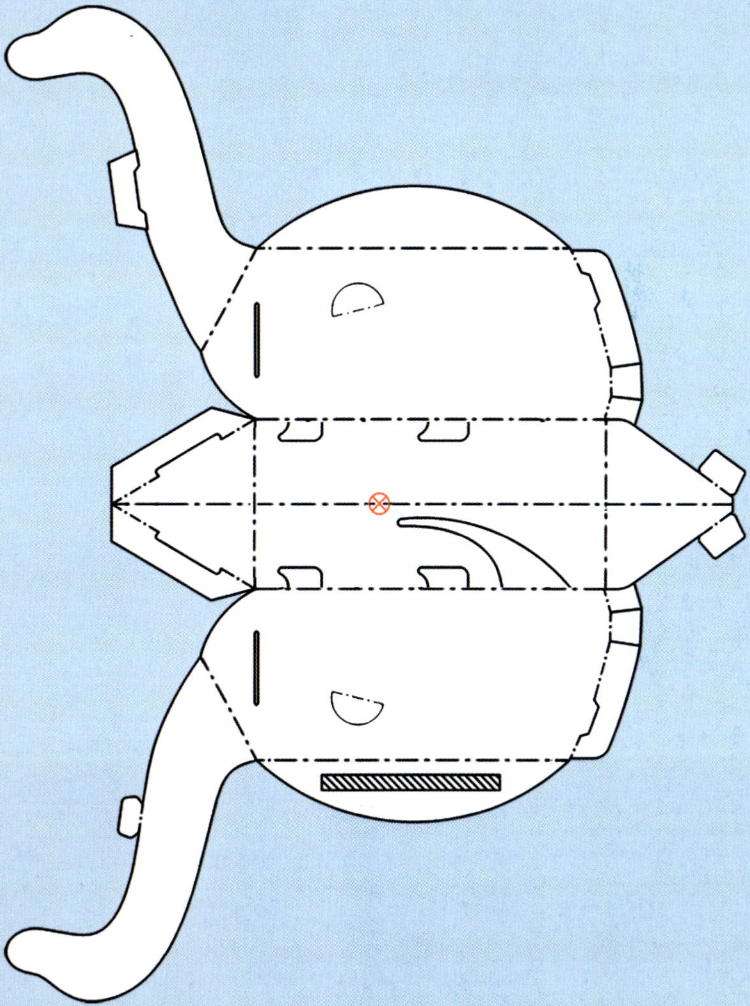

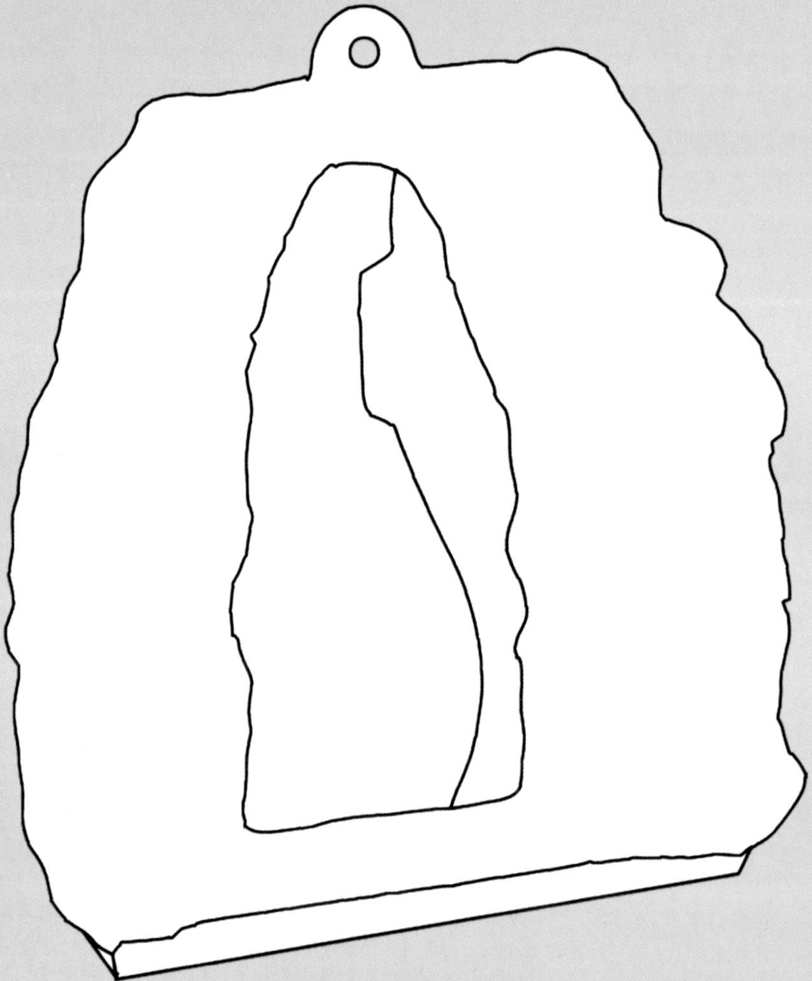

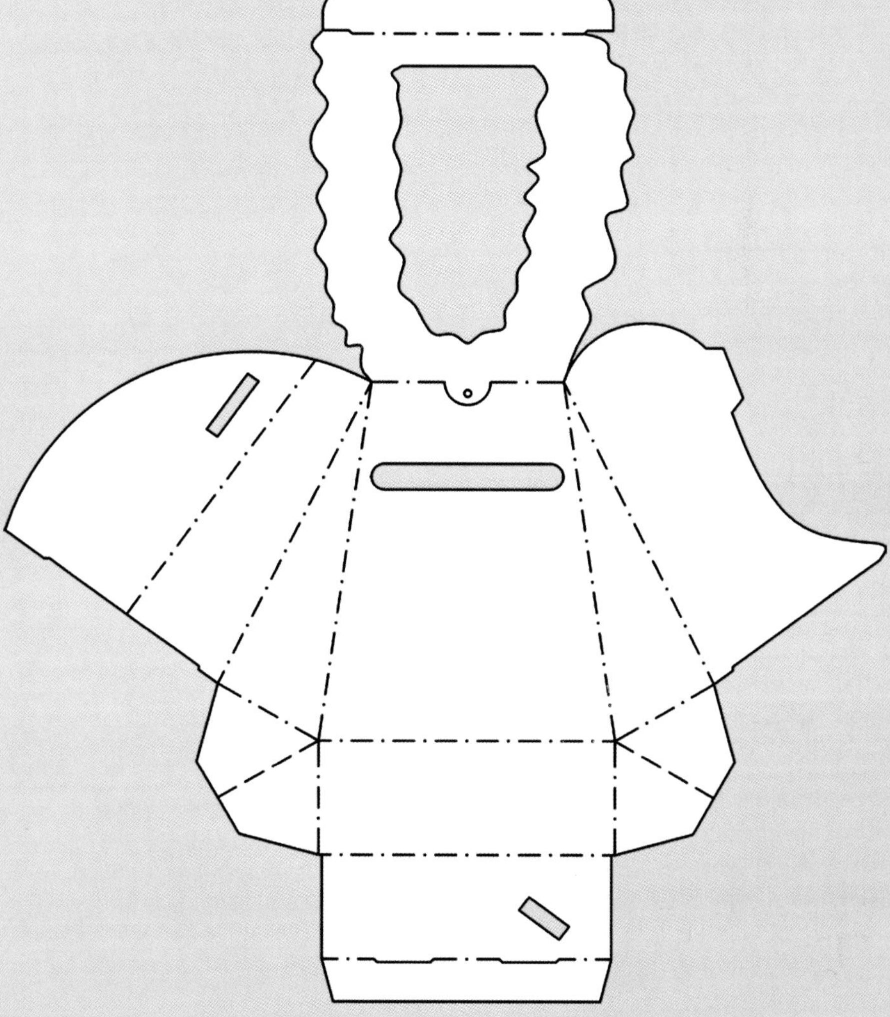

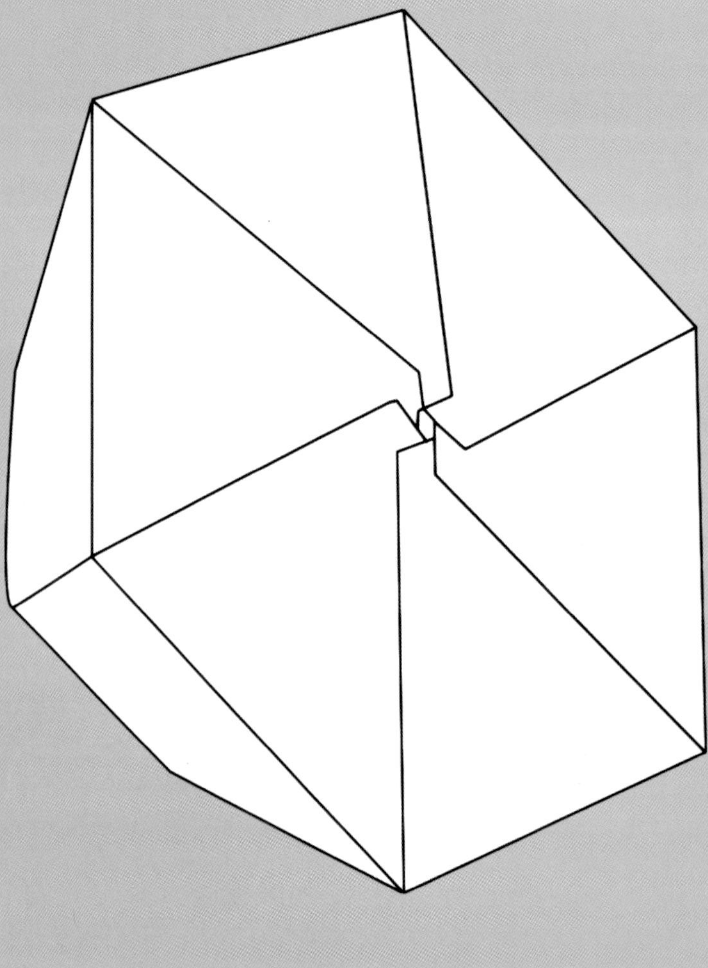

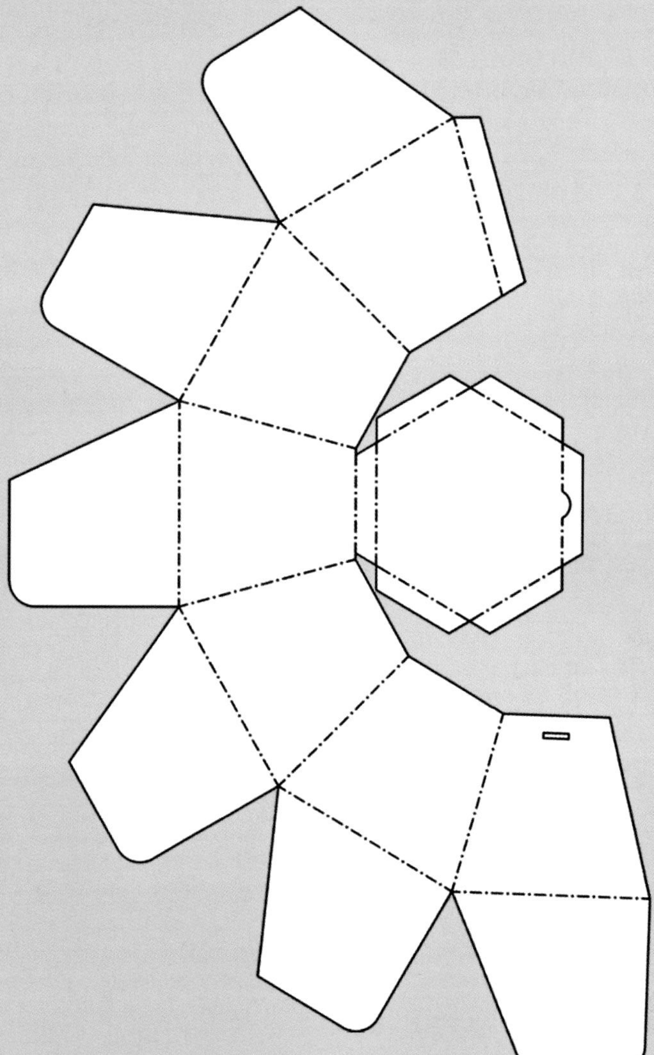

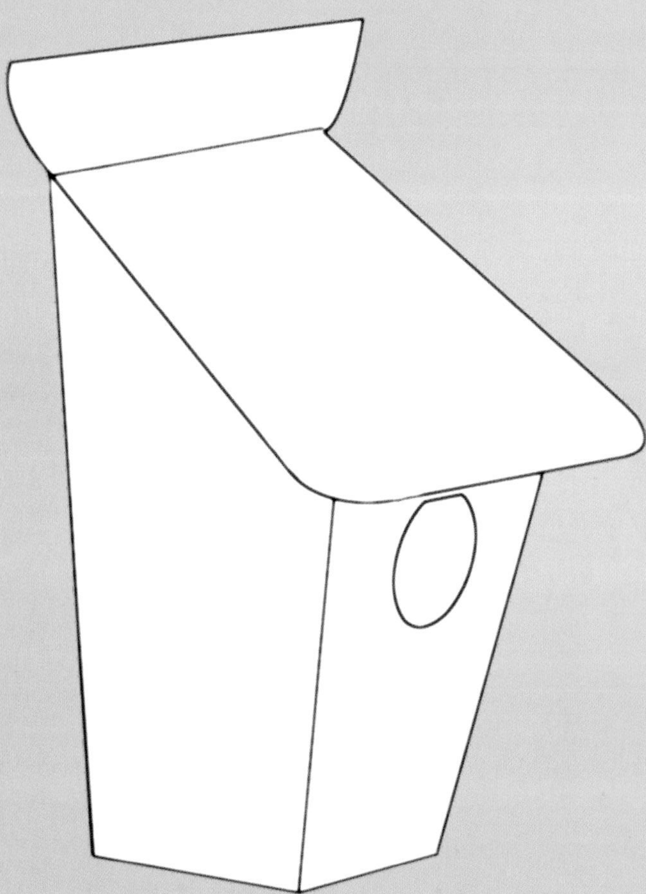

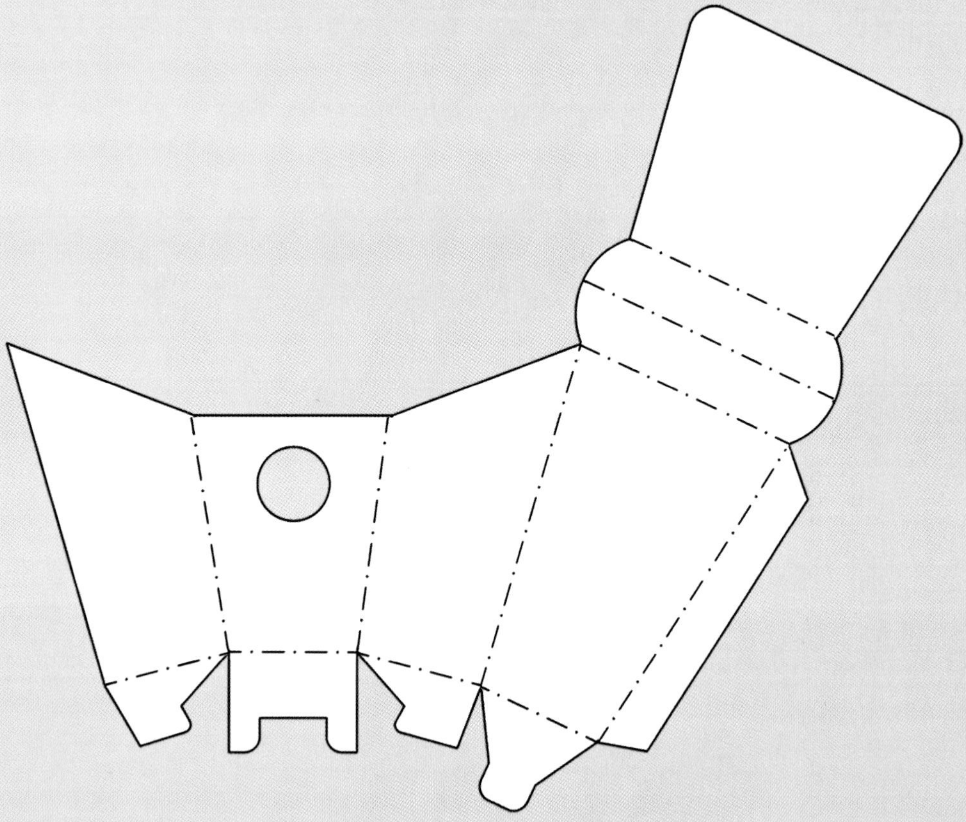

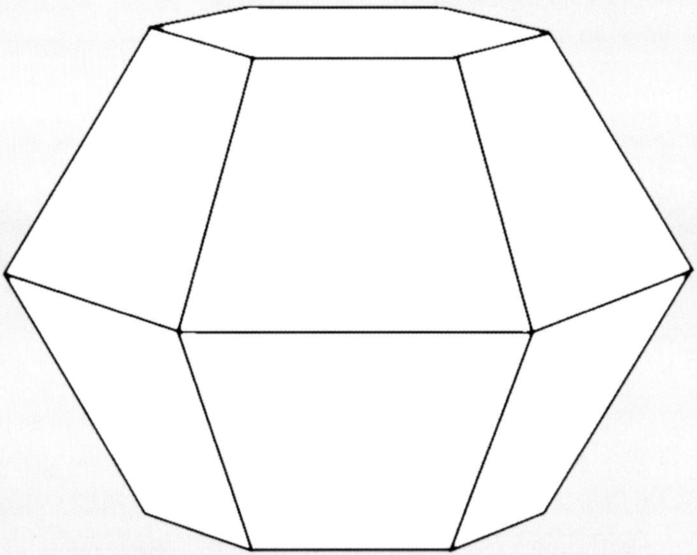

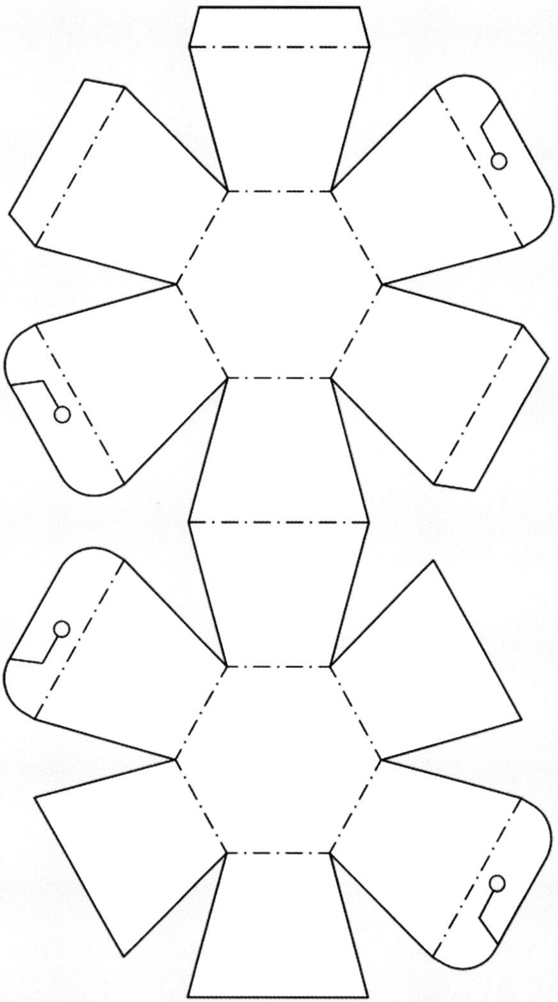

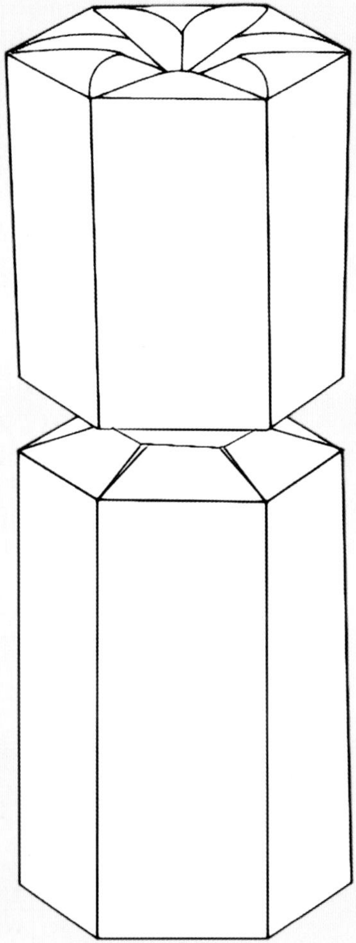

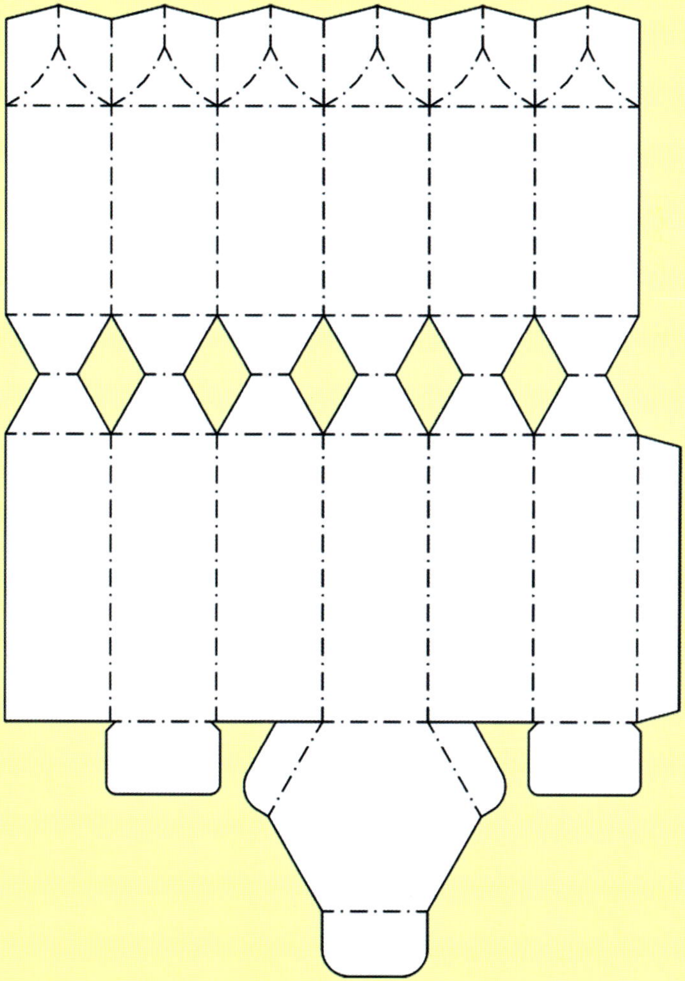

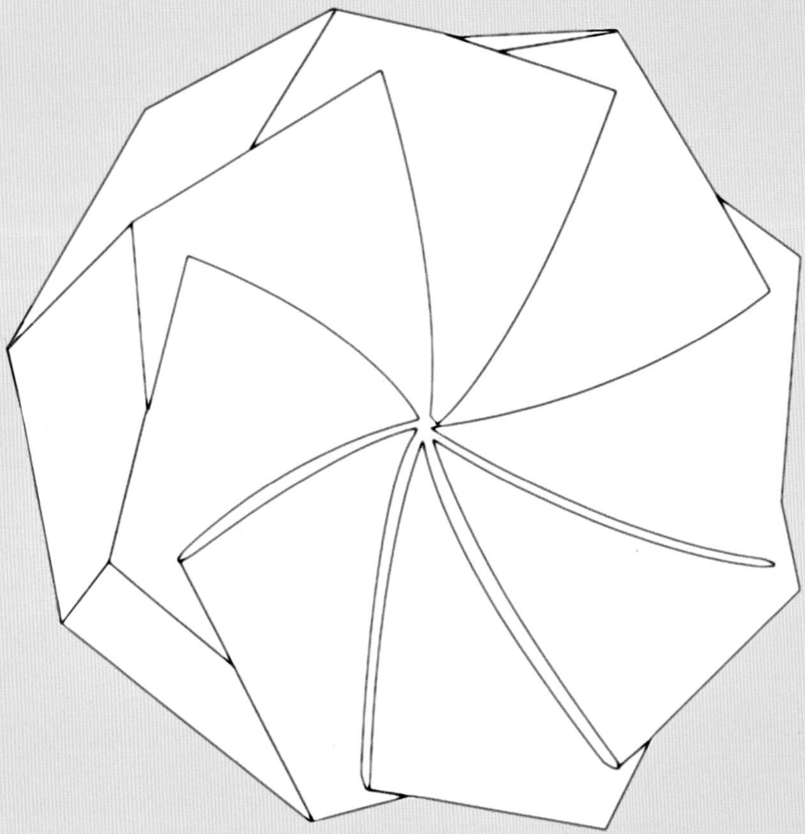

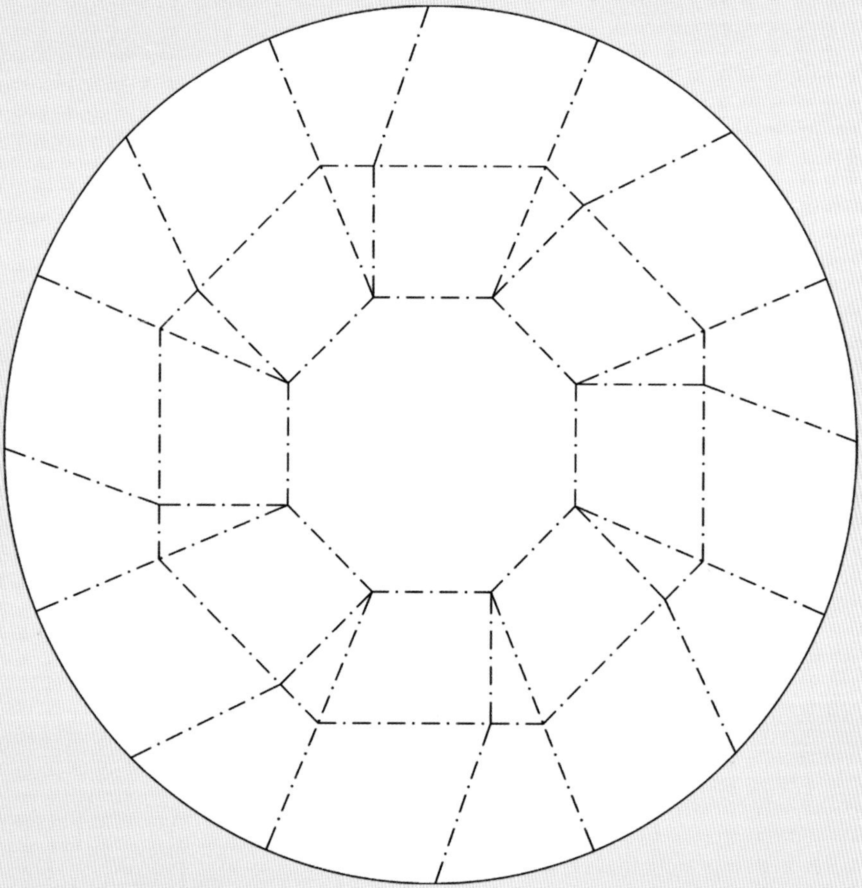

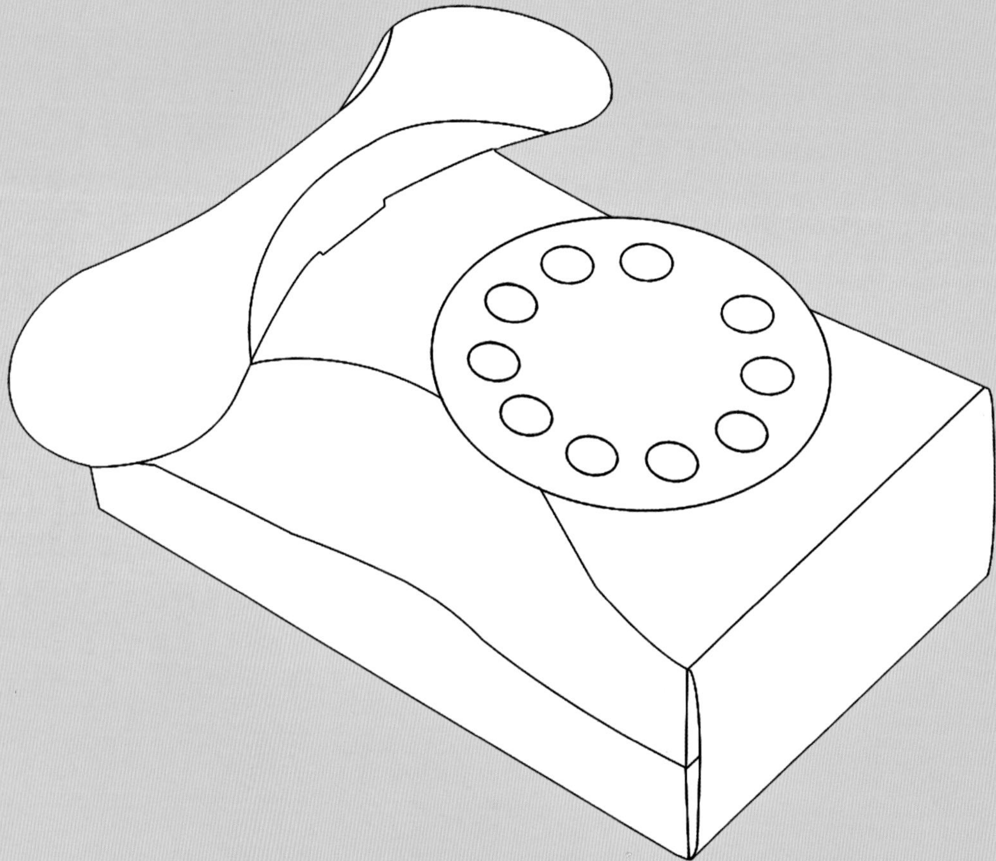

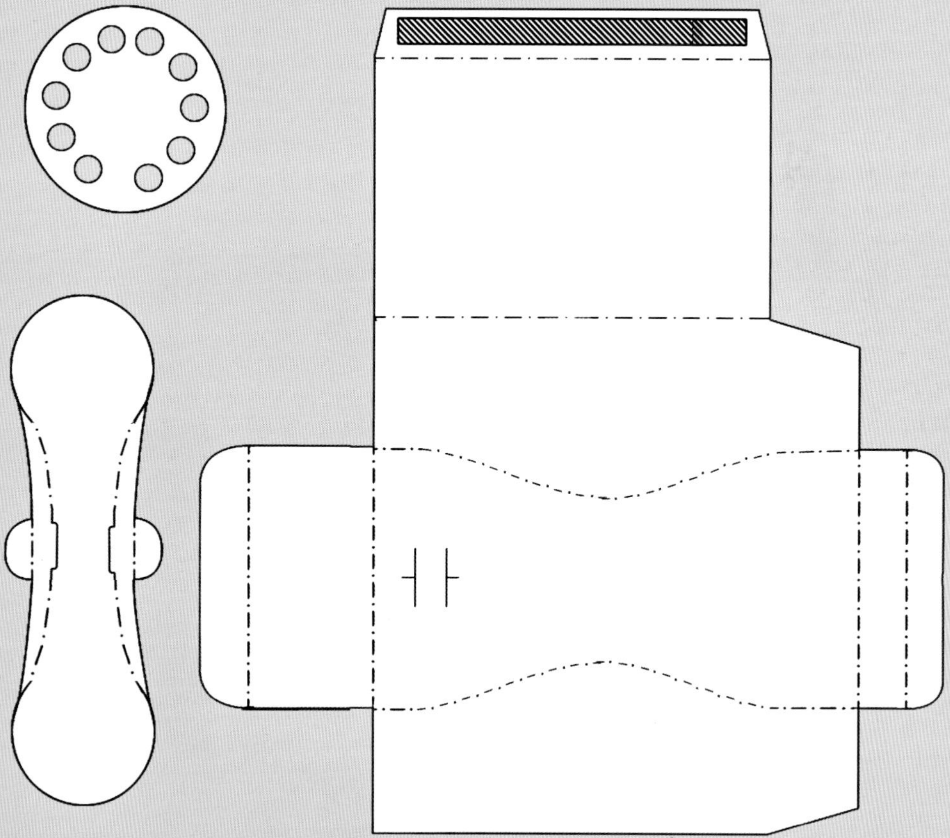

Carriers

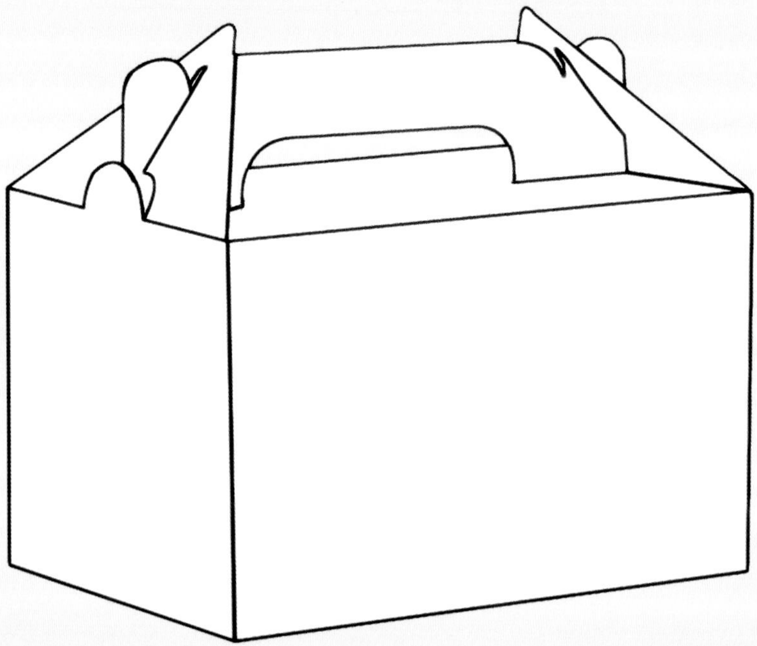

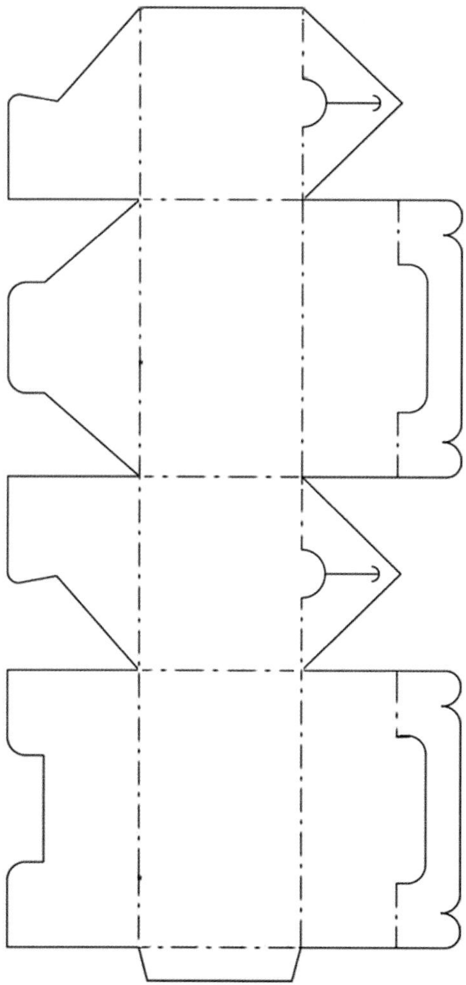

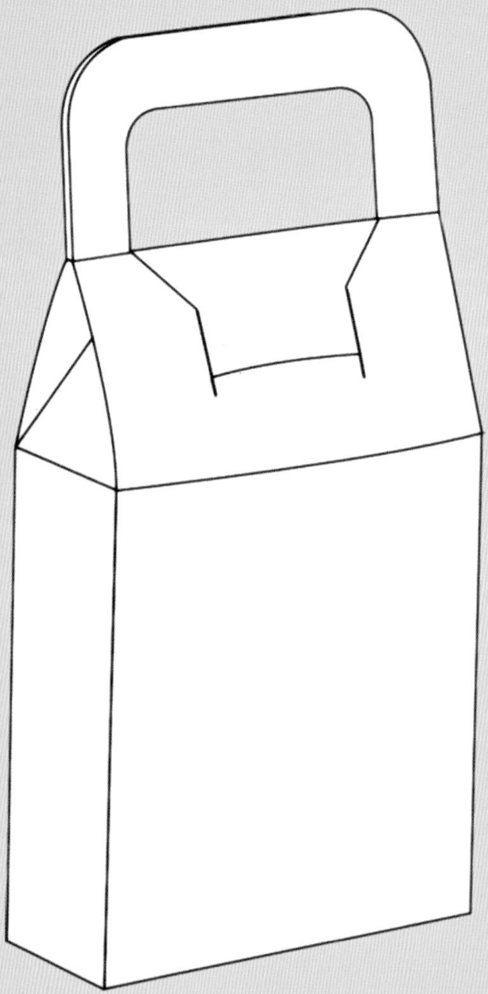

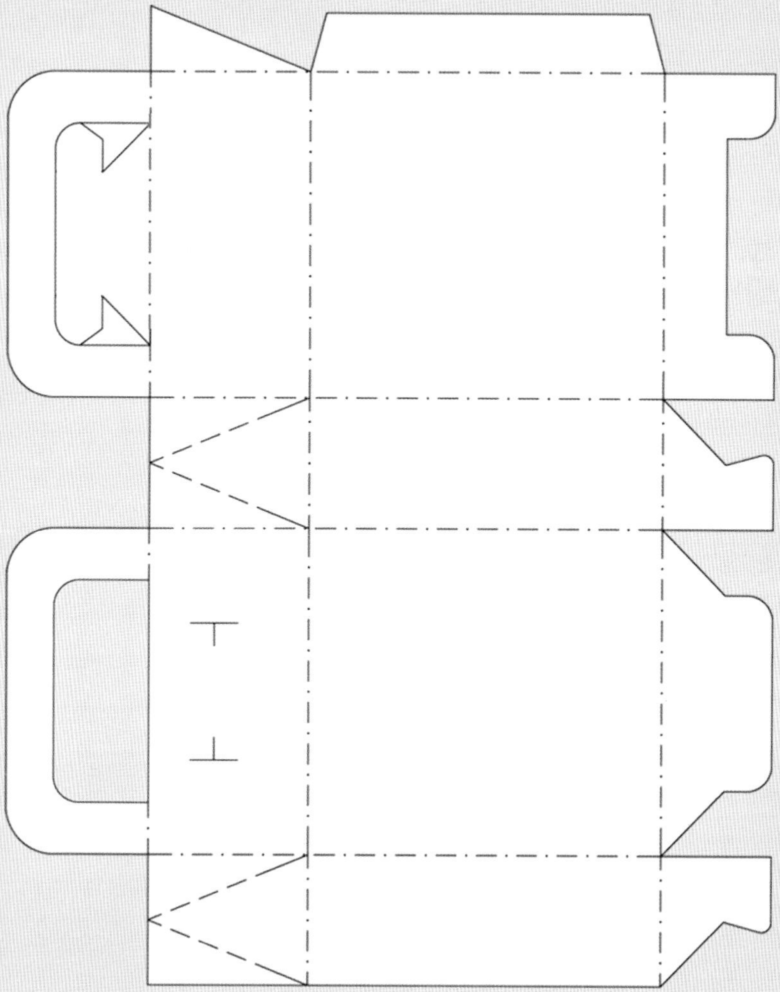

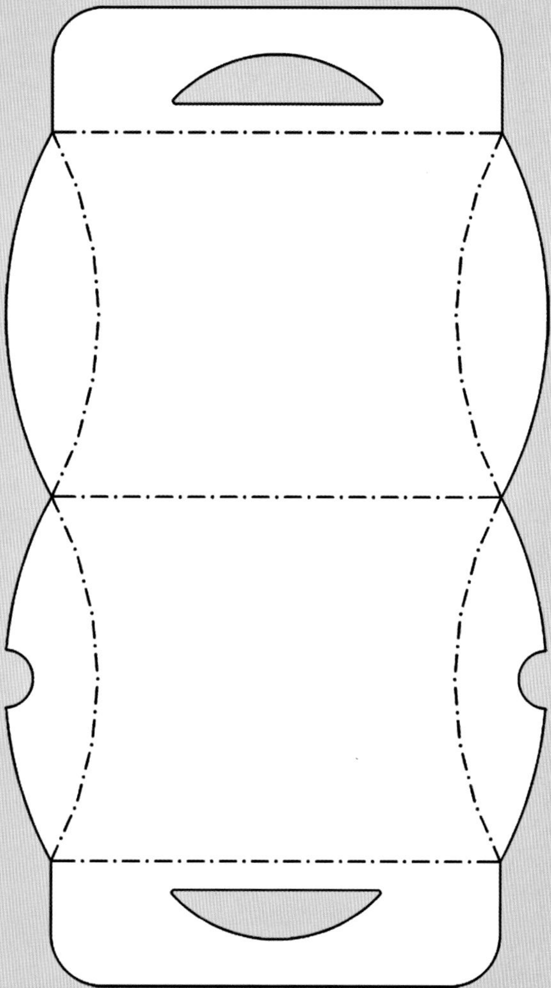

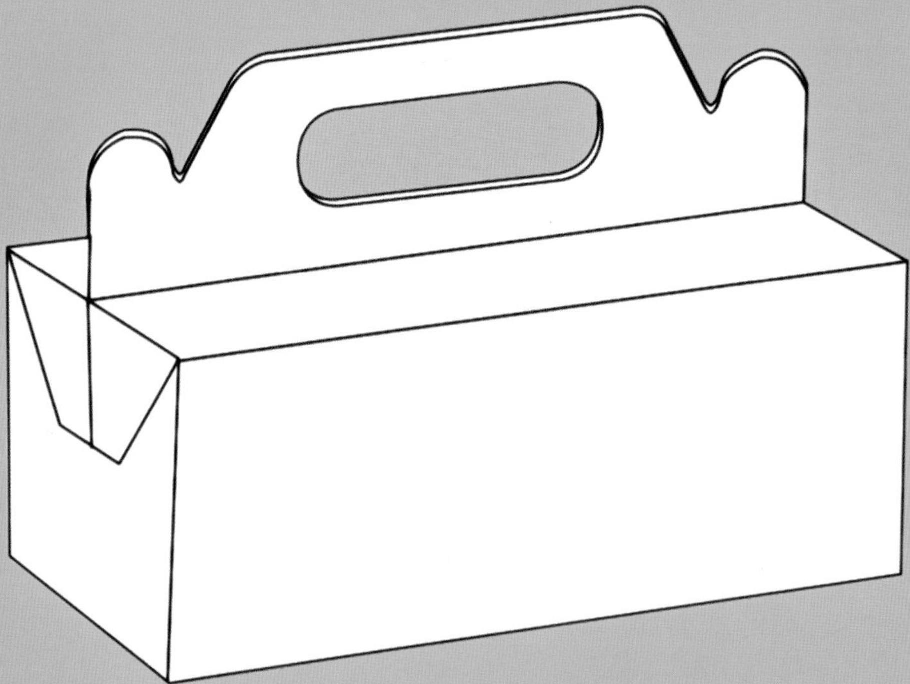

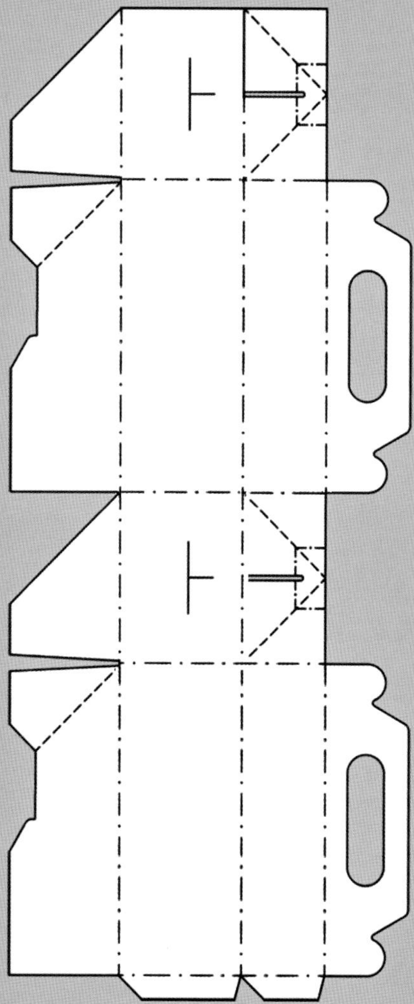

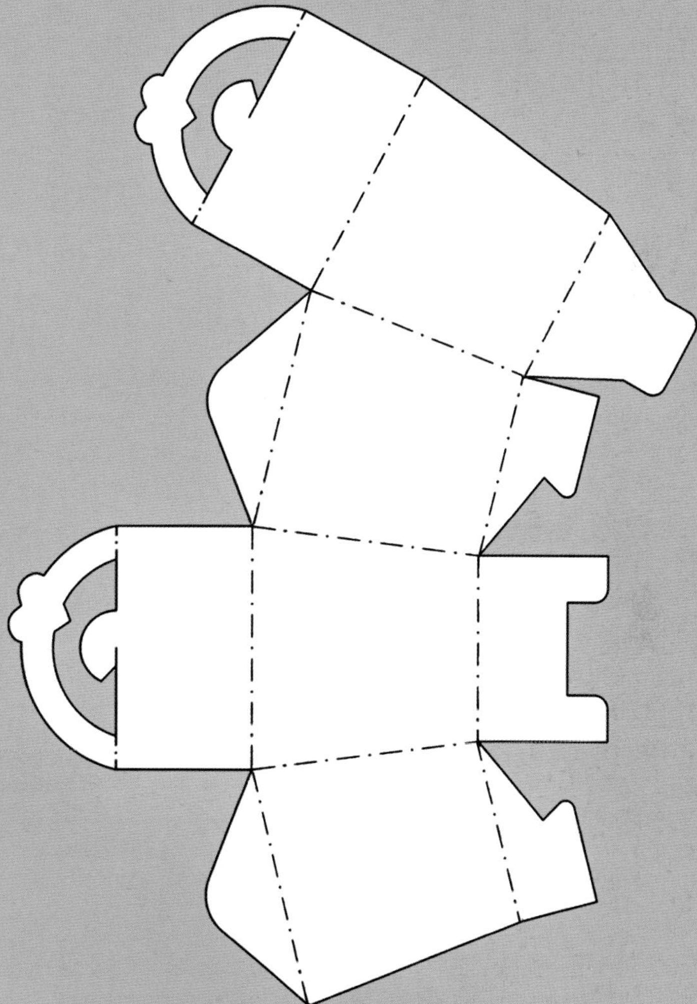

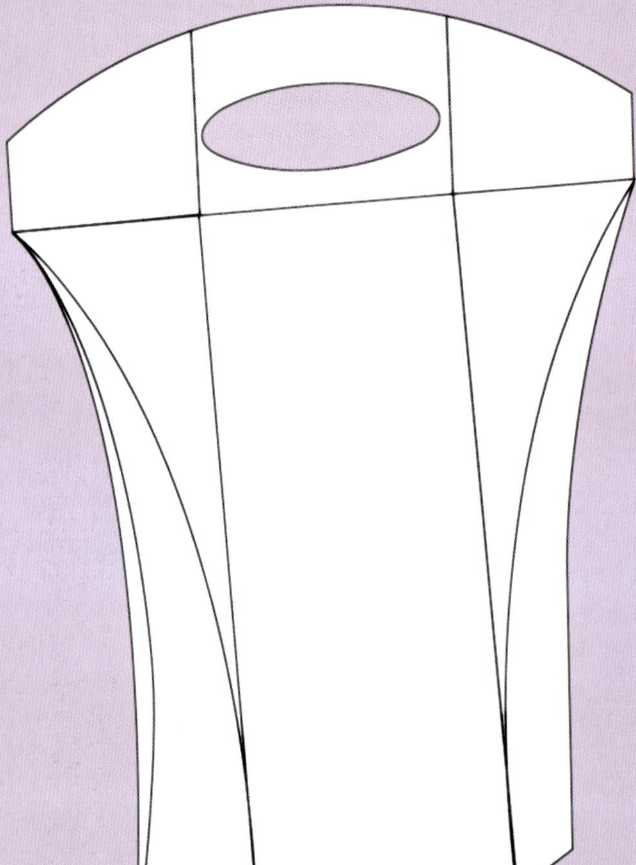

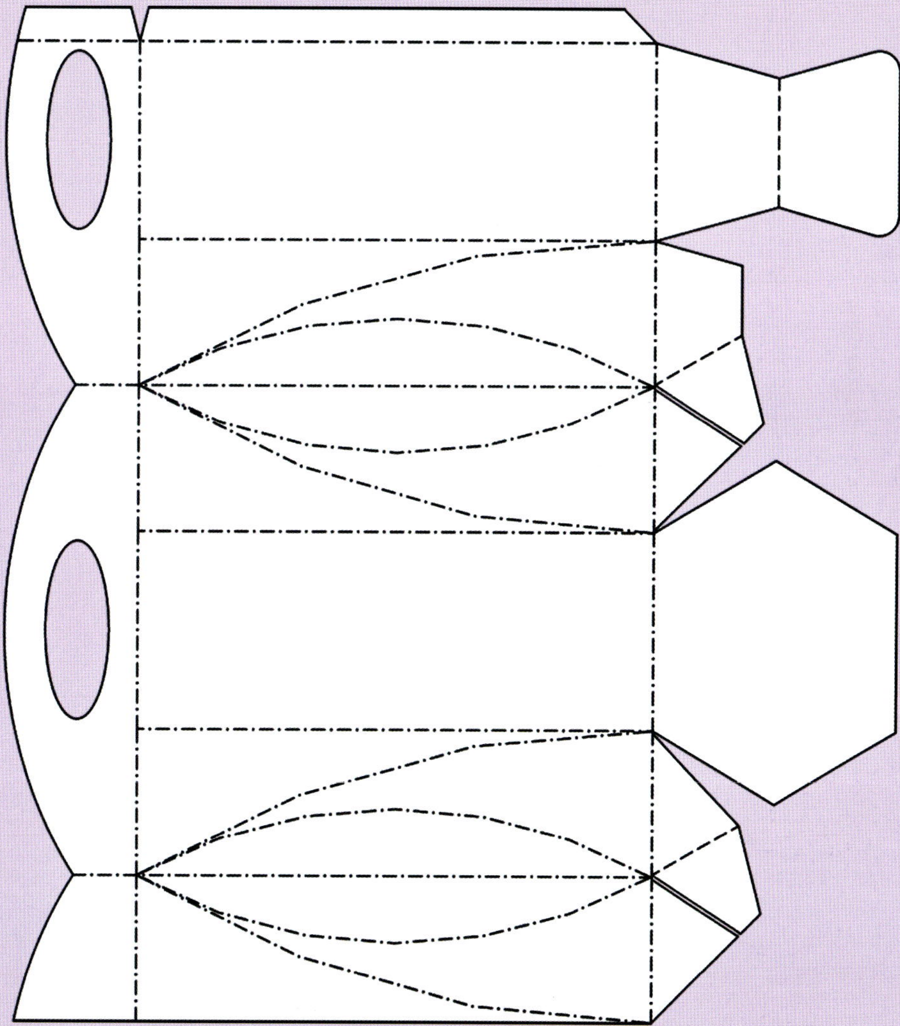

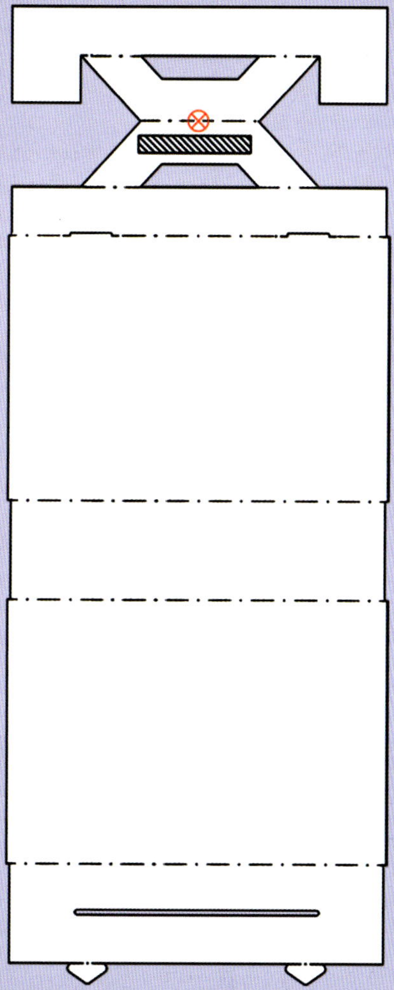

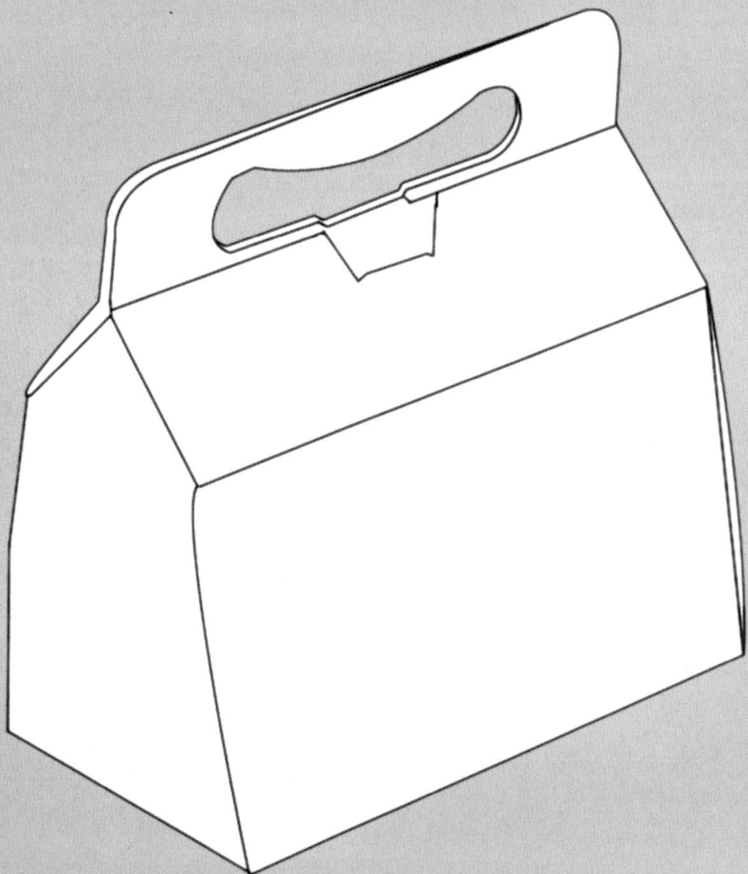

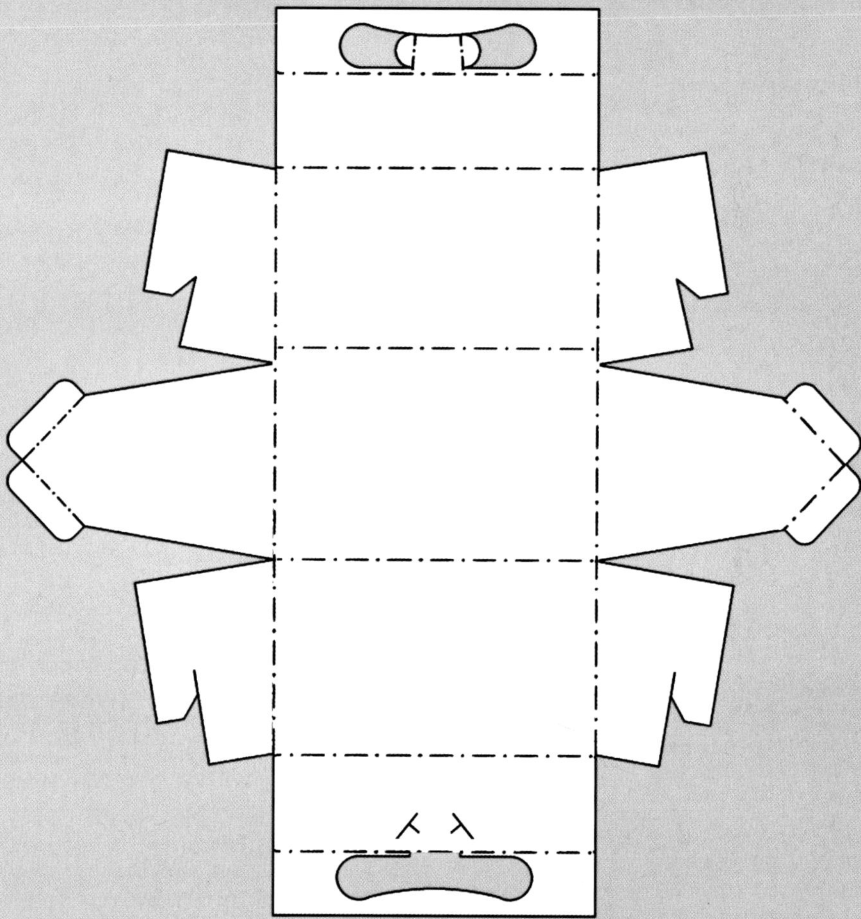

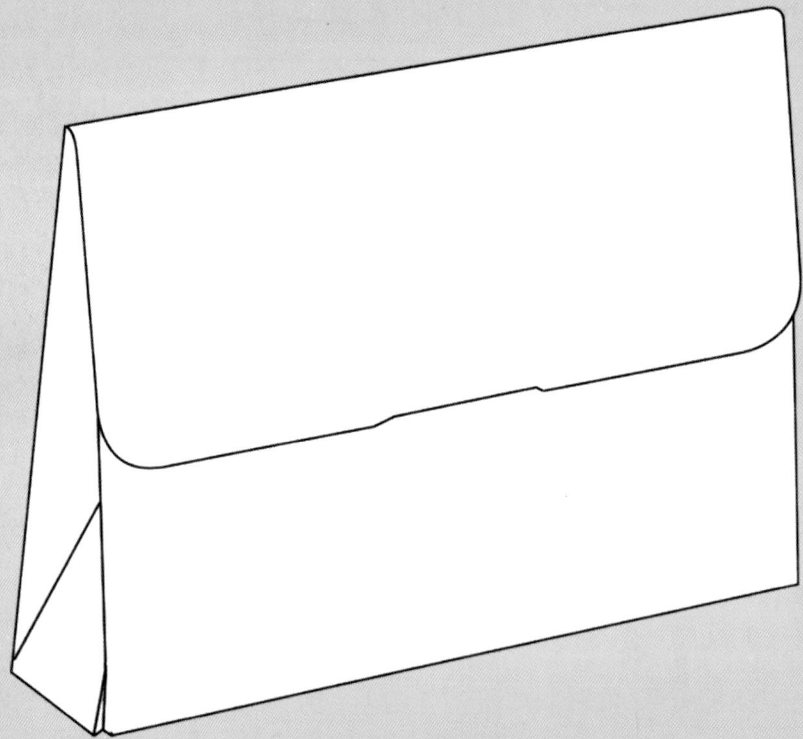

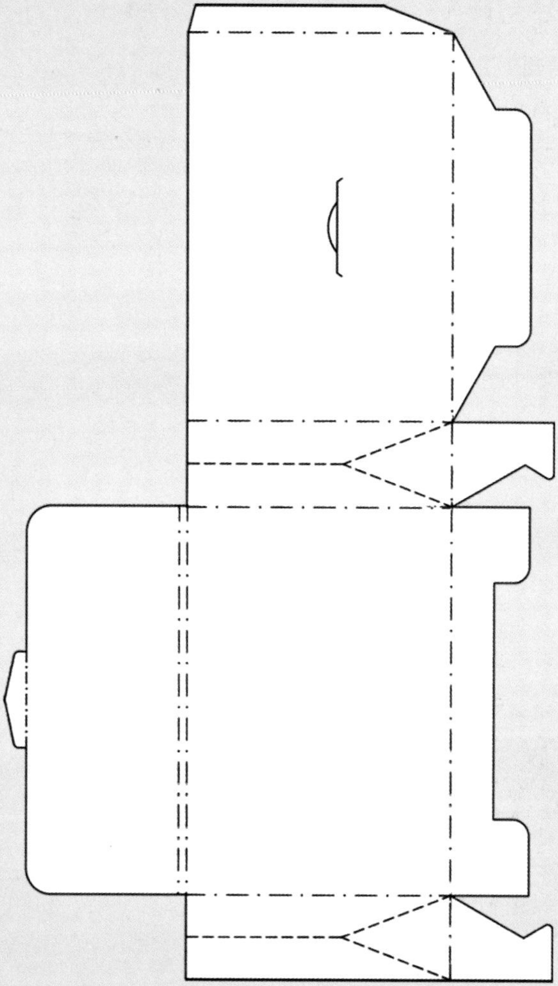

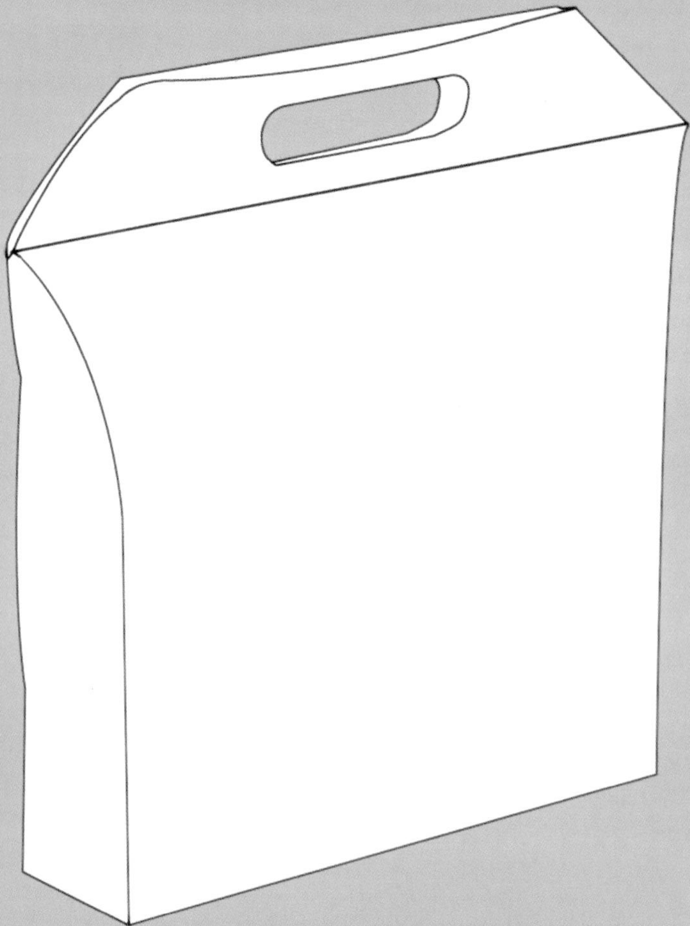

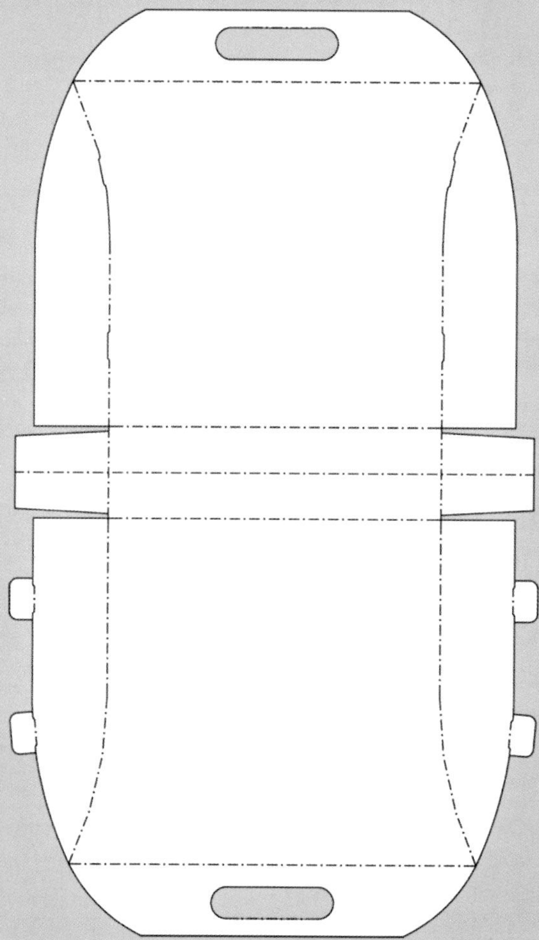

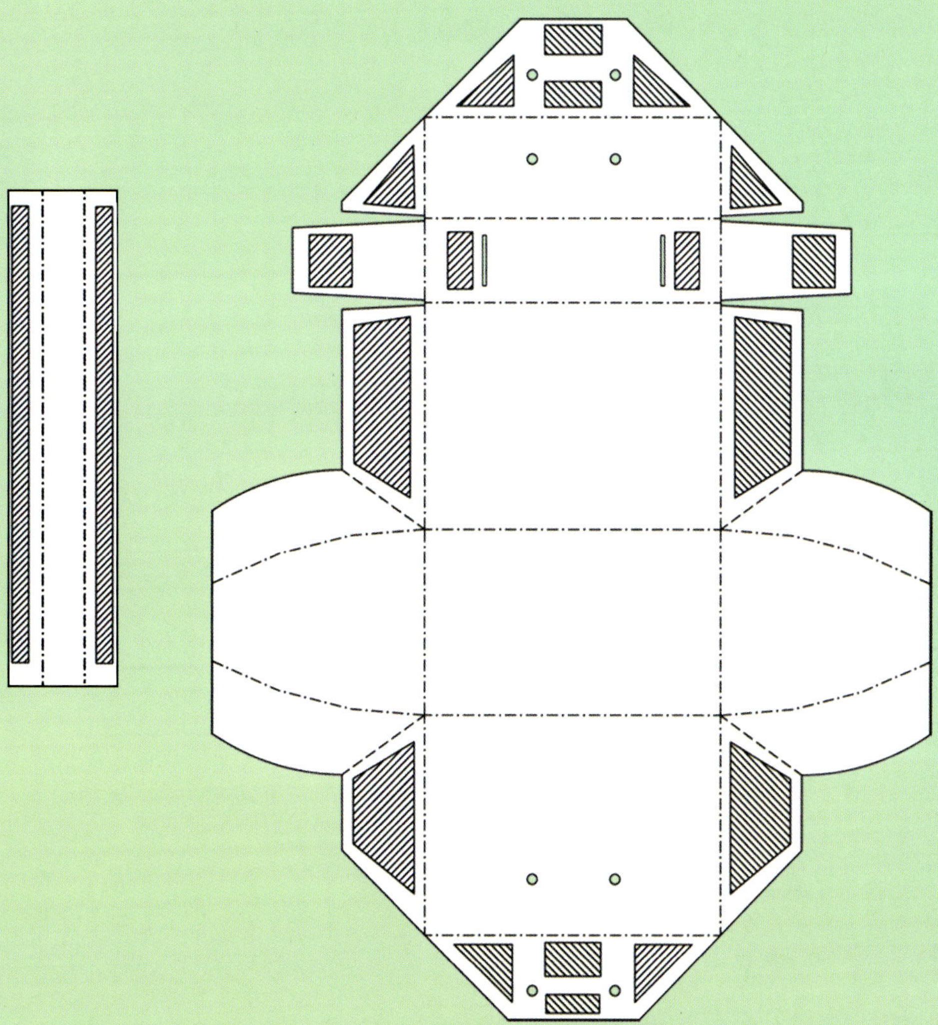

Gift Packaging

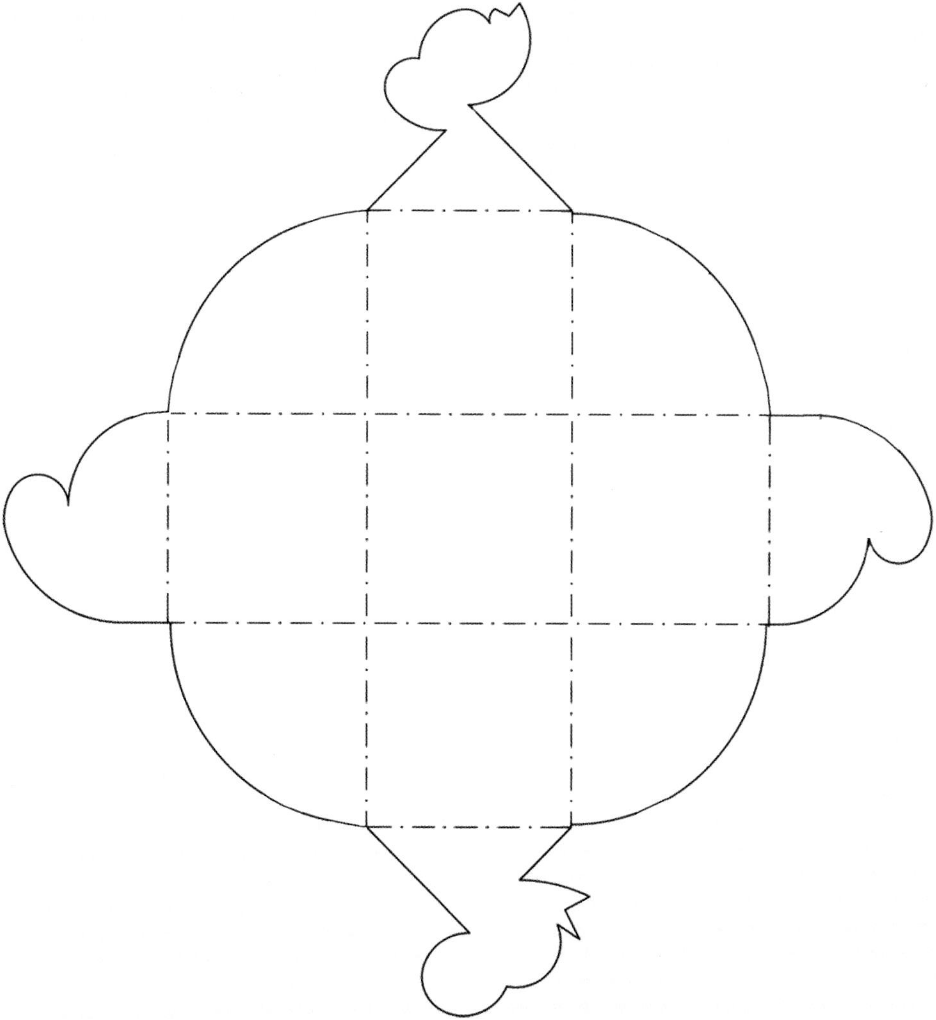

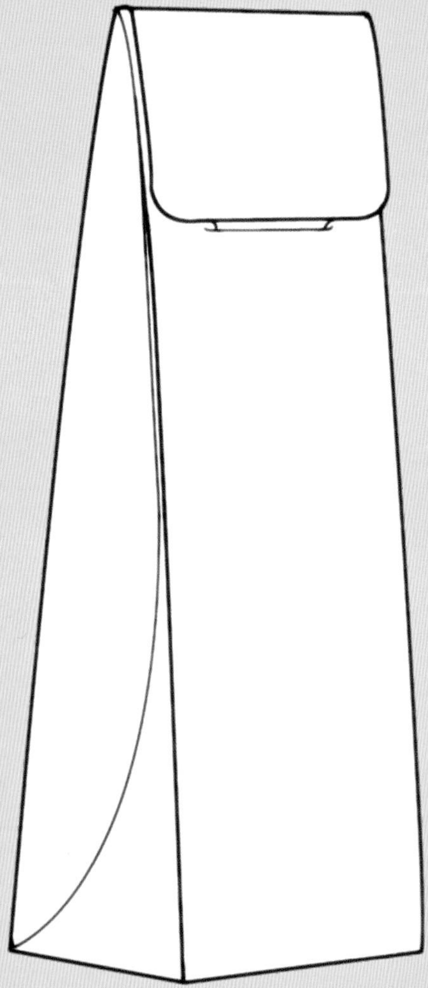

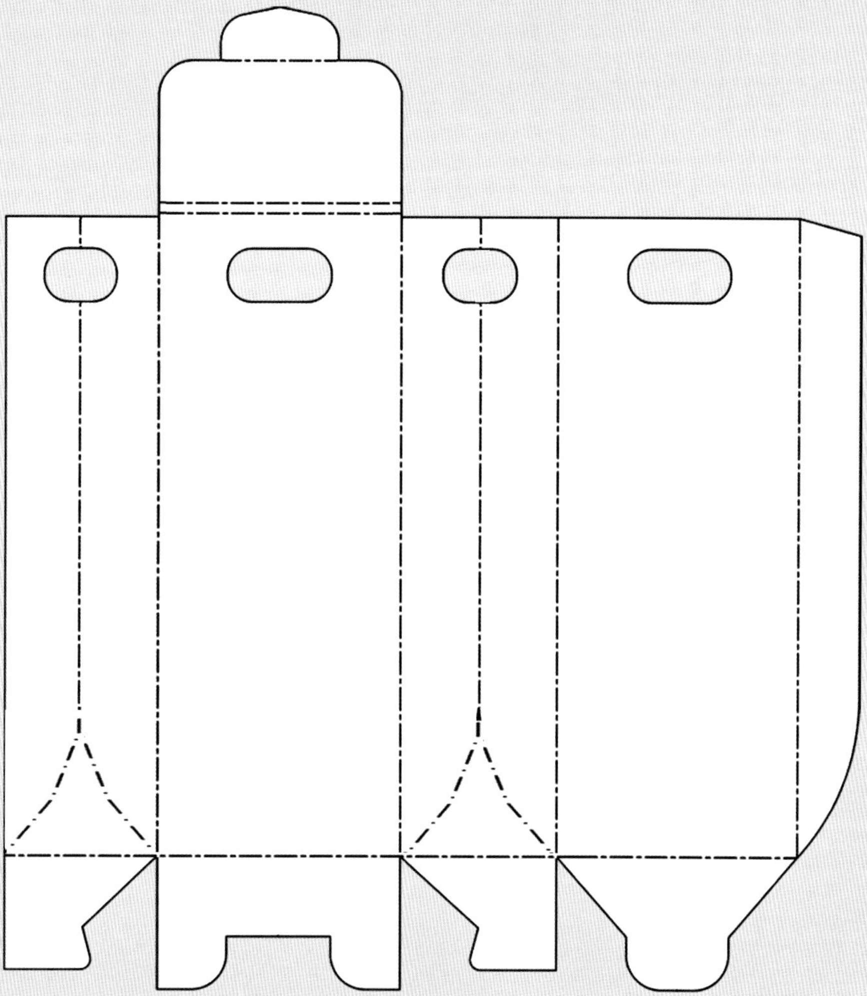

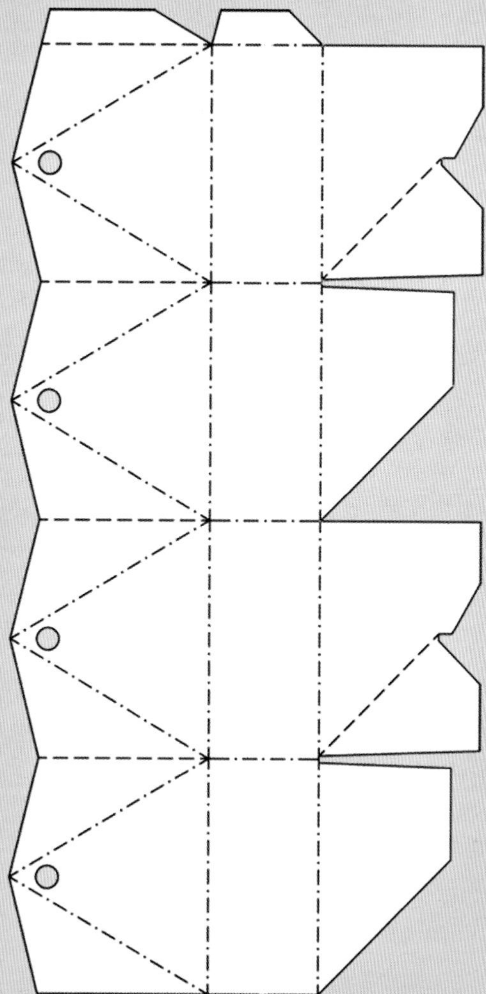

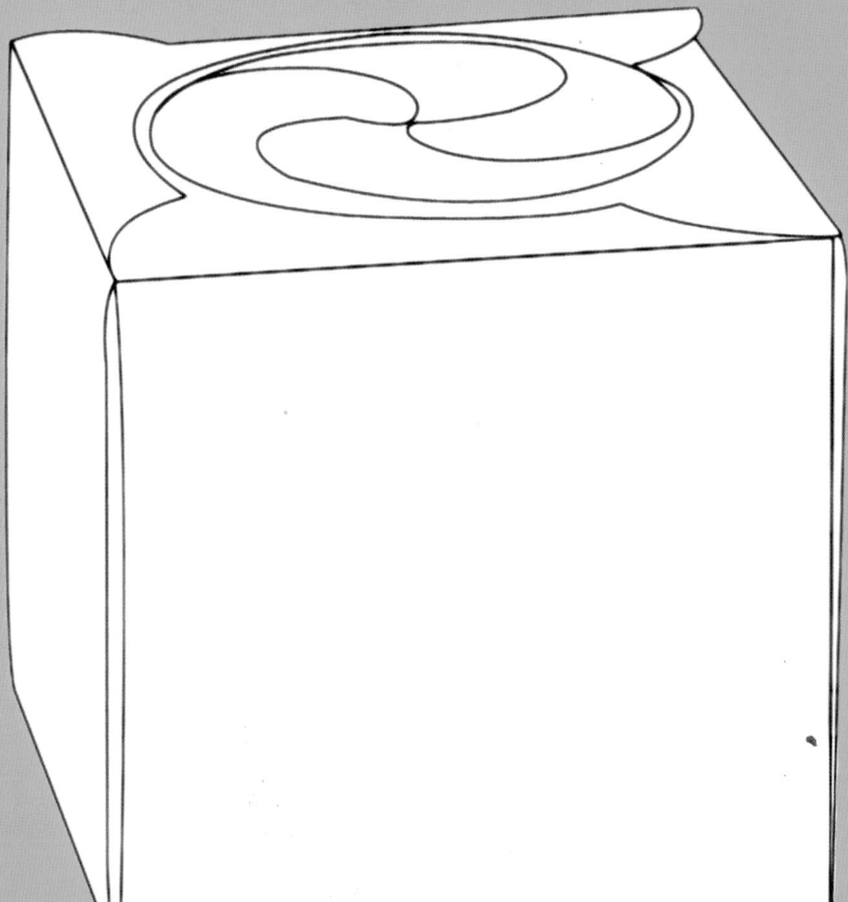

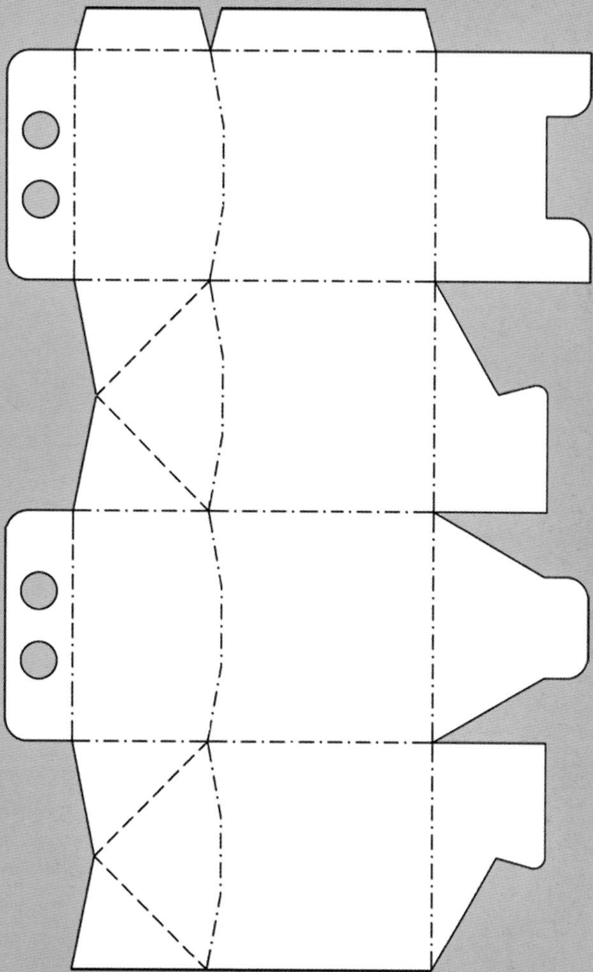

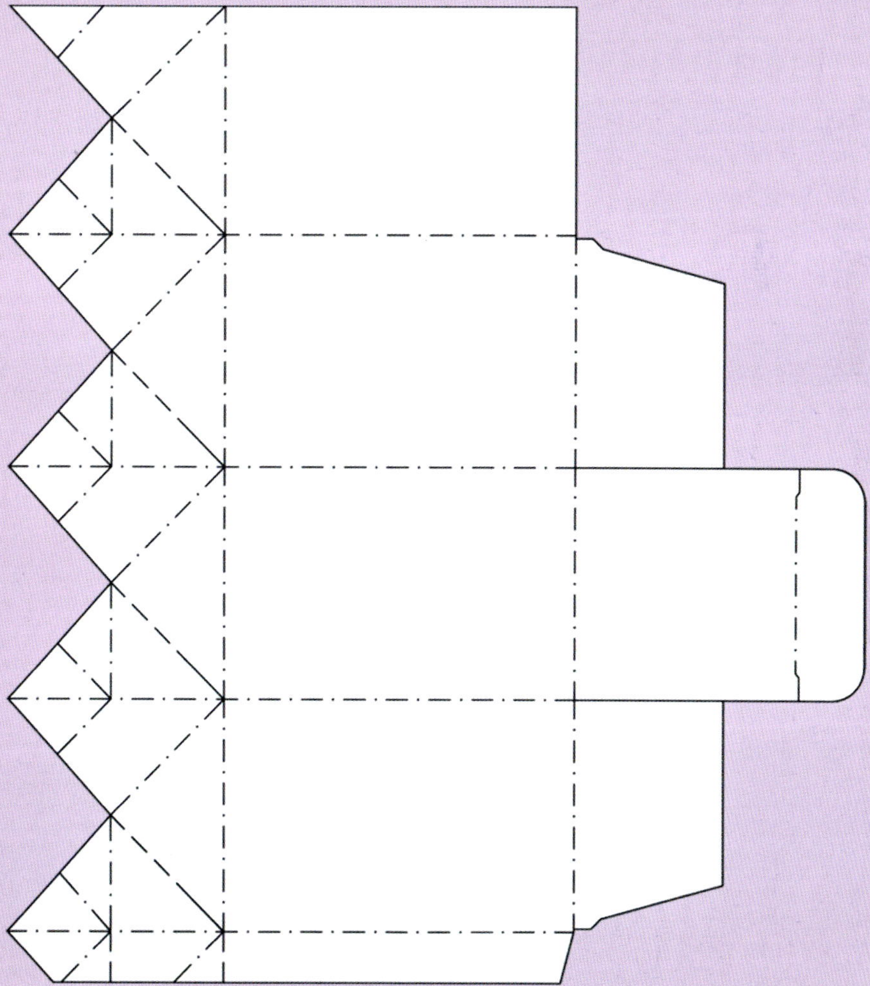

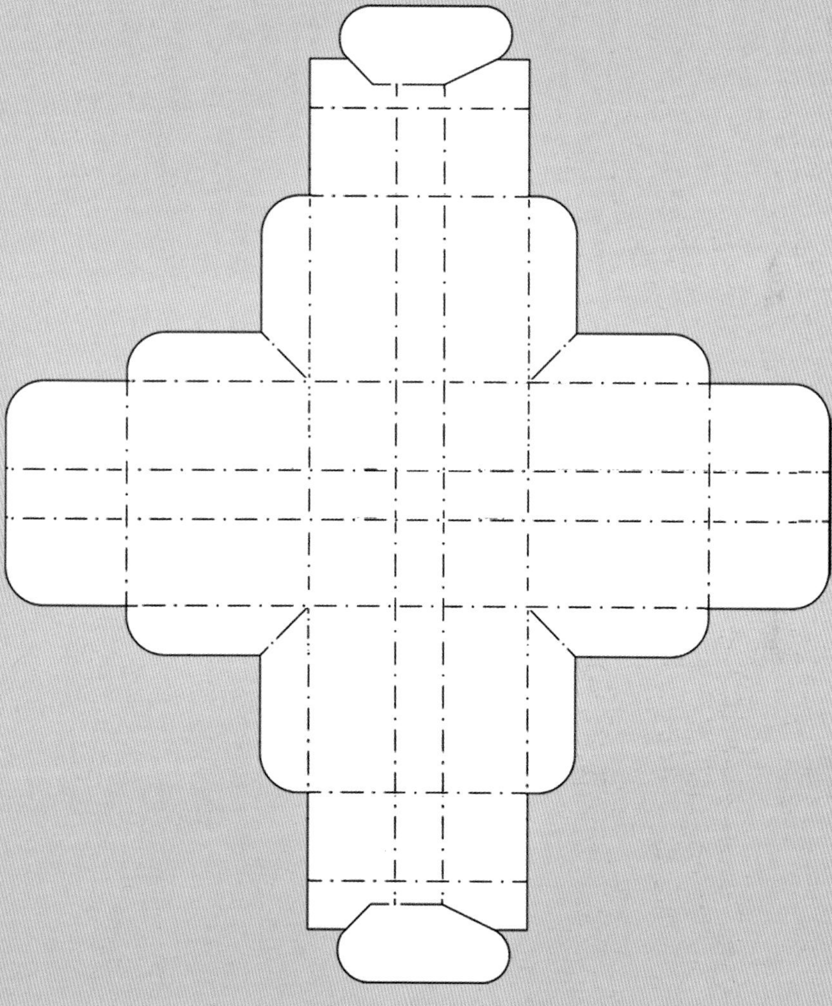

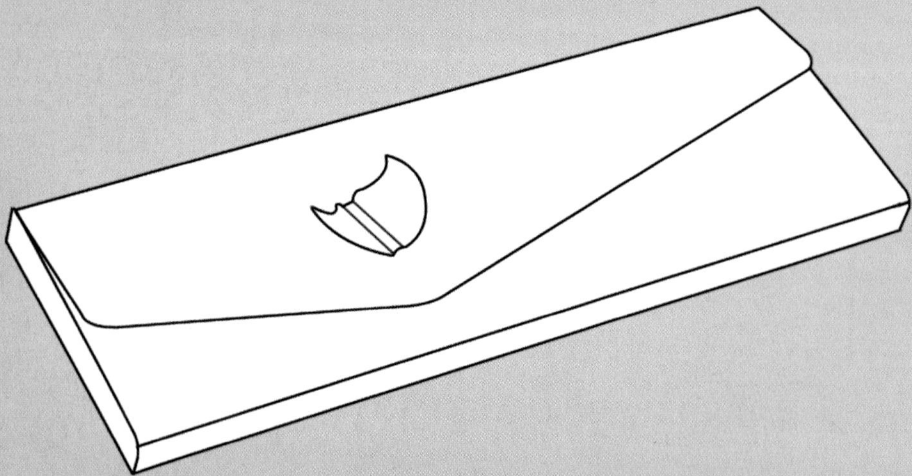

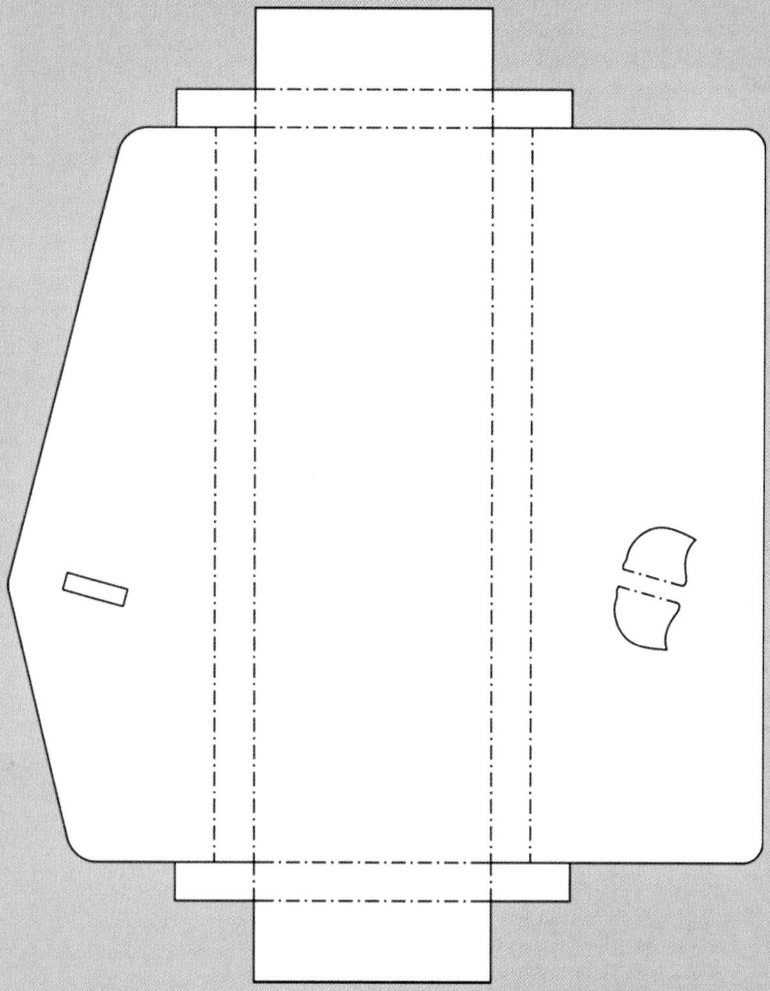

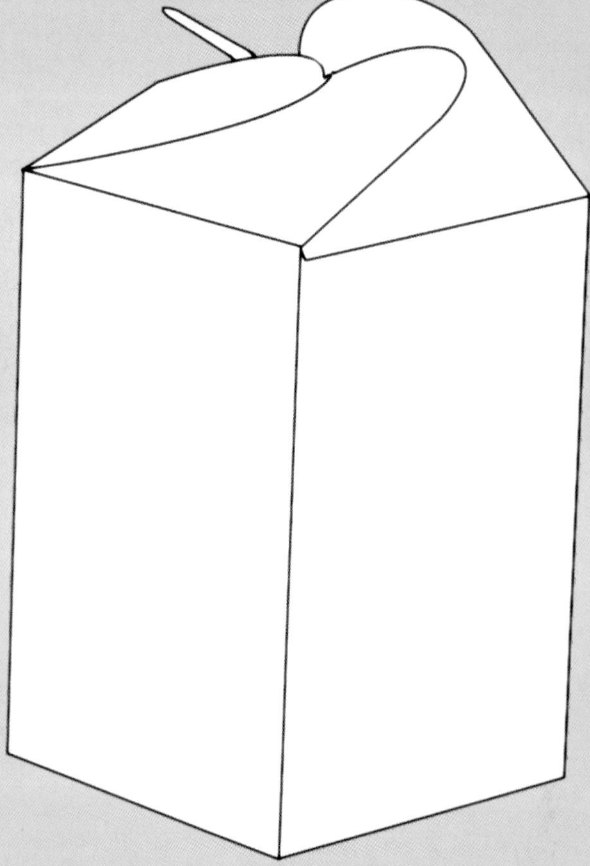

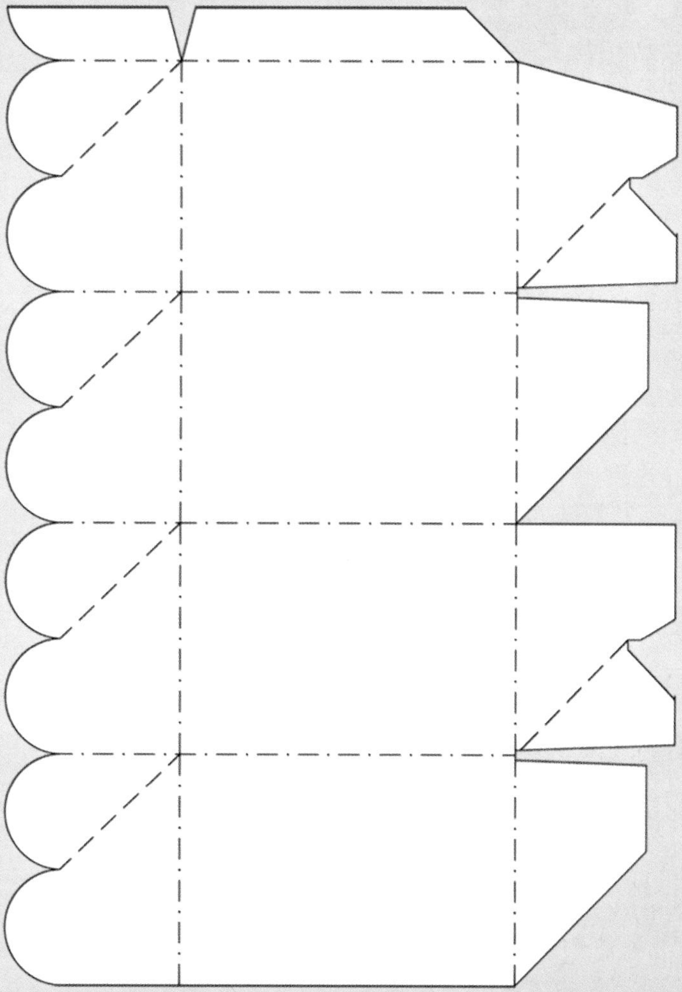

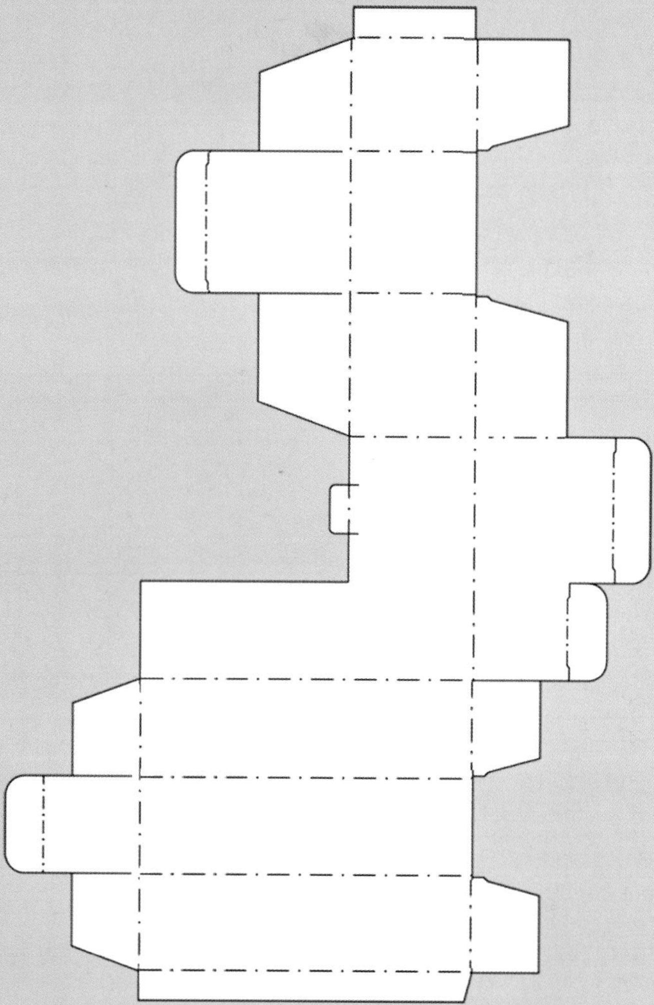

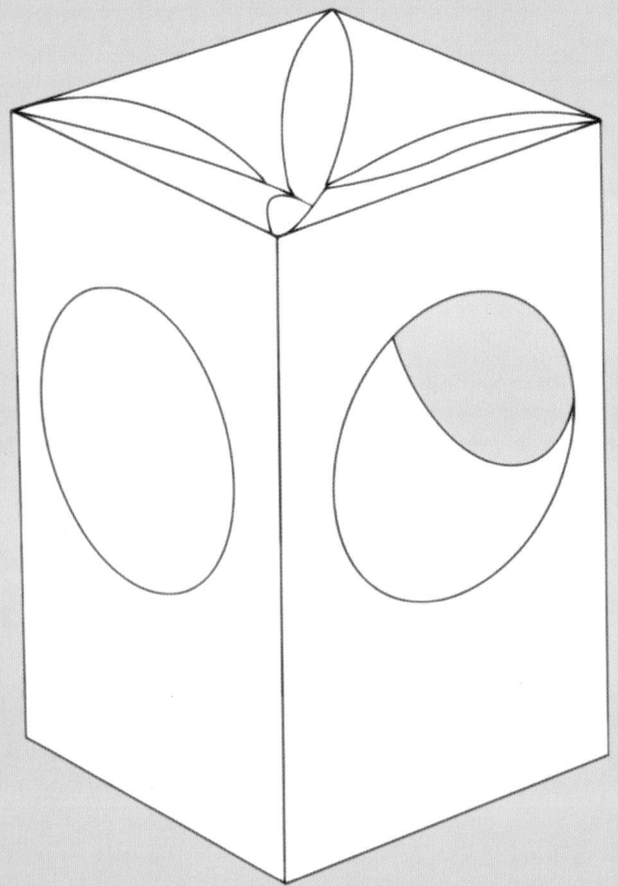

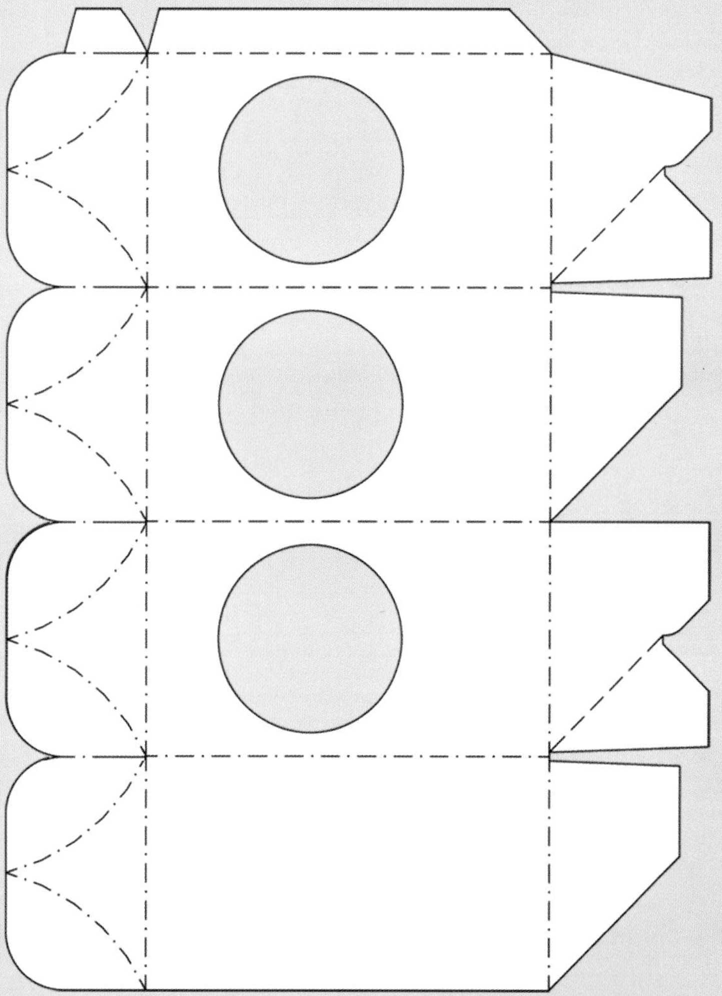

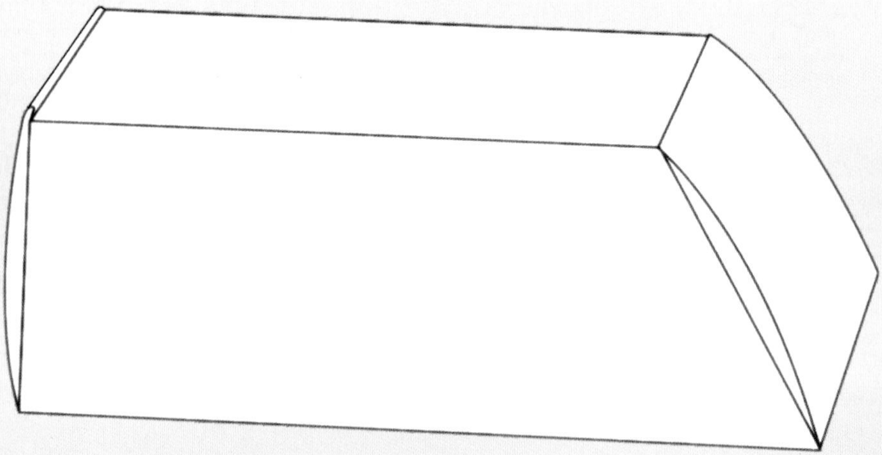

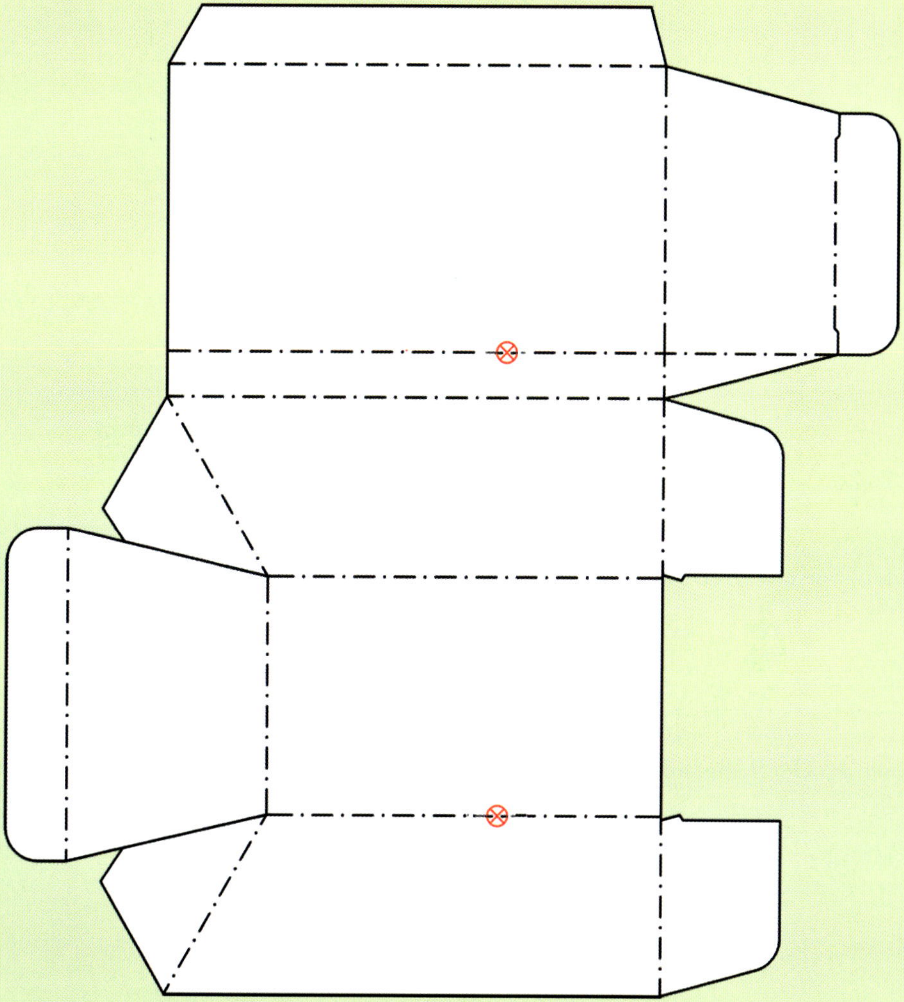

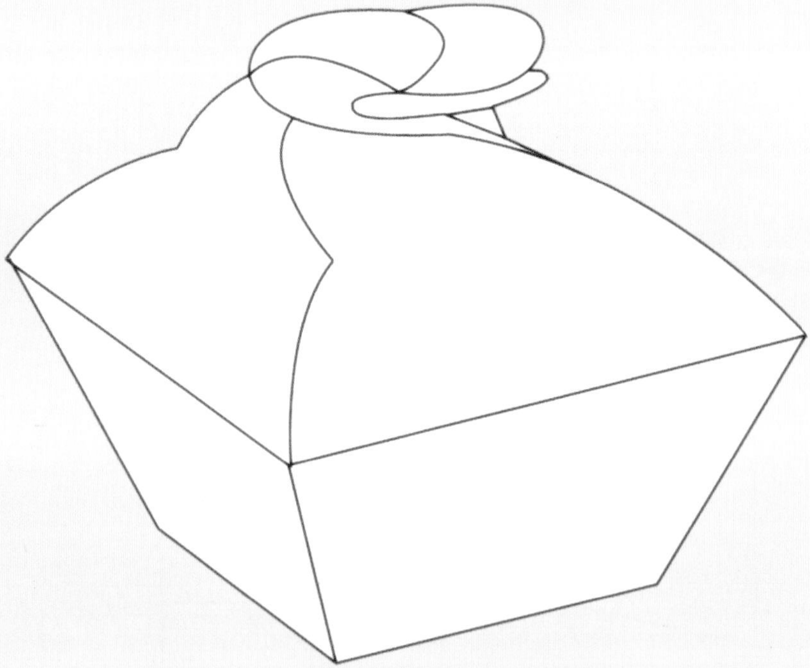

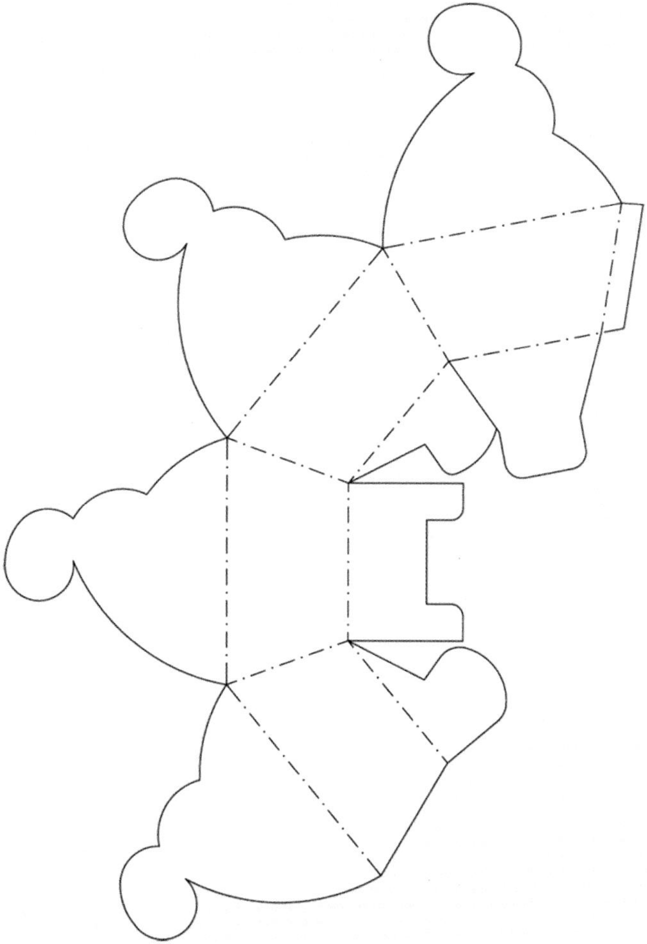

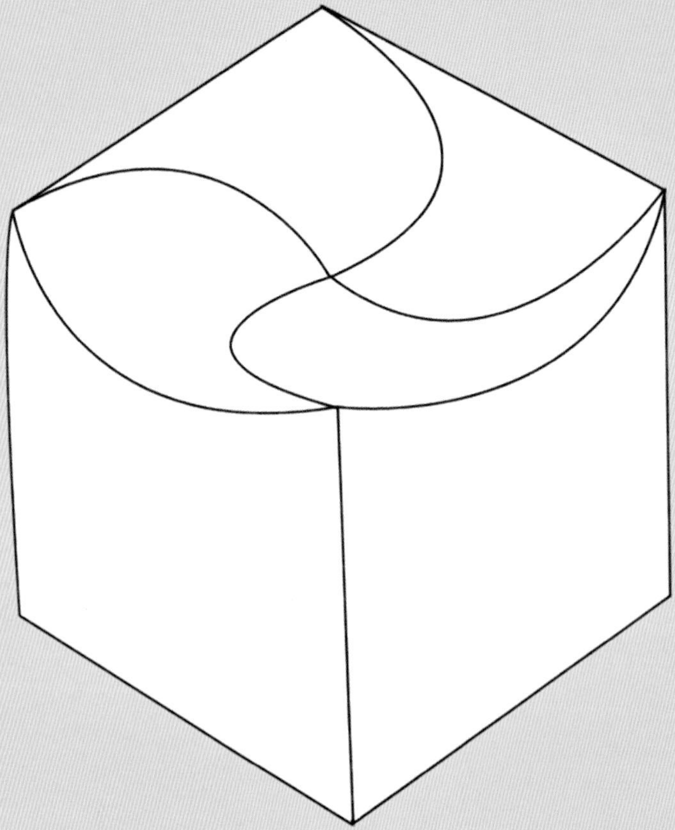

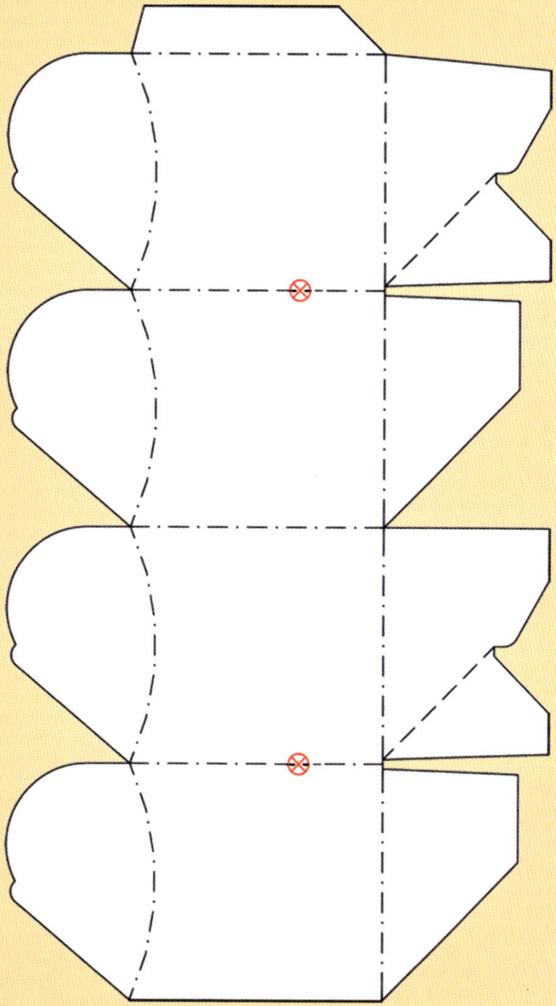

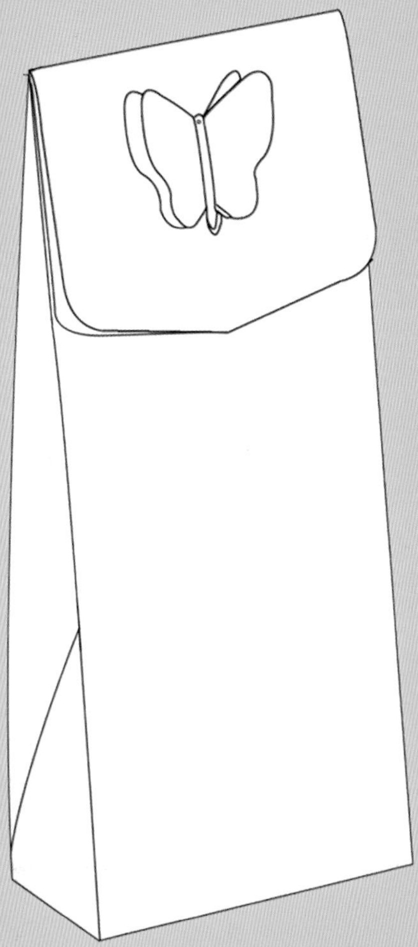

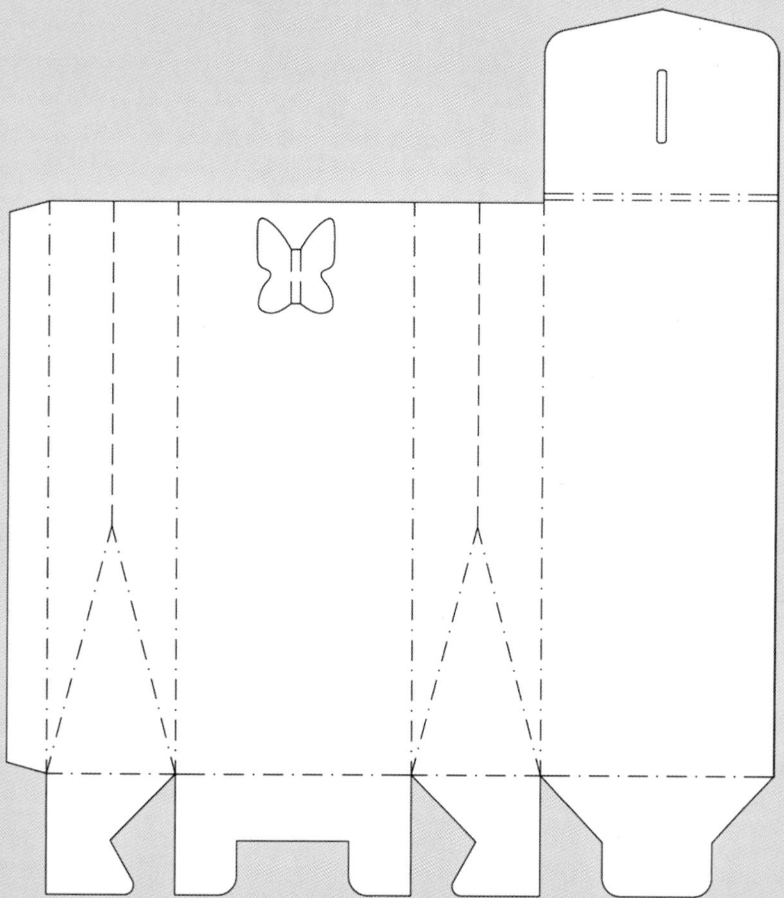

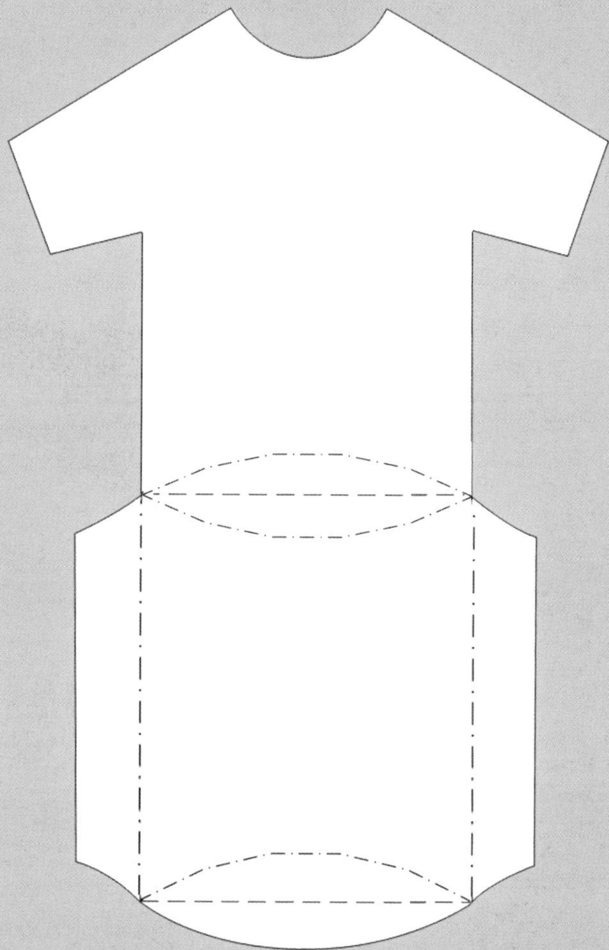

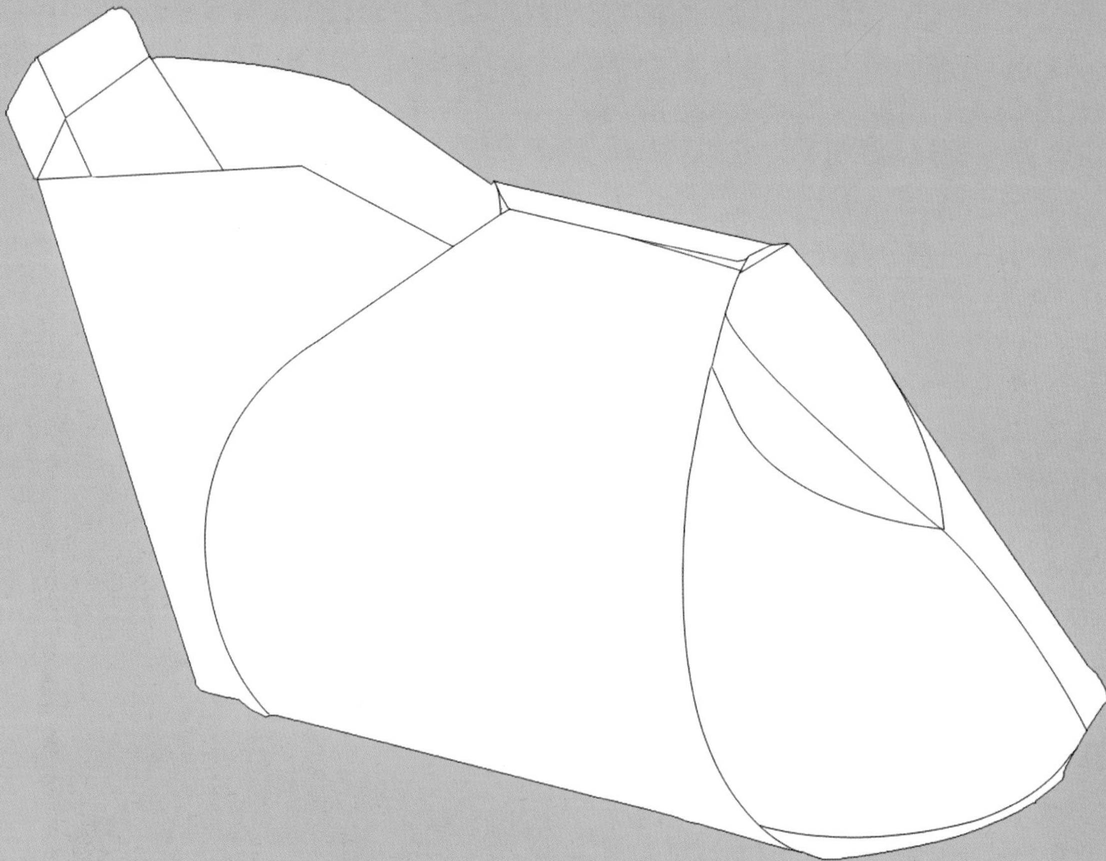

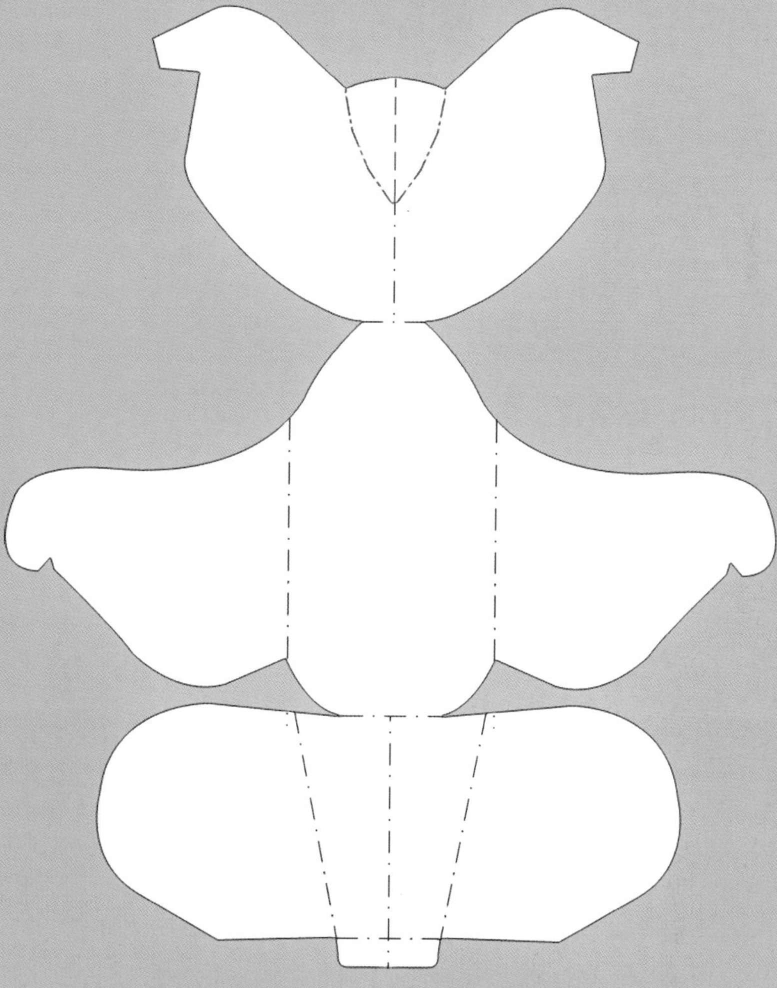

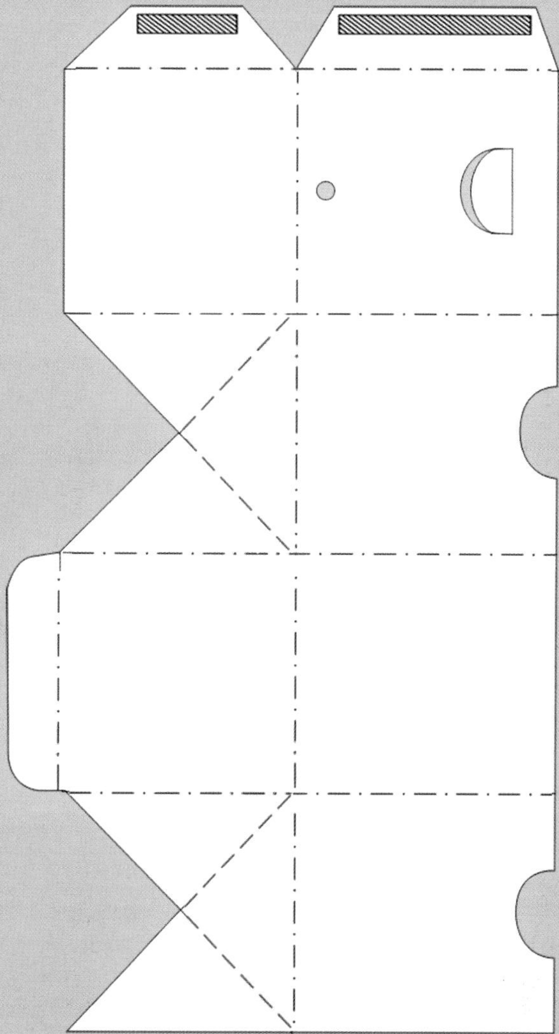

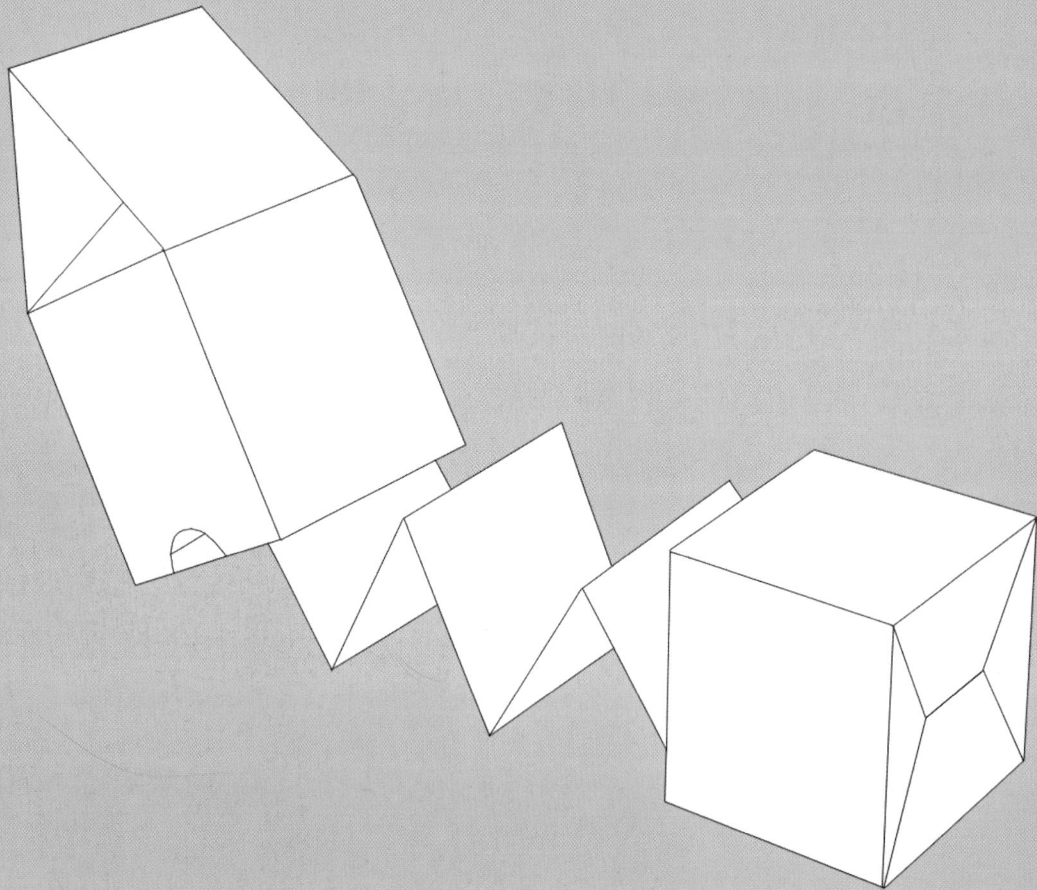

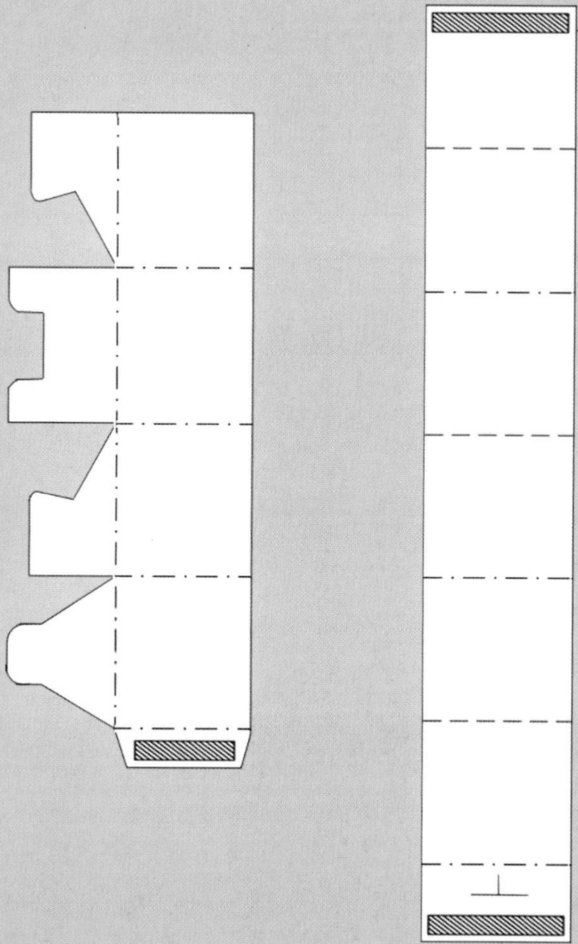

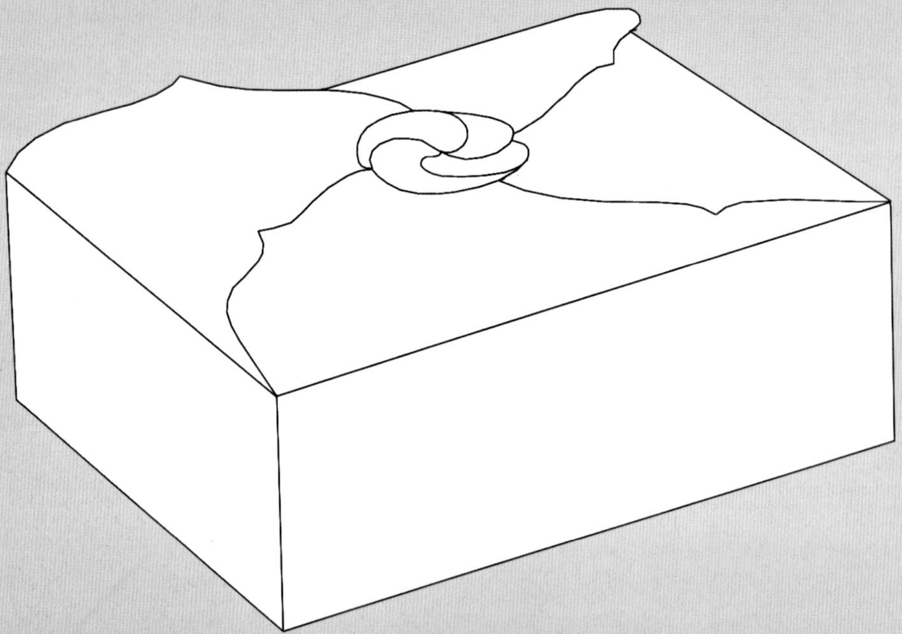

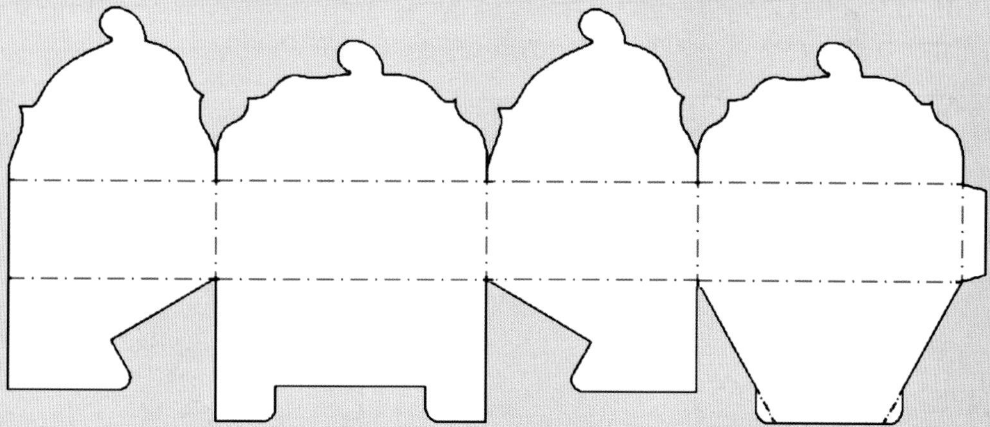

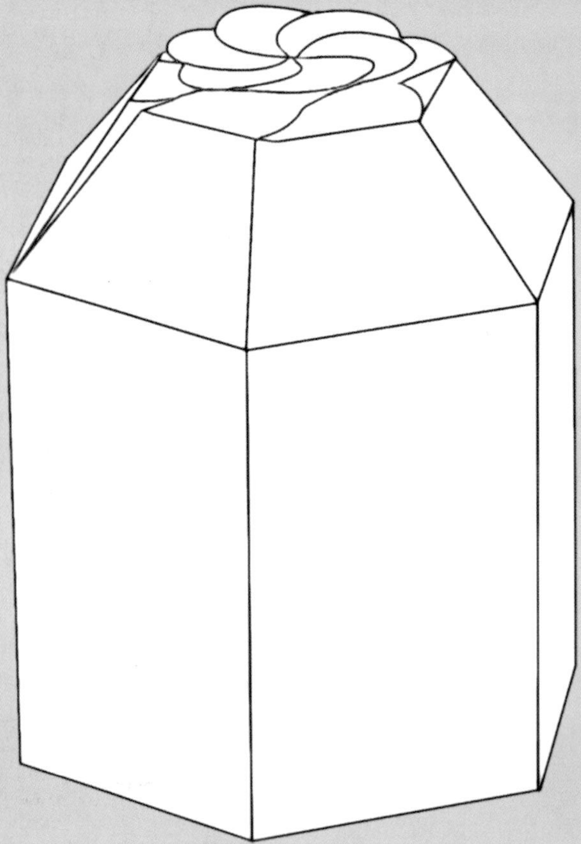

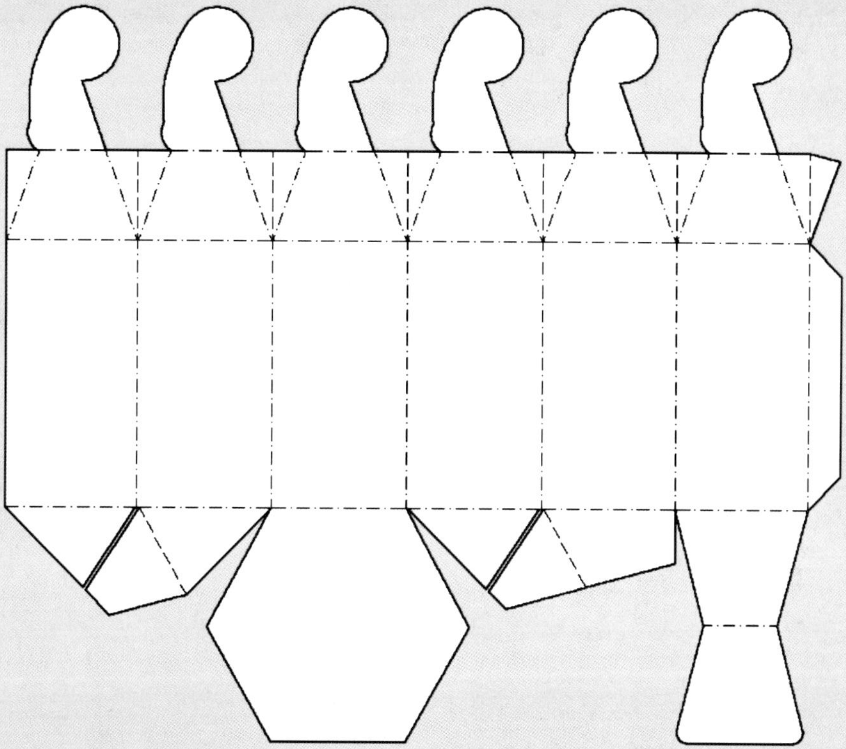

INDEX

P 032

P 034

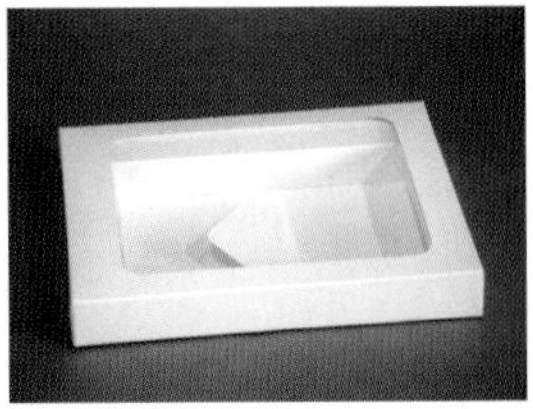
P 036

P 038

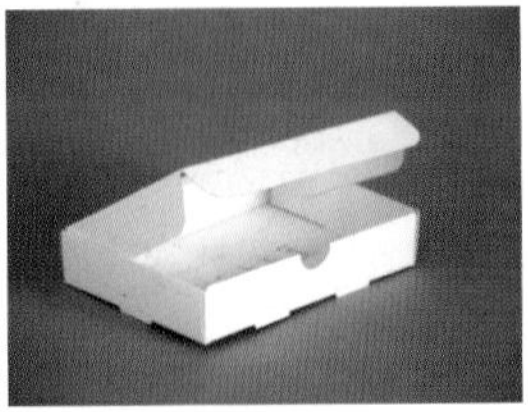
P 040

P 042

P 044

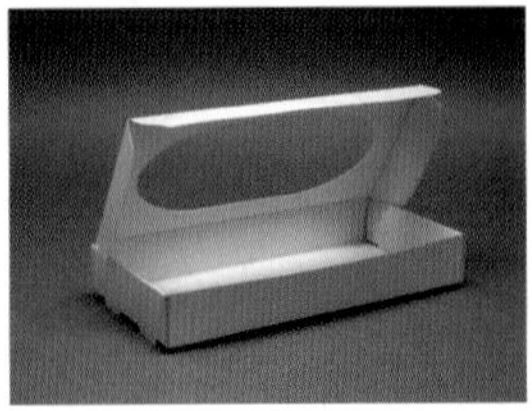
P 046

P 048

P 050

P 052

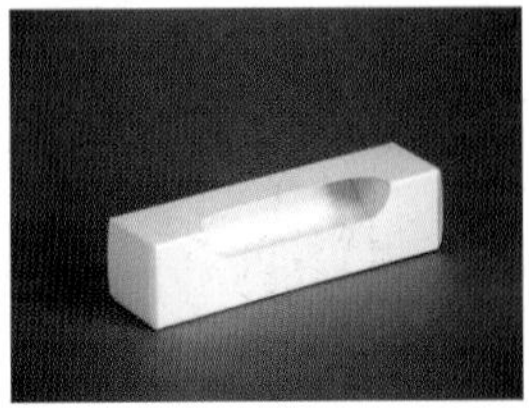
P 054

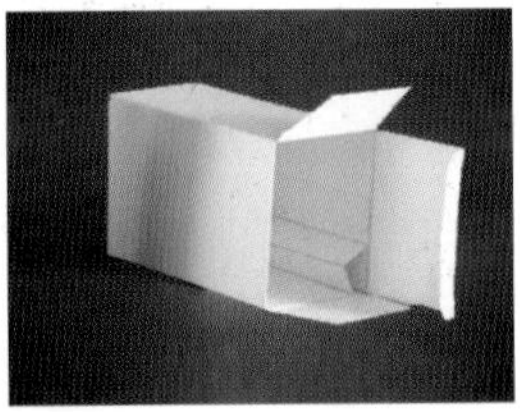
P 056

P 058

P 060

P 062

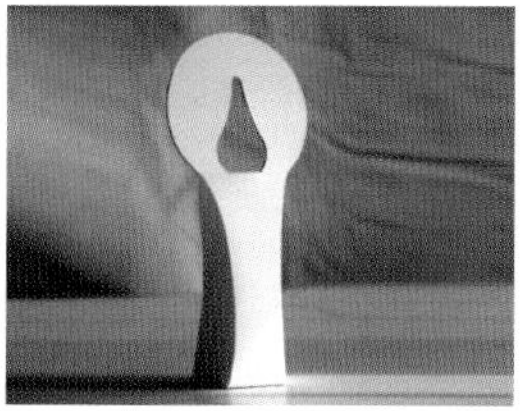
P 064

P 066

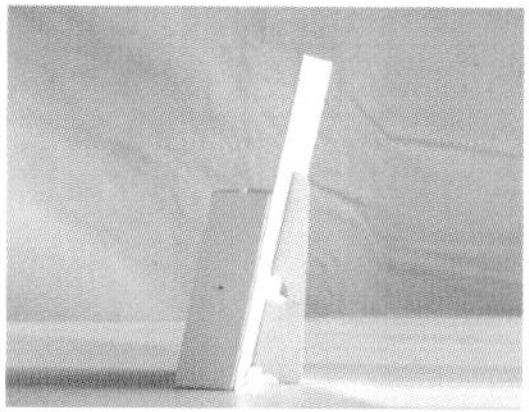
P 068

P 070

P 072

P 074

P 076

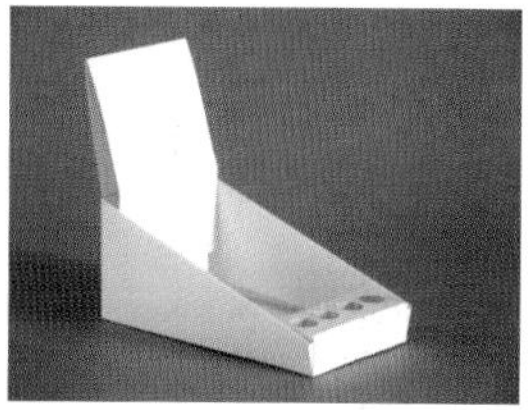
P 078

P 080

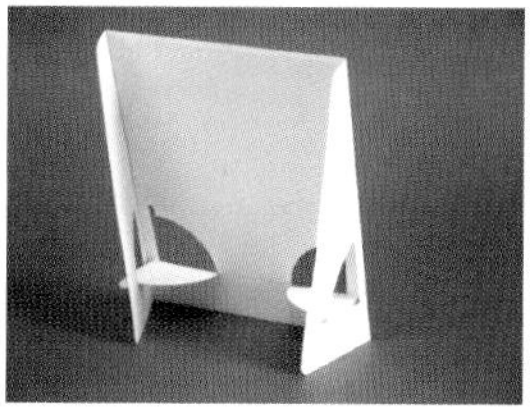
P 082

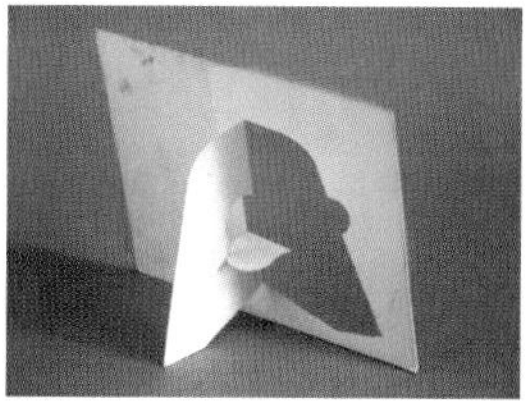
P 084

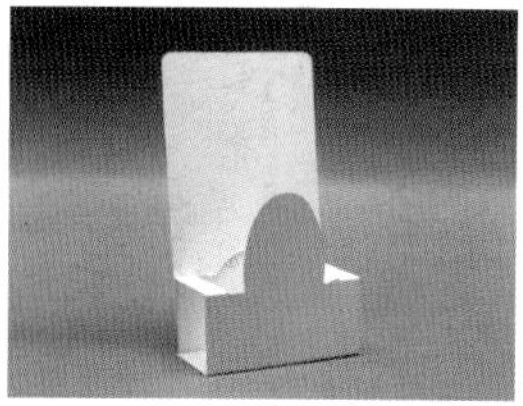
P 086

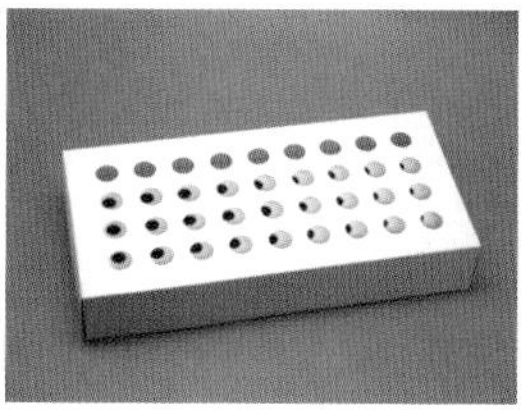
P 088

P 090

P 092

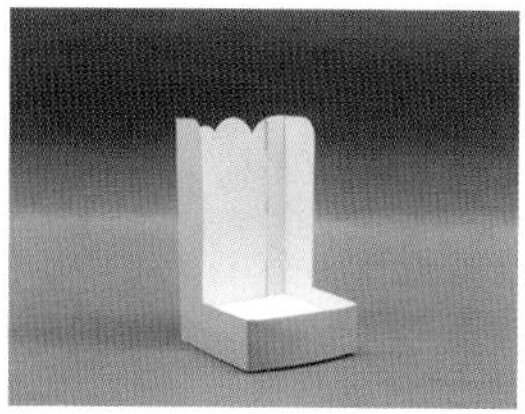
P 094

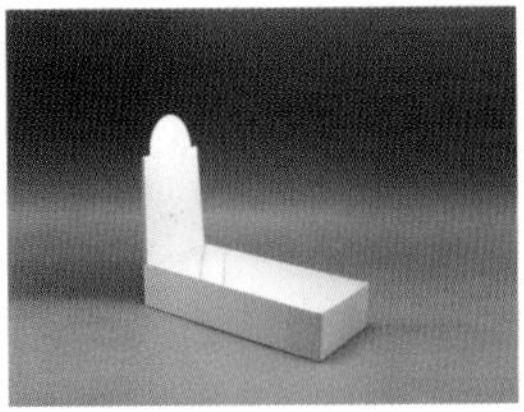

P 096

P 098

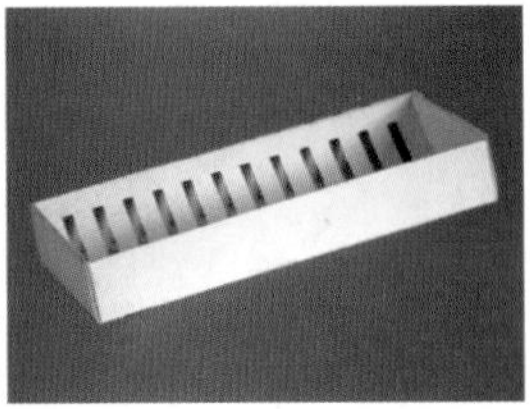

P 100

P 102

P 106

P 108

P 110

P 112

P 114

P 116

P 118

P 120

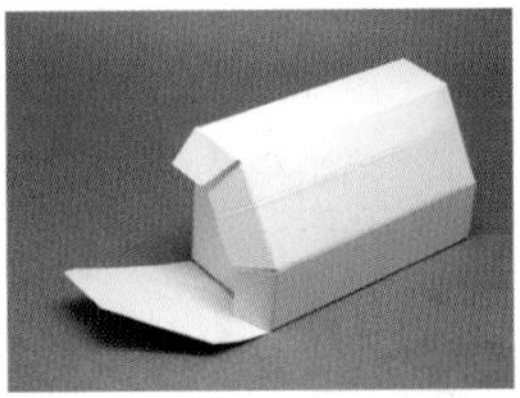

P 122

P 124

P 126

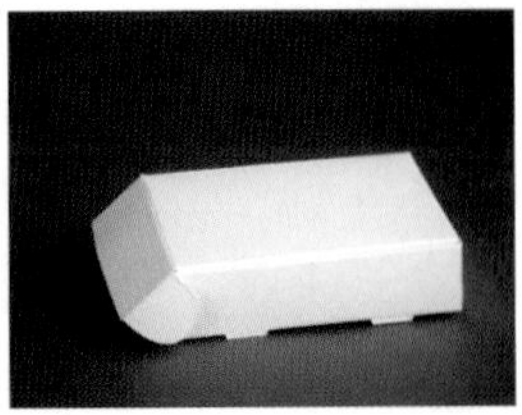

P 128

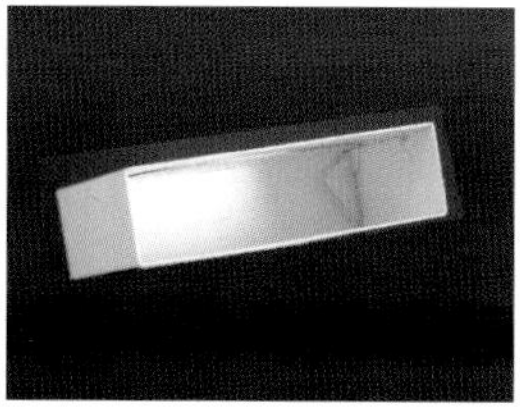
P 130

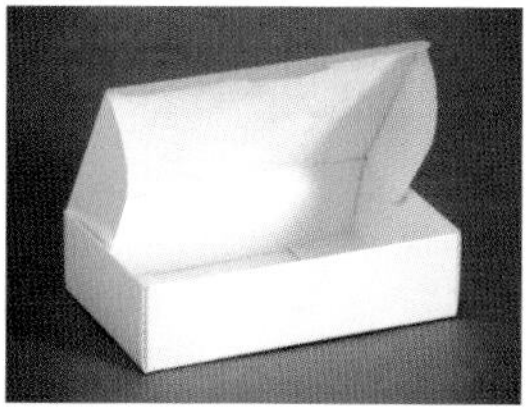
P 132

P 134

P 136

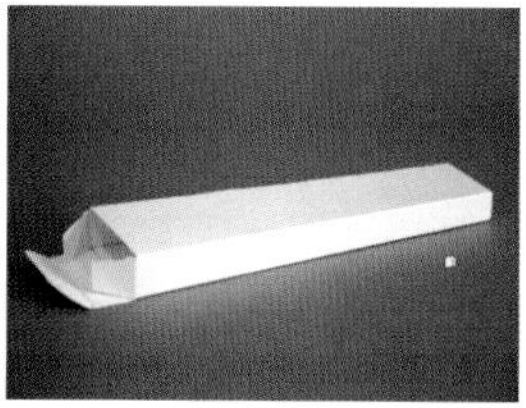
P 138

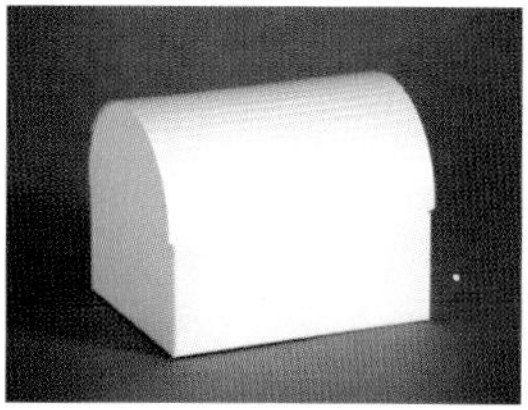
P 140

P 142

P 144

P 146

P 148

P 150

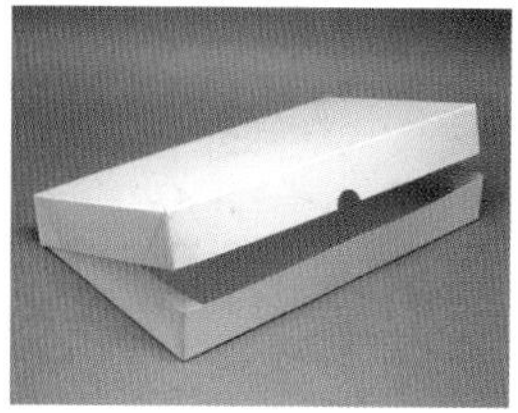
P 152

P 154

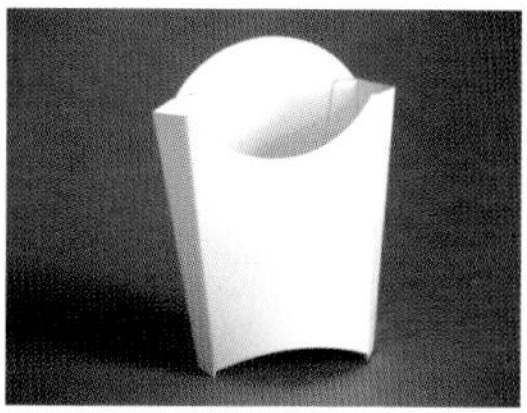
P 156

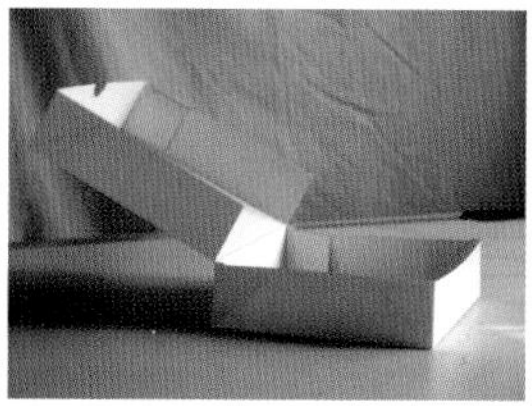
P 158

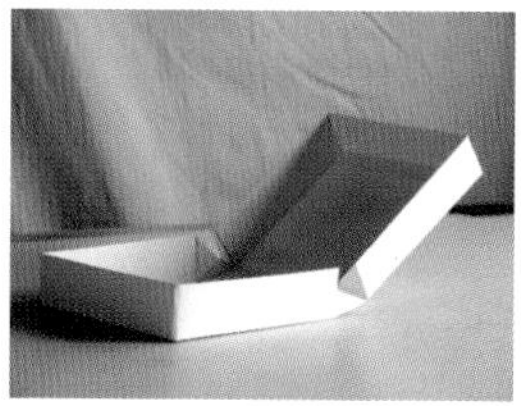
P 160

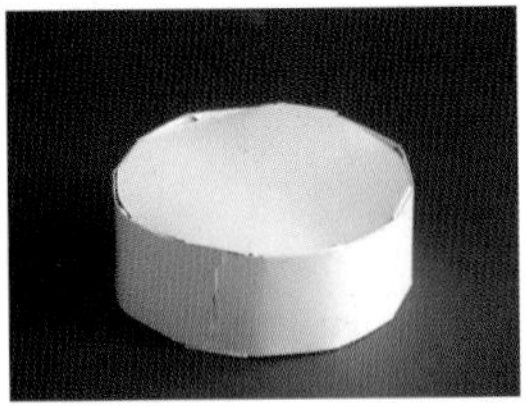
P 162

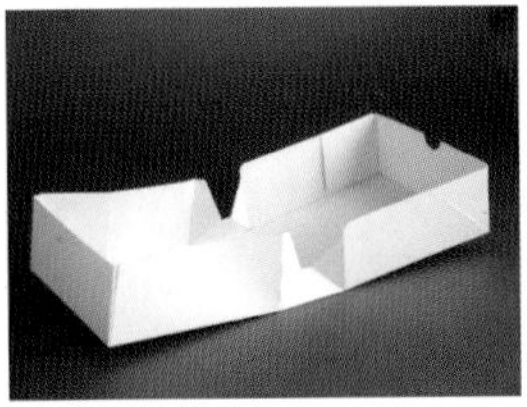
P 164

P 166

P 168

P 170

P 172

P 174

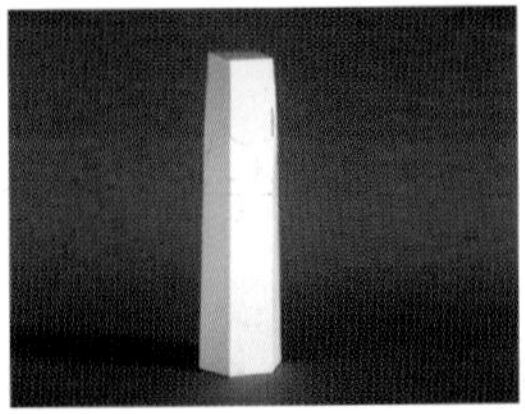
P 176

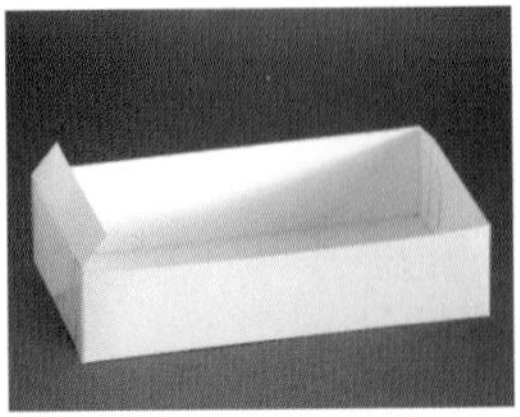
P 178

P 180

P 182

P 184

P 186

P 188

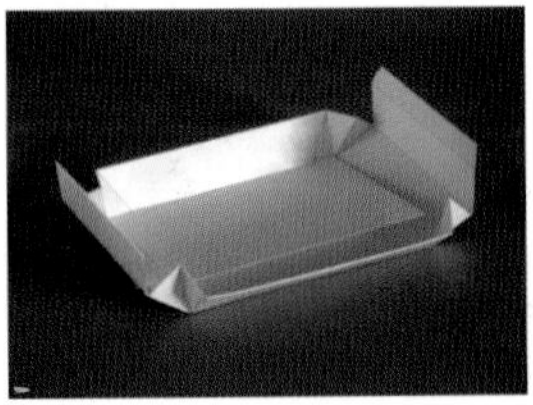
P 190

P 192

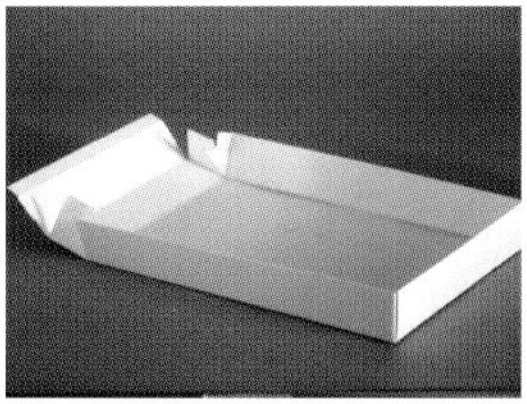
P 194

P 196

P 198

P 200

P 202

P 204

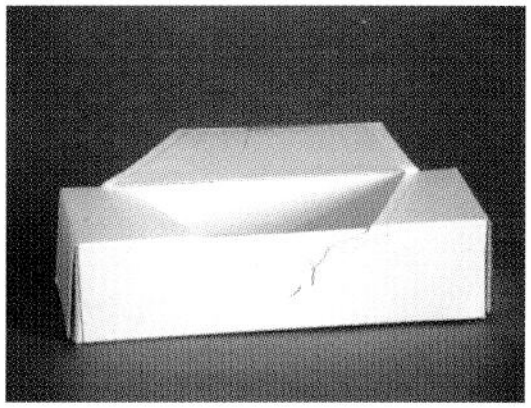
P 206

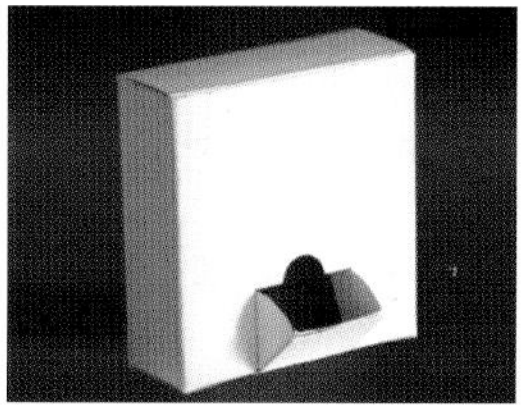
P 208

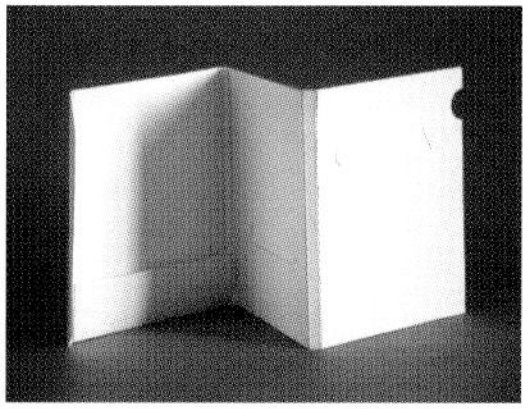
P 210

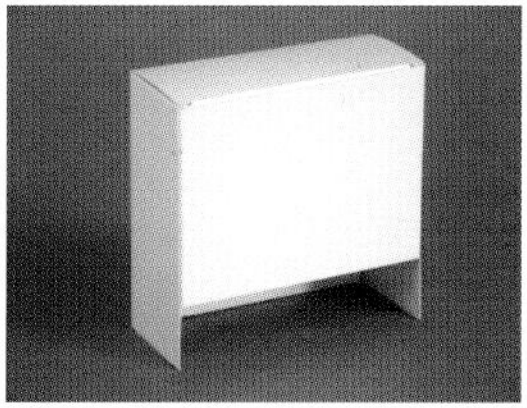
P 212

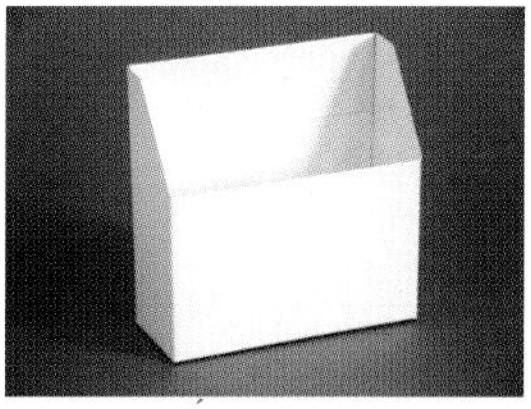
P 214

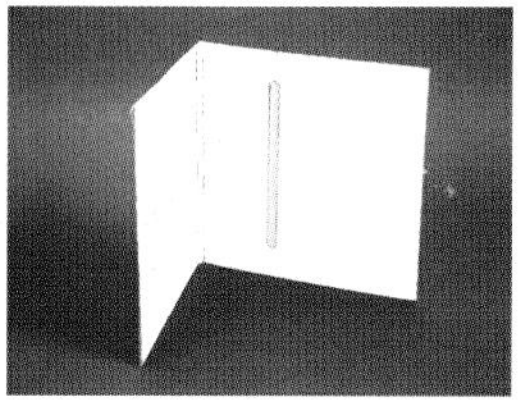
P 216

P 218

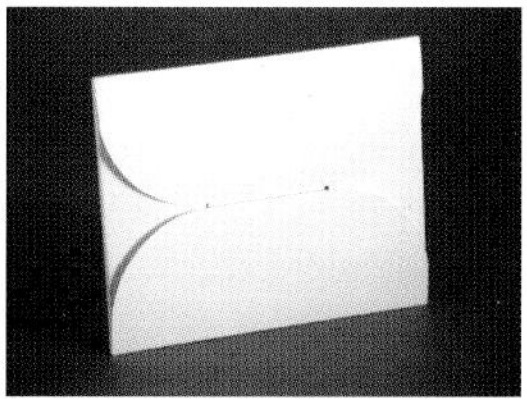
P 220

P 222

P 226

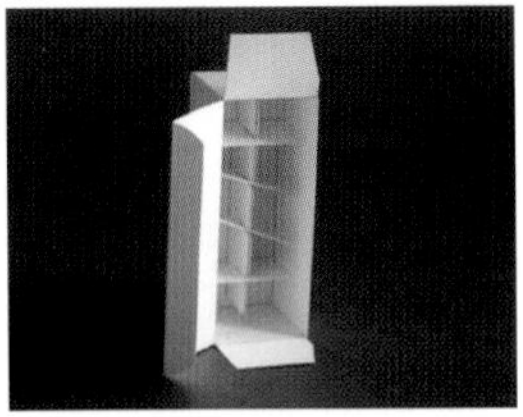
P 228

P 230

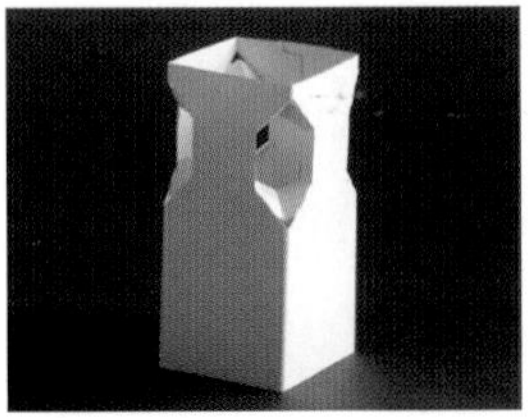
P 232

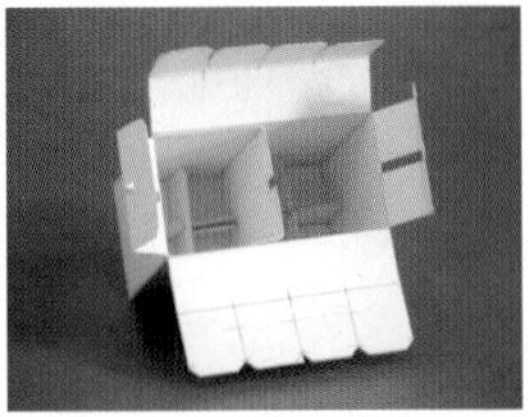
P 234

P 236

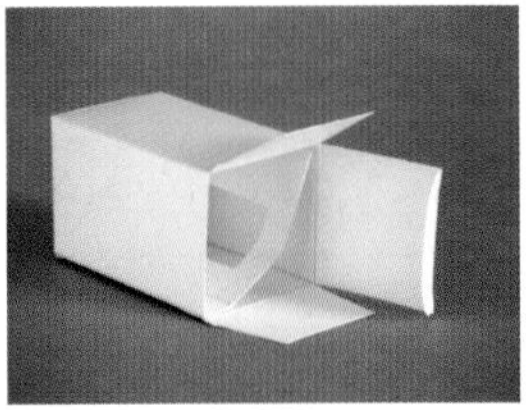
P 238

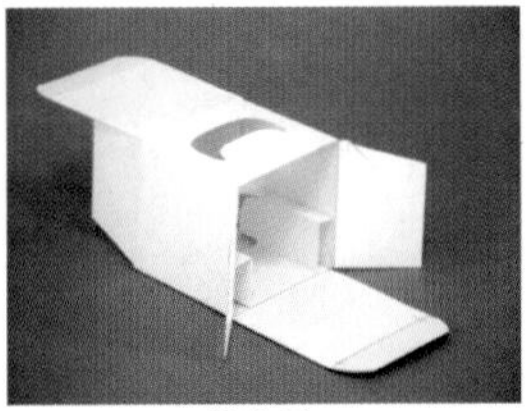
P 240

P 242

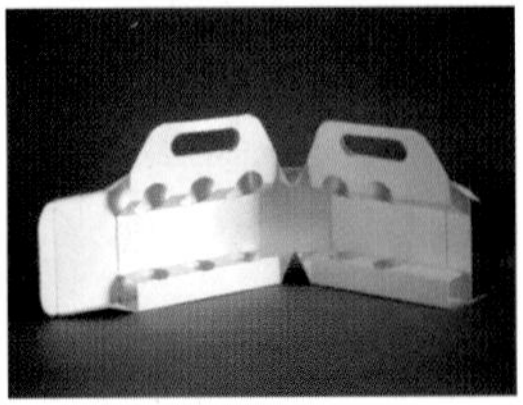
P 244

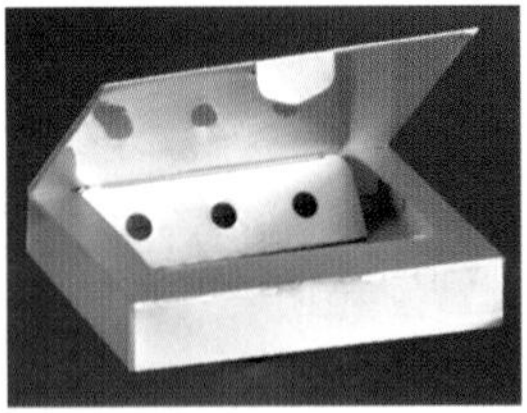
P 246

P 248

P 252

P 254

P 256

P 258

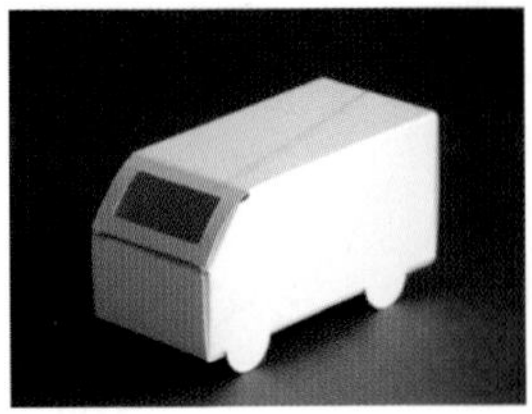
P 260

P 262

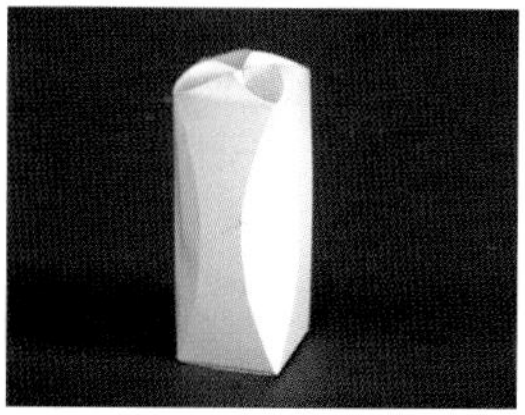
P 264

P 266

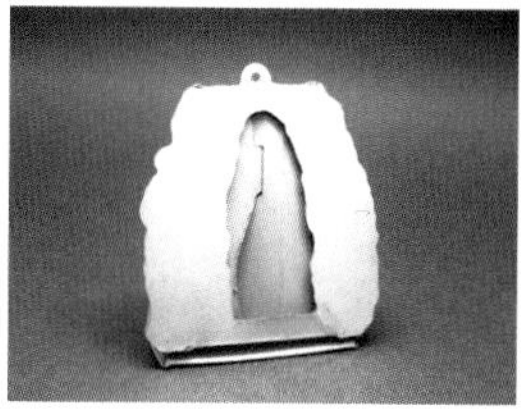
P 268

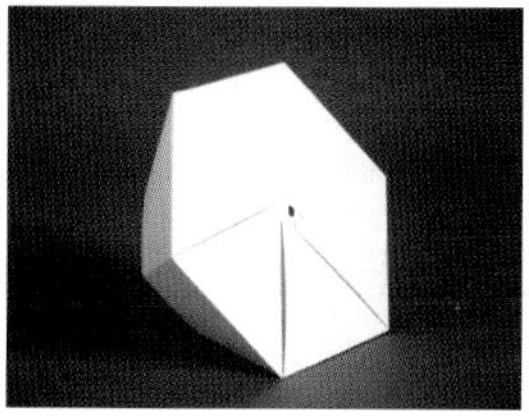
P 270

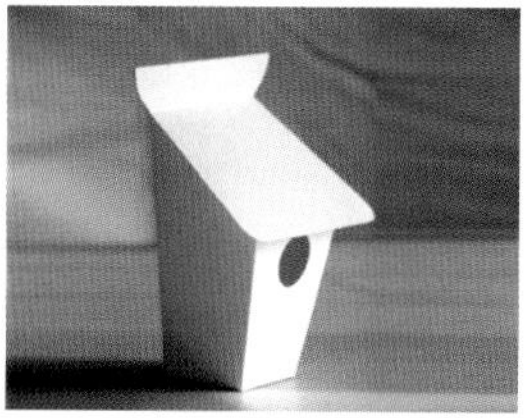
P 272

P 274

P 276

P 278

P 280

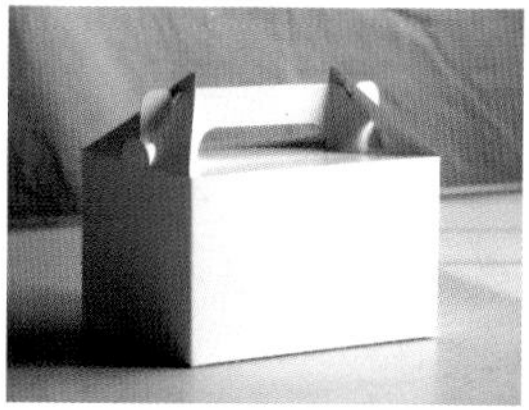
P 282

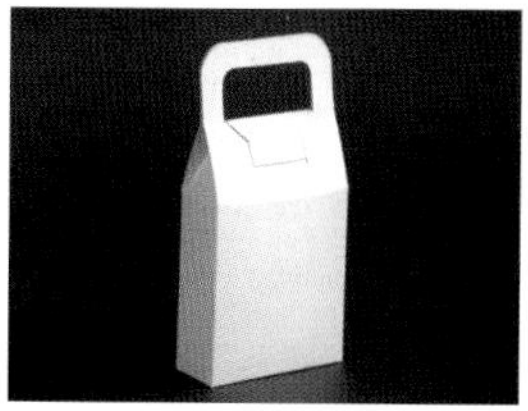
P 286

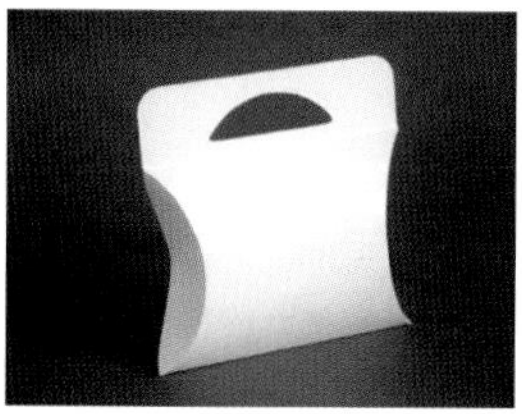
P 288

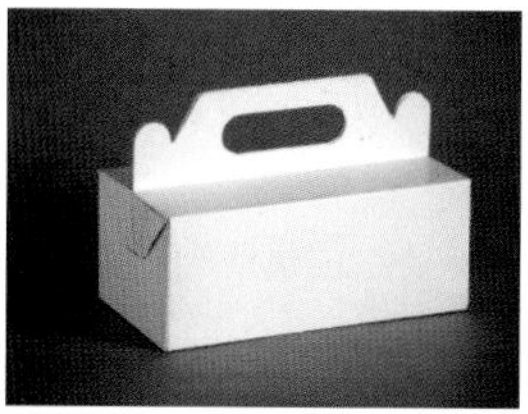
P 290

P 292

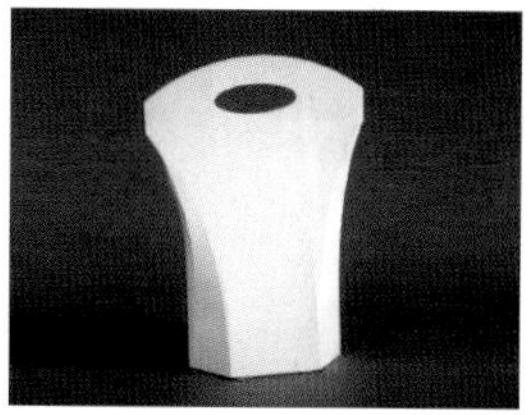
P 294

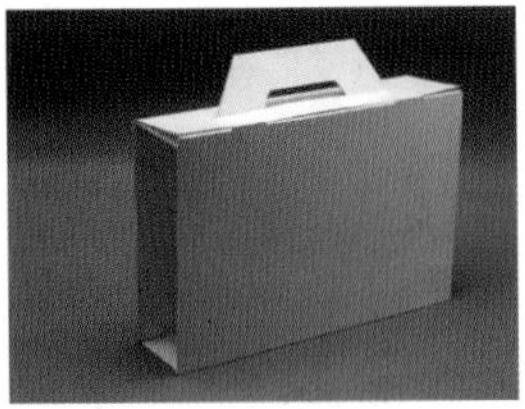

P 296

P 298

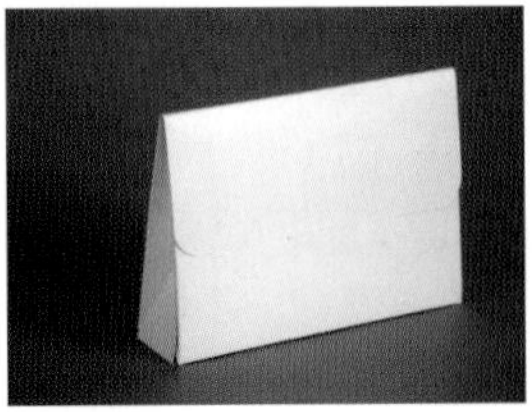

P 300

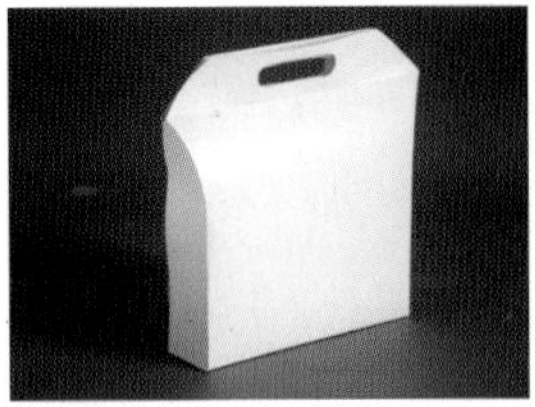

P 302

P 304

P 306

P 310

P 312

P 314

P 316

P 318

P 320

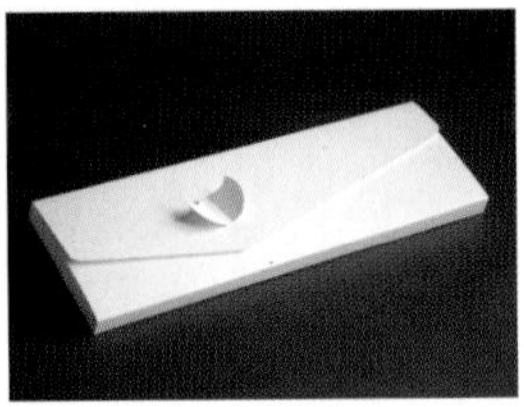

P 322

P 324

P 326

P 328

P 330

P 332

P 334

P 336

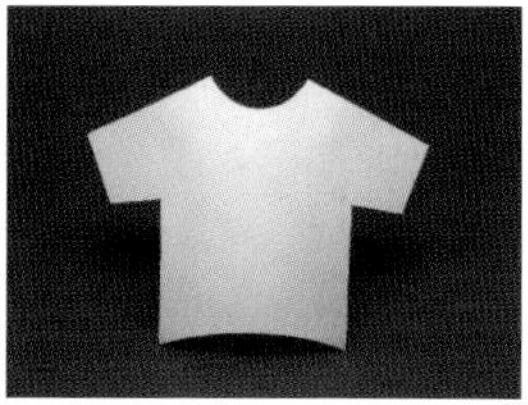

P 338

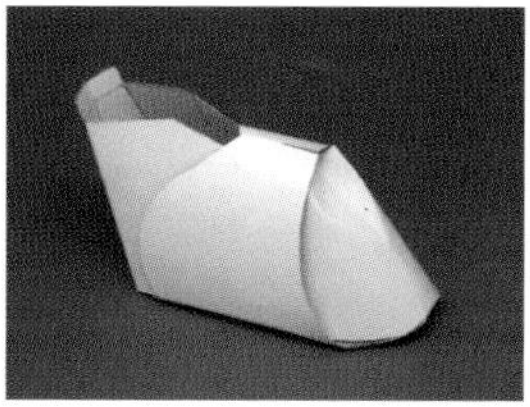

P 340

P 342

P 344

P 346

P 348